I0820987

RYDER CUP
RIVALS

ALSO BY HANK GOLA:

Hard Nose

Tiger Woods: An illustrated Biography

City of Champions

RYDER CUP RIVALS

The FIERCEST BATTLES *for* GOLF'S HOLY GRAIL

HANK GOLA

Author of *City of Champions*

TATRA PRESS

Ryder Cup Rivals

Library of Congress Cataloging-in-Publication Data application has been submitted.
ISBN: 979-8992215007
First Edition: July 2025 Tatra Press LLC

Distributed by Independent Publishers Group, Baker & Taylor and Ingram

Cover designed by Mimi Bark
Interior designed by Maria Ilardi Media
Cover photo: Mark Newcombe, visionsingolf.com

Special sales and permissions:
Chris Sulavik (Tatra Press) at tatrapress@gmail.com or 646-644-6236

Printed and bound in the United States of America by Sheridan Group (Chelsea, MI).
Tatra Press, 4 Park Trail, Croton-on-Hudson, New York 10525, www.tatrapress.com

To Lillian
My "A" Player

Contents

Foreword

How do I know the Ryder Cup is the most electrifying event in golf? It's because I hear it loudly and clearly from those normally indifferent to following golf. Even the majors don't guarantee the drama that seizes international viewers every two years. I liken it to the Olympics, which I've also been fortunate to broadcast over three decades. Both attract a wide viewership because they "look and sound" so spectacular and unique.

The Ryder Cup sends shivers up your spine. It's a football stadium on every hole and a bucket list item for every fan. Spectators can expect incredible drama and unrivaled emotion with the intensity ratcheted to lofty heights by behind-the-scenes turmoil that is inevitably stoked both on the course and in the respective team rooms.

I remember 1999 at Brookline. I was in a tower with Bernard Gallacher watching this whole thing unfold. I had to keep telling myself, "take a deep breath" because of the avalanche of momentum-changing moments that Sunday. Truly, though, it seems that every Ryder Cup has constantly challenged the media to report on it all.

That's where this fantastic read by Hank Gola comes in. He brings the energy of the Ryder Cup to every chapter. He takes you inside the ropes and behind closed doors with a front-row seat to the biggest pressure cooker in golf. Most importantly, Hank explains exactly why this event has meant so much, and why it continues to be one of the greatest spectacles in all of sport. *Enjoy!*

Dan Hicks, *Greenwich, Connecticut, April, 2025*

Introduction

I am a very small, though not inconsequential, part of Ryder Cup history. Having spent over twenty years on the golf beat for the *New York Daily News*, I was at Gleneagles in Scotland covering what would be my last Ryder Cup in 2014. The United States team had just been trounced yet again and, after witnessing the rollicking European celebration, came trudging into the interview room with shoulders slouched, a somber ritual many of them had performed before. All twelve of the vanquished, along with captain Tom Watson, glumly took their places on the raised podium, a microphone in front of each at the long table. It was the last place most of them wanted to be at that moment—being grilled by a roomful of critical reporters with most of the same worn, old questions.

I say *most,* because Phil Mickelson must have been rehearsing in his mind his theory on the meltdown—and he was itching to offer it up. Mickelson's answers are often calculated to provoke and as I sat there watching him pensively survey the room, he seemed poised to make a point. I was confident my question would give him the slight nudge he needed to do so. Asking questions of the winners is easy. Asking questions of the losers takes some crafting. You want to be fair to both your reader and the athlete. You can't lob up sympathetic softballs, because your readers want real answers. You can't come on too strong, however, or the athlete is bound to get so miffed that he or she replies with self-righteous scorn or, worse, not at all.

The great thing about writing from Europe is that deadlines are so generous, given the wide time zones, that a reporter has extra time to gather thoughts and plan the angle of a story instead of just reacting to the quotes. I was hoping my question would feed into the gist of my column–how the American team had lost its momentum so spectacularly–so I took a seat in front row to make sure the moderator would call on me. Several minutes later, he did. It turns out, I struck gold. As you will read in the 2016 chapter, Mickelson's takedown of the unfortunate Watson, whether just or unjust, not only created international headlines. It also opened the door to a re-examination of the PGA of America's approach to the Ryder Cup process. My only problem was that Mickelson always locks eyes with his questioner, and I couldn't scan the rest of the table, Watson in particular, to note their simultaneous reactions. As it turned out, most of them squirmed uncomfortably, except for Watson, who, with his hands folded, looked straight ahead as if to line up a putt.

"Phil, and anyone else who was at Valhalla," I had started, "can you put your finger on what worked in 2008 and what hasn't worked since?"

Mickelson pounced. What followed was what I described in the *Daily News* as the most fractious Ryder Cup press conference ever–and I think it still holds. It was also the most eventful, because it not only laid bare the internal squabbling of the US camp but also forced a renewed commitment of strategy and purpose. The famed "task force" was formed ahead of the American victory in 2016 at Hazeltine National in Chaska, Minnesota.

Not every Ryder Cup was as momentous as 2014. However, everyone who has ever played in a Ryder Cup has brought out some degree of the passion–and angst–displayed at Gleneagles. From the gamesmanship of Walter Hagen to the cunning of Seve Ballesteros, the emotion of Ben Crenshaw and the determination of Paul Azinger, not to mention the sometimes too exuberant galleries, nothing compares to the Ryder Cup.

Indeed, each of golf's majors possesses a particular charm; the Masters its unmatched environment; the US Open its difficulty; The Open Championship its unpredictable weather; and the PGA Championship's inclusion of club professionals in its field. But none can match the passion of the Ryder Cup. Playing for yourself is intense. Playing for your country and your teammates is transforming. As Chick Harbert, a member of the 1949 US team, once put it: "When I stood on the first tee and they played the Star-Spangled Banner, you couldn't have driven a nail into my ass with a sledgehammer." And that's back when the United States was routinely thrashing its poor cousins from Great Britain.

It's that core passion that I have endeavored to highlight by identifying those Ryder Cups that were either the most fiercely contested or pivotal and taking deep dives into them through both personal experience and research. Given that numerous volumes have already been written on Ryder Cup history (many of which I have sourced), I hoped to contribute to that collection by identifying those Cups that had the greatest impact. It was an easy task to recognize the raw emotions that were on display (win or lose) in those that I was privileged to cover. It was somewhat surprising, however, when my research revealed that no Ryder Cup was free from some controversy.

So, how to settle on the Cups that mattered most? First, I looked for turning points. Obviously, I had to begin with the original meeting in 1927, not without contention. I included 1937 as the first won on foreign soil and 1947, although a rout, for the reasons the United States had become dominant after World War II. The British win in 1957 snapped a string of US wins, but it was also notable as the last US defeat before continental Europe joined the fray. Jack Nicklaus' famed concession of 1969 had to be included, as did how the event was revived through continental Europe in 1983 and 1987, when Ballesteros first cast his everlasting shadow. The fight back from the US was encapsulated by 1991's War by the Shore, which set a new standard for intensity, followed by the give and take up to the present day, of '97, '99, '12, and '16. There were certainly other years worthy of review but, these cases—the tie in 1989 or the European victory in 1995, for instance—presented themes already covered in other chapters.

The reader will notice I left off with the 2016 Ryder Cup when, at the time of this writing, we are already on the verge of the 2025 competition. The US win at Whistling Straits in 2021 is certainly worthy of a chapter but the story line was essentially the same as 2016, a must win situation for the Americans. Much has changed since 2016, of course. LIV Golf has had a profound effect in terms of the limited opportunities its players have to qualify for teams. Indeed, Henrik Stenson's defection to LIV cost him his European captaincy in 2023. Similarly, Phil Mickelson, a darling of the New York fans, would have been a shoo-in to captain the 2025 US team at Bethpage. Additionally, the PGA of America is, for the first time, paying its players with a stipend in 2025, much to the dismay and disgust of their European counterparts. As Rory McIlroy put it: "I personally would pay for the privilege to play in the Ryder Cup."

It will be fascinating to see how it all shakes out by the 100th Anniversary of the Ryder Cup in Ireland in 2027. In any event, we can be certain it will be compelling. It aways is. To that end, I hope that I have conveyed in these pages some of the goosebumps I felt while covering it.

Hank Gola, *Parsippany, New Jersey, April, 2025*

Prologue

Make no mistake. Samuel Ryder, the British seed merchant who conceived, sponsored and gave his name to the Ryder Cup, may have done so in the spirit of comradeship and true, friendly competition. But the competition just as surely begged an answer to one question: which side of the Atlantic reigns over the golf world? Every golfer who has competed in the Ryder Cup has shouldered that charge into battle.

In the game's earliest years, this question was, naturally, moot. From the time the inhabitants of Scotland's eastern shores started whacking pebbles over sand dunes–and as the first courses began appearing in the 16th century–the game was the almost exclusive domain of British Islanders. It wasn't until the late 19th century with the explosion of leisure time that golf took root in the States, exported principally by Scottish professionals who saw America as fertile ground.

Those seeds first sprouted when John McDermott, a professional out of Philadelphia, became the first American-born player to win the US Open with consecutive wins in 1911 and 1912, and came into full bloom the following year when amateur Francis Ouimet, a twenty-year-old former caddie, shocked the pre-eminent English duo of Harry Vardon and Ted Ray in a playoff at The Country Club, across the street from his family home in Brookline, Massachusetts. At the time, Ouimet's victory resounded as thunderously as the United States hockey team's "Miracle on Ice" victory over the Soviet Union at the 1980 Olympics. It brought golf into the mainstream of American sports and ignited the trans-Atlantic rivalry.

The first "official" Cup in 1927 took place as Great Britain desperately clung to what it considered its rightful place at the top of the sport even as America kept churning out golf's best young players at a rapid clip. These homegrown American professionals–together with the great amateur Bobby Jones–would dominate the game for decades, until, at last, another generation of golf talent emerged in continental Europe.

The World War I years marked this power shift. Golf fell into dormancy in Great Britain with The Open Championship on hold from 1915 through 1919. Meanwhile, a fourth straight US Open victory by Walter Hagen in 1914 affirmed that homebred Americans could compete with the best Britain had to offer. Amateurs Jerome Travers and Chick Evans added to the US streak in 1915 and 1916. When the US Open resumed in 1919, it was the inimitable Hagen claiming the trophy for the second time. Beginning in 1922–and for seven of the next nine years–the claret jug, Britain's most cherished prize, would sail to America with either Hagen or Jones, a pair that exemplified the professional and amateur classes, respectively.

It was during this star-spangled era that George Herbert Walker, the maternal grandfather and great-grandfather of future US presidents George H.W. and George W. Bush, proposed another way to settle the argument. As president of the United State Golf Association, he had become interested in a match between the leading amateurs of golf's two foremost nations. In 1922, they competed for the Walker Cup for the first time. The US, led by Jones and Ouimet, began a steak of eight straight biennial victories with a smashing 8-4 verdict at the National Golf Links of America on Long Island.

Back in England, Samuel Ryder had become severely distressed by the turn in his country's golfing fortunes. Ryder was a self-made man guided by his passions–his work, his faith, his patriotism and lastly, his golf. Born in a small village outside Preston in 1858, the son of a gardener and a dressmaker of modest means, he would make his fortune producing and marketing penny packets of flower and vegetable seeds. His workaholic lifestyle contributed to poor health, and his Congregational minister urged him to take up golf when he was too old for cricket.

Ryder threw himself into the game with typical fervor, not only as a player at his home club, Verulam, but also as a supporter of British professional golfers. Ryder was sympathetic to their plight as virtual indentured servants of the clubs that employed them. This became particularly apparent to him when he befriended the three Whitcombe brothers–Ernest, Charles and Reg–on a golfing holiday. He was disturbed to learn they were unable to compete in The Open and other big events because they couldn't afford it; they were not paid while away from the club. A single remark from Ernest provided the spark that moved Ryder into action.

"The Americans come over here smartly dressed and backed by wealthy supporters," Whitcombe told him in an obvious reference to the sartorially resplendent Hagen, the first to earn a living exclusively from his tournament winnings and exhibitions. "The Britisher has a poor chance to compare to that."

This swelled Ryder's pride in the Union Jack. When World War I broke out, he had provided the British government enormous supplies of medicinal plant seeds needed for the war effort. He was now prepared to do anything for King and country to fend off what *The Guardian* called "the American menace." He and his brother James, partners in the Heath and Heather herb company, began to sponsor professional events–in both match and stroke play–picking up the expenses of every competitor with guaranteed prize money. As part of the Heath and Heather competitions, the Ryders considered challenging the American pros to a match as early as 1924, three years after the first informal matches, won by Great Britain, 9-3, had occurred at Gleneagles in Scotland. News of this planned match appeared in *The Daily Telegraph* in 1925.

By that time, Ryder had already hired as his private instructor Abe Mitchell, who he considered the best bet to defeat the Americans, on a healthy 500-quid salary plus another 250 quid for expenses. The unique arrangement was less about golf lessons and far more about affording the long-hitting Mitchell the same privileges as some of the American pros—chiefly, all the time necessary to prepare for tournaments.

It is supposed that during this period, Ryder made overtures to Hagen to assemble an American team to face Britain's best. Hagen was never one to turn down a challenge. In April, 1926 it was announced—to great fanfare in certain places—that Britain would host what the *Pittsburgh Daily Post* unabashedly proclaimed as "the greatest exhibition ever given." Hyperbole aside, the formidable team Hagen originally announced represented the best American golf could offer. However, by the time Hagen sailed for Britain on the *RMS Acquitania*, headliners Johnny Farrell, Gene Sarazen, Leo Siegel, Al Espinosa and MacDonald Smith were not included, partly due to havoc wreaked by a general strike paralyzing Great Britain in late May. They were substituted by English-born Cyril Walker (the 1924 US Open champion), Scottish born Fred McLeod, who had won the US Open twenty years prior, Emmett French, who finished his career with three tour wins to his credit, journeyman New England pro Joe Stein and Joe Kirkwood, an Australian-born trick shot artist who frequently barnstormed with Hagen.

No matter the makeup of the US team, the matches—prematurely referred to as the Ryder Cup on both sides of the Atlantic—were seen as part of the greater question. As the *Manchester Evening News* put it: could "British prestige be restored?" The newspaper fervently hoped for British victories in that year's Walker Cup, The Open Championship and the British Amateur as well, hoping to clear away the "black cloud" that had been placed "over the golfing supremacy our forefathers, by tiring effort, had gained for us.

"To arms then—with every weapon of the golf bag," the broadsheet begged. "Don't let us be of the type of golfer—not as uncommon as he ought to be—who starts out a beaten man."

Alas, John Bull ultimately held only the lesser of those four prizes. For the first time, America swept the Amateur (Jess Sweater), Open (Jones), and Walker Cup (a squeaky 6-5 victory). It came as little consolation to the Brits, that their side, with a full complement of their top players, embarrassed Hagen's makeshift squad, 13 ½ –1 ½, in the first of those events. The matches, eventually played at Wentworth, saw Melhorn securing the visitors' only full point. Enthusiastic galleries marveled at Vardon's wizardry and particularly enjoyed the spanking Hagen absorbed. George Duncan handed the Haig one of the worst single match-play defeats of his career, 6-and-5, after he and Barnes were trimmed, 9-and-8, by Duncan and Mitchell in foursomes. Hagen remarked that he "couldn't hit a balloon," let alone a golf ball.

"We are losing our hold on the British lion's tail," Allison B. Houghton, the US Ambassador to Great Britain, noted somewhat disingenuously as he presented the championship medals (not the actual Ryder Cup) provided by Wentworth to the winning side.

Not everyone agreed with Houghton's lament, including the *Minneapolis Sunday Tribune* which cautioned, "The results are not to be taken at their face value. The vagaries of golf must be considered in appraising the Americans' sorry showing. For one thing, the Americans were not acclimated. Further, they were unacquainted with the Wentworth course."

True, the Americans had disembarked just two days before the competition and had barely recovered their sea legs. Most of all, the US team was not representative of the country's best players. Ryder, too, realized it wasn't a fair fight and chose to withhold the actual cup before the matches were played. He nevertheless reveled in the post-match festivities, thrilled that his boy Mitchell had not only whipped Hagen in foursomes but also ripped Barnes, 8-and-7, in singles. Supposedly, Ryder raised a flute of champagne while toasting, "We must do this again," with all in attendance agreeing to a return match in 1927. But this tale appears tall. Ryder's involvement had already been secured, and the first unofficial Ryder Cup—without sanction by either the British or United States Professional Golfers Associations—eventually became an historical footnote in the annals of golf.

Over the next several decades, the Ryder Cup endured through war, terrorism, disease and even indifference. Once it was revived for good, however, it turned into a big-money, must-see event that, despite the occasional dustup, has developed into the pre-eminent competition between golfing nations.

So, which side supreme? The question is answered every two years.

1927

Hagen's Heroes

WORCESTER COUNTRY CLUB

UNITED STATES 9 ½, GREAT BRITAIN 2 ½

Samuel Ryder provided the trophy and his name to what has become golf's most absorbing spectacle. But it took Walter Hagen—a true force of nature—to create the unrivaled spirit of competition surrounding the Ryder Cup.

The Haig, or Sir Walter, as sports scribblers dubbed him, exemplified golf's growing professionalism in the decade known as the Golden Age of Sports. He was brash and antagonistic, a stark departure from the norm. While everyone loved Bobby Jones, who was all about the game, one either loved or hated Hagen, who seemed to be all about the money and the lifestyle it afforded him.

"I never wanted to be a millionaire. I just wanted to live like one," he unapologetically said.

Just as the rising tide of Tiger Woods lifted all boats as the 21st century dawned, Hagen was the storm that ushered in an era of prestige and wealth for professional golfers. Gene Sarazen, Hagen's fiercest rival, acknowledged as much after Sir Walter, having won eleven major championships and well over $1 million in earnings, died of throat cancer in 1969.

"All the professionals who have a chance to go after big money today should say a silent thanks to Walter Hagen each time they stretch a check between their fingers," Sarazen proffered. "It was Walter Hagen who made professional golf what it is."

Hagen arrived upon the scene with flash and an unflinching determination, intentionally creating his own persona. In doing so, he single-handedly elevated the stature of the professional golfer over the amateur. As in most sports, the amateur had long been looked upon as a paragon of sporting competition while the professional was scorned as a ne'er-do-well, sullied by profiting from sport. In Britain, the first professionals were working class blokes—club makers, caddies, and keepers of the green. To supplement their meager wages, they challenged one another to money matches which were anathema to blue-nosed guardians of the game. Even though early professionals such as Alan Robertson, Willie Park, and Old and Young Tom Morris were certainly admired for their skills (until Bobby Jones, just three amateurs had won the claret jug), they were nevertheless deprived of high social status, even by those who had handsomely profited by wagering on them.

Hagen broke that mold with relish. As a brash twenty-eight-year-old, arriving for the 1920 Open Championship at Royal Cinque Ports near Deal, he was denied access to the clubhouse and brusquely instructed to use the pro shop, where all the professionals shared its one available hook. For the rest of the tournament, Hagan arrived each day in a chauffeured Austro-Daimler limousine, parked it in front of the clubhouse and used it to change into the stylish golf shoes that accentuated the rest of his impeccable attire. Although the Haig finished the tournament tied for fifty-sixth place while the English and Scots dominated the leaderboard, he would soon launch an assault on The Open Championship with victories in '22, '24, '28 and '29. Likewise, he would transform himself into the preeminent figure of the first Ryder Cup events, and as the face of the US team. And the man the British wanted most to beat.

This was particularly true in 1927, the year of the first official Ryder Cup, thanks to lingering resentment from events held the previous year. Even as Britishers reveled in Hagen's sloppy defeats in the 1926 international matches at Wentworth, he continued to rankle his hosts. He had been buoyed by his comeback takedown of Ryder's man, Abe Mitchell, in a 72-hole, $25,000, challenge match, and then went on to Royal Lytham & St. Annes to be part of an

All-American top four at The Open, with Jones winning. When British reporters cornered Hagen at the Majestic Hotel at St. Annes, the Haig comfortably leaned back, held court, and filled their notebooks. They could barely keep up with him.

"When people ask me why it is that you Britishers get licked at golf, I've got only one answer and that is a question," he began. "Why, for glory's sake, don't the young golfers of this country go to work at golf? Why don't they treat it the same as work? They're too gosh-darned lazy, it seems to me. A lazy man cannot win championships at anything in the world today. He's got to work like hell at golf and then he's got to train himself to be a match player; to cut out the nerves stuff and tell himself there's a hole down ahead which he is sure he is going in, in the minimum number of strokes."

Hagen didn't stop there. He scoffed at the British ideal of a good sportsman and suggested that making the trip over was becoming a waste of time.

"Now I don't believe we Americans will come over here for the championships for a few years. What's the good of one coming over here if all we are going to do is beat one another? That doesn't do us any good. We could do that at home. I guess that we Americans will not be coming over here for a year or two as the novelty of winning your championship is wearing off. We will wait until you British win it yourself and then we will come back and see what we can do."

Although Hagen would soon become one of the first professional athletes to claim he was taken out of context by the press, the insult shocked his hosts—and drew even more ire from the New York papers.

"If Hagen was quoted correctly . . . he should be muzzled for the sake of American sportsmanship," the *Brooklyn Eagle* opined. "This overweening egotist has evidently no sense of the fitness of things"

"The spectacle of this loud-mouthed braggart giving lessons to Vardon, Braid and Taylor (the revered Great Triumvirate) and attempting to tell amateurs in England and Scotland how to pursue their sport is as offensive as it is ludicrous," the *Herald Tribune* chimed in. "Hagen's conduct is not representative of the game in the United States, and it would be difficult to imagine an American amateur insulting his hosts. Hagen is unique in professional ranks as a braggart."

"Showman" might be the more accurate description. Quite likely, Hagen's braggadocio was driven by an ulterior motive: there is nothing like stirring up some bad blood to stoke a rivalry. Hagen arguably remains the greatest match play golfer in history. Indeed, going into the '27 Ryder Cup, he had won three straight PGA Championships (then a match play event) and was headed for a fourth later that year. He didn't, however, cut a particularly intimidating figure. He was somewhat round with a high forehead. He had a whippy swing and could be wild off the tee. Yet his recovery shots were executed with steel nerves, and he played his best in the clutch.

Above all, Hagen was golf's most effective practitioner of gamesmanship, on and off the course. He rankled his opponents by showing up late for big challenge matches. He even kept President Warren G. Harding waiting for a friendly game. He would concede short putts early in the match and then suddenly force opponents to take them when the match was on the line.

Author O.B. Keeler captured that quality in his depiction of Hagen's challenge match against Abe Mitchell in 1926, for which Hagen was late, naturally. As the two men walked toward their shots, with Mitchell slightly away, Hagen said to his caddie, "Give me my mashie." Knowing that Hagen was familiar with the course, Mitchell also asked for his mashie and came up short. Having baited Mitchell into hitting the wrong club, Hagen asked for his mid-iron and landed it on the green.

Given Hagen's penchant for duplicity, it is not unreasonable to assume that his remarks back at the Majestic Hotel were more than a gratuitous gibe. He was not one for idle conversation, and usually had a practical (and often cunning) reason for his comments. Moreover, twisting the lion's tail made for great copy. Hagen helped create an undercurrent of tension that flew in the face of the grand ideal of sporting competition that has not quite accurately been attributed to that first Ryder Cup, all aimed at handing his team the advantage.

Although not of Hagen's making, a rift between the United States Golf Association (USGA) and the Royal and Ancient Golf Club (R&A) nearly prevented the event from taking place at all. While the Americans were at the 1926 Open Championship, they asked the R&A to reschedule its next Open from June to July to accommodate USGA's plans to move the US Open to June from July. The Americans were concerned that the July heat could be oppressive and that the course, without modern irrigation, could be baked out. The R&A wouldn't budge from its traditional date, however. The Ryder Cup seemed doomed with both sides digging in. If a Ryder Cup were to be played in 1927, it would need to be scheduled around the US Open. Otherwise, it would be impractical for the British team, which would have to make more than one voyage. The R&A's stubbornness so irked USGA secretary Herbert H. Ramsay that he was reported to have echoed Hagen's wisecrack. Because Americans had captured five of the previous six Open Championships, he asserted, it was well and good for the dignity of the Brits that no Americans would be competing for the claret jug.

In late November, the USGA made it official at its executive session at the Hotel Belmont in New York. The 1927 US Open would be played at Oakmont Country Club in Pittsburgh, and begin on June 20, in the same week the R&A scheduled The Open Championship at St. Andrews. The future of golf depended on the R&A's response. Fortunately, USGA president William Fowles played the diplomat with assurances that the USGA was uninterested in challenging the R&A as golf's rightful leader. "We owe them a debt of gratitude for the traditions they have preserved," Fownes granted. The R&A accepted the olive branch and in early January, the USGA announced at its annual meeting it had received a cable from the R&A with word it was moving its championship date.

With the path now clear, Worcester Country Club in Massachusetts was selected to host the Ryder Cup on June 3-4, allowing the event to stand on its own rather than serve as an opening act for the US Open at Oakmont. Worcester was a convenient journey from New York, where the Brits would land, about fifty miles west of Boston and a train ride to Pittsburgh. It was also considered among the nation's finest courses, built by the booming manufacturing city's captains of industry, and had elicited raves for its condition when it hosted the US Open just two years earlier.

Designed by Donald Ross, the Summit Course as it was also known, had been dug out of rocky farmland in 1914, and featured all the trademarks of the great golf architect. It was long for its era—over 6,600 yards—and presented players with thick rough and challenging greenside bunkers, twenty of which were scattered throughout the course after Ross toughened it up in advance of the 1925 US Open. The Brits, accustomed to playing run-up shots to greens at home, would have to contend with them.

Meanwhile, in Britain, it seemed that little could go right. The same day the scheduling issue was settled, George Philpot, editor of London's *Golf Weekly*, launched a campaign to raise £3,000 from Great Britain's golf clubs to support the British team, an appeal so miserably unanswered (just 216 of Britain's 1,750 clubs made contributions) that Ryder and Philpot each kicked in £500 of their own. At least Philpot's generosity earned him the role of team manager.

The funding woes were followed by an even greater crisis. Abe Mitchell, Ryder's great hope, fell ill with appendicitis and was ruled out for the voyage after his surgery. A powerful man with massive arms and strong hands, Mitchell was considered the most formidable member of the invading squad, "the uncrowned king of British golf," as one newspaper called him. Everyone was sure he was ticketed for a return grudge match with Hagen on singles day. "Let's hope our team can win but it is the play without the prince of Denmark," Ryder waxed.

The British team set off for America on May 21 without Mitchell and Ryder, who both saw the boys off with handshakes and backslapping at the Southampton port. Ryder had hosted a farewell dinner at his Verulam club, unveiling the handsome Cup for the first time. Ryder had selected Mitchell's likeness to adorn the top of the diminutive statuette and while Mitchell is long forgotten, his replica has indeed stood the test of time. Ryder commissioned it by contributing £100 ($500 in US dollars) with *Golf Illustrated* matching his portion and the R&A putting up another £50. Designed as a chalice, it was cast in gold on a wooden base by the prestigious London jewelry house of Mappin and Webb Ltd., standing just seventeen inches high and weighing about four pounds.

Back in the States, Hagen and the US selection committee wrestled with the makeup of its team, whether British-born pros would be included as they were in 1926 or if the roster would be limited to the "home-breds." To *Golf Illustrated* of London, it was clear-cut: "The fact remains that they are products of British golf and that they can no more be regarded as American players than an apple can be viewed as an orange by the process of hanging it on an orange tree."

The Americans concurred and, as it would turn out, assembled a much stronger squad than the '26 version. Of the ten players, including two alternates, eight were native-born and two–Al Watrous and Johnny Golden–grew up in the States after emigrating with their families from Eastern Europe. The team truly represented the first generation of US-bred golfers. They were, for the most part, the sons of immigrants, a colorful crew with nicknames, idiosyncrasies, and personality. They had self-taught swings and played an aggressive brand of golf. And they would forever change the game of golf from a gentlemanly pursuit into fierce competition.

Hagen himself was of German stock, the son of a sturdy Rochester, New York, blacksmith. Put to work at the age of five tending cows in the family pasture, he fashioned his own golf course, herding the cows to an area to graze and thereby creating a makeshift putting surface. He soon started cleaning floors at the nearby Country Club of Rochester (CCR), where he would eventually caddie for ten cents a bag. The resident pro, Andy Christy, saw promise in the youngster and taught him the game. Hagen turned pro at nineteen and won his first tournament, the Canadian Open, the following year.

For a brief time, however, Hagen considered quitting the sport and taking up his other youthful pursuit, baseball. While touring on the winter circuit in Tarpon Springs, he played some golf with a few of the Philadelphia Phillies during their spring training sessions. Pat Moran, the Phillies' manager, knew Hagen had played baseball and invited him to the team's workout, where Hagen performed well enough to earn an invitation to the next winter's camp. Hagen fully intended to concentrate on baseball instead of competing in the 1914 US Open at Midlothian Country Club in Illinois. But when Ernest Willard, a CCR member who was editor of the *Rochester Democrat and Chronicle*, overheard him talking about his plans, he offered to bankroll his trip if he entered the Open. Hagen took home the trophy and forgot about a baseball career. That he eventually became the sporting world's first millionaire demonstrated the wisdom of his decision. His wide stance, however, was a product of his baseball background.

Gene Sarazen was perhaps Hagen's biggest professional rival. Sarazen had come out on top in a 72-hole challenge match after Sarazen had won the PGA Championship and Hagen The Open Championship in 1922. Five years later, in March of 1927, Hagen got his revenge by whipping his "cocky" rival, 8-and-7, in another 72-hole challenge match in Florida.

Ten years younger than Hagen, Sarazen came from a similar background. Born Eugenio Saracini to Italian immigrant parents (upon seeing his name in the paper, he thought Saracini was too much like a "violin player"), Sarazen was marked by his father to join him in his carpentry business in Mamaroneck, New York. He was apprenticing for his father when he came down with a respiratory ailment and was advised by doctors that the sawdust-filled workshop would be poor for his long-term health.

Sarazen started to caddy and learn the game at the age of eight at nearby Larchmont Country Club. Years later, he was caddying at the Apawamis Club when he came to the attention of Al Ciuci, the pro at Beardsley Park, a nine-hole course across the state border in Connecticut. Sarazen didn't own clubs so he asked Ciuci if he could lend him a set to play at Beardsley Park. He offered him the course any time he wanted to use it. Ciuci went off to war and Gene went to Brooklawn Country Club to start his professional career as an assistant. He almost died in the 1918 flu epidemic but four years later, he shot a 68 to defeat Hagen and Jones for the US Open title, the first leg in his modern career Grand Slam.

Nicknamed the Squire, Sarazen had a cocksure manner and an infectious smile. Small-handed, he pioneered the interlocking grip, now a staple. He was short (5-foot-5) and stocky, but he created his power from a low center of gravity, a wide stance and a long backswing with lots of wrist action, particularly advantageous with hickory clubs.

Al Watrous grew up not far from Sarazen in Yonkers after emigrating with his Polish parents as a toddler. The family lived on Hog Hill, known originally for the wild pigs that fed on the abundant acorns (and later for the gin mills that supplied the local denizens). Watrous got his start as a caddy at Dunwoodie Country Club, where he buddied up with two other future pros, Joe Koval and Joe Devany. Together, they concocted a scheme to make more cash than the normal loop afforded them. They would meet the train that brought golfers from New York City. From the station, the players rode to Dunwoodie on the club's small horse-drawn wagon, which could not accommodate golf bags. It was a winding uphill road to the club; however, by taking a shortcut through the fields, the caddies could make two trips lugging bags to the clubhouse, earning 25 cents a bag.

According to Devany, "Al had an iron club, the shaft of which was sawed off to his size. He really went any place without it. He took it to church, occasionally concealing it in his shirt or trousers."

Watrous won Dunwoodie's caddie championship at fifteen and his first professional event, the 1922 Canadian Open, at twenty. His swing was distinctive. "I developed it from observation, you might say," he said. "I saw Bobby Jones when he was very young and Walter Hagen. I saw Harry Vardon. He was my idol. I was told I had a lot of Vardon's swing concepts."

The British golf writer Bernard Darwin described Watrous as having, "no tremendous power, but he had all the American virtues of smoothness and rhythm, and he was a very fine putter."

Watrous first caught Hagen's attention when Watrous took him to thirty-nine holes in their first-round match at the 1925 PGA Championship at Olympia Fields. A year later, Watrous held a one-shot lead over Bobby Jones with two holes left in the final round of The Open Championship. Jones hit one of his greatest recovery shots to beat him.

Bill Melhorn, the only American to win a full point at the 1926 competition, was nicknamed "Wild Bill" for the cowboy hat he wore, his wild stretches of golf and, most of all, his temperament. At the 1925 Texas Open, for instance, he perched himself in a tree and shouted out just as Bobby Cruikshank was bringing the putter back. "Melhorn does that sort of thing frequently," Ryder Cup teammate Al Espinosa said at the time. "A lot of us have spoken to him and asked him if he couldn't behave himself. But it hasn't done any good."

When Melhorn took the halfway lead in the '26 US Open, poison-pen columnist Westbrook Pegler of the *Chicago Tribune* wondered how on Earth the "prominent penitent" would keep it. "Melhorn," he wrote, "a loose-jointed, stoop-shouldered Texan, with a rather truculent manner, has been spotted, like quite a few others, as sort of a five-inning pitcher and he is expected to blow up at the very time when he should be prepared to defend his lead."

Melhorn (a native of Elgin, Illinois, not Texas) did indeed surrender his lead to Jones. Anyone who saw him putt would not have been surprised. He was the poster boy for the yips, the inexplicable affliction which causes the mind to override the hands to turn every routine putt into a nightmare. Melhorn's yips got so bad that sometimes he became paralyzed over the ball, unable to even pull the putter back.

He once took six putts from ten feet at an event in Miami. On another occasion, he putted off the green, leaving himself a 30-yard chip back.

Ben Hogan called Melhorn the best he ever saw from tee to green. Melhorn called himself the "world's worst putter."

"If I thought on the putting green the way I did for the rest of the game, none of the other guys would have won a tournament," he said.

A modern sports psychologist would also have had his hands full with Leo Diegel, a jumble of nerves who seemed to defy every theory about golfers and calm minds. Although Darwin called him a "golfing genius," Diegel had to force his mind to conquer his nerves. "I think people who say you can't play golf if you're excitable are all wrong," he explained. "I have made some great shots when my nerves seemed altogether out of control. I think an excitable person has to be keyed up to win."

Sarazen once wrote that Diegel, during a tournament, would go to bed too early, awake before dawn, then smoke cigarettes to calm down.

"Leo also is apt to worry about little things," the Squire noted. "I recall one tournament where he took a particular dislike to a tree on one side of the fairway. 'I wish they would cut that darn thing down; it's got my goat,' he told me, but I told him to forget about it. But he talked about that tree in his sleep and what do you think happened the next day at this hole? Why Leo took a full swing and hit that tree right in the middle."

Diegel bounded down the fairway between shots and, when hitting first off the tee, he would often find a high spot or jump up and down to get a better view of his next shot as the next player was preparing to hit. But the most eccentric thing about his game was the "arms akimbo" putting stance he developed in 1924. It was called "Diegling" and involved spreading his legs wide and splaying his elbows, crouching so that his chin touched the knob of his putter and bending his back so forward it was parallel to the green. From there, he started the stroke with his shoulders, becoming one of the first golfers to use a pendulum motion, deviating from the era's conventional wrist jab. When Diegel died in 1951 of lung and throat cancer from all his smoking, Hagen wondered, "how are they going to fit him into the box?"

Johnny Farrell, dubbed "Handsome Johnny" by legendary sports columnist Grantland Rice, was the picture of sartorial splendor, outdoing even Hagen. He wore it well. Tall, thin and debonaire with jet-black hair, piercing eyes, striking features and a ready smile, he could easily have starred in silent movies. Indeed, he once dated Fay Wray, the *femme fatale* whom King Kong hoisted to the top of the Empire State Building. Ultimately, he married a budding actress, Catherine Hush.

The son of Irish immigrants, he was born in White Plains, New York. His father, James, a dairyman, died when he was just four. At fifteen he quit school to work in the pro shop at Siwanoy Country Club, where he was inspired by watching Jim Barnes win the first PGA Championship in 1916. Three years later, he became head pro at Quaker Ridge Golf Club and played in his first US Open. Later to serve as the longtime head professional at Baltusrol Golf Club, Farrell had a fluid swing that was as handsome as he was. He won his first tournament at the 1921 Garden City Open and quickly established himself in the top level of American pros. He had more wins in the 1927 Ryder Cup year than any other player. He strung together an eight-tournament winning streak and, a year later, outdueled Jones in a 36-hole playoff at the US Open.

Joe Turnesa also came out of White Plains (incredibly, five members of the first US Ryder Cup team grew up in metropolitan New York, four in Westchester County). He was the third of seven golfing Turnesa brothers, together known as America's golf royalty. Their father, Vitale, was born in the small village of Potenza, Italy, and orphaned at fourteen. He lived as a shepherd in the countryside until, at eighteen, he had saved enough money to set off for America. Finding an Italian family from the Little Italy section of Manhattan to take him in, he worked first as a shoeshine boy and then as a steward on the Hudson River ferry.

He found his true calling by accident. According to stories passed down through his boys, he set out on foot to see some land just purchased by a relative in Westchester County. Before he got there, twenty-six miles into his trek, he came upon a field, was handed a shovel and found himself working on the construction of a new nine for the Fairview Country Club in Elmsford. There he would remain for fifty-two years, working his way up to greens superintendent with the labor supplied by his seven sons.

Joe outfoxed his father when it was his turn to operate the horse-drawn apparatus used to mow the fairways. He trained the horses to walk in circles, so he had enough time to practice with the mashie and balls he had stashed in the woods.

Tall and lanky, Turnesa had a sweet swing, and, for a time, he solved his woes on the green by putting one-handed. Turnesa was second to Bobby Jones at the 1926 US Open, in which he lost a four-shot lead at the final turn.

Then there was Johnny Golden, the least well-known of all the American pros. He was born in present day Slovakia and emigrated at age four, with his parents changing their name "Galdun" to Golden. Raised in Tuxedo, New York, where he caddied at the historic Tuxedo Club, he was the head professional at North Jersey Country Club when he won his first career tournament, the 1927 New Jersey Open. Golden was unerringly accurate off the tee, so Hagen valued him as a partner. When the two would later face each other at the 1932 PGA Championship, the match went forty-three holes before Golden poured in the winning birdie putt. Golden's career is often overlooked because of an early death at thirty-nine. Prone to respiratory illnesses, he caught pneumonia *en route* to Florida for the winter circuit and was mourned by all of golf when he died in 1936. O.B. Keeler wrote at the time that Golden, a man of few words, was the "most truly unobtrusive and most genuinely modest of all the golfers he had known.

"His modesty amounted to bashfulness," Keeler wrote. "I have always believed that his fine competitive game—unassuming and unspectacular as his own personality—would have carried him to greater heights had Johnny Golden possessed a slight measure of self-assertiveness."

Two alternates, Al Espinosa and Mike Brady, were named to the American team. Espinosa never got into a match (more about that later) and Brady was so miffed that he chose not to report for the matches.

The Brits left the selection process in the hands of the Great Triumvirate, James Braid, Henry Vardon and J.H. Taylor. They chose a team that averaged thirty-six years old, starting with fifty-year-old Ted Ray, who had atoned for his historic loss to Francis Ouimet at the 1913 US Open by winning the 1920 US Open at age forty-three. George Duncan, the only Scot on the squad, probably had the most moxie and was something of a Hagen nemesis. The highlight of his career came in 1920, when he came back from thirteen shots to win The Open Championship. Arthur Havers was the team's only other major champion (1923 Open Championship), although Fred Robson did have four top-ten Open finishes. Six-foot-five Archie Compston was a mercurial sort with a superb reputation in match play, and Aubrey Boomer lived up to his name as a long hitter. The roster was rounded out by Herbert Jolly, the last-minute replacement for Mitchell, and George Gadd, who never got into a match.

All but Jolly arrived at the Hudson River pier on May 27 after six uncomfortable days in rough, high seas (Jolly arrived at Worcester on the eve of the matches). Ray, named captain during the trip, led the team off the gangplank, puffing on the trademark briar pipe that he continually clenched in his teeth during a round. Behind him, no doubt sweltering in their English tweeds, walked the rest of the team. There was no rest for the weary. A fleet of limousines immediately took them to City Hall where they were greeted by New York City mayor Jimmy Walker. A police escort, with sirens at full blast, brought New York traffic to a halt as the team was then whisked to the Westchester Biltmore, today's Westchester Country Club. There, they sat through ponderous speeches at a welcoming dinner, and afterwards were taken to the Biltmore's floodlit green for a putting exhibition. The next day, they were treated to a baseball game at Yankee Stadium where Babe Ruth failed to hit one of his then-record 60 home runs. The hospitality was suspect, however. British observers considered the arrangements typical gamesmanship by Hagen to tire out his adversaries and cost them practice time. In any event, the contentiousness did not abate for the rest of the week.

As American golf correspondent Lawrence Perry concluded: "It might be said that this grand international event, among those whose more or less ulterior purposes was the drawing of the two great English-speaking nations together in that closer bond of relationship, which is supposed to be affected by sporting competition, was not altogether unmarred by ruffled feelings as between the rival bands of athletes.

"Saying this the writer hastens to add that nothing occurred which need cause any fears of war or even a break in (diplomatic) relations between Great Britain and the United States. On the other hand, there were little bobbles–as George Duncan, the dour Scot, would say–of irritation."

Those bobbles began to grow after the British team finally arrived in Worcester on May 30, four days before the matches began. Hagen reintroduced a request to play a fourball (better ball) session instead of foursomes, the alternate shot game that was much more familiar to the British. He also wanted each of those fourball matches to count for two points and each of the eight singles matches just one. Ray refused and then refused again when the American captain suggested that extra holes be played to settle matches tied after the requisite thirty-six holes and that a ninth singles match be played to avoid the matches ending in a tie.

Even the announcement of the lineups led to controversy. Ray assumed they would be released simultaneously. Hagen delayed his and was accused of changing his order to create advantageous matchups. According to Duncan, Hagen visited the British team's hotel and asked Ray for his foursomes pairings and order of play. Ray unwittingly handed them over and Hagen set up his lineup accordingly. "Walter Hagen outwitted us," Duncan admitted. "I don't blame Walter for what he did; in fact, I rather admire him. He has always been a skillful, intelligent fighter, and as captain of the American team, he was entitled to use his wits. Unfortunately, we were not clever enough for him."

Meanwhile, Watrous had declared himself out because of a sore thumb that affected his grip and Espinosa was set to take his place. "But Watrous changed his mind, so Hagen changed his team, Espinosa changed his clothes and Ray changed his disposition," Davis Walsh wrote in the *Boston Herald.* No doubt there were a few frosty looks across the tables when the teams enjoyed a pre-tournament banquet at the Hotel Bancroft, the British team decked out in tuxedos, the Americans in what the Boston Globe referred to as business suits. It was perhaps one more way to make the visitors feel slighted.

Who knows whether Hagen got into the heads of his adversaries? Duncan thought so. But as it turned out, the first official Cup would wind up with more drama off the course than on it. The week dawned with perfect weather and the competition attracted surprisingly large and enthusiastic galleries at $2 a ticket, more than the $1.65 cost of a box seat at Fenway Park. Spectators warmed to the British team during practice sessions, relishing the novelty. The British players obliged, bantering with fans as they walked along the fairways. When they begged Compston to hit a few wind cheaters, he obliged. "Aye, it's the Scotchman's shot you want," he said, setting his big frame behind the ball and sending a few brassies on their way barely ten feet off the ground.

Television would have loved the spectacle. The sunshine beamed upon the stately Tudor clubhouse and the bright white bunkers provided a perfect contrast to the emerald lushness of the fairways and greens. Meanwhile, the American team's attire added to the relaxed, endless-summer ambience. While the Brits went conservative with the lion of Trafalgar emblazoned on their sport shirts, the Americans flaunted their casual individualism.

Hagen, in white plus fours and a dark blue sweater, was among the more modest. Farrell was decked out in cream and green tones,

Turnesa with purple socks matching a purple sweater (that warred with his orange necktie), and Melhorn in a combination of greens.

"The Americans completely outclassed the Britons in the matter of personal scenery," wrote Ralph Troast of the *Brooklyn Eagle.*

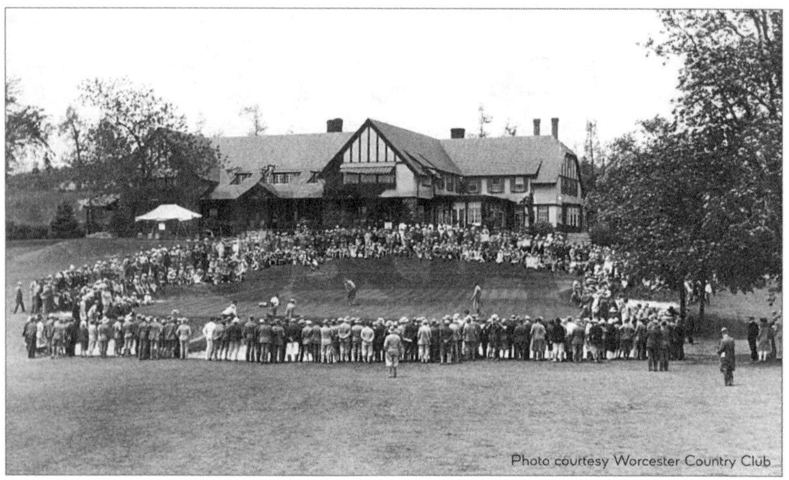

Photo courtesy Worcester Country Club

The grand scene at the eighteenth green, framed by the Worcester Country Club clubhouse. Few matches ended here as the US dominated play.

"One's ears are ringing yet with the ah's, oh's and other endearments tossed so deftly upon the air by the maids and matrons."

Unfortunately, although the setting was grand, the golf was not. Ray, concerned his team was fatigued, had called off the last afternoon practice session on the last of the three practice days. Writing in a syndicated column for the *News Service,* Hagen joked they were retiring for tea so as not to disrupt their routine. It didn't help. On the first day of competition, the US beat them at their own game, "Scotch foursomes," the format the Brits insisted on playing. None of the eight pairs broke par. Yet, by the end of the first day, the Americans had overcome their own spotty play and held a 3-1 advantage.

Even the injured Watrous came through with Gene Sarazen to take down Havers and the late-arriving Jolly, 3-and-2. Hagen was not at his best—on the eighth hole, he hit a green side bunker shot out of bounds onto the railroad tracks—but his putter was hot, and he and Golden managed to beat Ray and Robson, 2-and-1. Meanwhile, Farrell and Turnesa dispatched Duncan and Compston, 8-and-6, after the British duo combined for an 81 over the first eighteen holes. In the lone British win, Boomer, playing the most impressive golf of the day, teamed with Whitcombe to drub Diegel and Melhorn, 7-and-5. Pairing the two temperamental Americans turned out to be a disastrous decision. The jumpy Diegel hit enough practice shots for a full round before teeing off and spent the entire lunch time on the practice green. Melhorn didn't help Diegel with his putting and Diegel didn't help Melhorn at all.

It was, however, the most lopsided of matches that created the most controversy and ill feeling. On the very first hole, Turnesa's long drive ran under the footbridge just short of the brook. Farrell could barely put a club on the ball, so it was clearly an unplayable lie. Farrell asked Duncan what should be done while the official accompanying the match summoned a referee, who allowed Farrell to drop the ball one club length, giving him an easy pitch to the green and securing the hole. Duncan smiled witheringly and fumed internally, brooding as he struggled the rest of the day. Some later claimed the incident irreversibly altered the complexion of the entire match, but it's difficult to grasp how losing the first of thirty-six holes made much difference in the 8-and-6 thumping.

The singles matches turned out to be anticlimactic, although bad feelings resurfaced when Hagen attempted to substitute Espinosa for Melhorn, whom he felt had played poorly in foursomes. Melhorn, never one to take an insult lying down, suggested that Hagen bench himself for his own poor play. Ray, meanwhile, bristled.

"My goodness, this is not American football, Hagen," he huffed, rebuffing his own impulse to insert George Gadd into the singles for Jolly. It would have run contrary to British sporting tradition that those who start a game finish it. However, it was evident that whatever the lineups, Ray's team, needing to win five of the eight singles matches, had run out of petrol.

Golden led the way with an 8-and-7 win over the unfortunate Jolly, who was jolly bad. Diegel put on a recovery clinic from some awful lies, draining long putts, and downed the plodding Ray, 7-and-5. Farrell, in the best-played of all the matches, recovered from four down through nine and took down Boomer, 5-and-4, while Watrous defeated Robson, 3-and-2. Melhorn played his match with something to prove and, placed in the leadoff spot, provided a 1-up win over Compston. Hagen beat Havers, 2-and-1. The only British points came when Duncan sank a 30-foot birdie putt on the final hole to edge Turnesa, 1-up, in the anchor match and Whitcombe managed to halve with Sarazen after being 5-up at one point.

With a disappointed Samuel Ryder back in England, the first presentation of the Ryder Cup—displayed unceremoniously on a plain wooden table—found Ray handing it over to Hagen. The American team locked arms and admired the trophy as their captain held it in front of him. The Brits consoled themselves with their chance to do better at the US Open at Oakmont two weeks hence, although they were painfully aware they would need to do better on Oakmont's even more sinister greens. Before presenting the Ryder Cup, Ted Ray told the crowd, in between puffs on his pipe, that the Americans, as a team, were "the greatest putters the world had ever seen." It was almost out of resignation.

"It is no use attempting to disguise the fact the Americans are fine golfers," Gadd wrote for the *Evening Standard.* "They have mechanized all shots and reduced putting to a fine art. Our men looked uncertain when they took their putters in hand while their opponents were absolutely deadly."

Yet W.E. Mullins, writing for the *Boston Herald,* noted that the Americans were also the better iron players, especially when stiff breezes that should have favored the visitors showed up for the Saturday singles. Duncan admitted that his team had struggled with the swirling winds. In examining the cards, Mullins found that the two directly downwind holes, the third and twelfth, were dominated by the home side in the six matches won by the US. The Brits won the twelfth hole only once in twelve chances and the third only twice. They had more trouble judging distance with their low-ball flight, because they weren't getting as much run as they were accustomed to on links courses back home. The Americans, with their higher trajectories, were landing on the greens and sticking.

Both Gadd and Harold Hilton, the Englishman who won the 1911 US Amateur, saw the result as further proof of America's growing dominance of Britain's sport.

"I would sum up the vital difference in this way," Gadd wrote. "The British golfer, whilst hoping to do well, plays chiefly to get all the pleasure possible out of the game. The American, on the other hand, sets himself to the task of playing well enough to win and until he achieves his purpose, he hammers away at the game with a wonderful capacity for taking pains and enviable patience."

Hagen reduced that assessment by comparing the Brits to boxers and the Yanks to brawlers looking to land the knockout blow. The Americans are focused squarely on birdies, he opined. The Brits are satisfied with pars.

"In Great Britain there is much talk of the game for the game's sake," Hagen wrote in his syndicated column. "This is very wonderful, and everyone has it in mind. We all enjoy the game for the game's sake, but golf is the professional's business, and it is certainly no crime to keep everlastingly hitting that ball at the hole."

Hilton, in a column headlined "America's supremacy," simply embraced the inevitable.

"The truth is that American golf has developed in an extraordinary manner since 1911," he admitted. "I saw it coming when I was there. I remember dwelling on the future of American golf and suggesting that America could turn out a team of twenty-five years and younger who would defeat teams of similar age in this country. Sadly enough, my premonition has come true!"

An editorial in the *Edinburgh Sun* headed "A Golf Eclipse" came to a similar conclusion.

"British golf made a poor show in the Ryder Cup competition in America, and it is difficult to find any satisfactory plea of extenuation," it said. "The absence of Abe Mitchell was certainly serious, but it was not vital. He could not have carried the entire side on his shoulders. It is much better to admit that the more capable side won, and that the verdict was strictly according to the book."

The editorial also noted that British golf was in one of its "leanest periods" with "plenty of competent players but few geniuses" and that British-born golfers residing in America could have made an "infinitely bolder bid."

"If there is any justice in the law of averages, however, Britain's day of glory will return," the editorial asserted, adding that something must be done to "counteract the Almighty dollar. Even the longest of lanes has a turning."

The paucity of the British talent pipeline added to their consternation. Hagen was the only member of the American Ryder Cup team over thirty. The British weren't cultivating a new crop of young golfers in large enough numbers. The Britain teams did all they could to eke out victories in the next two Ryder Cups on home soil, but, clearly, the talent gap kept widening.

The British Ryder Cuppers stayed to compete in the US Open, and then followed with a short tour of Canada. Compston (seventh) was the only one to finish in the top 28 at Oakmont, where native-born Scot Tommy Armour defeated native-born Englishman Harry Cooper in a playoff, lending credence to the *Edinburgh Sun's* theory on the relative strength of the expatriates living in America. The team left Montreal and sailed home aboard the *Empress of Scotland* in time to prepare for The Open Championship at St. Andrews, where Bobby Jones defended his championship, defeating Boomer and Englishman Fred Robson by six shots in another humiliating blow to British prestige.

The British players had to comfort themselves with the wonderful reception they received while in the States—much better, indeed, than they were accustomed to at home.

The team had been "submerged by hospitality and kindness," Havers said as the team returned home. "America was a world of luxury and plenty . . . even the clubhouses were luxurious, with deep-pile carpets, not like the run-down and shabby ones at home, which is all most of us really knew."

Did Hagen simply treat his guests in the style in which he was accustomed, or did he soften them up as one part of his ever-present gamesmanship? The Ryder Cup was off to a rousing start.

DAY 1
FOURSOMES
Walter Hagen/Johnny Golden (US) defeated Ted Ray/Fred Robson (GB) 2-and-1
Johnny Farrell/Jim Turnesa (US) defeated George Duncan/Archie Compston (GB) 8-and- 6
Gene Sarazen/Al Watrous (US) defeated Arthur Havers/Herbert Jolly, (GB) 3-and-2
Aubrey Boomer/Charles Whitcombe (GB) defeated Leo Diegel/Bill Melhorn (US) 7-and-5
United States wins session, 3–1
DAY 2
SINGLES
Bill Melhorn (US) defeated Archie Compston (GB) 1-up
Johnny Farrell, (US) defeated Aubrey Boomer (GB) 5-and-4
Johnny Golden, (US) defeated Herbert Jolly (GB) 8-and-7
Leo Diegel (US) defeated Ted Ray (GB) 7-and-5
Charles Whitcombe (GB) halved with Gene Sarazen (US)
Walter Hagen (US) defeated Arthur Havers (GB) 2-and-1
Al Watrous, (US) defeated Fred Robson (GB) 3-and-2
George Duncan (GB) defeated Jim Turnesa (US) 1-up
United States wins session 6 ½–1 ½
UNITED STATES WINS RYDER CUP, 9 ½–2 ½

1937

The Kids Break Through

SOUTHPORT & AINSDALE GOLF CLUB
UNITED STATES 8, GREAT BRITAIN 4

The first four Ryder Cups failed to determine whether Great Britain or the United States could claim the mantle as the world's greatest golfing nation. The Americans were scoring wider margins of victory, but, until one team could win on foreign soil, the stalemate would persist. A convincing US win at Ridgewood Country Club in New Jersey in 1935, though, signaled an imminent seismic shift.

The return match in 1937 would tilt the competitive balance for decades. A second generation of American golfers, born just before Francis Ouimet struck the first blow for his country, would go on to claim Ryder Cup after Ryder Cup. Ralph Guldahl, Byron Nelson and Ben Hogan were Texas-born, Sam Snead in the hills near Hot Springs, Virginia. Each of these future American golf legends came into the world between November of 1911 and August of 1912, and all but Hogan, who would certainly play his part later, made their Ryder Cup debut in 1937 when they were twenty-five years old. Combined, they would win seven of the next thirteen US Opens, eight of the next fifteen Masters and seven of the next fourteen PGA Championships. It was obvious that Great Britain wasn't producing young golfers of that caliber.

The introduction of steel shafts allowed for the modern, grooved swing that the younger American players mastered. Theirs was more of a power game than the "feel" game of the British. Likewise, golf was becoming more of a sport than a game in the States.

British pros were still bound to their home clubs, stealing away occasionally to compete and often in just one-day events. American pros were becoming independent contractors. They now played a nearly year-round circuit for prize money that made them tournament-hardened with more opportunity to practice and hone their swings. They were professional golfers. The Brits were golfing professionals.

"In general, American professional golfers are much more studious and 'method-conscious' than their British rivals," Horton Smith, a member of the '37 US team, wrote. "This leads to greater uniformity of style and, I think, [a] more sound and fool-proof swing, especially when under pressure, as always happens in important events."

Signs of the more modern approach by the US team were everywhere. For the first time, Walter Hagen would not be crossing irons with the Brits, even as his formidable presence would be still felt as the non-playing captain. The Haig's putting touch had gone dry. "Whiskey fingers," he called it. The selection process now included opportunities to play one's way onto the team. The tournament committee of the PGA of America named the first six players, including the 1936 US Open champ (the little-known New Yorker Tony Manero) and PGA champ (Denny Shute) with the other berths allotted to Gene Sarazen, Henry Picard, Johnny Revolta and Horton Smith. The final four spots would go to the four best aggregate scores from the two qualifying rounds of the PGA Championship and the four rounds of the US Open, then considered the two US professional majors (the Masters was not at the time). Long-hitting Ed Dudley, the head professional at Augusta National, joined Snead, Masters champ Nelson and Guldahl, the 1937 US Open winner, as qualifiers, proving the wisdom of the new selection process.

That left the ten-man US team with four rookies, compared with just two on the British side. Coming off the 9-3 American romp in 1935, the stage was now set for the first team to win on foreign soil and eventually to a run of American dominance that would lead to the inclusion of continental European players to make the Cup more competitive.

Everyone felt the United States was sending its strongest team yet to Southport & Ainsdale Golf Club on the west coast of England. Still, no American Ryder Cup team had been able to master the difficult weather and strange conditions that had always flummoxed them away from their shores. The match was still considered a toss-up.

Even Grantland Rice, America's foremost sports columnist, favored the Brits. He quoted Charles Lacey, the English-born touring pro from Long Island, whose brother Arthur was on the British Ryder Cup squad, waxing on the prospects of British player Henry Cotton.

"To my mind Cotton is the greatest golfer in the world today," Lacey went on. "I played against him over tough conditions where he had a 64 and a 65 and I never saw anyone hitting the ball any better. He is a master of every shot . . . the remainder of the British team is strong. And they know local conditions much better than our men do—especially our younger stars who may find out what real wind is when it blows in from the sea."

Blowing, too, was American bravado.

Even before the teams were selected, Hagen predicted an American sweep of the Ryder Cup and Open Championship while Fred Corcoran, team manager and future PGA executive, taunted the Brits. "We are bringing a winning team," he said. "In fact, we only brought the Cup over here for you to get a look at it and see for yourselves that we are taking good care of it."

"If we don't win this time we'll never win over here," said the veteran Sarazen, whose confidence was grounded in the three twenty-five-year-olds. He pointed to the arrival of a "new school" that would send the "old timers" to a "nice easy chair on the clubhouse porch."

"You can have your Hagens, Armours, Coopers and Sarazens this year," he had said at the start of the season. "I'll take those three hungry kids—Ralph Guldahl, Sam Snead and Byron Nelson—in the books every time they start. I'd like to settle right now on a third of their total winnings."

Guldahl was the most hyped of the trio at the time. He was handsome "as all get out," to quote one writer—broad shouldered at 6-feet-2, 175 pounds with wavy black hair. He played in a starched shirt and necktie and often in fashionable colors, like the blue and cream attire he sported while winning the US Open at Oakland Hills in Michigan. The press that week lapped up Guldahl's humble beginnings and return from golf oblivion, writing him up as a Horatio Alger story. Here was someone, born to Norwegian immigrants, who nearly died from double pneumonia at age eleven, a blessing in disguise when doctors advised plenty of sunshine to aid his recovery. A caddie's job at Lakewood Country Club in Dallas fit the prescription, and, in four years' time, the healthy lad was setting course records with an improvised yet perfectly grooved swing. His backswing was fast, his shoulder turn was wide, his wrists were cocked early, and his right elbow flew. But all the moving parts worked.

Guldahl won the Dallas City Championship and skipped his high school graduation to play in the Texas Open, where he finished in eleventh place and opted to pocket his $87.50 winnings to turn pro. Success came quickly. Two years later, in 1931, he won the Santa Monica Open as a nineteen-year-old, a feat unmatched until Jordan Spieth won the John Deere Classic in 2013. That led to a prestigious position as the head pro at the St. Louis Country Club. Then, at the 1933 US Open at North Shore Country Club near Chicago, a frantic fourth-round rally propelled him to the seventy-second hole, where he needed a birdie to win and a par to tie amateur Johnny Goodman, the "Hobo of the Links." He got neither when he missed a four-foot putt, leaving Goodman as the last amateur to win The Open.

Most distressing to Guldahl, who still took the $1,000 first-place prize money, was that he wasn't selected to that year's Ryder Cup team, with the final spot reserved for the US Open champion before Goodman's victory. Although Guldahl's second-place finish was the best among the professionals in the field, the spot went to 1931 US Open champ Billy Burke, due largely (and ironically) to Sarazen's lobbying efforts.

The young Guldahl left his job at the club to play the tour full-time, but he couldn't shake the tag as the guy who yipped the four-footer at North Shore. One anonymous pro allegedly snarked, "Once a runner-up, always a runner-up; golfers never come back after a bust like that." Another pro weighed in on Guldahl's plight: "He's just shot himself through the heart. As a star golfer, this boy is dead from now on."

It first appeared as though those naysayers were right. A 1934 slump dragged into 1935 and, without any earnings to support his wife, Laverne, he returned to his native Texas to give lessons, which he did well—and to sell cars, which he did poorly. When their infant son, Ralph Jr., better known as "Buddy," took ill, they scraped up $27.45 to move to California, where Ralph picked up work as a carpenter on movie sets. He was no longer a PGA member; he couldn't afford the $25 annual dues. But then his luck turned. He met actor Rex Bell (Clara Bow's husband) and comedian Robert Woolsey and began giving lessons to the Hollywood set. Their fees and encouragement put him on a comeback track with a string of money matches at a nine-hole course in Palm Springs, whereafter Bell and Woolsey staked him $100 to enter the 1936 National Open qualifier in Chicago. With his clubs in hock, he found an old putter in his parents' attic in Dallas and headed "flat broke" for Chicago. Once there, he fatefully met a sporting goods executive who lent him a new set of clubs. He took those sticks to Olympia Fields to nab one of fifteen qualifying spots by one stroke.

A year later, Guldahl's confidence was restored after three wins preceding The Open at Oakland Hills. There, as Snead was accepting congratulations as the clubhouse leader with a remarkable score of 283, Guldahl was lining up a 60-foot putt across the lumpy expanse of the eighth green. The roars as it fell told Snead he'd been tied for the lead, but Guldahl still had US Open demons to shake—and Snead would come to know all about US Open demons. Guldahl made the turn needing to shoot one-over on the back nine for the win. Grantland Rice was on the tenth tee when Guldahl arrived.

"If I can't win now, I don't deserve to win," Guldahl told him. "If I can't break 38 on this last nine, just write a story about me saying that I'm a bum. But I'm not going to be a bum again."

Guldahl picked up two more strokes over the next eight holes and arrived at the eighteenth green surrounded by four thousand spectators. There, he paused to pull out a comb and fix his wavy black hair, alternately described as a distraction to calm his nerves or as preparation to accept the trophy well-coiffed. He finished two shots ahead of Snead when he knocked in a climactic two-footer to set the tournament record and earn his ticket to England.

So did Snead, who was playing in his first US Open. He would go on to finish second three more times, denied the one trophy he needed to complete the career grand slam. He had closed out his round with an eagle after hitting what he'd call as good a wood shot as he ever hit, 235 yards to the green with six feet of backspin. After sinking the eight-foot putt to a thunderous reaction, he was mobbed by the thousands who were following him, the radio men thrusting microphones in his face. USGA officials were so sure his score would stand up that they hustled him through the clubhouse kitchen to a secluded back porch. On the way, Tommy Armour told him, "Laddie, you've just won a championship worth more than a seat on the stock exchange." Everyone, except for Guldahl, felt he'd clinched it. He waited under a tree listening to the gallery roars.

Despite his disappointment that year at Oakland Hills, Snead was a phenom who came out in 1937 the way Arnold Palmer did in 1954 and Tiger Woods in 1997. He energized the sport when it needed it the most. The tour was struggling when he burst out of the Appalachian hills to set the winter circuit on fire and become golf's top drawing card, a story too good to be true and one that could never be repeated. His embellished hillbilly charm appealed to the galleries, drawing them in. An incredible athlete, he could kick a ceiling from a standing start (and reveled in demonstrating it) and hit a ball off the tee longer than anybody before him. In contrast to Guldahl's herky-jerky motion, Snead's unusual flexibility and double-jointed wrists enabled a swing of pure butter, or, as he once said, "like sorghum molasses pours from a jug." He made the game look easy. "I just watched a kid who doesn't know anything about playing golf, and I don't want to be around when he learns how," Sarazen said when he got his first glimpse of Snead, and he couldn't have been more correct.

Snead was born the last of six siblings on a beautiful spring day, perfect for golf at the nearby Homestead Resort, where his father worked maintaining the boilers. He was given the first name Samuel after his maternal grandfather and the middle name Jackson for his grandpappy's friend, Confederate general Stonewall Jackson. While his strict Methodist father ensured the family never went hungry (including dirt farming on the side), Sam's childhood was a backwoods existence—hunting racoons in the Back Creek Mountains and ducking gunshots from moonshiners when venturing too close to their whiskey stills. He was a self-described "peckerwood kid."

"When the chores was finished all of us Snead kids scattered for the hills. We were rounded up on Sunday the way they call hogs," he wrote in his book, *The Education of a Golfer.* "My mother, who had a good, strong voice, would let out a war whoop that could be heard over the next mountain and when we struggled in, they scraped off the mud and wood ticks and put us into clean clothes for churchgoing."

Snead would shag balls for his brother Homer, twelve years older, but he couldn't get his hands on Homer's mid-iron, because Homer took it everywhere. So he fashioned a rudimentary club out of a maple limb, which he used to knock around stones, then improved on it by attaching a beat-up clubhead to a buggy whip. The flexible rigged-up shaft led to his impeccable tempo and timing, teaching him how to feel a pause during the backswing.

"People think growing up in the hills was a handicap I had to overcome," he wrote. "In a lot of ways, it gave me a big advantage that has lasted me to this day. Just like with that stick, I'd had to overcompensate for just about everything: sticks for clubs, acorns for balls. When I finally got my hands on the real things, the regulation stuff seemed like a dream."

Snead started caddying at The Homestead when he was seven, barefoot with a bag slung over each shoulder, a sight for the well-heeled visitors who played the mountainous course when not luxuriating in the hotel's natural springs. But as he grew up—slender and strapping—his swing became something to behold. He achieved his first bit of notice when he outdrove Johnny Goodman and the long-hitting Lawson Little and Billy Burke in a four-person match at The Greenbrier, where he'd gotten his first big break as an assistant. And by 1936, he'd made his way to his first pro tour event in Hershey, Pennsylvania, dropping jaws by driving the 345-yard opening hole of his practice round.

His sixth-place finish set the stage for his winter circuit breakout in Florida and out west. Hailed in an *Oakland Post Enquirer* headline as "unknown," he won the first of eighty-two career victories at the Oakland Open, edging Guldalhl by two shots as the only player to break par. He added another win in Bing Crosby's tourney in San Diego. By the time the asters and the turtleheads started blooming back home, the guy who had to bum a ride to California returned with $4,150, third on the winter circuit money list.

But not everything was coming up so sweetly. Snead felt jinxed by a series of bizarre (and almost comical) circumstances that conspired against him. A year earlier, he had reported to the wrong site for PGA Championship qualifying, assuming he was required to qualify out of Virginia, not West Virginia. Then, when motoring to a tournament in Thomasville, Georgia, he took a wrong turn and ended up in Thomasville, Alabama. He was disqualified for signing an incorrect scorecard at Pinehurst. He was injured in Florida and somehow lost the feeling in his hands while leading a tournament in Charleston. But the worst snafu would take place at the Metropolitan Open at Forest Hill Field Club in Bloomfield, New Jersey, playing before the New York crowds and media for the first time.

Face to face with the biggest press contingent he'd seen, he charmed them and predicted that the jinx would end that week. "Hexed hillbilly predicts win over blue ribbon field," read one headline and he started to make good on the promise by tying Jimmy Hines for the first-round lead with a 68. Snead had a morning tee time for the second round, setting a tournament course record with a 65. But morning rains turned into afternoon downpours and, after the course became unplayable, the Metropolitan Golf Association considered its options along with all the complaints. Today the decision would be easy. Play would be suspended until the next day. But Max Kaesche, chairman of the MGA, ruled that all scores would be wiped out and the entire round would be replayed. Egged on to join a walk out in protest by several players, Snead remained but finished third to Hines by three shots, with a second-round 70 in place of his nullified score.

Immediately afterwards, he was installed as the 8-1 favorite to win the US Open, even though no rookie had ever won the national championship. It took Guldahl's great finish to add to his streak of bad luck. Still, he'd qualified easily for the Ryder Cup with the top aggregate score of 430, two shots better than Guldahl and Dudley. Nelson came in fourth at 432. Snead long maintained that a group of veteran players had attempted to keep him off the team, among them Paul Runyon, who had been left off. But the qualification system was in place and well known. Runyon's gripe was more sour grapes. "If he can't find Pittsburgh or Thomasville, Georgia, how can he possibly find his way to England?" Runyon sniped. But there was no keeping Snead off the roster.

Like Snead, Nelson emerged from rural America, only from the cotton fields of Texas. Like Guldahl, Nelson defied the child mortality rates of the era. His mother, Madge, was barely eighteen when she became pregnant, and Nelson was such a big baby (twelve pounds, eight ounces) his mother's labor lasted all day and into the night. The doctor, who came in from out of town, didn't think he'd survive and was just trying to save Madge. But his mom refused to give up. The doctor used forceps, breaking the infant's nose and, according to Nelson, leaving two dents in the side of his head. Thought to be stillborn, he was placed on a nearby table. A few minutes later his grandmother, who was cleaning him up, shouted, "Doctor, this child is alive." And so, he was.

Nelson's father, John, was a cotton farmer who had inherited a 160-acre farm at the age of six after his parents died of consumption. John was a hard worker, shorter than his son but with big hands, as Nelson explained in his autobiography, *How I Played the Game.* John moved the family from Waxahachie to a leased, two hundred sixty-acre farm overlooking the San Saba River. To serve as a good example to his father's hired hands, Nelson worked his hands to the bone in the fields with the sun burning his fair skin.

Times got tough when the boll weevil infestation hit Texas. The family moved again, this time to the railroad town of San Angelo and later, to Fort Worth. But Nelson remained a rancher at heart and, eventually, he'd leave competitive golf behind to run one.

"I think it was those early years when we moved to the city that I began to think about someday just having a ranch of my own out in the country," he wrote in his book. "My earliest and happiest memories, after all, were all associated with being out in the country, shoeless and happy as could be, a little fella riding that coal-black horse to school and back. That sort of thing stays with you."

Nelson's first exposure to the game came from caddying, like most players of the day. He had no idea what golf was when he asked a few schoolmates how they had come by a few extra coins. Nelson was twelve and had just survived a life-threatening bout with typhoid fever when he walked over to Glen Garden Country Club on the southwest side of Fort Worth and into the sport that would define him. There, he joined a caddie yard that included another squirt by the name of Ben Hogan.

He shot 118 the first time he ever played—the Glen Garden caddies were allowed to play at the Christmas party the club threw for them—but he was hooked. Two years later, he won Glen Garden's caddie championship after a nine-hole playoff against Hogan. He turned into one of the best amateurs in Texas (along with Hogan) and, out of a job in 1932, he made the decision to turn pro in Texarkana, Arkansas, two years after Hogan. Nelson's professional career took off faster than his rival's. After turning pro in high school, Hogan scraped by without winning a pro tournament until 1940, missing US Open cuts in 1934, '36 and '38. Nelson, meanwhile, attracted enough attention to be invited to the 1935 Masters, where he finished in a tie for ninth but, more importantly, got the break he needed.

George Jacobus, president of the PGA and the head professional at New Jersey's Ridgewood Country Club, needed an assistant and attended the 1935 Masters seeking one. He and Ed Dudley, the head professional at Augusta were tight, and Dudley knew Nelson from Texas and Arkansas. Jacobus was impressed with the soft-spoken Christian's demeanor and offered him the job. A few months later, Nelson found himself as one of the organizers of the 1935 Ryder Cup at his new home course, following all the matches with keen interest.

"It got me to thinking about getting to be a good enough player to make the team," wrote Nelson, who admitted in his autobiography that he was impressed most by the outfits the American team had been given. "It gave me that much more motivation for working on my game."

He became even more motivated when the Ridgewood caddies laughed at his aspirations of making the team. "Quit dreamin' Byron," they told him. But they laughed a little less after losing an impressive bet against him. A flagpole stood about one hundred feet away from the pro shop and the caddies challenged him to hit it from the slate terrace in front of the entrance. Nelson had played off plenty of bare lies in Texas, so he eagerly took on their nickels and dimes with more than just a bit of confidence. He missed his first attempt by six feet and then nailed the pole with his second shot. A plaque still marks the spot.

Today, Nelson is considered the father of the modern golf swing. No one adapted to steel shafts better. Where hickory shafts twisted and torqued, requiring a lot of hand action, Nelson stood more upright and used his lower body to achieve a dip that kept his clubface on plane through impact, resulting in consistent accuracy and power. When he won the Masters in 1937, he set a then-first round record 66 by hitting every green in regulation and reaching each of the par-five holes in two. His swing was so consistent, the USGA named its testing machine "Iron Byron."

"The mechanics of my swing were such that it required no thought. It's like eating. You don't think to feed yourself," he explained.

The three twenty-five-year-olds—Guldahl, Snead and Nelson—gave the American team a new look, pulling the squad's average age down to thirty, one year younger than the Brits. More importantly, the three newcomers kicked the talent level up a notch. Each was a future Hall of Famer. Although the British team included the last four British Open champions, it fielded only two players with winning Ryder Cup records—Charles Whitcombe (3-2-3) and Percy Alliss (2-1-1)—with the other six veterans at a combined 1-10-2. Sam King and Welshman Dai Rees (later to become a Ryder Cup fixture) were the two Ryder Cup rookies while Henry Cotton, unquestionably the best British golfer, was the biggest addition to the roster. He had played in only one Ryder Cup, going 1-1-1 in 1929 at Moortown in England, having been made ineligible for the next due to the Cup's residency requirements (he had worked at a club in Belgium). Samuel Ryder and the Brits refused the American PGA's suggestion to include Cotton on the 1935 team that traveled to Ridgewood. Now he was hailed as Great Britain's talisman.

There was some trepidation surrounding the finalization of the British team in early June, starting with Charles Whitcombe's selection as the playing captain. Most observers favored George Duncan, the wizened Scot who won The Open Championship in 1920 and Britain's playing captain in 1929. H. Lascelles Carr of the *Western Mail* worried that Hagen, without having to worry about his own golf game, would outfox Whitcombe at every turn.

"It was only after a great deal of controversy that the present plan was settled and I, like most golfers who have taken part in team engagements, cannot help but feel that America, with that arch-schemer Hagen to look after the players' interests in the role of non-playing captain, will have an enormous advantage as regards leadership," he wrote.

Then there were questions about the team itself, with so many of the top players struggling with their games. Again, Carr expressed his concern: "When I spoke to one of the selectors after the meeting ended yesterday, he said, 'Our lot would have been much easier six months ago. During the present season those players with reputation have been strangely out of form while members of the younger school have fared well in one tournament, only to disappoint in the next'."

Carr closed the article with the classic stiff upper lip.

"Now that they are selected, they can start to weld themselves into a happy team, ready to fight to the last ditch," he concluded.

In contrast, it was a pretty confident group of Americans who gathered at the Hotel New Yorker to be feted by the PGA before their departure. They were issued official team outfits–blue slacks and white blazers with a pair of black and white dress shoes and matching ties. As they entered the ballroom for an extravagant dinner, they were greeted by an orchestra belting out the Star Spangled Banner..

Everyone but Hagen, who would meet them in London, gathered at New York's Chelsea piers for the six-day trip across the Atlantic on the aptly named *SS Manhattan*, the same luxury liner that had carried the victorious US Olympic team to Germany the previous year. Six wives and little Buddy Guldahl accompanied the team with the three youngest American players admittedly apprehensive about the crossing. In fact, Laverne Guldahl had told reporters her husband feared winning the US Open and making the Cup squad because of his seasickness.

Although Nelson said it was smooth sailing, Snead said he got queasy, an opportunity the veterans seized on to haze him. According to his autobiography, they told Snead the cure was celery stalks and hard rolls and no other food, plus two hours of dancing nightly in the ballroom. He complied, "and darned if it didn't work," he marveled.

They also introduced Snead, as a former prizefighter from Virginia, to a burly passenger who challenged him to spar. When Snead admitted that he'd been in the ring a few times, the man thumped Snead's chest and told him he'd "work him in." Snead had no idea the man was Tommy Farr, the British heavyweight champ who would give Joe Louis all he could handle in their prize fight at Yankee Stadium the next month.

Pranking Snead and playing shuffleboard kept the team entertained until they neared Plymouth, their destination on the English Channel near the southwest tip of England. Seagulls greeted the ship in arabesque flights as it came within sight of the Cornish coast. Boredom shifted to ingenuity and an impromptu practice session that distracted other passengers on the deck taking in the wild cliffs of the Penwith Peninsula and its skeins of gulls. The team collected eight dozen golf balls, headed to the top deck and took aim, looking for birdies. Reportedly, no one bagged one.

They soon boarded a train to London, where Hagen waved to his men as they stepped onto the platform, joined by H.W. Barbour, the mayor of Southport, and R. Mackenzie, a British selector decked out in full Scottish regalia. Hagen removed the Ryder Cup from its bespoke case and handed it to the mayor.

"We must not drop it this time," he said, "because I want it back in good condition." Hagen had arranged for a practice round at the private course on the lavish estate of his friend, the legendary host Sir Philip Sassoon, in nearby Kent. There, the entire traveling contingent was treated to an elaborate lunch. They stayed in London long enough for photographers to capture Buddy Guldahl practicing golf on the hotel roof, and caught an overnight train to Southport. Although it might sound like a hectic schedule, it was the earliest a US team had arrived for the Ryder Cup. They would have more practice time on the golf course most Britishers hoped would confound them, just as the Southport & Ainsdale had four years earlier when Shute's three-putt on the final hole gave Syd

Easterbrook and Great Britain the victory in one of the closest Cups ever contested.

Hagen had been afforded a grand view of that scene, watching as Shute and Easterbrook walked up the eighteenth fairway from in front of the big window of the clubhouse while chatting with Edward, the Prince of Wales, and future—albeit briefly—monarch. Spectators had been herded away to clear the prince's vantage. Hagen was aware that Shute needed only to two-putt from 30 feet to give the US its first win on British soil. Shute did not know it. But since the US captain was tied up with the prince, he dared not leave him to apprise Shute of the situation. Shute played for the birdie and went five feet past then missed the comeback. Easterbrook holed his two-footer to return possession of the Cup to Great Britain for the last time in a long while. Shute shook it off by defeating Ryder Cup teammate Craig Wood in a playoff to win The Open at St. Andrews, but British golf fans could believe that S&A would hold some sort of "hoodoo" over the Americans when they returned.

Designed by the great James Braid in 1906, S&A was at the time more prominent than its neighbor, Birkdale, which, flouting its "Royal" designation, hosted the Ryder Cup in 1965, and became a regular part of The Open rota. S&A played entirely as a links course despite its slightly inland location and was just a ten-minute walk from the Ainsdale rail station that brought in record crowds from Liverpool. While it stretched out to 6,900 yards to a par of 73, the course would still favor the home side. The British Isles had experienced an extended drought leaving the fairways, only 40 yards wide, running hard and fast, optimum conditions for the British style of play. Several holes were memorable, starting with a rare par-three opener. It was there in 1933, when Hagen, taking the club back for a practice swing on the tee, nearly clocked Britain's non-playing captain, J.H. Taylor. The stodgy Taylor, already miffed since Hagen had twice failed to appear to exchange the order of play, glared in contempt, at which Hagen stingingly replied, "I wouldn't dare come that close to you."

The second hole, named "Terrace," afforded the best viewpoint for spectators, an enormous sand hill behind the green. The tee box on the par-three eighth had been moved back into the neighboring cemetery to lengthen the hole for the two Ryder Cups. Named "Plateau," the hole was just that, set on a hill, and offering an extremely difficult recovery shot to anyone coming up short. The famous "Gumbley's," the sixteenth, measured 490 yards along the railroad tracks over waves of sandhills with the second shot taken blind over a huge cross bunker fortified by railway sleepers, placed 100 yards in front of the green. The fairway on the seventeenth, named "Ainsdale," was strewn with bunkers and had gnarly rough along its entire left side with its green perilously close to an out-of-bounds railway fence. The closing hole was beautifully framed by bunkers in front of the clubhouse where Hagen and the Prince of Wales had watched Shute's misfortune two years previously.

The Americans had little issue with their first on-site practice sessions on Friday, when Guldahl came out firing with a 67. But Saturday ushered in those treacherous winds that make links golf so challenging. Writing for the *Associated Press,* Scotty Reston sent an ominous report back to the states.

"Bounded by a graveyard and a terrifying range of sand dunes and swept for the first time in a week by a stiff wind, the Southport & Ainsdale course frightened America's picked professional golfers today into a full realization of the task that lies ahead of them . . . the sub-par scores that has marked the Americans' first tussles with the layout were conspicuously absent today."

Henry Longhurst, who would become well-known to American television audiences for his commentary, wrote how the visitors, "with their brightly hued clothes and unfamiliar air," were more colorful than their opponents, but added, "after watching them fairly closely I came to the conclusion that they were not playing golf any better."

Longhurst was especially critical of Snead. While admitting that his "wide, elastic sort of swing" sent his drives a "positively frightening distance" and with "such accuracy that a reasonably alert goalkeeper could have fielded them on the first or second bounce," he wasn't as taken with Snead's iron play which he called, "encouragingly unimpressive."

Meanwhile, he lavished praise on Cotton's "phenomenal" practice round. Accustomed to the conditions, Cotton played his own ball and made the turn in 30 on the way to a brilliant course record 64. Afterwards he said he still wasn't satisfied with his game even after eight birdies. It was enough to turn H. Lascelles Carr's angst into swagger.

"His (Cotton's) play among that of a bevy of champions all at the top of their form has been outstanding–so outstanding, in fact, that he has instilled fear into the hearts of the Americans," Carr joyously penned. "Not only that, but Cotton's return to the best golf he has so inspired the rest of the British team that none of them will accept the suggestion of defeat. And there is good ground for that confidence.

"Padgham (who shot 68 in his practice round) has recovered his putting touch. Charles Whitcombe is a rock of steadiness and a fine captain. D.J. Rees, Wales' gallant member of the side, is reeling off 68 and 69 with disdainful ease and Alliss, Cox, Lacey and Burton are all hitting the ball a long way and very straight."

That "ball" was also an issue for the Americans, or at least everyone thought. With Great Britain hosting, its smaller ball (0.06 inches less in diameter but the same weight) was in play. It flew farther than the American ball but could be more difficult to hit, especially because it didn't set up as well on the tighter lies of linksland. As they adjusted, the Americans had an easier time Sunday before the southwesterly winds started blowing again Monday.

"British hopes rose with the wind and the prospect for a gale for Tuesday silenced all talk that the invaders might win in a breeze," the *AP* reported.

Hagen, however, was cleverly mixing up his combinations for the opening foursomes matches and decided to pair youth with experience, while leaving Smith and Snead out of action for the day. As Longhurst had observed, Snead was fighting a hook and might have had his partner hitting out of the scrubby overgrowth that the English call rough. Hagen explained to reporters that Snead was too long for fairways that seemed to run forever. At the same time, though, he had a surprise for the British in the metronomically straight Nelson.

While the British were expecting Hagen to lead off with the seasoned Sarazen and Shute against Cotton and Padgham, Hagen, guessing that Whitcombe would lead off with his strength, sent out good friends Nelson and Dudley in what was seen as a sacrifice to the hosts. Indeed, a week before the matches, Whitcombe predicted: "I don't care who plays against Henry in the Ryder Cup. That fellow is going to finish second." Now, the headline in the local Southport paper read "Hagen Leads Lambs to the Butcher." But Hagen was thinking nothing of the sort. He told Nelson: "Byron, you've got a lot of steam. A lot of get-up-and-go. And Dudley needs someone to push him. So, I'm going to put you two together. You can get him fired up."

Whoever came up with the lambs headline had no doubt never witnessed a demonstration of Nelson's accuracy before. Nelson, matched up against Cotton in the alternate shot format, drove it beautifully and put his ball inside Cotton's on every par-three. The match was supposed to set the tone for the Brits. Instead, it shocked their senses with the Americans' 4-and-2 victory. The same Southport paper came back with a "Lambs Bite Butcher" headline the next day, lamenting a 2 ½-1 ½ deficit and wondering how the Americans had done it with wind gusts so strong they kicked up sand into the faces of the estimated fifteen thousand spectators, bundled up in overcoats and long skirts.

As it was, most of the damage the Americans wrought occurred in the afternoon. When the team adjourned for lunch after the first eighteen holes, the Brits were ahead in two matches with the other two all square. But in a precursor of what was to happen, Nelson and Dudley fought back to even the match by winning the sixteenth and seventeenth after twice being two holes down. Cotton, Britain's great hope, lost his magic. He sent his second shot burrowing into the rough at Gumby's, the sixteenth, losing to an American birdie. Rattled, he then missed a putt inside two feet on seventeen.

The momentum continued after lunch. The Americans climbed out to an early four-hole lead, and, by the time they reached the pivotal sixteenth, they had the Brits dormie three. Cotton's second shot found the Gumbley's bunker and destroyed any chance of winning the hole.

Guldahl was paired with Manero. They were one down to Cox and Lacey after eighteen and two down after six holes in the afternoon round. They won the next two holes to pull even and, once more, Gumbley's bit the home team. Lacey hooked one off the tee and missed the green with his approach into seventeen, giving the US a 2-and-1 victory.

The only British win came from Alliss and Burton over Picard and Revolta. Rees, the only player on the British squad not born in England, kept his team in it when he coolly sank a par putt after Whitcombe, eliciting audible gasps from the crowd, sent the first putt seven feet past. That halved their match against Sarazen and Shute.

The Brits knew they couldn't match up against the Americans man for man. Now, they would have to win five of the eight singles matches the next day. It all came down to taking down Cotton in the swing match. Hagen was patting himself on the back for his prescience.

"I still think we'll win by eight to four," he said, doubling down on his pre-match prediction. "That boy Nelson certainly has it. I knew Dudley would come through and Nelson told me yesterday that he wouldn't trade places with anybody but wanted to play the toughest the British had. Well, I wondered then, but not anymore.

"You've been telling me I'm a mastermind, so I guess I'd better go into a huddle with myself and figure out tomorrow's lineups," he continued before dashing away.

"He's the boy who did it, not me," Dudley said, deflecting the praise to his partner. "I want Walter to put him in against Cotton in the singles tomorrow."

Cotton was nonplussed.

"I missed four iron shots this morning that were costly, but I was pretty satisfied with my play this afternoon," he told the American press. "Nelson played splendid golf. I do feel your side's mistakes were a bit less costly than ours, but that's simply the rub of the game."

Whitcombe, thankful that Rees bailed him out, called it "a great day's golf. We shall be fighting hard tomorrow."

When tomorrow came the drought broke—and did it ever. The *Times of London* wrote that "more deplorable conditions than those of the morning are hardly conceivable. The sky was black with never a break, the light was bad, the ground was rapidly getting water-logged."

But here, again, the Americans stole the advantage, not because they were more accustomed to playing in those more typical British conditions, but rather because the PGA had provided them with rain suits and towels. The Brits, in their more cumbersome gear, carried only umbrellas for protection—and they weren't holding up very well.

As on the first day, there was a narrow window of hope for the Brits. Padgham, who would be defending his Open championship at Carnoustie in two weeks, insisted on leading off, drawing Guldahl, the reigning US Open champ. Guldahl played splendidly. He was 6-up after eighteen before coasting to an 8-and-6 victory, almost assuring that the Brits would need to win five of the other seven matches. At lunchtime, the long shot had possibilities with the US up in four, Great Britain three and one all-square. When King halved with Shute, Rees beat a struggling Nelson, 3-and-1, and Cotton rebounded by beating Manero, 5-and-3, Britain had evened things up, 4-4. Its hoped were short-lived, however, as the Americans turned it on, winning the final four. Snead, finally in action, was the most impressive, beating Burton, 5-and-4, in a match of big hitters. Whitcombe had said before the matches that Burton's opponent could be "written off" while the Liverpool papers noted that Burton's long driving "has terrified and unnerved many opponents." Snead, however, must have unnerved Burton by hitting it past him, although he did have to recover from a gaffe on one of the early holes when he failed to check his ball before taking his shot. The West Virginian must have been shocked by Burton's proper English as he claimed the hole, telling Snead, "Beg your pardon but you've just played my ball."

It was Sarazen who secured the clinching point with a 1-up win over Alliss in a dramatic match filled with great shots, terrific momentum swings and good fortune. Sarazen started hot in the morning to win four of the first five holes, but Alliss battled back to go 1-up at the break and 3-up when they made the turn in the afternoon. Hagen strolled with the match and kept telling the British fans Sarazen would win. Three straight Sarazen birdies squared the match and after Alliss once again nudged ahead with a par win at thirteen, Sarazen answered by rolling in an 18-foot putt at fourteen. The golf gods smiled down on the Squire at the next hole. His tee shot at the short fifteenth bounded through the green and would have finished in a bunker had not a female spectator failed to move. Instead, the ball got caught up in her skirt.

"What am I to do?" she asked frantically, before standing up and shaking free the ball, which rolled back onto the green, ten feet from the hole. Alliss two-putted for par before Sarazen rolled in the gift birdie.

Sarazen caught another break when his tee shot on seventeen bounced off a spectator onto the fairway, allowing him to halve the hole with a 10-foot par putt after Alliss rammed home a 30-footer over a stymie, forcing the match to the thirty-sixth hole. "How he sank that putt, Hagen and I will never know," Sarazen said. Then, on the last, Alliss' 10-foot birdie effort stayed on the lip, giving Sarazen the point. Sarazen claimed that the rub of the green went both ways and that during the morning round the stewards in charge of crowd control had moved Alliss' ball back inside the out of bounds stake on the fourteenth hole.

He was quoted as saying: "That's when I made up my mind to beat him," although the authenticity of that comment is questionable.

The home crowd, an estimated 12,000, was left to console itself with Rees' gallant showing. When he finished off Nelson, he was lifted on their shoulders and carried off the green. Rees went on to play in nine Ryder Cups and captained five.

Hagen, accepting the trophy from Lord Wardington Beaumont Pease (Samuel Ryder died the previous year), proclaimed the moment as "the biggest thrill of my golfing life."

Braced against the cold by an ascot around his neck, he continued: "We have won that beautiful gold trophy for the first time on American soil," before someone from the crowd reminded him with a sharp yell, "British soil."

Hagen, however, was always known for his great recovery shots.

"British," he said, correcting himself while putting a finger up to his mouth. "You can see how well I feel at home.

"I want to congratulate captain Charles Whitcombe for the grand showing he has made with all the boys," he went on. "They have done their very best I know, and the matches were very, very close. It was only toward the last two matches that I didn't have to eat the cigarettes. I could smoke them."

The Americans had had a cheery time, especially while enjoying the English beer (but not the food), as numerous newspapers reported. They now owned a 17-7 advantage in the last two Ryder Cups and would go on to win five more in succession. Clearly, America had become the best golfing nation in the world, a point that Gayle Talbot of *the New York World Telegram* gleefully drove home without mercy.

"England's professional golfers, though fine fellows personally and uniformly kind to their mothers, simply can't take it very well under pressure," he wrote. "That's the painful and reluctant conclusion drawn after watching them–with a couple of notable exceptions–fizzle out like damp firecrackers in the concluding stages of the Ryder Cup matches."

The British press, while not going as far as Talbot, was forced to admit that the Americans were the better team. *Golf Monthly* wrote that "the deportment of every man cannot be overpraised" and that the visitors "presented a splendid spectacle of athletic youth."

Louis T. Stanley, one of the deans of British golf writers, opined that "the British team dressed like workmen and played at the game. The Americans dressed like golfers and worked at the game." Bernard Darwin, perhaps the most prominent British golf writer of all time, lamented that his prediction of a British win was predicated on the Americans' unfamiliarity with the links-style course and the conditions. He criticized Whitcombe for pairing Cotton and Padgham. But in the end, he admitted it would have made little difference.

There were various theories why the US won handily, mostly surrounding how the relative lack of competitive golf available to the British golfers placed them at a disadvantage when the going got tough.

"It might sound a little uncharitable, but the fact remains that this is the first time the American golfers have come over in time to have adequate practice for the Ryder Cup match and the first time that they have given the impression of taking it really seriously. For once they ran into form *before* The Open Championship," the *Evening Standard* noted. "The frequently quoted opinion that they are better putters remains true, but no one who watched them in action at Southport could possibly doubt that they were better all around. With the exception of Cotton, the British team looked like golfers in the making–promising material one might say. The Americans are the finished article."

George Duncan, the man some wanted to captain the team, boiled it down to the short game, which, much down the road, would become a European advantage.

"It seems that, at least until recently, the British player, missing the green with his second shot on a par-four hole or with his tee shot on a par-three, sort of unconsciously resigned himself to losing a stroke," he observed. The greedy and hard-headed American, however, resigned himself to nothing of the kind. His attitude was that he'd get down in two from where he was, by gum. So, he worked away at his chipping and developed clubs for it and studied his putting with a thousand different kinds of putters.

"In a word, the American was all for taking up any slack in the long game by rolling three strokes into two and two into one when he got within short pitching or chipping range of the flag."

Cotton regained a measure of British pride by beating Shute in a special 72-hole match for what was billed as the world professional match play title. A week later, he won The Open Championship in even more wretched weather at Carnoustie, upsetting many predictions that the claret jug would be handed to a member of the US Ryder Cup team. Only three–Nelson, Dudley and Smith–finished in the top ten. For Dudley, it marked three top tens–in the two Opens and the Masters.

But the '37 Ryder Cuppers weren't through with making headlines. After arriving back home over turbulent seas, Guldahl made things even stormier by calling the British fans "bum sports."

"If the British golf customers are sportsmen, then I hope I never see this tight little island again," he said. "As far as I'm concerned, I wouldn't swap a Texas cactus plant for the whole of England."

Guldahl, who cruised to his two victories at Southport, claimed that the British fans never cheered until the Americans made a mistake. He went to watch Manero's match after his own finished and claimed that the gallery, which was not cordoned off at the time, refused to give Manero room even after he requested it. Dudley joined in, claiming that a spectator intentionally knocked Alf Perry's ball back into play during their singles match. Shute alleged a woman knocked Rees' wayward shot toward the green with her handbag.

"British antipathy to Americans reached a new height during our visit," Dudley submitted. "There was a different feeling toward us this year. There was not the same sporty good fellowship which had been showered on us in previous years."

The British players were livid. Many wondered why Guldahl waited until he returned to America before unloading. Perry called Dudley's claim a lie and asserted that his ball had hit a ridge. Cotton said he was astounded and called the statements undignified. Padgham, Guldahl's singles victim, called his comments disgusting. Lacey, who played against Guldahl on the first day, fumed: "Perhaps it would be a good thing if he doesn't come back. I thought he was a rather difficult fellow."

Charles Lacey immediately appealed for Jacobus, as PGA president, to take some action, with initial comments to the media attempting to straddle the line.

"I wish to say that Ed Dudley, the acting captain, and other players were all extremely complimentary about the sportsmanlike attitude of the British team," Lacey told *The Daily Telegraph*. "They were all full of praise for the officials, the press and for the fine hospitality they enjoyed. They realize, of course, that the officials could not control the excited feelings of the gallery. They tell me the galleries in England are bigger than over here and include more people who come for the spectacle but know little about golf."

Jacobus, simultaneously embroiled in a power struggle within the PGA, was under pressure to do more. He tried to extinguish the brush fire with telegrams to the team, requesting the offenders to retract, apologize for or clarify their remarks, while hinting at suspension. He also cabled the British PGA, which had been unsatisfied with his initial comments.

"I am calling on the American players to clarify or retract their statements and they will," he promised, adding that he was grieved by the turn of events. "We consider the sportsmanship of Great Britain as fine as anywhere in the whole world and I am going to leave no stone unturned in an effort to straighten out things, mostly for the sake of the people of Great Britain."

Guldahl was playing in a tournament in Chicago that week, where he offered a half-hearted explanation and explained to Jacobus that his words were taken out of context.

"I still think, however, that the galleries did things which were not sportsmanlike but that is likely to happen anywhere," he said. "My statements may have given a wrong impression. I was critical, certainly, but I was hardly trying to indict the entire British sporting public."

Other team members seemed to comply with Jacobus to a degree.

Shute called the complaints "a lot of bunk."

"Gosh, what do they expect with four thousand or five thousand persons stampeding all over a course?" he asked. "Under those circumstances you can't have absolute quiet."

Horton Smith, the only member of the American team who did not get into a match, said that some complaints were "not entirely unfounded. Members of the gallery were responsible for some small annoyance, but I feel that they have been exaggerated. The gallery conduct was no different from that experienced in this country. The whole situation was magnified above its proper importance. I am sorry that all this has come up and regret any embarrassment it may have caused to my good friends in the British Professional Golfers Association or among British sports writers."

Hagen, who remained in Britain playing more exhibitions, advised the British to take no notice, and that "they will be back again." He called the allegations hot air from a bunch of players tired from their journey.

Snead, meanwhile, wired back to Jacobus: "I was treated very well. I have nothing else to say."

Sarazen had plenty to say to George Trevor of the *New York Sun.*

"I think ship news reporters have exaggerated what the Ryder Cup players said and egged 'em on to get a good story," he claimed. "If our boys were not misquoted, then they made fools of themselves. I'm sorry I came home ahead of the gang and wasn't on shipboard when they started sounding off.

"You don't know anything about golf crowds unless you've seen a mob of twelve or fifteen thousand persons swarm out from Liverpool. Naturally that Southport army yelled for the British players. What did our men expect? Would they like golf to be a sissy outdoor parlor game played in a church hush? I think we should have been flattered that the English crowds got so heated up. It was really a compliment to our golfing reputations. They feared our scoring ability and showed it."

Sarazen reaffirmed that he had no complaints to make and that his previous remarks about how this would be his last trip to England merely implied that he was getting too old. He even suggested to one British scribe that the tensions arose not with the American players but rather with the players' wives, claiming that things can go awry when wives travel with the team. Indeed, Guldahl's wife, Laverne, could be outspoken at times and was the darling of the sports scribblers when her husband won at Oakland Hills. They described her as a "brown-eyed, sun-kissed, slender blonde with the dental ad teeth and the soft Texas drawl."

"It's funny, but I don't care about making that trip to England any more than Ralph does," she told the press. "I don't think they have anything over there we haven't got here. A King? Oh, well, every American woman has her own king and Ralph's mine."

Although he betrayed no inkling of it at the time, a year later, Sarazen told Paul Mickelson of the *Associated Press* that he would never play on another Ryder Cup team because Jacobus had gone with Hagen, his bitter rival, over him for the '37 captaincy.

"The failure of Jacobus to name me captain of the team is an insult, a wound that will never heal," he said. "I think everyone would agree my record stacks up favorably enough with that of any other pro, past or present, to have given me a shot at that captaincy. I won every worthwhile championship, and I guess I did my share on every Ryder Cup team we ever had. But no, Jacobus didn't see fit to let me achieve my last and profoundest ambition."

Sarazen went on to say that with Hagen out of the playing lineup, he'd be named captain at last.

"But Jacobus named his bosom pal, Ed Dudley, playing captain and appointed Hagen non-playing captain to give me an insult that made me boil inside. I was ready to explode and quit last year when that happened, but I decided to turn it over in my mind. It's been almost a year since then and I feel the cut more strongly than ever."

Jacobus, who had been feuding with Sarazen, denied that politics had any part in naming Hagen captain. "I considered him the best qualified and most popular man for the position. There was no prejudice against Sarazen last year or at any other time," he stated.

The controversy was soon forgotten as the Ryder Cup was put on hold for ten years. Hitler's fascism was on the rise on the Continent as the teams met that June with demonstrations by his *Kriegsmarine* as Neville Chamberlain, in his first foreign policy speech, urged restraint toward Germany to avoid a larger European war. Two years later, Europe was thrust into armed conflict, and the Ryder Cup, scheduled for the Ponte Vedra Country Club that November, became another casualty of war.

The teams would have to wait until 1947 before they could resume their conflict.

DAY 1
FOURSOMES
Ed Dudley/Byron Nelson (US) defeated Alf Padgham/Henry Cotton (GB) 4-and-2 Ralph Guldahl/Tony Manero (US) defeated Arthur Lacey/Bill Cox (GB) 2-and-1 Charles Whitcombe/Dai Rees (GB) halved with Gene Sarazen/Denny Shute (US) Percy Alliss/Dick Burton (GB) defeated Henry Picard/Johnny Revolta (US) 2-and-1 **United States wins session, 2 ½–1 ½**
DAY 2
SINGLES
Ralph Guldahl (US) defeated Alf Padgham (GB) 8-and-7 Sam King (GB) halved with Denny Shute (US) Dai Rees (GB) defeated Byron Nelson (US) 3-and-1 Henry Cotton (GB) defeated Tony Manero (US) 5-and-3 Gene Sarazen (US) defeated Percy Alliss (GB) 1-up Sam Snead (US) defeated Dick Burton (GB) 5-and-4 Ed Dudley (US) defeated Alf Perry (GB) 2-and-1 Henry Picard (US) defeated Arthur Lacey (GB) 2-and-1 **United States wins session, 5 ½–2 ½**
UNITED STATES WINS RYDER CUP 9–5

1947

Reign in the Rain

PORTLAND GOLF CLUB
UNITED STATES 11, GREAT BRITAIN 1

Robert A. Hudson never won a Ryder Cup point, not even a hole. His handicap never dipped below fifteen. But Hudson remains the most underappreciated hero in Ryder Cup history. If the event owes its existence to Samuel Ryder, it owes its survival to this good-hearted entrepreneur from Oregon.

Hudson's life story mirrored that of many professional golfers of his time. He was self-made and hard-working. He toiled away at a wholesale grocery company in Portland at fourteen, about the age those would-be pros started to caddie. He rose up the ranks to city sales manager at nineteen, about when those golfers were turning pro. A year later, he risked all his savings to start the Hudson-Duncan Company, a fruit-packing concern. Soon after, he introduced the Piggly Wiggly supermarket chain to Portland. He liked to joke that he was "just a prune merchant. Nobody yet has asked to see my pits."

Hudson was fifty-seven before he witnessed professional golf, watching Byron Nelson and Jug McSpaden play an exhibition in 1943 at his course, the Portland Golf Club. When the cash-strapped organizers of the first Portland Open were about to cancel the event for the next year, the civic-minded Hudson saved it with $15,000 of his own money. Northwest rains pelted the tournament throughout, but Hudson never lost his optimism or his new-found love for spectator golf. One participant marveled at his spirit: "I'd play in one of his tournaments if I had to go around in a rowboat. He's the

Robert Hudson, the man who saved the Ryder Cup

only one not kicking about the weather, and he's the guy taking a financial bath."

Hudson was the right man at the right time for the Ryder Cup, which had been on a ten-year hiatus since 1937. That year's US victory in England revealed a growing gap between the two major golfing nations, and the war had only widened it. British golf, particularly on the professional side, had taken the bigger hit. The Open Championship had been cancelled from 1939 through 1945 while, in America, only four US Opens, three Masters and one PGA Championship, had been lost. UK coastal defenses had commandeered links golf courses. Fairways were converted into airfields, as at Turnberry, remnants of which still exist. Radar stations, anti-aircraft batteries, anti-glider ditches and mounds were strategically situated where golfers once strategized approach shots. The Richmond Golf Club in Surrey set up temporary golf rules to include relief from shrapnel and the replaying of any shot disturbed by a blast. At Royal Liverpool, part of the neighboring ground was set up as a minefield against a possible German invasion. No one dared venture there to recover wayward balls.

Southport, home to the 1937 Ryder Cup at the Southport & Ainsdale Golf Club, was in a direct line of attack as one hundred thirty-five air raid alerts sounded during the Luftwaffe's deadly blitz on Liverpool, twenty miles to the south. Seventeen people were killed and sixty-six more injured during nine enemy raids and one hundred thirty-one homes were seriously demolished. Incendiary bombs fell on the links at neighboring Birkdale Golf Club, a future Ryder Cup and Open site, and on a nearby home for blind infants.

The UK had emerged from the seven years of combat victorious but almost bankrupt and reliant on US loans. Draconian austerity measures went into place in 1947, including further cuts in food, fuel rations and foreign travel. No more than £75 could be taken out of the country, an amount later reduced to £25. Henry Cotton, the '34 and '37 Open champion, was able to accept his Masters invitation that April only after San Francisco businessman Eddie Lowery forwarded him a loan.

In a speech before the House of Commons, Oliver Stanley, the prominent conservative MP, suggested that the majority labor party had been waiting for help from America "as people once waited for manna from Heaven. It should inconceivable that this country should become permanent pensioners of the United States, committed to living forever on the dole. We would only be entitled to look for help, in the famous words of Mr. (Winston) Churchill, as a springboard, not as a sofa."

The British PGA had struggled to fund Ryder Cup trips to the US even before the war. Now, resources were as thin as a blade of fairway grass. Surely, it would be difficult to send a team to America in 1948, when the Ryder Cup was tentatively slated to resume. With the post-war economy booming in America, the US PGA was anxious to get it going even earlier. Ed Dudley, its president, had wired Cotton in November of 1946 with an invitation to bring the British team to America in the coming year, and—even with costs estimated at £5,000—the British agreed to make tentative plans. Cotton was named captain of the British team in January, and the US PGA selected Moraine Country Club in Dayton, Ohio, site of the 1945 PGA Championship, as host. As soon as February, however, Dudley could sense a reluctance from his counterparts in the British PGA.

"I think our challenge to England for a renewal of the matches is like a June-and-December romance," he quipped. "The thing has cooled. The fact is, the next ten days or two weeks will tell if the matches are to be held at all this year. Certainly, judging from the manner in which England is delaying the matter of setting the dates indicates the wedding won't ever come off."

The British PGA kept claiming a busy calendar of tournaments as an excuse, but stretched finances were nearer to the heart of the matter. The Walker Cup, for instance, had been renewed in 1946, but only after the USGA agreed to forfeit its turn as host and to play the matches in Britain. By June, the fate of the 1947 Ryder Cup was still unsettled. Moraine was now out because the British were unable to commit to a September date. Dudley insisted the matches would be played "if at all possible" but, as The Open Championship was about to begin at Royal Liverpool, Commander Charles Roe, secretary of the British PGA, announced a postponement of the Ryder Cup. Dudley wired Roe with strong regrets. When Roe replied that a November or December date might work, Dudley sent his promotions director, Fred Corcoran, to Hoylake with the hope of negotiating something. Finally, the Americans learned that the Brits would accept any date after October 25.

All the while, Robert Hudson remained on the periphery, patiently observing the British balking. He'd already put in a bid to sponsor the Ryder Cup at his home course with terms that were very favorable to the British. He'd pick up their entire tab and put both teams on his "full expense program" with free meals, free caddies, and free transportation for the wives. British pros began to pressure their PGA to remove any lingering doubts about going forward with the match. After all, once their travel to the States had been paid, they could remain for a time to go after prize money on the US winter circuit. The US PGA, meanwhile, dropped its opposition to playing the matches after October. In mid-August, Hudson was told he had landed the Cup, to be played the first two days of November.

In all, it would cost Hudson $70,000 and that was after he had laid out $35,000 to bring the PGA Championship to Portland in 1946. His explanation was prescient. "Some day when the country catches up on production we'll have shorter hours, and when we do a lot of people will turn to sports," he offered. "Sports is the proper thing. Sponsoring these golf events is a lot of fun for me. The Portland people get a chance to meet the top golf stars and to me that's a grand thing. Let other people buy yachts and racehorses. I'll have my fun in golf."

Hudson was at the head of the welcoming party when the *Queen Mary* docked in New York, delivering a sea-weary British team. The remnants of Hurricane Love may have made stomachs queasy, but at least those stomachs were full. On the first night of their six-day trip, they were served steaks, equivalent to a month's rations back home. Cotton downed two whole sirloins. Hudson ensured they continued to be well fed. He put the entire party up at the Waldorf-Astoria, where he hosted a dinner for one hundred. A press conference was hastily arranged before the dinner where Cotton poked fun at honorary captain Walter Hagen's new girth: "Won't you be seated Mr. Hagen . . . both Mr. Hagens?"

The Brits then headed into the Wedgewood Room for cocktails, where they feasted on Oysters Rockefeller, oysters on the half shell, smoked salmon and sturgeon followed by soup. Then came a parade of other courses, featuring steak, Virginia Ham, potatoes and asparagus with fruits and petit fours, coffee mixed with liqueurs, vintage champagne, whiskeys, and wine. If Hudson were scheming to fatten them up for the kill, he succeeded. "There were few survivors," wrote Lawton Carver, restauranter and sports editor of the *International News Service.*

"He knew we were broke, and he gave the PGA an open check to pay all traveling expenses," an appreciative Dai Rees, the Welsh Ryder Cup legend, explained. "And that is not all. Members of that British team, Henry Cotton, Arthur Lees, Fred Daly, Charlie Ward,

Jimmy Adams, Max Faulkner, Sammy King and myself, found it difficult to spend our own money from the moment we arrived in the States.

"Hudson showered us with generosity. We received wireless sets and wristwatches, among other things. He footed the bill at all our hotels; transport was laid on everywhere and he even provided us with pocket money."

The team could only marvel at post-war America's bounty.

"We find it difficult to believe that such an abundance exists in the world today," Cotton observed. "After our years of rationing, we have almost forgotten the days when eating could be done on a plentiful basis in the British Isles. We are all gaining weight and having a glorious time just eating."

"I have eaten more meat at one dinner here than I would get in a week on my ration in England," Roe noted. "And the ham and eggs served at breakfasts are equal to our monthly allowance. I still can't believe it is true."

After turning down an invitation to play a quick practice round at Winged Foot Golf Club north of New York City—a questionable decision—the Brits embarked on a three-day Union Pacific streamliner journey across the Continent, made more entertaining by Max Faulkner, who surprised everyone by reciting US history along the way. Hudson joined to make sure everything went well. The only thing he couldn't bestow upon his guests was an assured victory over the Americans. Ominously, for the Brits, the same day they pulled into New York Harbor, Ben Hogan arrived unannounced at the Portland Golf Club to begin his rigorous practice routine, stopping first at Larry Lamberger's golf shop to work over his clubs. He'd spent the previous three weeks hunting in northern Colorado and said he needed plenty of practice—but what else was new? "Hunting doesn't help your game, you know," he told the *Oregonian.*

Hogan was a favorite of Hudson's and vice versa. Hogan's pensive personality contrasted with that of the ebullient Hudson, but Bantam Ben shared Hudson's work ethic. Hudson was awed by Hogan's romp at the second Portland Open in 1945, where he won by fourteen shots over Byron Nelson (Sam Snead had won the first). Hudson also witnessed Hogan notch his first major title at the 1946 PGA held at Portland Golf Club with a 6-and-4 shellacking of Ed "Porky" Oliver in the championship match.

Hogan had been named US captain only a week earlier. The honor was somewhat surprising. A year earlier he had forced the PGA's executive committee to cede control of the Tournament Committee to the players to organize and oversee events, independent of any influence from PGA executives, by warning that a "civil war" could soon be on their hands. It was said he was the most loathed man in golf when he left that meeting. This was the first step to the eventual formation of the PGA Tour as an organization distinct from the PGA. However, if Hogan was the "most loathed" pro, he was also the most powerful. Although he was a Ryder Cup rookie (he was named to the symbolic 1941 team), he became the first man to captain the US team after Hagen had the honors six times.

In one way, the choice made perfect sense. In 1947, Hogan had distinguished himself—albeit temporarily—from Snead and Byron Nelson, together, the most dominant players in the game up to then.

Great golf champions, it seemed, often came in threes. There was the Great Triumvirate of Harry Vardon, J.H. Taylor and James Braid at the turn of the twentieth century, followed by Bobby Jones, Gene Sarazen and Hagen during the golden age of sports in the twenties. Jack Nicklaus, Arnold Palmer and Gary Player, the "Big Three," would rule in the '50s into the '70s. In the post-war years, arguments raged (and continue even today) about who was best—Nelson, Snead or Hogan. From 1937, when Nelson won the Masters, through 1954, when Snead won the Masters, they combined for twenty-one Grand Slam victories. But 1947 was the only Ryder Cup in which they played together, and that year Hogan was supreme.

Snead had won the first post-war Open Championship at St. Andrews in 1946, yet in 1947, he was mired in a slump marked by the "yips" on short putts. His controversial miss from thirty inches cost him another US Open, this time to Lew Worsham, in an eighteen-hole playoff. Nelson had won a record eleven consecutive tournaments in 1945 but, a year later, at age thirty-four, announced he was retiring from competitive golf. He made a cameo appearance at the 1947 Masters and finished tied with Frank Stranahan for second place behind Jimmy Demaret. However, instead of reigniting his competitive fire, it reinforced his resolve to remain retired. Retired, as well, was Ralph Guldahl. After winning a second consecutive US Open in 1938 and his only Masters in 1939, he was tabbed by Snead "the best player in the world." He might have made it a grand quartet. But he mysteriously quit the tour in 1942, just as Hogan was entering his prime—and that prime came later than most.

Hogan didn't get his first solo win on tour until 1940, by which time Nelson had won eleven times, including the Masters and US Open, and Snead had won seventeen times. He hadn't had an easy start in life. When he was nine, he witnessed his father, Chester, take his own life with a pistol blast to his chest, an experience that seemed to have cast a pall over the rest of young boy's life. He hawked papers at the Fort Worth train depot before hearing, at age twelve, that he could make a few coins (65 cents a loop to be exact) by caddying at the Glen Garden Country Club, where Nelson got his start. Hogan was almost too slight to carry a bag, but he used his fists to ward off bullying from other caddies. True to form, he spent his idle time beating balls on the range before taking his seven-mile walk home.

Hogan dropped out of high school before his senior year to turn professional, but it didn't go well at first. Battling a hook that worsened under pressure, he was filled with self-doubt. He nearly went broke a couple of times. But his inner resolve, along with the support of his wife, was ultimately central to his success. He got the break he needed when he became a protégé of the well-respected Henry Picard, who admired his relentless hard work. He teamed with Vic Ghezzi to win the 1938 Hershey Fourball and, after transforming his hook into a baby fade, his career took off with fifteen wins from 1940 through 1942. After serving as a physical education instructor for the Army in the war–the GIs under his charge were none too happy about how hard he pushed them–Hogan would win thirty-five tournaments, including three majors, over the next four years. When he dusted Nelson by fourteen strokes to win at Portland at the tail end of Lord Byron's historic 1945 season, he scoffed at his rival's nickname: "I guess this takes care of this Mr. Golf business."

Two years later, the two former Glen Garden caddies were teammates on an American team whose top half was as good as any the US ever fielded. Of the ten men selected, five were future World Golf Hall of Famers. The sides were stacked. Only Snead and Nelson had played in a Ryder Cup before and, at thirty-five, they were still younger than the average age of the Brits, who had just one Hall of Famer in Henry Cotton. The PGA, for the first time, used a points system to pick the entire team based on 1946 and 1947 results. That left them with the last two winners of the Masters (Herman Keiser and Demaret), the last two winners of the 1946 US Open (Lloyd Mangrum and Worsham), the 1947 winner of the PGA Championship (Hogan) and the 1946 winner of The Open Championship (Snead). They could even claim the winner of the only major played in 1945 (Nelson at the PGA). By contrast, Irishman Fred Daly was the only member of the British team to have won a post-war major. Cotton would win his third claret jug in 1948, and Max Faulkner would become the only other 1947 British team member to claim a grand slam title at the 1951 Open. That was it.

Nelson had played in only one event in 1947 with his share of runner-up honors at Augusta. His '45 season, with its record eleven straight wins, didn't figure in the points standings, but Nelson still earned enough to qualify for the team with his six wins in 1946. When Nelson confirmed his retirement to his 630-acre Texas ranch that year, he said he would play only in "special" events and the Ryder Cup and the Masters were the only ones he chose to enter. But he declared himself as sharp as ever when he got to Portland, having played a series of thirty-five exhibitions in two months, shooting between 63, with a course record at his old haunt, Ridgewood Country Club, and 68. His average score was 67.

Demaret and Mangrum comprised the other Hall of Fame duo. Demaret, Hogan's fellow Texan and closest friend, had won his second Masters that April to go with his 1940 green jacket. He beat out Hogan both for the 1947 Vardon Trophy with the tour's lowest scoring average and as that year's leading money winner and would finish runner-up to Hogan at the 1948 US Open. Demaret grew up so indigent he would say his family lived on "highway stew" (that is, roadkill) meals. He was full of one-liners and as flamboyant as they came, partial to bright golf clothes and fancy hats that earned him the nickname, The Wardrobe. But there was plenty of substance behind the flash. With his muscular arms and big hands, he was a powerful player whose shots could bore through wind with a low right-to-left fade. Hogan called him the best wind player he ever saw.

Mangrum was the fourth native Texan on the team, a pro at fifteen whose later physical appearance was distinguished by his thin mustache and a ubiquitous cigarette. Almost every player on both teams had served in the armed forces, mostly in non-combat jobs, although Dai Rees came under fire as a driver in the North African campaign. Demaret, for example, joined the Navy and was stationed near Corpus Christi, Texas. Ever the jokester, he wistfully characterized his wartime service: "You know we all had those famous mottos like, 'Remember the Alamo,' 'Remember the Maine,' and, of course, 'Remember Pearl Harbor.' Mine was, 'Nice shot Admiral!'

Nelson was the exception, deferring serving due to an improper blood coagulation condition. He and Jug McSpadden, however, did travel the country, doing over one hundred exhibitions to raise funds for the war effort. Herman Keiser spent thirty-one months at sea on the light cruiser USS Cincinnati. Only Mangrum saw combat, and he sought it willingly. After winning five pre-war tournaments and setting the Augusta National course record of 64, Mangrum was offered a comfortable post as the golf pro at Fort Meade. In typically snarly fashion, he told the Army he didn't join to play golf.

And so, in July 1944, he reached Normandy a month after the first troops hit the beach. On his way across the English Channel, he pulled a dollar bill out of his pocket and turned to a fellow staff sergeant, Robert Green. Tearing it in half, he gave one piece to Green and kept the other. "We'll put it together when this is over," he told him. Mangrum kept his half of the bill the rest of his life. He never saw the other half. His friend never made it. Somehow, Mangrum avoided joining Green as a casualty. But he came close.

At the Falaise Pocket, the decisive battle of the Normandy campaign, Mangrum was in an armored jeep moving down a slick, rainy road during a blackout. Suddenly, an oncoming truck came into sight, and his driver swerved to avoid it. The jeep rolled, pinning Mangrum and shattering his humerus and scapula. The injuries were beyond the medic's capability to treat, and he was given morphine to manage the pain. Mangrum lay in an ambulance from 12:30 a.m. until 7:20 a.m. as it crept stealthily toward the French coast, from where he was ultimately evacuated to an Army hospital at Leamington Spa in England. There, as the Army physician molded a cast around his arm and back, he offered a grim prognosis. Mangrum would likely never again be able to lift his arm above shoulder height. For twelve weeks, Mangrum wondered if his golf career was over.

"Not even the thrill I got from winning The Open equaled the one I got that day I found I could lift my arm," he would say in retrospect. "Imagine a golfer who couldn't do anything but swing like a hockey player."

Patched up, Mangrum returned to the fight with George Patton's Third Army, joining a motor cavalry company assigned to reconnaissance duty three to five miles in front of the infantry. There, following the Battle of the Bulge, he earned his first Purple Heart for a sniper's bullet in his knee. Near the end of the fighting, he won a second for taking shrapnel in his chin during action in Czechoslovakia. He was also awarded two silver stars and two bronze stars. He was one of only two soldiers in his original unit to survive the war.

In April, 1945, Mangrum wrote to Corcoran from near the front lines:

"Guess I have witnessed many things the other boys haven't had the displeasure of being in. I hope they never do, Fred, as it isn't fun at all. I never did know a grown man could get so scared. Sometimes we cuss and we pray. As a matter of fact, I would have cried at anything if I thought it would do any good. When shells are breaking all around you, if you have the time to think, you wonder if the next one will land where you are. I have cheated death many times and am quite lucky."

Mangrum had already earned his nickname, Mr. Icicle, before the war, but after his combat experiences, he grew even more steely. Remarkably, a year and two months after writing that letter to Corcoran, he won the 1946 US Open by surviving a grueling thirty-six-hole playoff against Nelson and Vic Ghezzi for the only Grand Slam title of his career. He needed to sink a nervy six-footer on the last hole and never flinched.

"An inch here and a half inch there is the difference between a dead sergeant and a live champion," he shrugged. "That's why I'm a fatalist. The ball is going in or isn't. Why worry? I don't suppose that any of the pro and amateur golfers who were combat soldiers, Marines or sailors will soon be able to think of a three-putt green as one of the really bad troubles in life."

After the big four of Hogan, Snead, Demaret and Mangrum, the remainder of the US roster wasn't too shabby, either.

Keiser was nicknamed the Missouri Mortician for his home state and his catatonic demeanor on the golf course. He had two other wins besides the Masters in 1946, never finishing worse than second in his six starts, and added another win in 1947. Worsham, the youngest player on the roster at twenty, won the Atlanta Invitational in 1946 and added the Denver Open to his US Open title in 1947 and would go on to win the money title in 1953. Ed "Porky" Oliver, who resembled Oliver Hardy of Laurel and Hardy fame, was the nemesis of Bobby Locke, the South African who otherwise ruled the tour in 1947. Oliver defeated Locke in a playoff at the All American Open and passed him for the win at the Canadian Open while setting the tournament scoring record. Herman Barron, forty-six and the oldest player on the squad, had won twice in 1946 and E.J. "Dutch" Harrison had won three times in '47 and once in '46. Nicknamed the Arkansas Traveler, he'd go on to tally nine top ten finishes in the four majors and would rank fifth on the list of players with the most victories (eighteen) without a major.

The British sent a relatively makeshift group against this array of talent. It was the best their islands could produce; there had been no possibility of nurturing golf talent with every resource dedicated to the war effort.

Cotton, whose career suffered the most, spent the war in the Royal Air Force raising money for the Red Cross, earning the Most Excellent Order of the British Empire for this service from King George VI. While he would win another Open at age 41 in 1948, he was far from his prime form at this Ryder Cup. Rees was probably the best British player at the time. He had the best stroke average on the team and had spent a productive winter season in the States, where he also picked up a set of American-made clubs. Daly and Adams, the Irish International champ for eight straight years, were next, but were mid-level at best. Faulkner, who played exactly two rounds of golf between the start and end of the war, was runner-up in the last two tournaments played before the Ryder Cup. Reg Horne finished second to Daly in that year's Open, Arthur Lees was fifth.

Nevertheless, the Brits put on a brave front.

"We didn't come over here to lose," Cotton said as the team disembarked in New York, calling it the best Ryder Cup team he'd ever played on. "Ask (Fred) Daly. He's an optimist as the Irish always are. He says it's in the bag."

He proudly added at his New York press conference, "I've brought a team of wonderful fellows. It's not a young team, as the youngest player is thirty-one and the average age is thirty-six and a half but, in spite of the seven terrible war years, we don't want to make any excuses. We want to win and hope to make a good showing. Win or lose, we shall play in the spirit we have always been taught and as Britain expects of us."

Rees assumed a similar stiff upper lip. "I don't believe we've ever had a team with as wonderful spirit as this one," he added. "Everyone likes everyone else and all we are thinking about is winning. We should have a fine match."

Back home, *The Guardian* was the exception to the general pessimism concerning British chances. The newspaper rationalized that because Bobby Locke had so much success in the US in 1947, the Americans could be beaten, suggesting that "the British may underrate themselves as they overrate the Americans.

"No one can support a strong case why Britain should win this match; equally no one can say categorically that Britain will lose it," *The Guardian* continued, with more hope than conviction. To that end, Leonard Crawley, a member of Britain's Walker Cup team working as an on-site correspondent for the *Daily Telegraph*, found one reason for optimism: "I have no doubt whatsoever that the standard of British professional golf has substantially improved this season."

The Americans opened as three-to-one favorites and, by the end of the week, they were bet up to five-to-one. As Grantland Rice wrote of the visitors, "If they can take the Cup back, it will be one of the greatest upsets sports has ever known."

"But then there was a guy who said Army would beat Columbia by 14 points too." wrote Hal Layman of the *Oregon Journal* with some sarcasm, referring to the Lions' busting of Army's thirty-two game winning streak that weekend.

If there was to be one real break for the Brits, it would come from the clouds. Rain. Hogan often said he would "dig it out of the dirt" with all his practice time; however, at Portland in 1947, he was sloshing it out of the mud. November is the wettest month of the year in the typically wet Northwest. Not even Bob Hudson's unending optimism could change the weather patterns. "It was like playing in India during the monsoons," Rees later recalled. Although the course took just an inch and half of rain the previous week, it had already been the rainiest October on record in Oregon. It then rained heavily on every practice day. There was some talk of postponement, but the matches would go on, to the delight of the visitors, for whom rain was just a normal part of golf.

"The duller the course the better," said Cotton, who won the '37 Open Championship at a rain-soaked Carnoustie. Many of his men said it was, "almost like home."

Even Ed Dudley, former Ryder Cupper and president of the US PGA, appeared to worry that the weather would tilt the advantage toward the British. "Henry Cotton, Dai Rees, Sam King and Fred Daly have been playing some excellent golf," he fretted. "And if this wet weather continues, they may be more than a match for our boys."

The Brits initially liked the course after shooting several scores in the sixties. Cotton even called it "easy." It wasn't surprising. The pros had been taking apart the Portland Golf Club course for years. Hogan set the 72-hole scoring record when he won Hudson's Portland Open in 1945 with a 27-under score of 261. Charles Congdon was 18-under when he won the 1947 event and Jim Ferrier was the first person to shoot 29 for nine holes during the 1946 PGA Championship stroke play qualifier. But the exception, and most accurate comparison, was the first Portland Open, played on a wet course in November in 1944. Snead won that with what was considered a miraculous one-over score of 289.

Crawley, allowed to play the course in advance as a Walker Cupper, called it "most picturesque and not too difficult" and compared it to the East Course at Wentworth in Surrey, a charming but not challenging 6,200-yard course where the unofficial 1926 Ryder Cup matches were held. Originating as a nine-holer in 1914, Portland Golf Club didn't have the pedigreed stamp of a golden age architect although its greenskeeper, Donald Junor, a legendary figure in the Northwest, made several improvements in the 1920s after the course expanded to eighteen holes.

"The course is not ideal for such an important match for it is not a severe test of golf and it is unbalanced," Crawley wrote, noting how the three par-five holes were lengthened and another par four converted into a par five for the occasion.

Easy or not, while the Americans were totally familiar with the golf course, none of the Brits had ever played it before–only three had ever been to the States–so practice time was both imperative and arduous. When the skies opened with even more fury on Wednesday, the second day of practice, the Brits braved the conditions, trying to figure out what angles they should play into the greens while getting comfortable with the larger American ball size.

"All the team practiced hard in the most trying conditions," Cotton wrote in his post-match report to the British PGA. "Incessant rain turned an already clayey course into a morass where deep footprints were left at every step–casual water lay in great pools all over the course and many bunkers contained water. During the four and half days left for practice prior to the event, hardly an hour was spent on the course without enduring sheeting rain, and so, apart from learning the layout of the course, no useful intensive practice, particularly of the short game, was possible. This we knew was our weakness only too well."

The Americans, meanwhile, could afford to sit out all of Wednesday and pose for photos with their new outfits and leather golf bags, emblazoned with the Ryder Cup emblem and the name of each player. The ever-flashy Demaret showed off his togs the next day, with a yellow cap, yellow sweater, blue turtleneck and "feather" red pants. He and the rest of the team looked the part of a winner.

Cotton, searching for any edge, provided some controversy on the eve of the competition by calling for an inspection of the grooves on the Americans' irons. The USGA instituted groove restrictions in 1942, but rarely enforced them during the war. At the same time, the USGA was trying to bring the PGA, with its separate set of rules, into compliance. So, after being lenient in the first post-war Open in 1946, a crackdown began at the 1947 US Open at St. Louis Country Club. Richard Tufts, chairman of the USGA's Committee on Balls and Implements, explained that "we've noticed this year that the game is running away and we're enforcing the rule to bring it in line here." Officially, the scorings could not be wider than one thirty-second of an inch, and the distance from one groove to the next at least one thirty-second of an inch. Tufts found so many non-confirming irons that one of the buffing machines in SLCC professional's Alex Ayton's shop caught fire from overuse. Snead, in fact, had every one of his irons rejected.

Surely Cotton noticed how the American players were able to spin shots back to the hole on the wet greens. He also was aware that Hogan had been involved in a bit of give-and-take with the USGA over his grooves. So, Cotton played his hunch, a bad one as it turned out. The clubs were deemed legal. Moreover, Hogan didn't forget Cotton's gamesmanship. When the next matches were played in England at Ganton in 1949, Hogan, as non-playing captain just months after his near-fatal automobile crash, challenged the British clubs and Bernard Darwin, chair of the R&A rules committee, was summoned from the comfort of a pre-dinner bath. He found discrepancies, forcing Jock Ballentine, the Ganton professional, to spend the night grinding away on the British club faces.

With his gambit having failed, Cotton appealed for divine intervention. He called the entire team together at the team hotel and, as Rees recalled in his book *Thirty Years of Championship Golf*, pulled out a bible when everyone was expecting a pep talk from their captain. "I think, gentlemen, that we should have a few moments for meditation," he said.

"I would not say that our team consisted of the most God-fearing men in the world, but they took Henry's attempt to seek inspiration in the right spirit, bowed their heads, and prayed," Rees wrote.

Cotton's invocation might have taken care of the Hell part but not the high water. Another inch or more of rain guaranteed that this would be the wettest Ryder Cup in history, and not to Cotton's benefit. As it turned out, there was a limit to dull. When the teams arrived at the course for the 9 am start, they encountered puddled fairways and water in every bunker, some knee-deep. Hudson had asked Cotton not to postpone the matches unless the weather made playing impossible and Cotton, who called Hudson's generosity "almost embarrassing in its largesse," wanted to save him the thousands of dollars per day he would have lost. Such was his respect for Hudson's generosity. The captains had also agreed to play by USGA rules with special rules if needed. However, after meeting to discuss any changes, the only concession was allowing embedded balls to be lifted but not cleaned. Golfers were allowed to take relief from casual water, as per the rules, but otherwise, they had to play the ball down and weren't permitted to clean the ball until they reached the green. They did not opt to allow free relief from water-drenched bunkers. It was either splash out or take an unplayable lie and a penalty shot. The rule is the same today, although local rules usually apply. The difference today is that water in the bunkers always necessitates a delay while the water is pumped out until play can resume. Essentially, then, there were water hazards on every hole. *The Telegraph's* Crawley described the conditions as the worst he'd ever seen.

It wasn't long before British resolve began to slacken. Rees had expressed optimism over the draw, saying it "could not have been more perfect" for his team. "If we picked man-to-man competition, we would have named our players exactly as the draw came out," he declared. But it soon became apparent from the first match that nothing would go the visitors' way.

If the Brits were counting on the wet conditions to favor them, they received an ominous sign on the first hole of the first match between Cotton and Lees and Oliver and Worsham. Cotton's opening tee shot was fine, but Lees splashed into a waterlogged bunker on his approach. Forced to take an unplayable, the hole was lost to the American par–and the day went downhill from there.

As two more spells of driving rain added to their misery, the Brits, who traditionally played the ball on the ground, couldn't get any roll to match the Americans' superior length off the tee. Hitting

Photo courtesy Portland Golf Club

From left-tonight, Great Britain's Fred Daly, America's Sam Snead, Britain's Charles Ward and Lloyd Mangrum of the US are set for the rain prior to their Day 1 foursomes match, won by the US, 6-and-5.

into the greens was all carry, another foreign concept to the visitors. The Americans threw darts and spun them back toward the hole, especially on pitch shots.

It was a shooting gallery in more ways than one for the Americans, who swept all four matches with only one match going the full thirty-six holes.

"Those Americans, they just pitch the ball past the pin and back it bounces," Cotton said, looking back at the play. "None of the greens at home would hold that sort of shot. We pitch and run up. The only way for us to beat them would have been to put the pins on the far edge of the greens."

Crawley concurred. "Though the course was totally unfit, the Americans played magnificently and clung more miraculously to 'old man par,'" Crawley wrote. "It was their short game and astonishing ability to improvise that won the day. On the sodden greens their approaches pitched past the pin, sat down, and then, as a rabbit temporarily stunned, scuttled back, often fifteen feet, towards the hole before lying dead. The British approach shots seemed to be struck just as well but were usually on the short side and burrowed straight into the turf."

The Americans totally separated themselves on the greens. The Brits simply couldn't drop the bigger American ball in the hole. Cotton had the worst time of it. He seemed to be faced with every important putt, and he missed them all. He took fifty-four putts in twenty-seven holes and fell, 10-and-9, after being down six holes at the 18-hole break. It matched the record set by Hagen and Denny Shute in their thumping of George Duncan and Arthur Havers in 1931. The final hole of the match was quintessential. Oliver drained a 30-foot birdie putt through the wet turf before Cotton missed a makeable eight-footer for the birdie that would have extended the match. It was his eighth miss between three and eight feet that day.

The second match was almost as lopsided. The long-hitting Snead and the steady Mangrum put on an early display of accuracy and shot-making against Daly and Ward and jumped out to another six-hole lead. A two-under par front nine led to a morning round of 71, the only under par round of the day. With the pressure on, Daly and Ward kept missing greens and slogged to a morning round 77. Mangrum closed out the match with an 18-foot putt on thirteen for the 6-and-5 win.

The other two wins required comebacks. Rees and King, the strongest British pairing, led Nelson and Barron, 3-up, two holes into the afternoon round after Nelson hooked his second shot into a watery bunker. Barron took off his shoes and managed to blast out, but the ball rolled back into the trap and the hole was conceded. After remaining 1-down going to the last nine holes after a brilliant downhill chip by King, Nelson's putter got hot. His eight-foot downhill putt to square the match on eleven seemed to unnerve the British. Rees pulled his tee shot on twelve and King came up short of the green, leading to a bogey that put the Americans ahead for good. After splitting the next four holes to maintain the 1-up lead, Nelson hit one to eight feet on the par-three seventeenth hole, seven feet closer than the putt King was facing. As Nelson stepped onto the green, he had a thought: why not concede King the birdie?

Barron, he later recalled, looked at Nelson like he was "completely crazy." But Nelson simply said, "Herman, I have no doubt at all that you will make this putt." It was another example of the Americans' confidence in the final result. Barron obliged, of course, to wrap up a hard fought 2-and-1 victory.

Finally, Hogan and Demaret, longtime partners and considered the strongest American pairing, had to come back from 4-down after nine against Faulkner and Adams. Faulkner's superb 2-iron into the first green got the British pair going and an equally impressive approach by Faulkner into nine sent them out with a blazing 33. The Brits gave back two holes by the lunch break when they double bogeyed the par-five tenth and conceded on the fourteenth to shift the momentum. The Americans recovered by shooting their own 33 on the third nine to go 2-up but, gamely, Faulkner and Adams came back to square the match with a birdie on fourteen. Hogan and Demaret then got a break on sixteen as Demaret's drive found a fairway bunker. Everyone approached, expecting to find the ball in water, but somehow it ended up dry. Hogan took advantage with a superb 6-iron shot to twelve feet and Demaret dropped the birdie putt to regain the lead. The Americans closed out the match on eighteen when both Adams' tee shot, and Faulkner's approach found watery lies in the sand. Hogan chipped close for a "gimmie" par that won it, 2-up. It was the only match to go to the final hole over the entire competition.

Sunday was more of the same–golf-wise and weather-wise. Cotton reported that the course "had been trodden into a quagmire" and that a good lie "was a matter of luck." Hogan, who was secretly nursing a sore back, kept himself and Barron out of the singles, knowing he wouldn't be needed, and put Harrison in the leadoff match and Keiser in the last. He then he scurried from match to match in a foreshadowing of Seve Ballesteros at Valderama. Cotton stubbornly stuck with the same eight players, leaving out Horne and Green. It took just three matches before Worsham won the clinching point by finishing off Adams, 3-and-2. In what was regarded as the feature match of the day, Cotton fared little better than he had on Saturday, losing 5-and-4 to Snead. The captain seemed to fume inside, as he lost four of the last five holes.

It was left to King, who played the best golf for his side all week, to prevent a complete shutout with his 4-and-3 win over Keiser (and that was after the Mortician took sixty-three putts in thirty-three holes). That match was the exception as the Sunday scorecards told the tale of the 11-1 US romp. The Americans were one-under par over 246 holes. The British were twenty-five over.

After cooling off, Cotton was gracious at the ceremony where Hudson presented Hogan with the Ryder Cup.

"I can offer no excuses. The Unites States team is, I believe, the best in their history and when you play badly against top-flight competition you must expect to lose," he said. "Although we were defeated, I'm just as proud of my team as I would have been had we won.

"I congratulate Ben Hogan and his team on their fine play. In my heart I did not expect us to win," he conceded. "I hope the matches will continue to be played and will never again be interrupted. The course itself did not give us particular difficulty but rather it was the continued rain which caused most of our troubles. It poured constantly during the days we were scheduled for practice, and we were unable to accustom ourselves to the playing conditions."

As usual, Hogan was brief with his remarks.

"When the British win the Ryder Cup, it's kept in close custody but I'm going to take it home with me," he joked.

A few of the Brits let their frustrations spill out. Faulkner called the course "slop" and joined Lees and Green in their assertion that the matches would have been postponed by the wiser heads in England had they been played there.

"They should have the course for a diving regatta," Lees complained.

The reaction back in the UK was harsh. The British had already taken a beating on their own soil that same year. They were routed in the Walker Cup, watched Americans Willie Turnesa walk away with the British Amateur and Babe Didrickson Zaharias with the British Women's Amateur. The Ryder Cup just added to the disgrace.

John MacAdam of the *London Daily Express* called the defeat in Portland "disheartening" and "most humiliating." He chided his countrymen for thinking that golf is "a game you play" and challenged them to "recast most of their ideas or get out." Cotton was criticized for not allowing his team to practice on the *Queen Mary* or at Winged Foot before they left New York.

Geoffrey Cousins of the *London Star* lamented the string of American victories. "British postwar golf has touched rock bottom with the writing of this final forlorn chapter in a tragic year which has seen United States victories in four of the five big international meetings," he wrote. "It is hoped that Cotton and his men will bring back with them the lessons which will enable us to regain our shattered prestige. In the early summer of 1949, the Ryder Cup match will be played on a British course. Between now and then we need work."

"There can be no excuse for the eclipse," the *Daily Mail* thundered.

"So ends our blackest year," bemoaned the *Evening Standard*.

Crawley, the only British journalist to witness the competition in person, was more realistic. He wrote that none of the Brits played poorly by their standards. "The plain truth is we were outplayed by a new generation of American professionals to whose masterly skill at the game we have not, at present, an effective answer," he concluded.

Dick Burton, then 1939 Open champion and a member of the '37 team, shared that grim assessment of the new golfing landscape. "It is hard to say where we are to get men capable of beating the Americans unless more is done for the younger players. This is the time to start building for a better future unless we are content to be a fifth-rate nation in sport," he warned.

Years later, Rees nailed it better than anyone in his book: "To put it mildly, we were massacred. Altogether it was a shattering experience to be so outclassed. But we had just been engaged in a war that had exhausted our physical and moral resources, as well as leaving us badly out of practice. I think it was a mistake to match ourselves against the Americans so soon afterwards."

Cotton held with the same assessment in his book *This Game of Golf*: "In sport only wins count–excuses, however genuine, mean nothing, but the dice *were* loaded against us on this occasion. I do not regret any more than the other players on the team do, having made the journey. Visiting our great neighbors was a treat and our beating deserved."

Interestingly, the mismatch prompted Lester Rice, the well-respected golf editor of New York's *Journal American*, to suggest that the makeup of the British team expand to players from across the British Empire, including Australia, South Africa and Canada. Hogan, writing his syndicated column, said it was an "idea worth considering." Thirty years later, after Great Britain and Ireland had lost sixteen of seventeen Cups, Jack Nicklaus suggested that the rest of Europe be included.

As cut and dry as the '47 matches were, the usual (and by now traditional) post-match squabbles ensued. Ghezzi, the New Jersey pro who won the 1941 PGA and lost to Mangrum in the '46 US Open playoff, called together some sports writers to air his grievances with the PGA Tournament Committee, which was now run by the players themselves. Ghezzi had been named to the three ceremonial Ryder Cup teams during the war and claimed he "was robbed" of a spot on the '47 team. He maintained the committee didn't use the results of two of his better tournaments (he finished twelfth in the point standings) and argued about his disqualification from the Houston Open, which cost him potential points after he refused to allow his grooves to be checked. He charged that the organization was being run to suit one man, Ben Hogan, ironically his partner when they won the Hershey Fourball in 1938.

At the same time, Hogan was facing what he called "utterly false" accusations spread by anonymous postcards sent to PGA members across the country. Among other charges, they asserted that Hogan resented Nelson's inclusion on the team. Hogan accused

Fred Corcoran, who was ousted from the committee when the players took over, of planting the stories and said he'd be willing to settle the score "man to man" with Corcoran.

"The statement that I am sore about Byron being on the Ryder Cup team is malicious and ridiculous," he countered. "On the contrary, I was very happy to see him on the team but above and beyond any feeling of mine was the rigid and fair points system that automatically put him on the team."

Both brushfires were doused at the November meeting of the PGA in Chicago after Ghezzi was threatened with expulsion from the organization for publicizing his gripes.

Bob Hudson, meanwhile, kept extending his largesse, sending Christmas food baskets to each member of the British team, a tradition he kept up for the next ten years. In 1949, aware of continued food shortages in the UK, he shipped over a half ton of meat to feed the US team including fresh butter and eggs, half a dozen Virginia hams, thirty pounds of bacon, and some six hundred pounds of Texas sirloin steak. The Americans shared the bounty with their opponents.

Hudson co-sponsored the 1951 Ryder Cup at Pinehurst and was instrumental in bringing the 1955 Ryder Cup to Palm Springs, his second home. Each time, he funded the British team's trip. The US PGA placed Hudson on its advisory committee, where he was instrumental in shaping policy and an appreciative British PGA granted him a seat on its board.

With the possible exception of Samuel Ryder himself, no official had a greater impact on the Ryder Cup or was as beloved on both sides of the Atlantic.

DAY 1

FOURSOMES

Ed Oliver/Lew Worsham (US) defeated Henry Cotton/Arthur Lees (GB) 10-and-9
Sam Snead/Lloyd Mangrum (US) defeated Fred Daly/Charlie Ward (GB) 6-and-5
Ben Hogan/Jimmy Demaret (US) defeated Jimmy Adams/Max Faulkner (GB) 2-up
Byron Nelson/Herman Barron (US) defeated Dai Rees/Sam King (GB) 2-and-1
United States wins session 4–0

DAY 2

SINGLES

Dutch Harrison (US) defeated Fred Daly (GB) 5-and-4
Lew Worsham (US) defeated Jimmy Adams (GB) 3-and-2
Lloyd Mangrum (US) defeated Max Faulkner (GB) 6-and-5
Ed Oliver (US) defeated Charlie Ward (GB) 4-and-3
Byron Nelson (US) defeated Arthur Lees (GB) 2-and-1
Sam Snead (US) def Henry Cotton (GB) 5-and-4
Jimmy Demaret (US) defeated Dai Rees (GB) 3-and-2
Sam King (GB) defeated Herman Keiser (US) 4-and-3
United States wins session 7–1

UNITED STATES WINS RYDER CUP 11–1

1957

The Empire Strikes Back

LINDRICK GOLF CLUB
GREAT BRITAIN 7 ½, UNITED STATES 4 ½

Before Seve Ballesteros, before Colin Montgomerie, before Ian Poulter, there was no greater Ryder Cup hero from the other side of the pond than David James Rees, better known as Dai.

From 1937 through 1967, Rees was involved in ten Ryder Cups—nine times as a player, five as captain. Before continental Europe joined Great Britain and Ireland, there was no more formidable linksman than the wee Welshman, all five-feet-seven of him. He played with both Percy Alliss and Peter Alliss, Percy's son. He was on a team that went up against captain Walter Hagen and captained a team that squared off against Jack Nicklaus. Even after his official Ryder Cup career ended in 1967, he was ubiquitous in an unofficial capacity at Royal Birkdale in 1969.

Rees was immersed in the game from his boyhood in the Welsh countryside, where he was born in 1913. His father, David (also Dai, for short) was the golf professional and his mother, Louisa Alice, worked as the stewardess at the Barry Club on the Leys near Gileston in the Vale of Glamorgan. The family lived in the old clubhouse, known as the Old Ship Inn. Dai's backyard was the practice green. The place was unhurried, until new steam train routes began to carry members to the course on weekends. The locomotives mesmerized Dai. He reveled in the undulating white billows of steam, the thunderous air trumpeting of Bangham whistles, the nearly palpable rumbling and chugging of a train on the track.

He was also enchanted by all things golf. At age four, his father gave him his first club, a sawed down "baffy," described by Rees in his 1968 autobiography *Thirty Years of Championship Golf* as "a number four wood with a brown, stained, hickory shaft and grip as thick as that of a cricket bat." Rees made for a charming sight as he fiddled with his new toy and a few beat-up gutty percha balls on the practice green, where R.J. Middle, the club champion, would take a break from his putting to play with the boy. With Dai Sr. busy with his all-encompassing job, Middle became somewhat of a mentor. On Dai's fifth birthday, Middle took him by the hand to the twelfth hole, a 300-yard downhill par four. Middle teed the ball atop a mound of wet sand and stepped back as Dai took his first swing. Three more whacks put him sixty yards out. "Go on," Middle encouraged as Dai took back the baffy for a fifth time. They both looked on in astonishment as it rode along the fairway, onto the green and into the hole for a bogey. Even Tiger Woods as a childhood prodigy couldn't boast of that. For his entire career, Rees was magic with a fairway wood in his hand.

Rees was compelled to turn pro at fifteen, after the Royal and Ancient rejected his application to play in an amateur tournament. He had worked as an apprentice for his father, and that, in the eyes of the R&A, voided his amateur status. It hardly mattered to his career. He adopted a unique baseball-type grip with all ten fingers on the club, which suited his small hands. He had also developed an effective and powerful flick in his swing because, as a youth hitting balls near the clubhouse, he wasn't allowed to hit full shots near the windows. That's how he picked up his first win at age twenty-one at the *Daily Mirror* Assistants Tournament. It was 1935, and he had hoped the victory would earn him a spot on the Ryder Cup team that would travel to the US. He was bitterly disappointed when Bill Cox, whom he had beaten by one stroke, was chosen instead. Rees wanted nothing more than to make that trip. He loved the gutsy competitiveness of match play. It fit his personality as a scrappy, undersized, overachiever. Yet, as he later explained in his book, that never changed his overall philosophy from stroke play.

"My method in match play has always been simply to play against the course rather than against my opponent and to anticipate his performing great feats rather than hoping he would commit vast blunders," he wrote. "I have never minded losing a match, provided I have played well. If someone has outplayed me, he is welcome to victory. I always try to go boldly for the correct shot, rather than easing up and playing safely."

His method was good enough to compile a 7-10-1 Ryder Cup playing record, remarkable considering the routine thrashings that the British team was taking during that era. If anyone could lead a team against all odds, it was Rees. He never lost his enthusiasm, despite being on the losing end nine times in ten. Even fate would not deny him that one magical win and it came at a critical time when the very existence of the Ryder Cup was being called into question as a one-sided exercise in futility.

The US hadn't lost since 1933, including three straight in the UK, and the talent gap seemed immense, with Americans winning thirty-five of the forty-eight major championships played since World War II. Interest in the Ryder Cup had waned, particularly in the States. It became more of a low-key event next to any of the three majors played in the US, and particularly so in 1957. The Cup was scheduled for the week of the World Series, when the Milwaukee Braves and New York Yankees would go at it. Hank Aaron and Warren Spahn, Whitey Ford and Mickey Mantle were a lot more appealing to the American sporting public than Jackie Burke and Tommy Bolt pitted against some British guys they'd never heard of.

Great Britain needed its version of Robert Hudson to save the Cup and into that void stepped Sir Stuart Goodwin, a Sheffield steel magnate and a vice president of the British PGA. Diabetes struck him as a young man, but, as one of the first patients treated with insulin, his life was spared. As the grateful Goodwin accrued his fortune, he gave back through philanthropy. Just like Hudson, Goodwin had developed a passion for golf in middle age after watching Rees and Fred Daly square off in an exhibition at Lindrick, his home club in Yorkshire. He previously had sponsored tournaments around Britain and, with the PGA cash strapped as usual, he gladly provided the £10,000 necessary to stage the Ryder Cup. His one caveat was also Hudson's, that the matches would be played at his home course.

Rees, named captain for the second straight time, was optimistic about his team's chances, an outlook that was not completely idle. The US had doubled up his British side, 8-4, at Thunderbird Country Club near Palm Springs two years earlier but, of the eight lost matches, four went at least thirty-four holes. That was after Britain had nearly reclaimed the Cup at Wentworth in 1953, when Peter Alliss and Bernard Hunt, both young players, suffered mishaps on the thirty-sixth hole to present the US a slim one-point victory.

Rees returned from the '55 matches aboard the *Queen Elizabeth* feeling good about the team's performance in the California desert, and more so, its spirit. Few Britons shared his enthusiasm. Skeptics were calling for the Brits to abandon the folly of challenging American superiority. It cut him deeply.

"I have never heard a more stupid suggestion, especially after our latest performance," he retorted. "This was the first time when playing in the States for all the British golfers to play with fire and determination. I feel that my team would have beaten that same American side on a British course."

Two years later at Lindrick, Rees was anxious to put those bold words to the test against an American team that was arguably weaker than either the 1955 or 1953 editions—neither of which was considered particularly strong either. Perhaps the US PGA took victory for granted and got in its own way with a watered-down selection process that centered around its one major, the PGA Championship. Either out of arrogance or self-absorption, it exempted the last two winners of the PGA (but no other major) while excluding anyone who had not played in the last two PGAs. This left eight spots available through a points system for first and second place finishes in tour events. It also cut off qualification in July, one week after the PGA Championship, in essence making its event the most important tournament of the year.

When the dust settled, long shot Lionel Hebert captured the automatic spot for the PGA winner after he defeated Dow Finsterwald in the last PGA to be contested as a match play event. Meanwhile, Jimmy Demaret and Cary Middlecoff, who would have qualified through the points system (Middlecoff was second to Doug Ford, Demaret seventh), were excluded by skipping the PGA. Their absence may have seemed a moot point, given American dominance in Ryder Cup play. But there is no denying they would have contributed. Middlecoff, who had played in the two previous Ryder Cups, was unquestionably among the best American players of the day. The Memphis dentist won the 1955 Masters, the 1956 US Open, and lost the 1957 US Open in a playoff. He chose to cross the Atlantic for his first Open Championship at St. Andrews, where he finished fourteenth, and the turnaround felt too tight for him to enter the PGA two weeks later. Demaret was left off despite three tour wins in 1957 and a 6-0-0 record in his three Ryder Cup appearances. He doubted he had the stamina for a potential 36-hole final in the PGA.

Julius Boros, another strong American player, never had a chance, having failed to qualify for the PGA Championship out of North Carolina. Arnold Palmer and Billy Casper–although second and fourth on the PGA money list during the summer–were deemed ineligible, because they hadn't finished their mandatory five-year PGA apprenticeship. Additionally, Ben Hogan and Sam Snead were left off the team after playing too few events, thus accruing too few points. Hogan wasn't in good shape anyway. He was bothered by back issues and hadn't played since May. He missed the cut at the Masters and withdrew from the US Open with pleurisy. However, Snead, who finished fourteenth on the points standings, had a better case with two wins in 1957, including the Dallas Open a month before the Ryder Cup but after the points deadline. A round of sixteen loss to Finsterwald in the PGA hurt him, and he decided against playing in the Eastern Open in Baltimore–the last tournament where points would count–essentially surrendering his chances.

Neither Snead nor Demaret was pleased.

"Imagine picking a team to represent this country and leaving off players like Snead, Ben Hogan and Doc Middlecoff," Demaret huffed, leaving himself out of the discussion. "I could have picked a better team blindfolded."

A less surly Snead said if he'd picked the team, it wouldn't have been this one.

"We are picking our teams not on their ability but on the number of tournaments they play in," he stressed.

"Snead didn't make it because he picked his tournaments," Demaret said sharply. "And he has won more tournaments than any golfer alive."

Snubbing Demaret and Snead so angered Lawson Little, the 1940 US Open champ and former chairman of the PGA Rules Committee, that he wrote a letter of complaint to *United Press International* golf writer Oscar Fraley.

"There is no question in my mind but that Snead and Demaret, from the way they played this year and because of what they have done for the game and for the PGA, should have been honored with places on the Ryder Cup team," Little insisted. "The rule which requires a player to play in the last two PGA Championships to be eligible for a Ryder Cup berth is a petty and small way of trying to force players to play in the championship. Actually, the best way to get players to support the PGA Championship is to make the event attractive, not try to do it by legislation."

Jackie Burke Jr., the playing captain of the US squad, would have certainly named Demaret to the squad had he had the captain's pick of later years. He and Demaret were like brothers. When Demaret's father died, Burke's father, Jackie Sr., the first club pro in Texas history and runner-up at the 1920 US Open, became a father figure for him. Thirteen years older than Jackie Jr., Demaret even babysat him. Earlier in 1957, they co-founded Champions Golf Club, future site of the 1967 Ryder Cup, back in their hometown of Houston. Demaret would have been invaluable to Burke in many ways, not the least of which may have been as a foursome partner.

Burke was the most accomplished member of the 1957 squad. He won both the Masters and the PGA Championship in 1956 and was bringing a 6-0-0 record into the '57 matches. Like many of his golfing peers, he started late with a stint with the Marines interrupting his career at twenty. After the war, he considered a job in the Texas oilfields, then held positions at Hollywood Golf Club in New Jersey and Winged Foot and Metropolis in New York. He finally broke through with four wins in 1950, starting with the Bing Crosby Pro Am, and five in 1952, including a stretch of four wins in four weeks.

Burke wasn't the most powerful player off the tee or the most impressive ball striker. But he knew how to manage his way around a golf course and never got ahead of himself. He was superb under pressure, especially on the greens, where he was arguably the best putter of his generation.

Burke would go on to captain the 1973 US team to victory and, at age eighty-one, serve as Hal Sutton's vice-captain at Oakland Hills in 2004. He expressed his reverence for the Ryder Cup in his 2006 book, *It's Only a Game.* "The Ryder Cup to me has always been most holy. During my heyday in the 1950s it was really the focal point of my year. As a player, I used it as my chief frame of reference. Week in and week out, all I tried to do was play well enough to make the team."

Burke also revealed the Americans were well aware of the mental edge they had held over the opposition.

"It was hard for them to look across at Sam Snead, Ben Hogan and Cary Middlecoff and not feel distress, especially when they knew our guys meant business," he wrote. "We knew the Brits were a little intimidated and we took advantage of it. We beat them badly most of the time."

Of course, there was no Snead, Hogan or Middlecoff in 1957. Burke was still optimistic with a team hardly devoid of talent, although it was missing depth, a deciding factor in previous Cups. The roster still included three of that year's four major winners in Doug Ford (Masters), Dick Mayer (US Open) and Hebert (PGA). Burke could choose his lineup from among the then three-time tour winner Finsterwald, who was being called by some the "the new Ben Hogan," hot-tempered Tommy Bolt, who would win the US Open the next year, '54 US Open champ Ed Furgol and Art Wall, who would win the Masters in 1959. Fred Hawkins, who was fourth on the 1956 money list when he won his only tour event, the Oklahoma City Open and Ted Kroll, who won four times in '56 and was runner-up to Burke at the PGA, rounded out the team, which Peter Alliss called "a lot less menacing."

Similarly, when the British press looked at the final squad, it breathed a sigh of relief. The *Daily Mail* warned that the selection "may be regretted," calling the American team "workmanlike but by no means an unbeatable one."

Noting the conspicuous absence of Hogan and Snead, it said, "Neither of them has qualified for a place and that has brought smiles to the faces of our selectors. It was said, when those two great players were in their prime, that the British team were two-thirds beaten before they started."

"It was generally agreed that the Americans were a vulnerable team," Rees wrote in *Thirty Years of Championship Golf.* "How could they be otherwise without Ben Hogan, Sam Snead and Carey Middlecoff?"

Rees knew he had a big advantage in Ryder Cup experience without them. The ten-man American roster included six rookies. Only Burke and Kroll had played in more than one. The British team had twenty-four Cups worth of combined experience with Peter Mills the only rookie. That might suggest that the Brits were old and past their prime, but the average age of the teams was identical—thirty-five.

As Brian Belton put it in his book, *The Ryder Lions,* the British players were "disparate but dedicated," largely selected on merit. The team, officially known as the British Isles after the inclusion of players from the Republic of Ireland in 1953, may have been unheralded, at least in the States, but they were seasoned.

Eric Brown, the best player in Scotland—and that's always saying something—was a grizzled match-play performer who owned

Ryder Cup wins over Lloyd Mangrum and Jerry Barber and had recently won the Dunlop Masters. Max Faulkner, the only British winner of The Open Championship (1951) in nine years, was quirky but confident, a veteran of three of the previous four Cups. Harry Weetman was a bull of a man—"as strong as an ox," according to Faulkner—who demoralized Snead by out-driving him with a 1-iron when he came from 5-down to beat him in their singles match in 1953. Smooth-swinging Irishman Christy O'Connor was the British Match Play champion that year and would go on to become one of Europe's most accomplished players. Though hot-headed, he often turned that to his advantage. Alliss, at twenty-six the youngest player on either team, was considered Britain's golden boy, if he could ever emerge from under the shadow of his accomplished father. He would achieve more as a commentator and master of repartee than as a player, but, at the time, he was motivated and formidable.

Rees considered Bernard Hunt, who would compile a 4-3-3 singles record in his ten Ryder Cup appearances, his most consistent player. Hunt's father was a pro and his younger brother Geoff would be a Ryder Cup player in 1963. Ken Bousfield, six times a Ryder Cupper, had the best short game on the squad. Irishman Harry Bradshaw, who came close to winning the claret jug in 1948 before losing to the inimitable Bobby Locke in a playoff, had a three-quarter swing with a loop at the top and an odd grip with three fingers of his right hand overlapping his left. But he was consistent and knew how to get the ball in the hole. The twenty-six-year-old Mills, the last man in, was seen as the weak link.

With his team assembled, Rees set his eyes on exploiting every opening with as aggressive a captainship as any British captain had yet waged. It would be the first time a home captain set up the golf course against his opponents. Lindrick, a blend of heathland and moorland, was the third consecutive inland course to host the Ryder Cup since the war. Then, as now, it wended its way through gorse, heather and silver birch with perfectly manicured fairways and well-bunkered greens presenting a more familiar look to the American player than the quirky and unpredictable links courses of The Open Championship. At first, this was considered a problem. Several British critics called for the site to be moved to a more favorable location. But Rees, knowing Lindrick to be a second-shot course, thought otherwise. If the matches couldn't be played on a links course, he would make sure Lindrick played like one.

At Ganton in 1949, Rees was appalled that the Cup committee kept the course well-watered and almost lush, as the Americans would prefer it. It appeared to him the committee nabobs were being generous hosts at their own peril. Rees persuaded Sir Goodwin to hand him control of the course. He gave orders to set the fairways as narrow as 35 yards across in some spots and to border them with six to ten yards of intermediate rough, long enough to stymie the Americans from imparting their famous backspin. After the galleries trampled down the rough during the first practice rounds, he had the ropes moved further back. Instead of cutting back the deep rough as was done in the most recent matches, Rees had it play as it was.

Rees ordered the fairways to be left unwatered for three days to get them to play hard and fast to accommodate running shots. He wanted the greens hard to hold. Then, he made sure that any American shots bounding off the greens would find trouble. American teams had been winning with their ability to get up and down. But Rees had a special type of grass, known as "jag grass," grown to two-inch height behind the greens. The tangled lies would negate any advantage the Americans had in the short game. Rees was well satisfied when he saw Jackie Burke advance the ball no more than a foot on two tries during a practice round. The night before the matches, he sent the greenskeeper out to use a brush harrow on the rough to toughen it even more.

"At Lindrick all the British team were very straight hitters in the classical English style," Max Faulkner recalled years later. "They hardly knocked a ball off the fairway in the whole tournament while the Americans were taking irons off the tee and still hitting it in the rough. They were all at sea with their approach shots onto the hard greens and kept running through the back into the jag grass."

There was one piece over which Rees had no control. Lindrick was set up at 6,541 yards, or at least it was supposed to be. The fifth tee wasn't on club property but rather on the edge of a bordering wood. Lindrick had been renting it for the equivalent of $425 per year so golfers could cross a small stream and play the par four at 416 yards. However, just before Ryder week, Laura Sidd, gratuitously referred to as a "farmer's wife" in the headlines, banned golfers from her property. Evidently, there was a flap over payment. She had asked for an additional £100. The club declined.

"I'm finished with this golfing lot," she snarled. "I've told them they cannot use my land anymore."

The fifth, then, was shortened by sixteen yards.

Rees took one more precautionary measure before play started. He recalled his first Ryder Cup in 1937, when captain Charles Whitcombe told him, "Don't watch these Yankees practice, Dai. It will only put you off." It was his first experience with the mental side of match play, not letting the opponent get into one's head, and, more recently, not being bothered by commentary in the press. From 1947 on, every Ryder Cup was preceded by the angst of Fleet Street. Rees knew the effect it had on morale, so he called the news boys together for an impromptu press conference where they expected some sort of news. Instead, he asked them not to build up the Americans until they showed superiority on the course. Not surprisingly, they complied and played it straight. Their Union Jacks were showing, and they were willing to help the cause.

The timing was perfect. Morale was up across the spectrum. Rationing had ended altogether in 1954, and British industry was producing most of the goods the UK needed. "Let's be frank about it," newly installed Prime Minister Harold MacMillan declared in July. "Most of our people have never had it so good." It could be viewed as an overstatement compared with the standard of living of their American cousins—only one in five British households owned a washing machine, for instance—but wages were on the rise and unemployment had eased. In fact, a 2017 study by Warwick University determined that 1957 was the happiest year of the century in Britain. It didn't report how the victorious Ryder Cup team factored into that happiness, but did show that Britishers were looking to the future instead of lamenting the past.

The Cup provided a chance to showcase the burgeoning prosperity. Post-war British teams had always been well-treated in America. Now they would repay the favor. Rees met the Americans at London Airport and entertained them at his South Herts Golf Club, where they were presented with plaster casts of Harry Vardon's classic grip, followed by an elaborate welcome dinner thrown by the mayor of London. According to *Golf Illustrated* magazine, a fleet of Jaguars was made available to the visitors during the week. That included the five American wives and one fiancée who came along. They stayed in the players' rooms at the team hotel, but the British wives were barred. That did not go over well with the British wives, particularly the always outspoken Freda Weetman, who railed that the forced marital separation would be the cause of a Great Britain defeat. The British PGA, perhaps recalling that Lord Wellington was without female comfort at Waterloo, wasn't swayed.

"We were treated like novice monks," Alliss recalled in his book *Peter Alliss—Reflections of a Life Well Lived.* "The Americans, on the other hand, arrived with all their ladies in all their glory: fur coats, high heels, jewelry, beautifully coiffured hair, full makeup—the lot. I'm not sure if our wives were left out because the PGA couldn't afford the extra cost, or perhaps they had to stay home because authorities feared we might get up to a bit of hand holding (or worse) in the middle of the night. This of course might upset the rhythm of our putting—or worse—throw off our delicate pitch shots from a bare lie over a bunker to a downhill green."

Who knows what they were thinking, but either way, it didn't go down well.

"It was absolutely ridiculous to see grown men kiss their loved ones at the front door of the hotel," O'Connor added. "The Americans, naturally, thought this was a great joke."

Perhaps Rees was smirking inwardly, for it added to both the Britishers' resolve and the Americans' complacency. Burke jokingly complained to the British press. "Our wives have all gone shopping at Harrowgate. Boy, is it difficult to keep your mind on the game when they are out throwing the cash around." Of course he didn't mean it, but his comment was indicative of a carefree attitude. Indeed, Burke had raised a few British cackles at the welcome dinner when, referring the string of American victories, he predicted: "I see no reason to doubt that this match will go the same way."

The PGA, in fact, failed to cancel the insurance on the Ryder Cup itself, confident it would be returning to the States. Smug? Perhaps. But then, even with Rees's finagling of the Lindrick course, nothing the Americans encountered during their practice rounds gave them pause. Given the choice, they opted for the smaller British ball, because they got more distance out of it. They also loved the conditions and respected the course, which they compared to Merion, site of the 1950 US Open.

"Some say it is short but is a very exacting test of golf that calls for a lot of finesse," Furgol said.

"It is short, but it doesn't play that way," added Mayer. "The greens are very tricky to read, and every hole is an interesting one."

Burke called it a "golfing paradise" with "perfect" turf and "flawless" greens.

"We've nothing like it in the States," he marveled. Augusta National was not yet the immaculate paradise it would become.

Even with cold weather early in the week, the American practice scores were good, particularly Burke and Kroll, who recorded a 67 and 66 in their alternate shot rounds Wednesday and Thursday. The condition of three of his golfers who fell ill during the week was Burke's biggest worry. Finsterwald and Hawkins, who quit after playing only a few holes on the final practice day, were down with suspected food poisoning, while Mayer was reportedly dealing with symptoms of the Asian flu. Burke even delayed handing in his foursomes lineup until he was certain of their availability, and he didn't look all that confident at the exchange with Rees.

Rees also had a couple of minor concerns. Harry Bradshaw's strained back required a brace (the papers called it a "plaster") and Brown would have a wisdom tooth extracted after a sleepless Tuesday night. He rushed off to the dentist Wednesday after combining with O'Connor to shoot a remarkable practice round 69. The next day he wore a scarf over his mouth but otherwise seemed unbothered.

When Rees met with reporters at that impromptu press conference, he exuded complete confidence. "I don't think we have ever had a better chance." He added that he was hoping for at least a split of the alternate shot matches because he believed his team matched up well in the singles.

"They are all playing in top form and are rarin' to go," he said.

So were the visitors. Yet the fifteen thousand people who braved log-jammed roads to mob the course in anticipation of British glory would leave dismayed. All that optimism, all that preparation, went for naught. Even Rees's well-thought-out tactics failed, partly because the greenskeeper, for some reason, was on the wrong schedule and believed the matches would begin a day later. With the greens left uncut for an extra day, the Americans were able to put their approach shots on a string. They putted as well as they always had and, before the morning mist gave way to brilliant sunshine, ran away with leads in all four matches, winning three.

That Rees's pairings appeared favorable just added to the frustration. He led off with Alliss and Hunt, confident that they would be eager to bury their mishaps from 1953. But they never had a chance against Ford, considered the American with the best short game and Finsterwald, a rising star. The Americans birdied the first two holes and parred the third to take a two-shot lead and went out in 32 even while driving into the harrowed-up rough six times. They were 4-up through fourteen and even though the Brits twice closed the gap to one hole at one point, the Americans never gave up their lead in a 2-and-1 victory.

Rees put himself in the second match with Ryder Cup veteran Ken Bousfield and won his first Ryder Cup foursomes match ever, 3-and-2, over Wall and Hawkins, rallying after finding themselves 1-down with nine to play. Hawkins had elected to play safe with an iron off the tenth tee and found a bad lie in a fairway bunker, allowing the Brits to win with a par and even the match. Hawkins then flubbed a chip shot on number eleven and the Brits charged through the opening. A 15-foot putt by Bousfield saved the match with two to play.

The third match involved Burke and Kroll, who had played so well in their practice rounds, against Faulkner and the muscular Weetman, the longest-hitting British pair. Kroll, who lost to Burke in the championship round of the 1956 PGA, was 3-0 in his previous foursomes matches, twice as Burke's partner. Both pairs played poorly over the first eighteen holes with the US 1-up. The Americans took control over the next nine holes and cruised to a 4-and-3 win. In his reporting, veteran writer Leonard Crawley noted that Faulkner, the fashion plate of British golf, was "completely outdressed by an astonishing-looking caddy in a scarlet sombrero and sky-blue pullover."

The final match lacked that sort of color but was even more one-sided as the Celtic combination of Brown and O'Connor couldn't find the fairway and went down to a 7-and-5 defeat to Mayer and Bolt. The Brits were overwhelmed as Mayer and Bolt put up a 67 in the morning and made eleven threes and a two over the thirty holes. Brown had to admit they played "supremely well." Meanwhile, Crawley called Brown and O'Connor's play "indescribable," and added, "this was sad business because one had hoped for great things from Brown and O'Connor." He noted Bolt and Mayer were in "complete harmony from the time it began until they went home for tea early in the afternoon."

With their side down 3-1, Crawley and the other hometown

sports writers, after agreeing not to pump up America's chances, reverted to the usual pessimism. "Britain Were Left at the Start," read the headline in the *Liverpool Daily Post.* "Dazzling Golf by Americans," screamed the *Evening Standard.* "The Old, Old Ryder Cup Story," fretted the *Daily Telegraph.*

Leslie Edwards of the *Daily Post* sounded the familiar alarm with a hand-wringing analysis: "The melancholy conclusion is that we have as little chance of winning the Ryder Cup today as the lady from the grange has of collecting her rental fee for use of the fifth tee.

"Only the greatest optimist will be expecting Britain to swing the match by getting the necessary wins in singles. The bleak prospect is that against opponents who yesterday showed themselves to be a shade better in all departments, we shall be lucky to win two or three matches."

They needed five and a half out of the eight points available. But they were down by the same 3-1 count in '53 and nearly won. Rees was always confident in his team's singles chances and was still certain it could win. Now his team would be called upon to repay that confidence—but not before an internal squabble threatened to tear everything down. Rees would call it "one of the most bitter incidents in the history of golf."

In his book, Rees recounted that as he was changing his shoes in the locker room after the day's play, he ordered Bousfield and Faulkner to gather the squad at the hotel. "Get the rest of the team together. We've just got to rouse some enthusiasm."

Everyone cleared out as Rees looked over the scorecards from the day's matches. Faulkner and Weetman stood out for their big loss against Burke and Kroll. Rees jotted down seven names, five of the six players who had lost but "played confidently," plus the two men who sat out the foursomes, Mills, the Ryder Cup rookie, and Bradshaw, with his sore back. That left one final spot between Faulkner, Weetman and O'Connor.

Rees hadn't seen many of the matches outside of his own, so he asked for feedback. He didn't want to make the call on the last man by himself. All eyes were on him at the head of the table as he shuffled his papers.

"Well, fellows, I needn't tell you how disappointed I am in today's result. It's the same old story, the Yanks have got off to a better start," he said glumly. "We're three-one down and we've got a big job ahead of us tomorrow."

Rees then startled everyone out of their doldrums by pounding his fist on the table. "But I'm absolutely sure we can win. We *can* beat this lot," he said.

Rees told them he had a good idea of the eight men he wanted but put it up for discussion. Here is his account of what then unfolded:

"Bernard Hunt chipped in: 'Well, you've got all the cards there, Dai, so you can tell for yourself who's hitting the ball good. Peter and I lost, two-and-one, but I feel we played well against Ford and Finsterwald. We had to be to lose by that margin over thirty-six holes.'

On the other side of the table, Peter Alliss nodded his head in agreement.

Max Faulkner suddenly spoke up: 'Well I shouldn't play tomorrow. I played rubbish today.'

Harry Weetman followed this immediately with a spontaneous and sincere remark: 'I should not play either. I played badly.'

'I had hoped it wasn't going to be necessary for me to play myself,' I said. 'I was hoping to be able to skip up and down the course tomorrow egging you on. But as I'm playing so well, I feel I must play. I've also decided Ken should play and I'm giving chances to Harry Bradshaw and Peter Mills for I feel that if a chap is in the team he should get a game, unless he's in appallingly bad form.'

Rees then read out the seven names and said, *"That leaves one place and it's between Max, Harry and Christy."*

According to Rees, Weetman quickly said, "Well, you must play Christy. He's the match play champion."

That settled it, so far as Rees was concerned. Weetman and Faulkner were both volunteering to sit it out, it appeared. Rees decided on the order of play and met with Burke to exchange lineups. When he returned, he sensed an unusual hubbub. The bar was buzzing, and a newspaperman stopped him and requested a statement. Weetman, known for being outspoken, had been overheard saying he'd never again play on a Ryder Cup team captained by Rees.

Now, according to Weetman's account ten years later, he didn't intend his words for public consumption. He claimed he was trying to cool down with a drink at the bar with a friend and that a reporter had eavesdropped on them.

"I dared to breathe a suggestion of criticism against that sacred institution of British golf, Dai Rees," he told the *Daily Mirror*. "I was angry, and I meant it. I thought he had set about his job of captaining our Cup team in a quite misguided way . . . if a captain won't pick his team–the most basic task–he has no right to be doing the job."

Rees always felt that Weetman, while at the bar drowning his sorrows, was egged on by friends and family, particularly by his wife Freda. Perhaps, over the next decade, Weetman's memory had been become blurred. Yet it's odd that if Weetman was aware that he had been overheard, why didn't he simply make it clear he was off the record? In any case, reporters could scarcely believe the prize quote was dropped into their laps, as reported by the *Daily Herald*:

"I shall never play in another Ryder Cup match as long as Dai Rees is captain. I did not mind being dropped but it was the way it was done. Rees told us there was one place left among three of us, including match play champion Christy O'Connor. I naturally said, 'You must play the match play champion.'"

While all this was going on, the Americans were feeling relaxed with their 3-1 lead. It seemed inevitable they would win at least three of the eight singles matches to keep the Cup. Burke, who hardly drank, celebrated with a glass of wine and decided to leave himself out of the singles while bringing in the two members of the squad, Hebert and Furgol, who hadn't played in the foursomes. Art Wall was the other man out. At least one English paper also gathered that the Americans had celebrated a bit too much beyond Burke's one glass of wine. In any case, they felt they had little reason for concern, given the way most of them had mastered the course and, in particular, the greens.

By morning, everything changed—almost miraculously. A strong southeasterly wind arrived, drying out the course overnight and adding an element of unpredictability that became more befuddling as the day wore on. When Rees arrived at Lindrick, Jack Jacobs, the club professional, happily announced that it was "a different course." On Friday, the first hole, for instance, had been driver, wedge. It would now require a long iron to reach the green. The greenskeeper who had screwed up the watering schedule took Rees aside and informed him he had cut down the greens to favor the Brits and used the brush harrow once again on the rough. Rees was also happy to see his team in high spirits after the Weetman uproar. It had galvanized them in an us-against-the-world mindset. Rees later wrote that the squad resembled a team waiting to run out onto the Wembley pitch for an FA Cup final. Alliss only reinforced Rees's mounting confidence when he mentioned to him that one writer believed the potential of a comeback so unlikely that the writer had vowed to cover himself with one hundred tons of compost if they managed to pull it off.

"Nothing will give me greater pleasure than to bury his head under a big pile of shit," Alliss asserted.

When the American team arrived, Burke requested that Kroll, the No. 2 man in the singles lineup against Mills, be replaced. Kroll, Burke explained, had a case of "red ass"—a chafed posterior, irritated by the coarse pants the American team had been issued. Kroll, an Army sergeant, was a veteran of the Anzio landing in World War II. He was wounded four times and received three purple hearts. Now, what Burke called "the sorry condition" of his back side was preventing him from playing a game of golf.

At first, Rees found it incredible, and, according to Burke in *It's Only a Game,* Rees demanded that a doctor confirm Burke's malady. "That hacked me off," Burke wrote. "I thought it was small of him not taking me at my word."

Rees's account differed. He later wrote that he had demurred by calling Kroll's real issue a "painful internal complaint." But he added: "Technically, I could have claimed a walk off for Peter. I did no such thing. The Ryder Cup is above such pettiness." Rees was further surprised to learn that Burke was taking Kroll's place. The incident was just the beginning of what would soon become a truly astonishing match.

While Rees had been tipped off about the greens speed and passed the information onto his players, the Americans were oblivious. Having arrived at Lindrick understandably overconfident, they three-putted the first green in six of the eight matches. By the time they adjusted, they found themselves trailing. That fueled a rowdy crowd estimated at twenty thousand, with up to six thousand sneaking through the gates.

"The atmosphere was magnificently partisan," Rees later wrote. "The whole North of England seemed to be at Lindrick that day and by 11:30 a.m. (two-and one-half hours in), the gatekeeper had run out of tickets. As the home players proved, one after another, that they had the beating of their rivals, explosions of applause went off like exploding bombs on all parts of the course. It was wonderfully inspiring, an atmosphere unique in my thirty years of the sport."

The first two matches got the spectators going early and set the tone for the entire day. Having sent off firebrand Tommy Bolt against Eric Brown in the first match, Burke removed his dressy overcoat and prepared himself for his unexpected match in the No. 2 spot. He recalled the scene in his book in a section entitled, "Take nothing for granted."

When asked whom he was facing, Burke replied that it was Peter Mills and that he had never heard of him.

"I have," somebody from the gallery shouted. "He has a reputation for having a very shaky putter."

That was all Burke, one of the game's most proficient masters of the greens, needed to hear.

"Waiting to tee off with no warm-up, I felt pretty good about handling Peter Mills," he wrote. "Well, Mr. Mills proceeded to birdie three of the first seven holes. On the other holes, he left every approach putt four feet short, and then made the tough putts for par. I couldn't get it going, and Peter Mills just killed me, 5-and-3."

Rees admitted he fretted over the spot Mills was in, playing his first (and only) Ryder Cup match against America's best player, who had not lost in seven previous Ryder Cup matches. But, as Rees noted, Mills played the game of his life and was never intimidated. According to Mills, Burke even resorted to bits of gamesmanship, at one point unwrapping a golf ball from "crackling" paper while Mills was over his shot. To no avail.

"You've got to expect that sort of thing," Mills said. "I just took my time. The longer you wait the wilder they get."

Mills's patience paid off. He played a remarkably steady round and waited for Burke to make mistakes. He did, and in an uncharacteristic fashion.

As all this was happening, Faulkner, unlike the stewing Weetman, had accepted his role and acted as de facto captain. With Rees tied up in his own match, Faulkner sprinted from match to match providing updates and encouragement. "Those were the days before walkie-talkies and scoreboards," Bousfield recalled later. "All of us playing out there would have no idea what was happening in the other matches if it wasn't for Max. He was marvelous."

It was said the biggest lift came after Mills won the tenth hole to go 5-up, especially given the action in the opening match between Bolt and Brown.

Leading off with the Scot was a stroke of genius by Rees for he anticipated that Burke would open with his most explosive (in more ways than one) player. The volatile Bolt was aptly named. Bad shots, bad breaks and bad lies sent him cussing, often followed by the main attraction of his show, club throwing–at times out of anger, at others in showmanship. The crowds loved him and encouraged him to fire away. Often, he obliged. Demaret once joked that Bolt's putter "spent more time in the air than Lindbergh." Leonard Crawley found him entertaining. He described him as "the hardest boiled golfing egg on the North American continent. Incorrigible and yet delightful."

Bolt was born in Oklahoma, and his mother died shortly thereafter. He played his first golf barefoot, sneaking onto the Lakeside Country Club in Shreveport, Louisiana, during the winter months when he and his pals went unnoticed. He caddied a little, hustled some (he called his pigeons "mullets") and worked in construction before a stint in the US Army as the head pro at a golf club in Rome toward the end of the war. The course was just sixteen holes thanks to Benito Mussolini. Il Duce needed to keep his golf-loving industrialists happy, but he had two outer holes plowed to prevent the proletariat from noticing.

Bolt went bust playing craps on the troop ship home, hustled some more, got noticed as a good stick and somehow found his way to the PGA circuit. Success wasn't immediate. He once had to sell his clubs for $100 to cover traveling costs for the next tournament and took a job giving lessons at a North Carolina driving range. But you can't hide talent. Bolt persevered and won his first tournament, the North and South Open, at Pinehurst in 1951, beating all the Ryder Cup players from both sides from the previous week. He was thirty-three at the time, although he lied about his age and shaved off two years for the record. He could finally make a living playing golf.

Bolt was so desperate to cure his hook, he took three weeks out of the 1955 calendar and spent them with Ben Hogan, the malady's most famous conqueror. His career really took off after the Hawk's ministrations. "I didn't really learn to play golf until then," Bolt said. "He told me what his secret was. It was the left hand moving over on top of the club to eliminate the fear of hooking."

It's a shame that Bolt is remembered more for his temper than his game. Hogan called him the best ball striker of his day. He also had many friends on tour–Hogan being the closest–and he had a soft spot for golfers in need. But he was also quick to unleash his legendary wrath upon those he didn't like.

The balding Brown was also no wallflower. He played with a chip on his shoulder and resented when broadcasters at Lindrick called the team "English." He was a Scot, aye, but he hated Americans more, not in general, but certainly on the golf course. Henry Cotton, previewing the Ryder Cup for *Golf Illustrated,* commented: "I have always had a lot of admiration for Eric Brown because he is one of those people who has come up the hard way and has retained the courage to call a spade a spade and not be a tiring sort of yes man. He has never had an elegant golf swing, but he has the courage to attack the ball all out, and has learned to play the hard way too, that it pays to control the ball through the green."

Brown may not have needed added motivation. He'd have a bit of revenge going for him after losing to Bolt in alternate shot. But Rees supplied it anyway.

"I know you've never lost to a Yankee yet and have no intention of doing so today," he told him, noting Brown's perfect singles record. "Three-one down can quickly become three-two if you beat Bolt as I know you can and will."

This was the match the overflow crowd wanted to see and the gallery swelled around the first tee in anticipation. Like two prize fighters entering the ring, they were both late arriving. Demaret, who attended the matches despite being snubbed, cracked that the last time the two had been spotted "they were standing at fifty paces throwing clubs at one another."

It started out poorly for Brown, as in his 7-and-5 alternate shot loss with O'Connor against Bolt and Mayer. He hooked his first drive into the rough and botched a shot out of the greenside bunker, snarling at photographers who had snapped their shutters during his swing. But it was soon apparent that Bolt, like many of his teammates, couldn't figure out the greens. He was unable to get up and down from a bunker on the third—or from his position short of the green on the fourth and sixth. Bolt grew frustrated and the gallery was loving it. It was even over the top for Brown, who intervened and attempted to silence the spectators while Bolt was over a shot. On the eighth, however, the tenor changed. Bolt's pitch shot came up well short, and he slammed his wedge into the ground, bouncing several feet away, where his caddie retrieved it. After Brown found the green easily, he laid his club gently on the ground and smiled with stinging sarcasm at his opponent. The ill will continued at the ninth where Bolt's approach shot went through the green and into the gnarly jag grass behind it. He snarled to Brown that if it had been the Scotsman's ball, someone would have kicked it into a better lie. Brown told him to stop his moaning, which gave the British supporters even more license to misbehave.

"You cannot prevent a golf crowd from spotting your idiosyncrasies or your momentary expressions and they had quite clearly noticed Bolt's tendency to grumble about unfavorable lies and bad luck," Brown explained.

After going 3-up, Brown concluded that Bolt was slow-playing him. The gallery agreed and began to heckle Bolt even more vociferously. But Brown had an idea. He whispered instructions to his caddie—a short, stocky gent with a bowler cap—who then dashed off to the clubhouse. The caddie returned with a folding chair. Brown lounged in it as Bolt interminably negotiated his shot. The stunt infuriated Bolt and egged on the gallery to cheer his bad shots and missed putts. Roars for other British successes resounded throughout the course only intensified the spectator's heckling of Bolt. They were clearly under his skin, and they knew it.

Bolt stayed in the match with a few fine recovery shots before lunchtime but still had four holes to make up in the afternoon. He narrowed the deficit to two at one point but was again 3-down with four to play at the 351-yard fifteenth, where the wheels finally came off. Bolt hooked his drive into deep rough, slashed out violently forty yards short and compounded this error by pitching to the back of the green. Brown was on in two and, after running his long putt nine feet past, it was obvious Bolt would lose the hole. As a way of conceding, he walked up to his ball and swatted it off the green.

There was no handshake. "Can't say that I enjoyed the game," Bolt said to Brown. "I imagine not," Brown retorted. "Because even you knew when the games were drawn that you never had an earthly chance of beating me."

Bolt took it out on his 6-iron. He broke it over his knee, steel shaft and all, and headed into the locker room, where a grizzled old attendant commiserated: "Jolly bad luck, Bolt. You put up a jolly good fight. I'm sorry to see you lose." To this, Bolt whipped off his cap and hurled it to the floor. "The hell with that," he sneered. "You're glad I lost."

A gaggle of reporters had followed him in with open notebooks which he filled with a litany of complaints about the spectators, describing their behavior as, "the most disgusting display of partisanship I have ever known. The crowd actually cheered every time I missed a putt or hit a loose shot. It was demoralizing."

Burke was also there and tried to intercede.

"Relax, Tommy, forget it," he begged.

"If you like to lose," Bolt snapped. "I don't."

The Brits were up in seven of the eight matches through nine holes, then up in five, down in two with one even after eighteen, which would have been enough to win the Cup. The US needed a furious rally; however, learning that their toughest two teammates had lost the first two matches couldn't have helped. The British momentum continued to roll.

Rees did his part against Furgol with a brilliant 68 over the first eighteen holes. The two had become close while Rees was touring in America in 1946. Rees admired Furgol for his tenacity in reaching the top levels of golf with an atrophied left arm, the result of a fall from playground equipment as a child. Rees's team was up in the four matches ahead of him when he and Furgol arrived at the first tee. Rees was eager to get his match over as quickly as possible, which he did, 7-and-6, having made five putts of 25 feet during the match.

"You know, Dai, you boys are going to win this whole thing today," Furgol told him as they shook hands.

"Don't give me that, Ed," Rees replied. "It's one thing talking about it, and quite another doing it."

"Yes, you are, and although we won't like it, it will be a great thing for golf and the future of the Ryder Cup," Furgol said. "I've never seen a team with such a spirit as yours."

It was perhaps the most magnanimous exchange in a generally contentious day.

Furgol's prediction was spot-on and it wasn't even close. No American could stop the bleeding as the rout fed on itself (just as it would for the Americans at Brookline in 1999). *The Guardian* called the American response "a pathetic procession to defeat." O'Connor's 7-and-6 rout of Finsterwald was a microcosm of the day. It was a bitterly contested match and not without gamesmanship. At one point, Finsterwald picked up a putt inches away from the hole before O'Connor conceded. Later, O'Connor did the same. They were all-square through eighteen, but O'Connor, using a putter he picked up at the break, won six of the first eight holes in the afternoon as the wind picked up. The match turned on the par-three third and the par-four fourth, the twenty-first and twenty-second holes of the match. O'Connor was bunkered from the third tee but hit a brilliant shot to get up and down for a three while Finsterwald three-putted. "The American was clearly shaken," wrote Bob Ferrier of the Sunday Dispatch, adding that Finsterwald was then "shattered" on the next hole when O'Connor hit a gem of a recovery shot from the deep rough to the heart of the green. Finsterwald was even more shaken after O'Connor miraculously holed out from under a bush near the eighth green.

Again, there was no handshake. According to Belton in *The Ryder Lions*, Finsterwald had directed several "waspish remarks" toward the Irishman during the match and behaved boorishly. "The anger of some of the Americans was highlighted, too, by the reaction of Dow Finsterwald, after I murdered him. In spite of pleas from players on both teams my humiliated opponent was so disgruntled he declined to shake my hand," O'Connor said.

The Cup was clinched before any American point went up on the board. Just as Rees was running out to encourage Alliss in a match that he would go on to lose to Hawkins (the only US win of the day), a thunderous roar went up from the neighboring fourteenth green. Bousfield had clinched his halve to put Hebert at dormie-four to secure the last half-point necessary. He'd get the full point on the next green, knocking in an 18-inch putt.

With Bernard Hunt beating Doug Ford, 6-and-5, the Brits won in convincing fashion. All six of their victories went no further than the thirty-third hole. Hawkins's lone American win was by 2-and-1 with Mayer halving with Bradshaw and his back aching in the final match. The final score was 7 ½-4 ½ as the US experienced its worst defeat in singles. Aside from Rees, no one on the home side shot in the 60s in a complete round while Hawkins was the only American to break par on the day.

The Americans were stunned. Alliss recalled they "looked on in disbelief that they could have lost to this ragtag outfit." For once, their short games came up short. They had problems chipping with the smaller British ball, an issue when hitting from the rough as well, and never adjusted to the faster greens speeds. The sudden change in the weather, Henry Cotton noted in his syndicated analysis, was a major factor. Burke, Cotton said, had told him just before the matches began that his team was having issues with "crazy" angles and blind shots.

"Looking back, it seems as if the good Lord was gradually setting the scene for what will be known as 'the day of resurrection' of British golf because the wind of the night had already dried out the course considerably, and that the deceiving, dull light, ideal for television cameras, puzzled our visitors so much that they floundered from the word 'go,'" Cotton wrote.

Burke had complained about the inconsistent height of the flagsticks during the week and in trying to find more reasons for the debacle, second-guessed arriving eight days ahead to begin practicing. "We over-trained," he said.

"Being the captain of a losing team is pitiful," Burke said years later. "There's all kinds of reasons, none of 'em happy ones. Hurts like hell, but you've got to suck it up and hope you get another shot." He did, and won, in 1973.

Furgol, for one, admitted that his team was, "well and truly licked.

"It's tough to lose but then these British guys deserve a lot of credit," he said. "They came up a long hill."

US PGA president Harry Moffitt tried to play down the US team's complaints about the fans: "angry criticism of the behavior of the British spectators is unwarranted. I think the crowds, on the whole, were very sporting." But he also told the Brits at the dinner that night not to get too attached to the Cup. Burke took his lumps at the trophy presentation and offered a similar good-natured warning.

"We're probably the greatest American ambassadors that have ever hit these Isles," he said. "I'll tell you one thing. You had better bring a team with you when you come to the States because we'll be waiting for you."

At that point, the 1959 matches were the last thing on the winners' minds. Even Weetman was seen congratulating Rees with a handshake. The captain then took the Ryder Cup and posed with it, beaming. He was hoisted over the shoulders of his team and paraded through the cheering mob.

"It's wonderful. I think my whole team deserves the freedom of Sheffield, and of Britain, for their performance," Rees said. "This is the proudest moment I have ever had."

Following the dinner, which three American players snubbed, the Brits partied into the wee hours, finally running out of gas before sunrise. The tee-totaling Rees sought to drink as much champagne as possible to get tipsy but couldn't seem to find the tipping point. His caddy, "Little Mac" had better luck. He staggered onto a carpet and passed out.

"My wedding day apart, this was the most thrilling day of my life," Rees wrote.

For once, the British press could gloat, starting with the headline in the *Sunday Dispatch:*

"It's the Lindrick Miracle".

Golf Illustrated urged all British golf fans to let loose: "We have sustained so many golf defeats over a period of many years that we can be pardoned for feeling so cock-a-hoop."

Great Britain captain Dai Rees holds aloft the Ryder Cup after his team's stunning comeback. Photo credit Lindrick Golf Club

Writing for *The People*, David Williams called it "the most astonishing golf win of the century," although older American fans might argue for Francis Ouimet in 1913.

Bill Withers's lede in the *Nottingham Evening News* rubbed it in on two fronts.

"America got two big shocks last weekend–finding that Russia had satellites circling the earth and that Britain had golfers making equally impressive circles round their top ten professionals," he wrote. "You may try and excuse the American failure or at least at best find the reason for it–but the answer was that the British play got them rattled."

"We did not just beat the Americans. We trounced them and rubbed their noses in the soft green turf," Frank Pennick wrote in the *Sunday Express.*

"This was something more than a win at golf," declared Sid Bailey of the *Sunday Empire News.* "It burst the American bubble of sports supremacy. It was the greatest shot in the arm that British golf has had for many a day. It should inspire all our tennis and boxing and athletic lads to go out against the 'Damn Yankees' and do to them what Rees and his merry men did yesterday."

"Their names should be inscribed in the halls of St. Andrews," proclaimed John Ballantine, the *Daily Graphic* writer who would help Rees pen his autobiography.

Henry Longhurst, who provided the color commentary on the BBC broadcast, was tough on Bolt's conduct.

"It is possible for any man to radiate hostility, argue with the referee, break his clubs in half and pass vitriolic comments on the spectators and his hosts in general, but if he feels that way, someone should persuade him to abstain from contests calculated to foster good will."

Back home, the reaction was muted and almost indifferent, with the news of the loss largely relegated to the back of the sports sections. The World Series was on, and there was college football to report.

Herbert Warren Wind, the great American golfing sage, put it in matter-of-fact terms:

"Perhaps the real lesson to be learned from the loss of the Ryder Cup was the obvious one: on a given day a group of British pros, playing determined golf, are now again capable of defeating a team of excellent American pros who are slightly off their game."

About a week later, Bolt sat down for an interview with Ned Cronin of the *Los Angeles Times.* Cronin satirically suggested that "the Redcoats finally got even for what happened at Yorktown." Bolt had a different battle in mind. He hadn't mellowed.

"In the doubles we had someone we could talk to," he said. "The singles was something else again. We all found out how General Custer must have felt when he ran into those unfriendly Indians."

Speaking of Lionel Hebert, Bolt said he never felt so sad for a man, calling Hebert one of the nicest guys in the world. "After he finished, he came into the locker room and said, 'I don't know how any American could ever win a match in England. It was awful. I never felt so alone in all my life.'

"Individually, they are pretty nice folks," Bolt said of the British golf fans. "But get them together and they are about as miserable a bunch of people as you could ever have the misfortune to run into in a supposedly civilized world."

Forty-two years later, the Europeans would echo similar sentiments about the Boston fans who tormented them at Brookline.

Meanwhile, as the British Isles were reveling in the victory, the British PGA dealt harshly with Harry Weetman. It made an example of him with an unprecedented year's suspension, denying him a chance to make a living by winning a share of the £30,000 in prize money available during his suspension. He was, however, still eligible for The Open Championship, run by the R&A. The news was delivered over the phone while Weetman was playing in the Spanish Open. Freda, speaking for her husband, called it a "vicious attack, particularly so as Harry was given no chance of being represented at the meeting."

Weetman wrote letters of apology to both Rees and the PGA. To Rees, he said, "On reflection I now realize how untimely my remarks were at Lindrick and for this I am sorry . . . As you know, Dai, I am not a fellow to talk very much and I have never let anyone down yet, but I don't like unfaithfulness of any kind."

Rees responded that Weetman's letter left him "perplexed" in that he had refrained from making a genuine apology. "I assure you that I bear you nothing but good will, but I am not convinced it is reciprocated," he wrote.

To the PGA, Weetman wrote, "I can only say that I regret my action and hope that you and the committee accept this truly sincere apology." After the PGA brusquely replied that its

Executive Committee had reviewed his letter and "at present see no reason to alter their decision," Weetman said he was "almost beyond caring."

Rees would have a change of heart and intercede in April with a letter stating that he would be "personally glad" if the suspension was removed, and it was. Rees felt he and Weetman had reconciled but Weetman never let go of the grudge. Weetman eventually received redemption when he was named captain of the 1965 team. However, when Rees was again tabbed two years later, in commemoration of the ten-year anniversary of Lindrick, Weetman penned a critique in the *Daily Mirror*, calling the selection "ridiculous," and that the British PGA had an "almost hypnotic fascination with the dapper, fierce-tempered Welshman.

"I have every admiration for him as a brilliant tournament player with a lot of guts," Weetman added. "But not as a captain or leader of men."

"I suppose Harry and I are as different as two human beings could be," Rees wrote soon after. Both would die in automobile accidents, Weetman at age 51 in 1972 and Rees at age 70 while returning from an Arsenal football match in 1983.

The victory was undoubtedly the British Isles' biggest in international sports until England's 1966 World Cup victory. But while Lindrick stands as a remarkable example of Churchillian resolve, the American giant would not be caught sleeping again. The US PGA adopted a more sensible selection process, and the players redoubled their focus. As Burke promised, the return match at Eldorado Country Club two years later produced a convincing 8 ½-3 ½ win by an American team fortified by the addition of Snead, Middlecoff and Boros. It would take the European expansion to make the series competitive again.

Lindrick played its part in reviving interest in the Ryder Cup, keeping the flame alive for the enormous spectacle it would become. That was something Rees could not anticipate when he purchased a crate of champagne soon after the victory at Lindrick, not to be opened by anyone other than the next team to beat the Americans.

DAY 1
FOURSOMES
Doug Ford/Dow Finsterwald (US) defeated Peter Alliss/Bernard Hunt (GB) 2-and-1 Ken Bousfield/Dai Rees (GB) defeated Art Wall/Fred Hawkins (US) 3-and-2 Ted Kroll/Jack Burke Jr. (US) defeated Max Faulkner/Harry Weetman (GB) 4-and-3 Dick Mayer/Tommy Bolt (US) defeated Christy O'Connor/Eric Brown (GB) 7-and-5 **United States wins session 3–1**
DAY 2
SINGLES
Eric Brown (GB) defeated Tommy Bolt (US) 4-and-3 Peter Mills (GB) defeated Jack Burke Jr. (US) 5-and-3 Fred Hawkins (US) defeated Peter Alliss (GB) 2-and-1 Ken Bousfield (GB) defeated Lionel Hebert (US) 4-and-3 Dai Rees (GB) defeated Ed Furgol (US) 7-and-6 Bernard Hunt (GB) defeated Doug Ford (US) 6-and-5 Christy O'Connor (GB) defeated Dow Finsterwald (US) 7-and-6 Dick Mayer (US) halved with Harry Bradshaw (GB) **Great Britain wins session 6 ½–1 ½** **GREAT BRITAIN WINS RYDER CUP 7 ½–4 ½**

1969

The Concession

ROYAL BIRKDALE GOLF CLUB
UNITED STATES 16, GREAT BRITAIN 16

This was the year the world would spin on a new axis. In 1969, man walked on the moon. Others mooned the world at Woodstock. The Beatles released their final album, and the Amazin' Mets defied the odds to win the World Series. Midnight Cowboy would become the only X-rated film to win best picture at the Oscars while some 250,000 marched on Washington D.C. to protest the Vietnam War.

And at long last, this was the year Jack Nicklaus would make his Ryder Cup debut.

It seems incomprehensible. The twenty-nine year old had won his first major, the US Open, in 1962. He won the PGA Championship in 1963. He won the Masters in 1963, 1965 and 1966. He won The Open Championship in 1966 and the US Open again in 1967. That's seven majors and the completion of the career Grand Slam without a single Ryder Cup appearance.

The Golden Bear was the best player in the world, and arguably the best in history, but he wasn't seasoned enough to play for his country, according to entrenched and outdated PGA protocol. Great didn't matter to the PGA. Its decision-makers seemed more bent on preserving the five-year apprenticeship requirement than fielding the best pros to represent the flag.

The curious eligibility condition dated back to the organization's earliest days when almost every top playing professional outside of Walter Hagen was associated with a club. The PGA could be assured that new members, by apprenticing under established club professionals, could properly hone their craft. At the same time, the old boys didn't mind keeping the prize money to themselves and away from the newbies. Once in the exclusive club, PGA members made sure that potential Ryder Cup players paid their dues just as they had.

Apprenticeships originally lasted just three years. That's how Sam Snead was allowed on the 1937 Ryder Cup team. But it was upped to a more problematic five years after World War II. When Cary Middlecoff was deemed ineligible for the 1949 team, he called it "the silliest, most obsolete rule I ever heard of."

Two decades later, it was still obsolete–and even sillier in Nicklaus's case. Apprenticeship to what?

Nicklaus turned pro in 1961. He dutifully sat it out as the PGA named the 1963 and '65 Ryder Cup teams and looked forward to making the 1967 squad. Rules were rules and they had to be observed, he said, without protest. He cut one year off his apprenticeship by attending a week-long business school in February of 1966, where he learned the ropes of running a pro shop, selling shirts, giving lessons and running the club championship. But even that fell short of Ryder Cup eligibility.

The PGA also required that its members play in at least twenty-five tournaments per year before making the team. Nicklaus played in twenty-four in 1965 because the Miami Open–in which he had entered–had been cancelled that year. When the PGA agreed to count his 1965 season due to extenuating circumstances, it left him with a shorter period than other players to collect points. Additionally, although the 1967 Cup matches originally scheduled for the summer were moved to the fall, the PGA failed to extend the points period beyond April. This meant that Nicklaus's US Open win in June did not contribute to his points. Nicklaus would need to win the Masters for a third straight time in 1967 to make the team. He missed it.

"It's possible the matches will be played without any of the major champions. That would be a little silly, wouldn't it?" he noted at the time, and he was almost right. Masters champ Gay Brewer, alone, participated in those Ryder matches at Champions Golf Club.

Everything changed in two years. The touring pros were increasingly perturbed by the PGA's stranglehold over tournaments. "Just as we wouldn't presume to tell the PGA how to run its affairs, we think we should have the authority to run ours," Nicklaus wrote in his contemporary book, *The Greatest Game of All.* Acrimony intensified when, in August of 1968, Nicklaus, Frank Beard, Gardner Dickinson, Dan Sikes and Doug Ford spearheaded a group voting to form an organization independent from the PGA: the American Professional Golfers. Twenty-eight APG tournaments were scheduled for 1969; however, before any took place, the PGA–its hand now forced–relented to the formation of a Tournament Players Division (which would morph into the PGA Tour in the mid 70s). Divorce was fortunately averted, as was, most likely, the demise of the Ryder Cup.

The British PGA watched all of the upheaval with a wary eye. The Ryder Cup was more sacred on their shores, despite becoming so difficult to win. The notion of abandoning Samuel Ryder's tournament was unbearable. It certainly seemed to the Brits that the PGA of America wasn't giving the Ryder Cup a second thought, as it haggled with its touring pros. In January 1969, the Brits' patience with the dilly-dallying ran dry. They flew John Bywaters, the association secretary, to PGA headquarters in Palm Beach as their emissary. Several changes were floated. The Americans foolheartedly lobbied to move to stroke play to ensure all matches would conclude on the eighteenth hole, in a bid to entice the US television networks to broadcast the competition for the first time. They also suggested adding Commonwealth players such as Gary Player and Peter Thomson to those from Great Britain and Ireland. Bywaters nixed both ideas, although the two sides did agree on expanding team rosters from ten to twelve players.

Meanwhile, the British PGA did some creative thinking. It changed its selection process by reducing its apprenticeship period from three years to six months, thus securing young stars Bernard

Gallacher and Maurice Bembridge. Additionally, the points-based Order of Merit would be used to pick the first six players with the remaining six selected by a committee of captain Eric Brown, five-time captain Dai Rees and the leading man on the Order of Merit, Christy O'Connor. That opened the door to considering Tony Jacklin and young Peter Townsend, who competed mostly in America. The British press had long been clamoring for a less stodgy team. This would provide new blood.

Every move seemed advantageous. And, when Jacklin became the first Englishman since Max Faulkner in 1951 to win The Open Championship, British golf was awash with an optimism it had not experienced since the 1930s. The British press began hailing Jacklin as the world's best player. While such an assertion might seem to slight Nicklaus, Jacklin was playing better golf than anyone that year, especially Nicklaus. After a fallow 1968 season–excusable due to the PGA dustup–the Golden Bear had just one top ten major finish in 1969, a tie for sixth at the British Open. Coming into the Ryder Cup, he'd won only once, in February at the Andy Williams San Diego Open. The papers obsessed over his slump. *Sports Illustrated* ran a feature story pleadingly entitled: "WHAT HAS GONE WRONG, JACK?" All the while, Nicklaus characterized his game as "medium lousy." It was ironic that over the period of the three previous Ryder Cups for which he was ineligible, he was at the top of his game. In the first one he played, his game was on the skids.

Arnold Palmer, too, was off form. A lingering issue with his hip kept him winless since the previous September and, despite a gamely effort to accrue enough points to make the squad, the bum hip forced his withdrawal from the PGA Championship after a first round 82. It was his last chance at points. It would be the only team he missed in a run from '61 through '73.

That didn't render the US team toothless. Combined, they had already won $125 million in earnings that year. Billy Casper, Lee Trevino, Ray Floyd and Gene Littler would all have World Golf Hall of Fame careers. The roster was filled out by hardened, solid players such as Dave Hill, who won the Vardon Trophy for low scoring average. Still, of those, only Tommy Aaron would win a major in his career (1973 Masters). Other than Casper and Littler, this was a team of Ryder Cup rookies. What's more, Hill, Sikes, Dale Douglass and Ken Still, had never played in Britain. Floyd was the sole team member who had won a major that year (the PGA) as Masters champ George Archer and US Open champ Orville Moody failed to qualify. The team they would face balanced out the youth of Gallacher, Townsend and Bembridge with seven Ryder Cup veterans experiencing a total of twenty-nine Ryder Cups to the Americans' eight. O'Connor, Peter Alliss and Bernard Hunt all had played in seven. None had a winning record, but those three had a taste of victory over the Americans at Lindrick in 1957. And their appetite was whetted for another.

The British captain, too, was hungry. Eric Brown was long obsessed with beating the Americans, and he had a knack for it. He never lost a singles match in his four Ryder Cup appearances, including his fractious victory over Tommy Bolt at Lindrick and notching the only British singles win in 1959 over Middlecoff. Known as "Bad Boy Brown", he came up the hard way and played that way. His old Ryder Cup teammate, Peter Alliss, described him as "a bit abrasive, liked a dram and a cigarette, and didn't suffer fools" and wrote that Brown "was at his best as a match player, thriving on the greater element of personal combat in that form of golf." Brown approached his captaincy the same way and relished his matchup against another cantankerous competitor who excelled in the Ryder Cup cauldron.

Sam Snead, serving as captain for the second time, was 10-2-1 overall, 6-1 in singles, in his Ryder Cup career. His one singles loss came after blowing a four-hole lead with six to play against Harry Weetman, whom he dismissed as "a bushy-haired pro with just a fair reputation." Losing to such a player haunted him the rest of his life and he was assuredly reminded of it at Birkdale. "In my mind, I was ordering a nice thick steak for dinner when we walked up to No. 31," he wrote in his autobiography, *The Education of a Golfer.* "A good rule is never collect any trophies in your head until you have them in your hand." His competitive zeal wasn't confined to professional events. If a big-talking amateur was foolish enough to challenge Snead to a big-money Nassau wager, even he would see Snead's ruthlessness first-hand. Snead gave no quarter.

The golf course itself was a story. Royal Birkdale is arguably the best course ever to host a Ryder Cup. It isn't as ancient as the established shrines to the game. However, following a redesign by F.G. Hawtree and J.H. Taylor in 1932, it was quickly acknowledged as the best championship test in the British Isles, a masterpiece of links golf. Hawtree and Taylor redirected the eighteen holes in between, rather than over, the natural sand dunes along the Irish Sea, creating wind tunnels and natural viewing platforms. In prestige and importance, it dwarfed nearby Southport & Ainsdale, which hosted the '35 and '37 matches, and was later honored with its "Royal" designation by King George VI in 1951. It hosted its first Open Championship in 1954 and eventually became part of The Open rota. The Ryder Cup first came in 1965, the same year the club hosted its third Open.

While Birkdale was very much a links course, it was far from a typical one. It played as a par 74 (38 on the back nine) with five par-five holes, each of them reachable in two if the wind cooperated. Four of those were on the incoming six holes, including seventeen and eighteen, making for a dramatic match play finish. Three of the four par-threes were even-numbered holes, which made the choice of the order in alternate shot pivotal. The better driver could play the odd-numbered holes, the better iron player the even holes. The four finishing holes already had been toughened up for the 1965 Ryder Cup. They would require great golf under pressure. In general, Birkdale was not as quirky as some of the older links that had hosted Open championships and, as such, seemed to suit better the Americans' style of play. Its greens presented themselves as targets and didn't require as much guesswork on distances.

The format of play had changed since the home team won at Lindrick in 1957. In 1961, instead of four thirty-six-hole foursomes matches and eight thirty-six-hole singles matches over two days, the matches were reduced to eighteen holes with eight foursomes matches over morning and afternoon sessions on the first day, followed by eight morning singles matches and eight afternoon singles matches on the second day. In 1965, the event was expanded over three days with the addition of eight fourball matches, leaving thirty-two points up for grabs. The first day was devoted to alternate shot, the second to better ball and the third to two singles sessions.

Modern touches had also been added around the course, thanks to industrialist Brian Park, who subsidized the matches at Birkdale for the second straight time. Park aimed to make the Ryder Cup experience at Birkdale surpass anything the Americans had hosted. He had constructed two miles of walking paths and grass amphitheaters around greens. The matches had always drawn more fans in Britain and, to accommodate them, organizers used Birkdale's vast open spaces to build hospitality areas for concessions and a tented village with an exhibition area, a post office, a first aid station and the largest press building ever yet provided. The high dunes were perfect for spectating. To keep everyone updated, eight "good looking girls", as the *Manchester Evening News and Chronicle* called them, drove electric buggies, called Mini Mokes, alongside each match with four-sided signs that displayed the score from all angles. Park's original £30,000 pound investment in 1965 was bolstered in 1969 by first-time corporate sponsorship from cigarette firm Senior Service, whose slogan was "The Perfection of Cigarette Luxury."

Wives, too, were ever more a part of the Ryder Cup (although they were yet to wear matching outfits). Frank Beard's wife, Patti, was the talk of the course on the first day of play in her miniskirt, red tights and black boots.

Most of the American contingent, including wives, gathered in Washington, D.C. for the Pan Am flight to Heathrow. The US team had always departed from New York, whether by sea or air. But Max Elbin, chairman of the Ryder Cup Committee, lived in Bethesda, Maryland and wanted to bring business to the relatively new Dulles Airport. That gave newly inaugurated President Richard Nixon the opportunity to invite the team to the White House for a sendoff.

With everyone in dress attire, Nixon, taking a needed break from a Vietnam policy conference, showed off the White House putting green and handed out golf balls embossed with the presidential seal before asking for a putting demonstration.

To no one's surprise, old hustler Lee Trevino cracked, "What are we betting?"

"Nobody's betting around here," Nixon quickly replied with a feigned scowl. "The Treasury Department is right across the street."

Trevino's putt came up eighteen inches short. Miller Barber and Ken Still missed as well, and Snead was off by a full two feet.

"And finally, a new member of our team, the President," someone announced.

"Oh God," Nixon guffawed, before leaving his putt two feet short. "Well, anyway, it was on the line."

The American team landed via London at Ringway Airport in Manchester, where, decked out in their official team blazers and ties, they posed in front of the wing of their airplane. Eric Brown—appearing less official in a bucket hat concealing a bald pate—greeted them, and joined them with most of the British team for a joint press conference at the Prince of Wales Hotel in Southport—the US headquarters for the week. Hotel stays in the UK often required a certain amount of roughing it for the American players, as the unapologetic Hill, no Anglophile, bemoaned in his 1977 book *Teed Off.*

"Those folks are about two hundred years behind America in modernization, especially out where some of those seaside links are," he wrote. "We were in a hotel that had something like one hundred twenty rooms, and out of those one hundred twenty rooms there were twenty-seven private bathrooms. I was lucky—I had a private bath—otherwise I would have used the window before I'd have headed down the hallway at four AM. And that was one of the luxury hotels in the area."

In any event, Brown played the martinet once Jacklin and Brian Huggett disobeyed his orders by arriving late. They had played an exhibition in Huggett's native Wales earlier that day. "I say that if you're a member of any team you must be a team man and accept the rulings laid down," he said. Not everyone appreciated the upbraiding.

Brown's approach was certainly distinct from that of Snead, who followed the *laissez faire* captaincy of his old rival Ben Hogan. Two years earlier at Champions, Hogan gave his team a now-legendary pep talk that summed it all up, "Boys, there's nothing to being the captain of the Ryder Cup. You guys are all great players. Pairing is really easy. I'm going to pair together you boys who drive crooked, and I'm going to pair together you boys who drive straight. And the first ball's going to be hit by Julius Boros 'cause he don't give a shit about anything. So y'all just go play your game."

Hogan didn't require the team to wear the official uniforms and even told the colorful Doug Sanders he could "dress like a peacock" if he desired. "But let me tell you boys one thing–I don't want my name on that trophy as a losing captain."

At the formal dinner, Hogan waited patiently as British captain Dai Rees introduced each individual member of his team with a lengthy description of each man's accomplishments. Hogan introduced his men by name only, then announced, "Ladies and gentlemen, the United States Ryder Cup Team–the finest golfers in the world." He promptly sat down, confident his players would back up his words, which they dared not do in a 23 ½-8 ½ rout.

Snead's approach was even less hands-on. He seemed to spend most of his time before the matches charming the British press. He had one team meeting during the week where he asked his players to write down whom they'd prefer as partners, suggestions he didn't necessarily take. The esteemed *Sports Illustrated* golf editor Gwilym Brown was scorching in his appraisal of Snead's captaincy.

"A final hazard in the path of a routing US victory was the fact that the Professional Golfers Association of America had named Sam Snead as the team's nonplaying captain," he wrote. "There is no doubt that Snead has had a long and honorable competitive career. He is, at fifty-seven, still a wonder of a golfer. But he can also be a crude, sullen, cantankerous old buzzard, and he is as capable of leadership as Ebeneezer Scrooge. Snead's relationship with the majority of US tournament players has long been one of mutual animosity. He was the only player of any reputation to side with the PGA in its administrative squabble with the touring pros."

The "crude, sullen, cantankerous old buzzard" description could also be applied to Eric Brown, although, unlike Snead, he was a model of organization. Before vice captains became a regular part of the team, he asked his old captain, Dai Rees, to assist with everything from favorably setting up the course and pin placements to monitoring players during practice rounds.

Brown fired the first salvo on the first practice day when he ordered his players not to help search for opponents' balls in the rough. Brown claimed he was concerned about a rule penalizing players touching an opponent's ball, although that rule made an exception for balls touched during a search. Jacklin, for one, rebelled against the order, refusing to be a part of any "intimidation" tactics. Alliss later called it one of the "silly things" that was going on. The *London Daily Express* was even moved to point out Brown's unsportsmanlike conduct in an editorial: "Our records in both the Walker and Ryder Cup matches is such that some may be excused for wondering, if goodwill is to be deliberately stamped out, what is there left to play for?"

Peter Dobereiner, the well-respected golf correspondent for *The Guardian*, seemed to agree.

The UK PGA "fanned the air gustily and tried to pretend that it hadn't happened (an old PGA failing, this) but it had, thereby displaying a lamentable ignorance of the laws and the spirit of the game, not to mention the fundamental reason for having a Ryder Cup match at all," he wrote.

The controversy eventually abated but, as the American team saw it, Brown had set a contentious tone for the week.

Brown rescinded his instructions the next day, explaining that he had been misinformed of the rules. But Brown wasn't exactly being conciliatory. Everything he did or said during the week was aimed at toughening up his side, and to make his players believe that "they are playing twelve American human beings, not magicians.

"My contention has always been that our fellows, or most of our fellows, have stepped on the first tee with an inferiority complex. I want my boys to go in fighting right from the first tee," he asserted. "I want to massacre the Americans and that's the spirit I want to get through to my side, especially the younger ones."

His message resonated with enough of the team. Gallacher, who, at twenty was then the youngest-ever Ryder Cup player, confidently announced: "I'm not awed by the Americans. I think maybe they should be awed by me. I couldn't care less whether it's an American I'm playing or an Afghan."

"He had more of our guys believing that they could win," Huggett ventured. "Eric was strong compared to captains before him. 'We're going to beat this lot,' he said in the locker room. He was a bold one and he'd say bold things to you. 'Give them a whacking,' he'd say, and he'd use pretty strong words to back that up. Maybe we hadn't had enough of that before."

When the American Billy Casper told the press at the British Masters that the matches would be close, Brown responded with his own prediction (beating Joe Namath's brashness at Super Bowl III by four months): "He's dead right not to feel confident. Because I am completely convinced that we are going to win this one. This time the Ryder Cup is staying in Britain."

Brown's confidence was contagious. Despite the trouncing at the hands of Hogan's team in 1967, the press rallied around Brown and called for a repeat of Lindrick. Headlines like "I'm Backing Britain," "Go Along with Brown, Britain to Win," and "Rebel Brown is Perfect Choice for Captaincy," heralded his team. More than just guarded optimism had been uncorked.

"I think he will sell the British side to the public and perhaps, instill confidence in them, long before the match begins," wrote former British Ryder Cupper Dave Thomas in the *Daily Mail.*

"Britain has more chance now of winning the Ryder Cup than at any time since that sensationally unexpected success at Lindrick," Bob Rodney wrote in the *Daily Mirror.*" Ignore the psychological war of nerves that has preceded the action. The vital fact is that we are becoming as good as the Americans. Everybody thinks so. All history is bunk. Even the record of our past defeats."

"In a year when Jacklin has restored belief and pride in British golf with his Open triumph, I do not think it improbable that the trend will be taken a step further," Alan Parr wrote in the *Evening Telegraph*. "With warrior Brown in the driving seat I'm backing Britain for a win—and a convincing one, too."

The most unabashed British booster was Paul Trevillion, a writer and illustrator for *Golf Illustrated*, the world's oldest golf publication. Trevillion created "Ryder Cup Reggie", a tiger based on "World Cup Willie", the lion mascot that cheered on England's winning World Cup side in 1966. Trevillion debuted the tiger in May. "WE WILL WIN THE RYDER CUP," he promised, and he kept up the drumbeat through September. The campaign had its effect, even if only to annoy the US team. According to *Draw in the Dunes* by Neil Sagebiel, when Snead was introduced to Trevillion, he leaned in hard. "Have you ever heard of Jack Nicklaus? Billy Casper? Lee Trevino? Gene Littler?" Trevillion nodded. "Check the American team sheets," Snead sneered before walking away. Then, he turned back to make his point. "They are all playing."

Snead's audacity was to be expected if not forgiven. He'd never been on a losing Ryder Cup side in his seven appearances as a player, twice as playing captain. While he told reporters it would be "a lot closer than most people over here seem to think" and called the 4-to-1 odds "ridiculous", the inevitability of another victory must have pervaded not just his thoughts but that of the average American sports fan. That's if the average fan was interested at all. In fact, there was so little fervor for the Ryder Cup at home that it was never televised up to that point, something lamented by pro Max Elbin.

"It's a shame that an event as colorful as the Ryder Cup has never been televised in this country. Hopefully, someday it will be," he told Dick Slay of the *Washington Evening Star* without any way of foreseeing the blockbuster TV event it would become. The networks had been prime movers in forcing the PGA Championship to abandon its match play format. They had no interest at the time in bringing match play of any kind to the television screen. Not that anyone was clamoring for it.

The un-hyped Americans, then, went about their business. Nicklaus had arrived at Birkdale early to play a few holes on Sunday, before the rest of the team arrived around noon the next day. Snead hustled them out on the course for an afternoon session and what was, for most, a first look at Birkdale.

"My players were just feeling their way round, having a good time," Snead said. "They are trying to get over the time change. Tomorrow they will be lowering their sights and on Wednesday, we will know where we are going."

Brown, meanwhile, gave his team the afternoon off in what may have been a psychological ploy to keep their confidence up. "All the boys are playing so well it frightens me," he said. "The British are cock-a-hoop," wrote Fred Tupper of the *New York Times,* as he mulled over their new-found bravado.

Not everyone interpreted things the same way, however. Thomas Reedy of the *Associated Press* found the Americans relaxed. He noted how Trevino told jokes as he fired 5-irons down the practice range, that Ken Still (and Ray Floyd) took time off to visit a local gambling joint and that Brown, who seemed a bit excitable, insisted on playing a practice round with his boys, while Snead never picked up a club.

"The whole atmosphere was one of the rich assured they would win because this is how they get rich and the poor battling to prove something else," Reedy wrote. "The bookies who were once willing to put up one dollar against three on the Americans decided it would have to be one dollar against five."

And so the week began. The controversy over Brown's ball-searching edict blew over, at least in the media, and neither team had much to say about the larger American ball becoming mandatory. A caddie strike over wearing uncomfortable nylon "boiler suits" was averted on Friday. Even the weather seemed to be stuck in a still, anticipatory state. The vaunted winds never blew in from the Irish Sea, and the sun smiled down to give the course its distinctive hue. The only spot of rain was convenient for the US side after a long dry period. It made the fairways lusher and the greens softer. The best Dai Rees could do was move the pins toward the back of the greens to favor run-up shots.

"Thus far, Birkdale has not been a fearsome place," wrote Pat Ward-Thomas, the longtime golf correspondent of *The Guardian*. "It waits in peace for what should be a memorable three days, come what may."

What came first was a British charge. What came second was an American response. The thrusts and parries continued for three days in the most tightly-contested Ryder Cup ever fought. Seventeen of the thirty-two matches would go to the eighteenth hole, and the last of them, between Nicklaus and Jacklin, would settle it all. The first morning's matches established the pattern.

Brown had considered his pairings with great care. Snead didn't care much who played with whom. "They're all good players. At any time, any one of them might beat the rest," he explained. But as a veteran of the days when Ryder Cup matches went thirty-six holes, he wanted to make certain that his best players were well-rested for the singles matches on Sunday. So, he did the unthinkable. He benched Jack Nicklaus and Gene Littler in the opening foursomes session.

"I'm holding my big boys in reserve. I would much rather have Jack in the fourballs and singles than play alternate shots. He's the sort of player who can suddenly turn on the magic and make a magic rainbow," he said.

The Golden Bear had spent the week desperately trying to find the magic form that had eluded him for most of the season. Two days before the start of play, Nicklaus struggled to an alarming 40 on the front side of his practice round before bumping into Max Elbin at the turn. Elbin suggested a slight adjustment in Nicklaus' grip, and he fired a six-under 32 on the inward nine. Nicklaus said the tip helped get his left side through better. He followed that 72 up with a 67 in his final tune up. It seemed the Golden Bear had suddenly found it.

"I've had no match play competition since the Walker Cup and I want to prove myself on this," he said. Nicklaus was, then, appropriately stunned at being benched. When someone joked that he was washed up at age twenty-nine (the *AP's* Reedy called it a "pudgy" twenty-nine), Jack couldn't hold back. "Yeah, I'm through . . ." he scoffed. "If being twelve-under par for my last twenty-seven holes of practice means being through."

Brown, no doubt relieved, piled on. "Sam has left him out so we can get finished at night," he said in a jab at Nicklaus's tendency toward slow play. He also handed Snead a jar of bait to give to Nicklaus for some idle time fishing.

Back then, there was no elaborate opening ceremony fit for royalty. They simply gathered the two teams in front of Royal Birkdale's iconic, white art-deco clubhouse, raised the nations' flags and played the Star-Spangled Banner and God Save the Queen. Players on both sides confessed to stirred emotions and proudful tears, which hit Miller Barber the hardest. Barber, whom his teammates called "X", was a quivering mess. Unfortunately, he was supposed to hit the first ball of the week, playing with fellow rookie Ray Floyd against Neil Coles and Huggett, who had partnered together two years earlier. No doubt Brown had experienced first tee jitters as a rookie at Wentworth in 1953, so he shielded his younger players by sending his veterans out first, and then last, as anchors.

The visitors had honors off the first, a terrifying hole with a massive sand dune along the left side and out of bounds to the right. But as Coles and Huggett waited for the Americans to be introduced—another nervy moment—things were not going as planned for the Americans. The pair had settled on a strategy where Floyd would play the even-numbered holes, so he could attack the three even-numbered par-threes. But Barber didn't think he could pull the trigger on his ugly but repeatable swing.

"We go walking to the tee and X says to me, 'I can't hit it. I can't hit it',” Floyd recalled, which Sagebiel recounted in *Draw in the Dunes.* “I said. 'Pardon me?' He said, 'I can't hit it. I can't hit it. You gotta go. You gotta go'.”

Floyd tried once more. “What do you mean, X? You're playing the odd . . .” But before Floyd could finish the sentence, Barber protested again. So, Floyd stuck a tee in the ground and the Ryder Cup was underway. The kerfuffle mattered. The Americans won the first of the even-numbered par-three holes over a British bogey but Barber, fighting a push, missed both par-three holes on the inward nine. When Barber's second shot flew into a patch of willow scrub off the right side of fifteen, it set up the Americans for a third straight loss. Snead, aware of the order switch on the first tee, was fuming. His leadoff hitters were dormie and would lose, 3-and-2, with Coles playing the hero for the home side.

The British win was followed by two more from the youth brigade as Gallacher and Bembridge edged Trevino and Still, 2-and-1, and Jacklin and Townsend dispatched Hill and an admittedly nervous Tommy Aaron, 3-and-1.

Like Barber, Still felt the butterflies on the first tee and dreaded hitting the first shot. Luckily, he had Trevino as a partner. Merry Mex couldn't give an enchilada about being a Ryder Cup rookie or first tee jitters. He had outlasted Nicklaus in an eighteen-hole playoff to win the 1968 US Open and he'd win it again in 1971 along with The Open Championship at Birkdale. His one-liner, “You don't know what pressure is until you play for five bucks with only two bucks in your pocket”, is fabled. Even if some of his teammates were on unfamiliar turf, Trevino had a natural affinity for links golf, especially Birkdale, where he could keep the ball low, sheltering it from the wind between the big dunes.

“There's nothing quite like playing in the British Isles. Golf is in the air there. You breathe it in, like smelling home cooking. It makes you hungry. You want to play,” he wrote in his autobiography, *They Call me Super Mex.*

Still turned to Trevino. “Lee, I'm afraid I'm going to whiff it.”

Trevino came back with a light-hearted rejoinder. "Go ahead and whiff it and we'll get out of here."

Settled down, Still remembered his reputation for accuracy off the tee and sent his drive 280 down the middle, setting up the first of three straight birdies to start the match. A US bogey at the eighth pulled the Brits even and a 12-foot birdie putt put the Brits 1-up two holes later. Things took a bad turn when the golfers arrived at the thirteenth tee. With Still close by and in his line of vision, Bembridge asked him to move. Normally, not a big deal, but Still, for some reason, took umbrage and mocked the request by dramatically shooing everyone, including caddies and officials, to the opposite side of the tee box. There was a considerable amount of murmuring from the British fans; the stunt did not go over well.

Seemingly rattled, Still hooked his tee shot into the left rough and Trevino's shot from there plugged under the lip of the greenside bunker. Still's almost impossible shot caromed back to him and nicked his shoulder. "It hit you, didn't it?" Trevino asked. The stunned Still didn't answer. "Pick it up," Trevino told him. The Brits were 2-up with five to play. The Americans shaved one hole off the deficit but lost the match on seventeen where Gallacher, the man who said he didn't mind if he was playing against Afghans or Americans, confidently drained a six-foot birdie putt.

Jacklin and Townsend were simply too good in the third match. They were seven-under par for the seventeen holes the match lasted. Had they played eighteen, a par would have given them a 67 on one of the hardest courses in Britain, as Leonard Crawley of the *Daily Telegraph* noted. The barrage began with three straight birdies and culminated in a wonderful eagle after Townsend sent a 3-wood to within nine feet of the cup. Jacklin finished it off to the roars of the gallery. The Americans, who hadn't played poorly, won a single hole in the entire match.

A sweep of all four matches was now possible. It all hung on the last match between the veteran team of Alliss and O'Connor against Casper and Frank Beard, the leading money winner on the

American tour. The teams traded birdies on thirteen and fourteen to stand all square with four to play, then matched pars to send the match to eighteen, with much of the crowd of nine thousand looking on. Both teams made mistakes. Beard had a short pitch into the green but plopped it in the bunker while O'Connor left Alliss with an 18-footer for birdie after a poor chip shot. Casper came through with a nice sand shot to five feet that still gave Alliss a chance to win the match. Alliss always doubted himself as a putter. True to his sardonic wit, he ordered a license plate that read PUT 3 that was more apt than ever for this week at Birkdale. "Although I was striking the ball as well as ever, my putting, for whatever reason, was abysmal," he wrote in his autobiography, *"Peter Allis–Reflections of a Life Well Lived."* This time, however, Alliss put a very good stroke on the ball. The gallery held its breath in anticipation then let out a groan as it lipped out. Beard left little doubt with his five-footer and the US was able to take a half-point out of the morning, among the closest of all the half points that would become so crucial to the final score. As it was, the British found themselves leading the first session for just the fourth time with a three-point margin, their biggest in eighteen Ryder Cups.

"I am overjoyed," Brown said as he headed for a satisfying lunch. "This start is everything I had hoped for. We are cock-a-hoop now because we know that we can win."

The press, too, exulted. Ward-Thomas's inspired prose was worthy of Grantland Rice.

"Nothing can diminish the morning glory, no matter what the coming days may bring," he declared. "Never has a British team begun more impressively, not only in the winning but in the manner of winning. Here was youth in all its strength, pride and confidence. The golf of Townsend, just twenty-three, and the youngest player on either side having played in Walker Cup and Ryder Cup matches; and Bembridge and Gallacher was well-nigh beyond praise for its attack, quality of striking and composure.

"There was no wavering, no anxious starts; no tremulous finishes; and the Americans almost to a man were found wanting. They were outplayed in conditions which hardly could have been more sympathetic to them. Not a whisper of wind stirred beneath the overcast sky; there was no bounce on the fairways, the greens were holding and slow for the putting. The striker got what he hit without fortune and the British got the most."

As the Brits were preening during the break, the afternoon matches beckoned. Snead didn't spare curse words as he addressed his bedraggled troops loudly enough to be heard through the locker room door. There were "frayed nerves," Peter Willis of *Golf Illustrated* reported somewhat prematurely. For while down, the Americans were far from out. Snead had played somewhat nice in the morning, but he now rolled out a much more fearsome lineup. He kept together Casper and Beard, the pair that won the half-point, as well as Hill and Aaron, who had played well despite losing, 3-and-1, to the red-hot Jacklin and Townsend. Littler joined Trevino, a very formidable pairing, while Nicklaus and Sikes came off the bench as the anchor pair. The only change the elated Brown made was to substitute Peter Butler and Bernard Hunt for Alliss and O'Connor. Brown told the press he was giving the "old men" a rest, but, in reality, he had previously agreed with the BBC to make Alliss available as a commentator on the afternoon broadcasts. It was one of the first assignments for the future broadcasting great.

Naturally, the debut of Nicklaus was greeted with trepidation by the British galleries. While the morning matches were underway, Nicklaus and Sikes had hit the range to warm up for their afternoon match. A flock of spectators abandoned the matches to get their first glimpse of Nicklaus. The Golden Bear was impressive as he hit cut after cut but not as impressive as Sikes. He wowed onlookers by hitting a succession of 4-iron shots with a perfect draw, running them up to his caddie's bag from 200 yards out. An old Brit looked on with some consternation.

"Are you going to play this afternoon, Mr. Sikes?" he asked.

"I sure am, sorry to say," Sikes replied. Then, turning to Nicklaus, he joked, "Hey Jack, I'm getting frightened. I'm playing so well I may leave it all behind on the practice strip."

Nicklaus enjoyed his partnership with Sikes. He considered Sikes one of the best drivers of the golf ball and his long iron play was almost as good.

Sikes, a graduate of the University of Florida Law School, was instrumental when the touring pros broke away from the PGA in 1968. He took some of the pressure off the high-profiled Nicklaus, a fellow member of the Advisory Committee, by being the point man. Sikes had a quick temper and was somewhat aloof, but he also had a keen sense of right and wrong. When public courses in his native Jacksonville limited African American play to one day a week, Sikes forced their hand until a landmark court case opened play to everyone. After paving the way for the formation of the Senior Tour, he would sadly pass away at age fifty-eight.

Snead was counting on a point from Sikes and Nicklaus, but he'd have to sweat it out. In fact, that's all he and Brown could do as all four matches came down to the last hole with no one team opening more than a two-hole lead at any time. It did little to temper Snead's uneasiness when Hill and Aaron went 2-down through three in the first match, but the Americans turned it on from then, storming back to go 2-up at the turn, one of the three leads the US took on the outward nine, with the other match tied.

The tension was nearly palpable in the crisp air. British hopes soared when Coles and Huggett fought back to tie the first match on the par-five fifteenth. They'd gotten away with a bogey as the Americans made a mess of things, finding three bunkers before reaching the green. Aaron's blast never got out of the last of those, and the momentum seemed to shift to the Brits. The next two holes were halved, leaving it up for grabs on eighteen. Coles had the honors off the tee. He had a reputation as a superbly accurate driver but, perhaps feeling the pressure of the moment, found trouble in the left rough, leaving Huggett with no option but to chop out. Aaron took advantage with a perfect tee shot, allowing Hill to go for the green in two. His 3-wood shot fortuitously hopped over the front bunker and found the back fringe, still far from the pin. Aaron putted from there, leaving Hill with a tricky four-foot birdie putt to win the hole and the match. Hill took his time with the read then sent the putt on its way. The ball caught the lip and circled the cup before toppling in through the back door. "A shaky putt but a solid point to the Americans," wrote Peter Ryde of the *Times of London.* Such was the nature of this Ryder Cup. Had Alliss's final putt of the morning not lipped out, had Hill's not lipped in, it would have been a completely different outcome.

Littler and Trevino, the second US pair, seemed the calmest of the Americans, with their cool manifested in different ways. Trevino kept on a free-flowing banter with the gallery while Littler, nicknamed "Gene the Machine", displayed nary a hint of nervousness, as always. "The extrovert and the retiring. The puncher and the classic swinger," Ward-Thomas observed. It had to be a bit disconcerting to their opponents, Bembridge and Gallacher, who found this match a lot tougher than their first. After falling behind at the start, Littler and Trevino were able to rattle off three straight wins to go 2-up, including a chip-in from Littler on seven. The Brits, still in it after the Americans' brilliant 33 on the inward half, closed the lead to one hole a few times, the last with a birdie on seventeen to extend the match. But it was up to Gallacher to drive off the last, and he'd been pulling his tee shots all day. Another yank found trouble, forcing the Brits to lay up on the par five and after Trevino's second shot stopped inches short of the bunker, a brilliant chip from Littler secured the winning birdie. The US was within a point.

Two matches remained on the course, Casper and Beard against Jacklin and Townsend, Nicklaus and Sikes against Butler and Hunt. Each one was all square.

Casper and Beard failed to take advantage of several opportunities and were clinging to a 1-up through twelve, where Casper muffed a short putt that would have won the hole. Beard hit his approach into the rough on thirteen and, with the ball halfway in an old divot hole, Casper jarred his wrist on the shot, leading to a bogey that tied the match. Although he said the injury didn't affect him, Casper hooked drives on fifteen, where the teams halved, and seventeen, where the Brits went ahead for the first time. Townsend hit a beauty of a 3-wood just short of the seventeenth green and Jacklin's chip was stone-dead. On eighteen, needing to win the hole for a half-point, Beard hit a strong second shot that came up fifteen feet short. Jacklin's second put Townsend in a tough spot with a bunker to clear to a short-sided green. But Townsend's clutch pitch shot deftly cleared the bunker and stopped inches from the hole. When Casper was unable to sink his eagle putt, the home team secured a point that ensured their first opening day lead in twenty years.

The US desperately needed its best player to produce a point, or at least a half. A British win would put them up by two and with these matches being played on a knife's edge, every point was multiplied in value. Nicklaus and Sikes were tied with Butler and Hunt playing the last hole. The Americans had been tied when they bogeyed the sixteenth and were lucky to have escaped the seventeenth with a half after Nicklaus sprayed a second shot that had been engulfed by gorse. Unfortunately for the Brits, Hunt, an eight-time Ryder Cup performer, also made a mess of the par-five seventeenth. He pushed a drive, hit a mediocre pitch shot and finally missed a six-footer that would have insured his team of a half-point. As his teammates were losing their match on the green ahead of him, Nicklaus hooked his tee shot into the light rough. Advantage, Great Britain. Sikes, however, responded with one of the best clutch shots of the week, a searing wood that bounded up the fairway 250 yards, stopping just short of the bunker guarding the green. Hunt failed at his task once again with a second shot well wide of the green. Nicklaus, given the opportunity, wasn't going to let it pass. He pitched it to two feet and Sikes finished it for the winning birdie.

Still, Brown was ecstatic. "I must have walked miles out there," he said. "I feel great. It's the first time in twenty years we've led at the end of the first day. We went in as underdogs and finished ahead. If we can get another good start tomorrow, we'll be in with a chance."

Snead, though not completely satisfied with the day, managed a smile of relief. "I'm pleased that the margin is not more. I'm sure my boys are learning all the time about this course and will play better in the fourballs," he said. "I think they played well in the opening matches, too, but so did the British guys, who I think are the best team Britain's had for years."

Snead had reason for optimism. Fourball (or better ball) was an American game and, since it had been added to the Ryder Cup in 1963, the Brits had won just two of the twenty-four matches with five others halved. When Friday brought more ideal conditions, the US odds seemed enhanced. Snead, however, was forced to hold out Casper, who was receiving heat treatments for his injured hand, giving Dale Douglass his first match of the week. Brown brought in Alex Caygill and Brian Barnes off the bench and, to the surprise of many, split up Jacklin and Townsend after they'd won both alternate shot matches. He paired Townsend with O'Connor in the opening match and Jacklin with Coles in the last. He also saved Bembridge and Gallacher for the afternoon session.

"I'm blending youth and experience to see how it goes. It should work well," Brown explained, adding that Jacklin and Townsend would be back together in the afternoon.

Happily, for Brown, the British started fast again and added another point to their lead, winning two, losing one and halving the other in a better ball format suited more to the Americans, who had won seven of the eight fourball matches in '67. What's more, in their first heavyweight matchup of the week, Jacklin won a point from Nicklaus, who was once again paired with Sikes. Snead knew it would be another nail biter when Townsend birdied the first hole of the first match. While Hill and Douglas came back to tie the match three times, Townsend and O'Connor's five-under par inward half gave the Brits their first point of the day. Townsend hit another one of his brilliant wood shots onto the seventeenth and won it with a 12-foot eagle putt that earned the biggest roar of the day, announcing to the entire course that the Americans were in a spot of bother. O'Connor's eight-footer for birdie halved the eighteenth, surely a relief to him after a chronic shoulder injury had acted up and affected his swing on the third hole.

Playing with Barber again against Caygill and Huggett, Floyd's heroics saved the Americans from losing the second match as well. Neither side was able to edge ahead after Floyd tied the match at the ninth, halving the next seven holes despite opportunities for both sides. Britain finally broke the stalemate when Caygill made–and Floyd missed–five-foot birdie putts at seventeen. Yet, Floyd atoned by reaching the eighteenth with two splendid shots. The Brits were already in with a birdie when Floyd came through with an 18-footer for the eagle, halving the match.

Trevino was just as heroic in the third match with seven birdies. Cawley wrote that he "practically carried" Littler around the course. Alliss later said it was a match he and Brian Barnes should have won, but again, he couldn't match Trevino on the greens. Chattering away as usual, Trevino dropped a long birdie putt on seventeen to put the US ahead before wrapping up the full point when he birdied the last.

Anchor matches don't always live up to expectations, but this one did. It was a birdie fest that produced the lowest better ball scores of the day. Jacklin and Coles shot a nine-under 65, Nicholas and Sikes 66. Brown, continuing to push the right buttons, wanted to pit his best player against Nicklaus and felt that Jacklin could be helped by Coles' aggressive style of play against the long-hitting Nicklaus and Sikes.

Nicklaus and Sikes came out of the box hot. Sikes hit one to eighteen inches for a winning birdie on four and Nicklaus hit one to two feet on five for his second birdie of the day. The match turned on six where Nicklaus roped a 1-iron to within five feet but missed the eagle putt that would have put the Americans 3-up.

That reprieve opened the door for Coles, with a birdie on seven and Jacklin, with a birdie on eight, to even up the match. They would reach the last two holes the same way after Sikes sank a 15-footer birdie winner on fourteen and Jacklin responded with a birdie putt from the same length to halve fifteen. Now the Brits would have to find a way against the American bombers on the two closing par fives. Both Americans hit long irons to seventeen but found sand, settling for pars. Coles hit his favorite club, a 2-iron, which he said he "could make talk", and was left with two putts for birdie to win the hole. He left the first two feet short. The second, notably, was not conceded, but he rolled it in. The point went to Great Britain when both sides birdied eighteen.

The afternoon fourball matches became the most crucial of the week. The Americans knew they had to break the British momentum. The singles were always their strength, but first they had to get within striking distance.

Captain Brown could not have been happier. His strategy for pairing players—splitting up Jacklin and Townsend, for instance—was working perfectly, and it appeared he was outwitting Snead. Once again, Slammin' Sammy had befuddled everyone—especially his team—when he left out Nicklaus and Sikes after their 66. *Sports Illustrated's* Brown quoted an unidentified US player whinging: "Everyone's trying damn hard, but you could say that team morale is just about zero."

"It was a bad time for zero morale," *Sports Illustrated's* Gwylim Brown noted. "Fortunately, the US had two players, Lee Trevino and Dave Hill, who couldn't care if they were being led by Sam Snead or Shirley Temple. They infected their teammates with new verve just by the way they hurled themselves into every shot."

Snead, at least, was able to get Casper back into action after his morning heat treatments, pairing him with Beard, with whom he won just half a point in their two alternate shot matches. The other three pairings were new, including Hill and Still. Their matchup with Gallacher and Huggett turned out to be a combustible mixture, and one the US sorely needed.

It was a rematch of sorts of the first morning's foursomes when Still, playing with Trevino against Gallacher and Bembridge, made such a histrionic display over Bembridge's request to move out of his line of sight. Now tensions flared on the very first green of this second Saturday match. Huggett, about to putt, was distracted by Hill, who was moving slightly and by Still, who was standing unusually close to Huggett. According to *Draw in the Dunes,* the assertive Huggett turned to Still and barked: "I want you behind me from now on." Still scoffed and smoldered. Notably, the Americans won the hole to take the early lead. Then, at the third, Still's caddie wound up tending the flag for Gallacher, which was not uncommon in those days. Yet it seemed to get under Still's skin—as did, most likely, Huggett's long pre-putt routine. So, in what appeared as a masterful stroke of gamesmanship, Still waited stealthily until Gallacher was about to draw back the blade to pounce in, telling his caddie to hand over the flag to Gallacher's man. After Gallacher left his putt inches short, the Americans made him putt it, or as Leonard Crawley phrased it, "hole the tiddler."

Those incidents were just brush fires compared to the inferno that broke out on the seventh, where the US was 2-up. Hill had left his 30-foot putt short by sixteen inches. As he would have done on the American tour, he walked up and knocked it in, then picked up Still's marker at three feet, thinking the four was secured. But Gallacher, who had an eight-foot putt for par, immediately appealed to the match referee, David Melville, a local pro: "They can't do that. They've played out of turn." When Still offered to put it back, Gallacher snapped. "No, you won't. That's not good enough." Enraged, Still stormed off the green, fuming. "You can have the hole and the goddamn Cup."

The whole kerfuffle could have been avoided if there hadn't been so much confusion surrounding the rules of match play. Hill was entitled to replace his ball and replay the putt without penalty, and Melville told Huggett just that, according to Leslie Edwards of the *Liverpool Daily Post*. Huggett didn't accept the explanation, but the Americans, Melville noted, had walked off the green by then. "If they would have remained calm, nothing would have happened, but they blew their top," Huggett maintained. "What else could I do but give the hole to Britain?" Melville concluded. "They realized they had been too hasty," Gallacher later told Bob Rodney, the reporter. "But when we are given a hole, we keep it." Still, though, maintained that Melville announced "loss of hole" before they had walked off. To the crowd, the Americans appeared sore losers and on the next tee, the eighth, hell broke loose, with the British fans jeering and cursing the American pair. Still recalled a "pretty ugly" scene with "garbage, cans and bottles" being thrown. Then, as everyone walked up the fairway, Melville finally informed Hill of the correct ruling, that his ball could have been replaced. Hill lost it on the spot.

"I called the referee every four-letter word I'd learned since I was a kid," he recollected years later. "I felt we'd been cheated out of a hole."

"Insults were hurled back and forth," Rodney reported. "It seemed the players would come to blows before Dai Rees arrived on the eighth fairway and tried to calm them."

"Tried" was the operative word. "The referee's decision is always right, even if it's wrong," Rees told the Americans. "You get on and play the next hole." The advice did not sit well. Ben Wright later wrote it was the closest he'd ever seen to a fistfight on a golf course. Samuel Ryder, he fretted, must have been, "spinning in his grave."

Cawley chalked it up to passion. "We must remember that all four are born fighters who are not prepared to bow the knee to anybody," he wrote in the *Daily Telegraph.*

Still, in a 2011 interview, Still stuck to his guns. "We were right, and they were wrong and so was the referee," he said. "It was like an umpire blowing a call at home plate, calling the runner safe when it's clear he's out. I still get calls from the British press about that round. We were made out to be the villains and we were innocent. It was ridiculous."

Still wasn't particularly known as a hothead. To the contrary, he'd been counting his blessings after nearly losing his life two years earlier. When he assumed he'd shot himself out of the 1967 Houston Open with a first-round 78, he made reservations with Braniff Airlines for a late Friday flight back to Sea-Tac Airport.

"But on Friday I shot 2-under par 69, making the cut by two strokes," he recounted. "The plane I was to take from Houston was hit by lightning and all eighty-seven aboard were killed. I've always been a believer in never quitting, and it really came true in this instance."

Hill, however, had a temper just this side of Tommy Bolt. His book was titled *Teed Off* and that's how he played, with an edge. "When I get mad on the golf course, which is frequently, I feel mean," he explained. His behavior off the course could even be worse. Hill once came to blows with Chi Chi Rodriguez in the locker room, because he felt Chi Chi's interactions with the galleries distracted him from winning the tournament. In 1961, the PGA fined him $1,400 for his routine breaking of putters, which was half the check he earned for his first tour win in Tucson. At the 1970 US Open at Hazeltine, won by Tony Jacklin, he created the biggest stir of the week. At first, he declined a request to visit the press tent after shooting a 69. A few vodkas changed his mind before he was asked what he thought of the relatively new golf course designed by Robert Trent Jones.

"I'm still looking for it," he said. "All this course needs is about eighty acres of corn and a few cows. I want to come back in August and see how the crops are coming in. I bet they'll have a helluva harvest. My seven-year-old boy could design a better course. The man who designed this golf course held the blueprints upside down."

Hill, however, had the ability to channel whatever anger he was feeling. Birkdale's taunting crowds fueled his inner resolve and, shortly after his interaction with the match ref on the eighth fairway, he delivered a stinging approach shot to four feet. Still ran his longer birdie putt from the opposite side just past Hill's ball, but Gallacher quickly picked up Still's par putt, denying him the chance to show Hill the line. Still was incensed and the crowd stirred once more, but Gallacher was justified in conceding Still's putt. Hill made the putt, then told Gallacher he'd wrap a 1-iron around his head if he uttered another word. He played brilliantly the rest of the way even as the jeering persisted. As Hill sized up a 12-foot eagle putt to win the match on seventeen, Still said to his partner, "See those people up on the hill? Tell them this match is over." Only the sound of the ball dropping into the cup broke the silence. The four players shook hands, but Hill refused to shake Melville's, even at the urging of his wife. Even Leslie Edwards called it "a just result," thankful that the bad ruling wouldn't be a bone of contention "for as long as the Ryder Cup matches are played."

"It was very bad at the time," Huggett said years later. "It was almost as if we were prizefighters. I'm afraid Bernard and I were very fiery, as were they."

But, lo and behold, as Birkdale turned into a Roman circus, the Americans were erasing the two-point deficit, thanks to the fire in Casper's menacing putter. No doubt he and Beard, Butler and Townsend could hear the raucous match behind them as they tried to focus on their own tight contest. Things turned the Americans' way after the tenth, where Britain was 1-up. If Casper was feeling any pain in his wrist, it wasn't showing. A man known for his comebacks, he and Beard went on a birdie blitz to win on three of the last eight holes for a better ball 66 and a 2-up win.

With the score 7-7, the last two matches, Bembridge and Hunt against Floyd and Aaron, Jacklin and Coles against Trevino and Barber, hurried to finish. The morning session had taken five hours, an astoundingly sluggish pace for those days, and the afternoon sessions were creeping along as well. Lunch had been cut short to outrace the darkness, but it closed in, nonetheless. They probably should have suspended play—they later agreed to do so, if necessary, in the singles—but play on they did to everyone's peril. As Leslie Edwards wrote, "Conditions last night were almost farcical when the last two games came to the last hole. Thousands of spectators could scarcely see the hole, at a range of twenty or thirty yards; aiming second shots at the flag must have been almost like firing into nearly impenetrable mist."

The Scots might have called it, "in the gloaming." Automobiles were arranged with their headlights blazing to fight against the twilight, but these weren't heavenly shades of night falling. It was spooky dark. Executing shots was one thing, finding the hole was another. Hunt and Bembridge both had putts to win their match at eighteen, Hunt from ten feet, Bembridge from five. But it was pure guesswork, and both putts grazed the hole for the sixteenth halve of a match that ended all square.

Ten minutes later, the last group trudged up to eighteen. Trevino was uncharacteristically flustered, even after sinking a clutch eight-foot putt that halved seventeen to even the match. Willie Atchison, a spindly Scot, caddied for Trevino every time he played in the UK. They were quite a pair. Willie loved chatting it up with the galleries as much as Trevino did. Something must have seemed strange, then, when Willie's chatter faded away as they approached the final hole. Trevino told the story in his autobiography, *They Call Me Super Mex:*

"When we came to eighteen it was almost dark, and we were feeling a lot of pressure. When I got to the tee and I looked for my bag Willie wasn't there," he recalled. "The next thing I knew, here comes a guy carrying my bag and I've never seen him before. 'Where's Willie?' I ask. 'He was talking to someone coming up the hill,' the stranger said, 'and he slipped down and broke his ankle.' Now that's got to be a first in the history of golf.

"While I was trying to figure that out, I missed a putt to keep us from winning outright. Hell, the British should have given Willie a team blazer."

Everyone played their third shots into the green and, incredibly, when they were finally able to see the results, three balls surrounded the hole inches apart from one another. Jacklin was four and a half feet out, Trevino just inside that and Barber, who, for some reason, was still wearing sunglasses, the closest. The match official determined who was away, and, one by one, they all missed. An audible sigh of relief went up from the gallery. And so, an afternoon like no other in Ryder Cup history, full of brilliant golf and unprecedented controversy, ended with the US having fought back to tie the match.

"A hell of a match up to now," Snead said, while Brown admitted he was "a little disappointed." Nevertheless, going into the week, the Brits would have taken it.

"Hopes of a British victory must still be lively," Ward-Thomas wrote. "The peril of the fourball matches in which the Americans have always excelled, has been withstood. Furthermore, the

American performance has been lacking in lethal thrusts, saving strokes, and assumption of command. It has yet to arise to greatness and the burden is now upon them. The British have everything to gain."

For sure, lots of punters lined up at the Southport betting parlors to wager a few quid on the home team, a 2-to-1 underdog. Their lads had defied the odds so far and, as Ward-Thomas noted, there wasn't any separation in the quality of golf between the teams, reputations notwithstanding.

It was a quiet night, mostly, although Hill and Huggett resumed their argument in the hotel hallway while Trevino held court in the lobby, telling jokes, no doubt some at his caddie's expense. The draw for the eight Sunday morning singles matches had been set with Brown alternating his most and least experienced players, starting with Alliss, in what would be his last Ryder Cup match, and ending with Jacklin, who, along with Coles, would play in all six sessions. Brown saved Gallacher and Huggett for the afternoon, concerned they had been emotionally drained by their hostile match the afternoon before. Snead hoped to gain the momentum early and led off with the two men who had played the best golf so far–Trevino and Hill–the only two Americans who would play all six matches. Floyd and Nicklaus held up the rear with Nicklaus matched up against Jacklin for the second time in three matches. Snead's bench-the-Bear strategy was meant to keep Nicklaus fresh for the thirty-six holes, but, for some reason, Snead also sat Littler, among the most accomplished of the Americans, even though he had played just twice up until then. Perhaps the most interesting of matchups: Still facing Bembridge in the sixth game, with feelings still raw from their Friday morning dustup.

Snead mustered as much bravado as he could at the pairings announcement, declaring: "This is our front line, and I'll think we'll be the winners." He then turned to Brown. "Eric, I hope you come in second." Nine holes in, it was Brown, though, who looked like the genius once again as his boys led in six of the eight matches, the Americans in just one. There was a lot of golf still ahead, but if those scores held up, the US would be facing a practically insurmountable 22 ½-17 ½ deficit going into the final session. The Americans needed to play up to their reputations over the last twenty-seven holes.

Luckily for Snead, his front-loading paid off with three of the first four points of the day, but it was all Britain after that, as the hosts swept the last four matches. Hill continued his inspired play and made six birdies in fourteen holes to blitz Townsend, 5-and-4, in the first match to end. Trevino followed with a 2-and-1 win over Alliss, who had started the day with two straight birdies to get the partisan crowd going. Ultimately, though, Alliss' putter failed him again. He missed eight putts under ten feet.

O'Connor's shoulder held up well enough to dispatch an off-form Beard, 5-and-4, highlighted by a chip-in on eleven that put the Irishman 4-up. Then Coles overcame Aaron, 1-up, in a nip-and-tuck match. Aaron had come from 2-down to go 1-up through fifteen, but Coles rallied brilliantly. He evened the match with a 15-foot birdie on sixteen then hit a spectacular fairway wood inches away from the cup for an eagle on seventeen. A final birdie matched Aaron's on the last to secure the point.

Casper, America's wounded warrior, pulled his team ahead, 11-10, by showing his Hall of Fame mettle against Brian Barnes, who was playing his first match of week. Barnes, the son-in-law of Max Faulkner, was 2-up with four to play before Casper rallied with four straight birdies to win 1-up. Barnes lipped out an eagle putt that would have halved the match on the final hole.

Three matches remained on the course and the first ended in a shocker. Jacklin dusted Nicklaus, 4-and-3. Nicklaus may have been refreshed after resting but his putter was still a slumber. He missed a seven-foot eagle putt on the first hole, a three-foot birdie putt on three and an 18-inch par putt on six, where Jacklin took the lead for good. In all, he missed five putts inside five feet. He did manage to hole out a 75-foot putt from the fringe for eagle on thirteen, two holes before Jacklin closed him out to the crowd's delirious reaction. "Jack's playing like he would much rather be home fishing," Brown said to Trevillion, according to *Draw in the Dunes.*

Meanwhile, Still was attempting to put aside any memories of the prior days' incidents, but the crowd wouldn't let him. *Golf Illustrated's* Willis reported he "was taking a hammering from the gallery" and that "one fan nearly collapsed with laughter" after Still flubbed a three-foot putt on eleven. He must have felt as if he was being mocked by the mob on his way to the guillotine after Bembridge went 4-up through twelve. Yet, Still rallied as Bembridge faltered, winning four straight holes to tie things up with one to play. One more emotional twist awaited him. A new tee was put in play on eighteen and Still miscalculated the distance to the fairway bunker. His drive took one bounce and went in. It cost him a bogey and the match.

The Brits were assured of a lead going into the final session when Floyd and Butler arrived at the final hole of their lackluster match with the Britisher 1-up. Incredibly, Floyd hadn't made a birdie all day. He did here. But so did Butler. Another point was added to extend the British lead to 13-11.

Asked for his reaction, Brown said, "Joyous, jubilant, tremendous. How can it be anything else? Now I think we can win the Cup. The boys have done us proud. I'm feeling great about our prospects though my nerves are taking a hammering."

Willis reported that Brown was so excited he could hardly speak at the lunchtime press conference. Snead wasn't any more talkative because he chose to say little. Why should he? His favored squad need to win 5 ½ out of the last eight points available to win the Cup outright, five to retain it. The Americans had been stronger in the afternoon sessions all week long, winning them, 6-2, but the pressure was squarely on them here. Snead certainly didn't want to have his name associated with a Ryder Cup loss, especially since Hogan's name never was and, while he may have been outmaneuvered by Brown at times, he wasn't at this moment. His lineup made sense. He left out four players—Beard, Aaron, Still and Floyd—who had lost matches in the morning and brought in Sikes, who hadn't played in two days, Douglass, who had played only once, Barber and, finally, Littler. He led off with his two horses that week, Hill and Trevino, and finished with two of the generation's greatest players, Casper and Nicklaus, even if Nicklaus wasn't at his best.

Brown, however, made his first poor decisions of the week by distrusting his depth. According to *Draw in the Dunes,* Coles had told his captain in the morning he had only one round left in him, that he had "shot his bolt." Brown agreed that the morning match would be his last. But after Coles had played so brilliantly down the stretch to hold off Aaron, Brown sent him out again. He told Coles, "You must be feeling good." "But I wasn't," Coles noted—and he was playing against a well-rested Sikes.

Brown also should have seen that Bembridge had run out of gas in letting Still almost catch him in the morning. The captain had a fresh Bernard Hunt available to take either spot in the lineup. Hunt was a seasoned performer who had won 4 ½ points in the nine singles matches he'd played since 1953. But Hunt and Caygill, who had halved his only match that week, would sit out both singles sessions. Additionally, Brown put Barnes in the leadoff spot even though that didn't give Barnes much of a turnaround after just finishing his match against Casper. He forced down a sandwich and practically ran to the tee to face the red-hot Hill.

All three would lose their matches. Barber put the first American point on the board by boat-racing Bembridge, 7-and-6, in the most lopsided match of the week. Hill wasn't sharp in the first match, but Barnes was even worse. He bogeyed eleven, twelve, fourteen, fifteen and sixteen as Hill, 4-2 for the week, pulled the US even with a 4-and-2 win. Coles, in the five hole, fought hard but fell to Sikes, 4-and-2. At that point, the well-rested Gallacher, relishing his matchup with Trevino, had taken down the American stalwart, 4-and-2, and Butler had dispatched Douglas by the same score. When the steady Littler (3-0 for the week) beat a faltering O'Connor on the seventeenth hole, this most fiercely contested of all Ryder Cups came down to the last two matches, Casper against Huggett, Nicklaus against Jacklin.

As if on cue, Mother Nature weighed in. The wind the Brits had been eagerly awaiting all week finally blew in from the Irish Sea, and the warming sun was now obscured by clouds. Tupper noted how the weather "came in raging, with rain squalls." Cecil B. DeMille could not have orchestrated it better.

Both last two matches were tight affairs. Gasps filled the air when Huggett missed an 18-inch putt on the tenth, giving Casper the lead with a second straight bogey. But after halving the next five holes, Casper ran afoul of the ill wind that blew into his face and across the wide fairway on sixteen. His tee shot flew into a bunker, as did his approach, and he conceded the hole to Huggett, leaving the two closing par fives to decide things. Meanwhile, neither Jacklin nor Nicklaus was able to take control of their match, shooting 37 and 38, respectively on the front side. Jacklin's birdie gave him the lead on eight but a double on nine and a bogey on ten handed it back to Nicklaus, who then handed it back with a bogey on twelve. Jacklin heroically drained an eight-footer for par to keep things even on fifteen and their match headed to the final three holes.

Jacklin had the honors on sixteen where his tee shot, just as Casper's before him, was blown into a fairway bunker. The door open, Nicklaus responded with a monstrous drive that defied the wind and found the fairway. Jacklin couldn't recover and the Golden Bear's routine par—although nothing was routine at that point—won the hole. Both Huggett and Casper went just beyond the green with their second shots into seventeen but, while Casper executed a perfect chip to gimme range, Huggett left himself six feet short. *Sports Illustrated's* Brown wrote that Huggett "crouched over the ball for an eternity" before knocking it in to full-throated roars rom the gallery.

Back on the tee, Nicklaus pulled out a 3-wood. The wind was at his back, turning the 510-yard par five into a sure two-shot hole, and he safely found the middle of the fairway between two huge sand hills. Jacklin chose driver and he, too, hit it perfectly, ahead of Nicklaus' ball. Nicklaus, struggling so long with his game, knew he needed to dig deep to recover his championship form. With five bunkers guarding the green, there was enough danger to punish a wayward shot but the sound of the ball meeting the clubface of his

7-iron explicitly told the gallery that it was pure. It never left the flag on its way to the green, finishing about twelve feet short of the cup.

Now it was Jacklin's turn. Even though he was closer to the target than Nicklaus, he had to take more club, a 5-iron. He hit it low and came off it slightly, leaving the shot "in the laps of the gods," as the Brits say. The ball missed the green to the right and could have kicked anywhere. The gods complied. The fickle sphere fortuitously caromed off the sand bank and back onto the green, stopping about fifty feet away. Nicklaus still had the better of the situation, but at least Jacklin had a putter in his hands.

Sizing up the subtle slopes and breaks between him and the hole, Jacklin had to expect Nicklaus to make his eagle. "All I was trying to do was make the putt, but it was a bloody long way," he said. He stroked the putt with a long follow-through, as his caddie, Willie Hilton, tended the flagstick with Jacklin's bag slung over his shoulder. On it rolled, taking a slight left-to-right break midway there. With each turn it appeared more online, and the more online it got, the louder the gallery became, until it finally disappeared amid the loudest roar of the week.

"It's in! It's in!" Australian great Peter Thomson exclaimed to the BBC audience. Jacklin, as if he expected it, propped back his shoulders, waved and nodded to the appreciative crowd, as he strutted to the hole to pluck out his ball. Nicklaus still had a chance to halve the hole, but his attempt stayed right of the cup the entire way. Everything was even, although, up ahead on the final green, Huggett didn't know it. Casper was already in with a birdie four as the tenacious Welshman stood over a ball that he had run a delicate four feet past on his 30-foot try for an eagle win. He'd heard the roar from seventeen after Jacklin's triumph. It could only mean one thing, he thought.

"You know what certain roars mean and that was a winning roar. There was no doubt about that," he said. For sure it was. But Huggett thought the roar signaled that his teammate had won the match. To his mind, it meant he was putting for the half point that would win the Ryder Cup for Britain. When that putt, the biggest of his life, fell, he was beside himself in ecstasy.

First came an uppercut first pump—Tiger Woods before Tiger Woods—but audacious for Huggett's time. BBC broadcaster Henry Longhurst excused him: "Well, he has every right." Casper, who knew the score, extended his hand and Huggett took it, but the emotional drain left Huggett's knees wobbly. Casper walked him over to Brown. Huggett embraced his captain and started crying on Brown's shoulder.

"We've won! We've won," he said.

"Oh no," Brown told him. "We can still lose."

Jarred out of his rhapsody for the moment, Huggett joined his teammates and Casper his. They were among the thousands circling the final hole to watch Nicklaus and Jacklin play out what Jacklin called "an unenviable situation."

Each man hit a 3-wood off the tee and Jacklin, probably out of nerves, jumped ahead as he started down the fairway. Nicklaus hollered after him, "Tony." Jacklin waited for him. Nicklaus put his hand on his friend's shoulder.

"Are you nervous?" he asked him.

"Hell, nervous? I'm petrified," Jacklin said.

Nicklaus smiled. "I just thought I'd ask," he said, "because if it's any consolation I feel the same way you do."

The exchange calmed Jacklin down. It was another example of Jack's sportsmanship. But now a nervous Brown was making his way back down the fairway toward Jacklin. "You know what you've got to do?" he asked in his thick Scottish brogue. Ironically, Jacklin and Huggett were the two players that Brown had chastised when they reported late to the team hotel on the first day. Jacklin may have been thinking how much that didn't matter now.

"Yes Eric, I know what I've got to do," he said.

With the wind in their favor, reaching the green in two wasn't a problem. Nicklaus hit first and Jacklin responded, roughly equidistant at about twenty feet, from different angles. The gallery had rushed onto the fairway and had to part to let the two competitors through. The green was now entirely engulfed.

"These putts will decide the entire Ryder Cup match of 1969," Longhurst said, setting the stage for his TV audience.

Jacklin was away. He trusted the line more than the length and the putt never made it to the hole, stopping two feet short.

"Anguish Jacklin," Longhurst said, suffering with him, no doubt, while letting the player tell most of the story, as Jacklin let out a frustrated breath while holding his putter behind his head.

The great Jack Nicklaus now had a putt to win the Ryder Cup. He wasn't going to leave it short. He didn't. It raced five feet past. "Idiot," he said to himself.

"It was shocking," Jacklin said. "There was a pregnant silence all around the green."

So here stood Nicklaus. In his match that morning, he couldn't make anything from inside this distance. Now he faced what he described as a "downhill left to right slider which is probably the toughest of all putts." Plus, he said at the time, "I was terrified. I wasn't putting for me. I was putting for my country."

But Nicklaus was also the greatest player of his generation, perhaps of all time, and arguably the greatest clutch putter in history. If he ever needed a putt, he'd make it. And he needed this one. To no one's surprise, but against British hopes, it dropped into the heart of the hole. He paused momentarily, perhaps thinking about his next move. Then, before picking his ball out of the hole, he scooped up Jacklin's coin and handed it to him.

"I don't believe you would have missed that, but I'd never give you the opportunity," he told him.

The Ryder Cup was tied for the first time ever in one of the iconic moments in all of sports history.

"A gesture that was just unparalleled in our game," Jacklin called it.

"I don't know why but I quickly thought about Tony Jacklin and what he had meant to British golf," Nicklaus explained later. "Here he was The Open champion, he'd been their new hero and all of a sudden, I felt like if he missed this putt, he'd be criticized forever. This all went through my mind in a very, very quick period of time and I just made up my mind. Walk off here, shake hands and have it be a better relationship between two golfing organizations. That would be the right way to do it."

The two competitors walked off the green arm-in-arm. If Samuel Ryder ever envisioned the perfect personification of his founding ideal, this was it. Nicklaus had tied a pretty bow around a week of animosity and bad blood. The 1969 Ryder Cup is known fondly as The Concession when it could have been remembered as The Contention. Nicklaus had become the game's greatest sportsman. Nevertheless, while some eventually mellowed, Jack's captain and teammates were not feeling as benevolent at the time.

Jacklin would likely have made the putt, although some of similar and shorter lengths had been missed during the week. Certainly, it's more cutthroat at many country clubs' member-guest tournaments. Understandably, Snead, was incensed, more so behind closed doors than in public. Hell, he would have made Hogan putt it.

"When it happened, all the boys thought it was ridiculous to give him that putt," Snead said at the time. "We went over there to win, not to be good ol' boys. I never would have given a putt like that—except maybe to my brother."

Most of the American players remembered being shocked. As it was happening, Still turned to Beard and asked, "Is he doing what I think what he's doing?" Years later, Barber told *Golf Digest* that many felt the grand gesture was driven more out of vengeance toward Snead than magnanimity toward Jacklin.

"You've heard how Jack Nicklaus conceded the putt to Tony Jacklin on the last hole on the last day, the competition ending up tied. Jack has said that he conceded the putt purely out of sportsmanship, but I was on the team and none of us players believed that," Barber claimed. "See, our captain that year was Sam Snead. He sat Jack down in the morning the first day and in the afternoon the second day because he didn't want Jack to get worn out. Jack wanted to play and was upset about being benched. Most of us believe Jack conceded the putt at least in part to get back at Sam. And it worked, because behind the scenes Sam was furious that Jack didn't make Jacklin hole that two-footer."

"I thought a tie was a pretty good result," Nicklaus said. "My captain didn't necessarily think so."

As an aside, Snead's strategy to keep his Grand Slam winner out of two matches was not as foolish as it appeared. Nicklaus admitted he was never more tired than on the plane ride home after going toe-to-toe with Jacklin for thirty-six holes Sunday.

"That's when I decided it was time to lose weight. I told Barbara (his wife) to have my clothing altered," he said. "Four weeks later, I was 180. It may have been the best thing I've ever done."

The slimmed-down Bear finished the year winning the Sahara Invitational and Kaiser International Open Invitational after winning just once prior to the Ryder Cup, then turned it on for the entire decade of the 1970s. It was a personal metamorphosis. Afterwards, the only thing fat about him was his wallet.

Curiously, while Jacklin was appreciative and the Americans perplexed over the finale, the press hardly noticed the monumental moment. Ward-Thomas wrote the only "game story" which mentioned the concession, and then as a throw-away line in his last paragraph in *The Guardian.* Max Faulkner, the former Ryder Cupper, wrote of Nicklaus's "courtesy" in his syndicated column days later and Jack Rowe wondered about the golf shoe being on the other foot.

"(Brown) might have taken the attitude 'fair enough' but, somehow, I feel he would have pointed out, no doubt gently, that with the Ryder Cup at stake it would have been better to have kept the pressure on the Americans until the last possible moment," he supposed.

Most of the scribes—including all of the Americans—wrote that Nicklaus had made his clutch putt. That was that. There were no opinion columns lionizing him for conceding Jacklin's putt. It took years before it was recognized as perhaps the finest sporting gesture ever made. "The Concession" didn't enter the sports lexicon until at least the 2000s, shortly before Nicklaus and Jacklin collaborated on a golf course by that name in Florida.

One thing was clear, however. Nicklaus, as perhaps only he could have done, made the match impossible to forget.

The editor of *Golf Illustrated,* Tom Scott, nailed it. “Those who were at Birkdale and saw the final stages of this year’s Ryder Cup match will surely recall it again and again down through the years, for even if they live to be a hundred, I doubt whether ever again they will see a finish charged with so much emotion or filled with such drama.”

While all of Britain rejoiced over the outcome, the result meant that the US retained the trophy, although at the official dinner, in the spirit of Nicklaus’s concession, US PGA president Leo Fraser offered to share it. The Brits could keep it for one year before shipping it back to the States in time for the 1971 matches in St. Louis. At any rate, all of Britain was looking at the tie as a win and celebrated accordingly. The team threw a “moral victory” party after the dinner that night and invited the American team. Only Billy Casper went. According to *Draw in the Dunes,* they were dancing until the wee hours in the halls of the Prince of Wales Hotel.

To America, the tie was like kissing Miller Barber.

The country’s leading sport voice at the time was *Los Angeles Times* columnist Jim Murray. He used words like Hogan used a 3-iron and wrote a stinging rebuke of the team.

“I have a feeling they are on their way back from Gettysburg,” he began. “Don’t believe the communique that they ‘tied’ Britain, that the battle was indecisive. The 1969 Ryder Cup was a ‘tie’ only if you consider Caporetto to be one—or Waterloo.

“We were turned back, troops, and it’s getting to be a trend. I’m afraid we’re breeding a generation of hothouse golfers who can play the game only when the fairway is as wide as Rhode Island, the greens are watered, and the rough wouldn’t hide a snake and the nearest trees are two states away.”

Waterloo? The British raised Brown and his boys on a pedestal as they did the triumphant Wellington. Jack Rowe of the *Liverpool*

Post even advocated for making Brown permanent captain. Faulkner wrote that, coming after Jacklin's Open Championship, they had "beyond question re-established Britain as a leading power," adding, "the extraordinary thing about it is not that it happened, but the speed at which it happened."

Crawley predicted "wide repercussions on the game of golf all over the world.

"Ten thousand people breathless at the scene of the battle and still countless watching on the small screen could neither have wished for, nor envisaged, a more palpitating or engrossing struggle in any field of sport," he tapped out with a flourish. "A fresh wave of enthusiasm for this grand old game will sweep the country. On the other side of the Atlantic, whether they like it or not, they will have to take stock all over again."

Like most, Dobereiner considered the tie a crossroads for British golf.

"The benefits arising from the British performance will be considerable," he wrote. "I doubt whether we shall hear any more talk about expanding the Ryder Cup into an America versus the world to make it a more competitive contest. And from now on young British golfers need not feel any awe for the American super-golfers. In the past—and I suspect, slightly this time as well—the British have gone into the Ryder Cup matches psychologically one down. Next time the matches will at least start all square and then—who knows?"

Dobereiner's lofty hopes would fall flat. The 1969 Ryder Cup was Great Britain's last hurrah, even as Nick Faldo, one of those "young British golfers", supplanted Jacklin as the next English superstar. The Americans won the next four Ryder Cups by comfortable margins of six, ten, five and six points. To Dobereiner's dismay, the European continent, at Nicklaus's urging, was appended to Great Britain and Ireland in just ten years' time. The Ryder Cup's best years ensued. For fans of the ancient game, however, 1969 remains a fond memory.

"It was definitely a watershed year," Jacklin said. "No doubt about it."

As Ryder Cups went, it certainly had it all.

DAY 1

MORNING FOURSOMES

Neil Coles/Brian Huggett (GB) defeated Miller Barber/Ray Floyd (US), 3-and-2

Bernard Gallacher/Maurice Bembridge (GB) defeated Lee Trevino/Ken Still (US) 2-and-1

Tony Jacklin/Peter Townsend GB), defeated Dave Hill/Tommy Aaron (US) 3-and-1

Billy Casper/Frank Beard (US) halved with Christy O'Connor/Peter Alliss (GB)

Great Britain wins session 3 ½–½

AFTERNOON FOURSOMES

Dave Hill/Tommy Aaron (US) defeated Neil Coles/Brian Huggett (GB) 1-up

Lee Trevino/Gene Littler (US) defeated Bernard Gallacher/Maurice Bembridge (GB) 1-up

Tony Jacklin/Peter Townsend (GB) defeated Billy Casper/Frank Beard (US) 1-up

Jack Nicklaus/Dan Sikes (US) defeated Peter Butler/Bernard Hunt (GB) 1-up

United States wins session 3–1

Great Britain leads 4 ½–3 ½

DAY 2

MORNING FOURBALLS

Christy O'Connor/Peter Townsend GB) defeated Dave Hill/Dale Douglass (US) 1-up

Ray Floyd/Miller Barber (US), halved with Brian Huggett/Alex Caygill (GB)

Lee Trevino/Gene Littler (US), defeated Brian Barnes/Peter Alliss (GB), 1-up

Tony Jacklin/Neil Coles (GB), defeated Jack Nicklaus/Dan Sikes (US), 1-up

Great Britain wins session 2 ½–1 ½

Great Britain leads 7–5

AFTERNOON FOURBALLS

Billy Casper/Frank Beard (US) defeated Peter Butler/Peter Townsend (GB) 2-up

Dave Hill/Ken Still (US) defeated Brian Huggett/Bernard Gallacher (GB) 2-and-1

Tommy Aaron/Ray Floyd ((US) halved with Maurice Bembridge/Bernard Hunt (GB)

Lee Trevino/Miller Barber ((US) halved with Tony Jacklin/Neil Coles (GB)

United States wins session 3–1

Teams are tied 8–8

DAY 3
MORNING SINGLES
Lee Trevino (US) defeated Peter Alliss (GB) 2-and-1 Dave Hill (US), defeated Peter Townsend (GB) 5-and-4 Neil Coles (GB), defeated Tommy Aaron (US) 1-up Billy Casper (US) defeated Brian Barnes GB) 1-up Christy O'Connor (GB) defeated Frank Beard (US) 5-and-4 Maurice Bembridge (GB) defeated Ken Still (US), 1-up Peter Butler (GB) defeated Ray Floyd (US) 1-up Tony Jacklin (GB) defeated Jack Nicklaus (US) 4-and-3 **Great Britain wins session, 5–3** **Great Britain leads, 13–11**
AFTERNOON SINGLES
Dave Hill (US) defeated Brian Barnes (GB) 4-and-2 Bernard Gallacher (GB) defeated Lee Trevino (US), 4-and-3 Miller Barber (US) defeated Maurice Bembridge (GB), 7-and-6 Peter Butler (GB) defeated Dale Douglass (US) 3-and-2 Dan Sikes (US) defeated Neil Coles (GB) 4-and-3 Gene Littler (US), defeated Christy O'Connor GB) 2-and-1 Billy Casper (US) halved with Brian Huggett (GB) Jack Nicklaus (US) halved with Tony Jacklin (GB) **United States wins session 5–3** **UNITES STATES RETAINS RYDER CUP 16–16**

1985

Doing the Continental

THE BELFRY

EUROPE 16 ½, UNITED STATES 11 ½

It took some fifty years of Ryder Cup history before Great Britain (and Ireland) acknowledged it couldn't match the number of quality golfers being churned out in America. Yet, it took America less than a decade to realize that things were going to be different with continental Europe in the mix.

After hoping against hope for the random trickle of success, the 1985 Ryder Cup turned the tide. Once the Europeans got a taste of that champagne Dai Rees had set aside in 1957 for the next team to beat the Americans, their thirst became unslakable. At times since, it's been the United States that could use a little fortification.

Credit three men—Jack Nicklaus, Tony Jacklin and Seve Ballesteros—for making the inevitable occur following World War II, when American and British golf emerged spinning in different orbits: the US with furious momentum and the UK hobbling. The star-spangled rout that was the 1947 Ryder Cup made the distinctions painfully clear and led to the first plaintive calls to restore competitive balance. Some, including Ben Hogan, suggested adding Commonwealth nations such as Australia and Canada to the British roles. But the Brits were determined to cling to Sam Ryder's original vision. Sporadic successes in 1957 and 1969 helped them defend the status quo. A few Irish players were eventually included in the roster, and the team's name officially changed to Great Britain and Ireland (GBI) with the 1973 matches, but the United States continued to pile up victories.

When the US once again hammered GBI, 12 ½-7 ½ at Royal Lytham & St. Annes in 1977, the count stood 18-3-1 in America's favor. Interest in the States was practically nil. The American television networks never considered bringing the one-sided competition to the nation's screens, and American corporations were uninterested in sponsoring it. Somehow, the Cup still roused patriotic fervor in the UK despite the one-sidedness. There, crowds of at least 20,000 attended each session. If the Ryder Cup attracted 3,000 in the States, it was considered a throng.

Upon witnessing yet another US rout that year, *The Observer's* Peter Dobereiner bemoaned that such a success should not be wasted on an unappreciative public, sneering: "In America, the Ryder Cup now rates somewhere between Tennessee frog jumping and the Alabama Melon Pit Spitting contest."

Jack Nicklaus may not have put it quite that way, but he knew something had to be done to prevent the Ryder Cup from sliding into irrelevance.

"The Americans are quite happy to treat this match as a goodwill gesture, a get-together, a bit of fun, but here in Britain it's treated differently," he noted. "The people here seem to want a serious knock'em down match. If that's what's wanted, there has to be a stronger opposition."

Prior to those 1977 matches, some suggested that America be matched against the rest of the world. Nicklaus had a less drastic solution ready when he sought a sit-down at Lytham with John Stanley, the Earl of Derby, head of the British PGA and Ryder Cup Committee. Invite the rest of Europe.

"John," he told him. "Please don't think me presumptuous, but I want to be honest about this. The American players love to get onto the Ryder Cup team because there is no greater honor in sports than representing one's country. But the matches just aren't competitive enough."

Lord Derby took umbrage at first but soon saw the merit in Nicklaus' suggestion. Seve Ballesteros shared runnerup honors with Nicklaus as a nineteen-year-old at the 1976 Open Championship and was beginning to dominate the recently formed European Tour. He was a handsome, daring player, the likes of which had never been seen in Britain, a charismatic draw whose value extended beyond the golf course down commercial avenues. Lord Derby asked Nicklaus to draft a letter he could share with his fellow PGA officials. Nicklaus said his argument could be summed up in one sentence: "It is vital to widen the selection procedures if the Ryder Cup is to enjoy its past prestige."

The two PGA organizations agreed to discuss the plan at the 1978 Masters and approved it on the spot. Lord Derby made the announcement in late May, crediting Nicklaus for bringing his considerable gravitas to bear. Curiously, some of the old guard derided the change. Eric Brown, hero and then captain of the last two British teams to avert defeat, said it hurt him to see Europe join the fray and called it "mad and crazy" to scrap tradition.

"Continental golfers have little to offer," Brown scowled. "It is ironical that the British and American committees should come at a time when there are a number of excellent up and coming youngsters in the game, such as Nick Faldo, Mark James, Sandy Lyle, Howard Clarke, Sam Torrance and Ken Brown."

Brown was always a rally-around-the-flag type, but he was coming across as an aloof aristocrat, of the ilk that had once disparaged early professionals at the turn of the twentieth century. He was wrong, of course, especially the "little to offer" part. At first the Europeans didn't take over the roster. The guys Brown mentioned all played their part. Ballesteros was more of a special guest star on an overwhelmingly British team. Over the years, however, Nicklaus' wisdom became apparent as Seve's rising influence brought more continental players into the game. As Tony Jacklin noted then, Nicklaus always "had his ear to the ground" and anticipated the future. Ballesteros would become a Ryder Cup giant and transform it from a quaint little competition into the $5,000,000 enterprise it is today. He continues to inspire European teams more than a decade following his death from brain cancer in 2011 at just fifty-four.

At first, the European expansion had little impact. Ballesteros and compatriot Antonio Garrido were the only additions in 1979, when the US swept to a 17-11 win at the Greenbrier in West Virginia. Ballesteros had captured the claret jug at Lytham that year, but the two Spaniards managed only one point in four matches as partners, losing three times to the formidable American pair of Larry Nelson and Lanny Wadkins, two of the most successful US players in Ryder Cup history. Both also fell in the singles, Ballesteros, 3-and-2, against Wadkins.

Two years later, Ballesteros was left off the European team in a political squabble. He'd been embroiled in a controversy over appearance money and was deemed a non-member of the European Tour, costing him Ryder Cup points. By the time he became eligible again, his only path to the team was as a wild card pick. John Jacobs, the European captain, veteran Neil Coles and German star Bernhard Langer (who led the Tour's Order of Merit), formed the selection committee. Jacobs favored Ballesteros, but he was overruled. Ballesteros was judged unsupportive of the European Tour by the majority of its players. Half-witted as the decision was, Europe went into the Ryder Cup without the best European player, with Langer and Spain's Cañizares and Manuel Piñero representing the continent.

Would it have mattered? Probably not. The Americans brought arguably the most powerful team ever assembled to Walton Heath. Eleven of the twelve players had won or would win a major with thirty-six combined grand slam titles. Nicklaus, Lee Trevino and Larry Nelson went unbeaten. Nicklaus and Tom Watson didn't let any of their foursomes or fourball matches get past the sixteenth hole. Europe took an 18 ½-9 ½ shellacking.

Then came 1983 at Palm Beach Gardens and there went American superiority. The people running the Ryder Cup for Europe finally came to their senses and realized they weren't going to snatch the Cup from America's clutch without Ballesteros, who was stubbornly standing on principal and wanting nothing to do with the event. Seve was still feuding with both the European Tour and the PGA Tour over his ability to pick and choose the events he wanted to play. They needed someone who could convince him otherwise, and, in a twist of fate, that turned out to be Tony Jacklin.

Like Ballesteros, Jacklin been snubbed by the 1981 selection process. He considered his Ryder Cup career over, still steaming from being bypassed for Mark James, just two years after James had been fined along with Ken Brown for their escapades at The Greenbrier.

"James (ironically to be named the 1999 captain) behaved abominably at the '79 matches, which was the first European match," Jacklin told *ESPN* years later. "He was disruptive. He let the whole side down. Even the Americans knew something was going down and it was a major factor. Doing childish things, being bloody-minded about the whole thing. It tore down any team spirit."

Jacklin was then understandably stunned when Colin Snape of the British PGA and Ken Schofield of the European Tour approached him and told him the players wanted him to captain the side against Nicklaus. Jacklin said his first instinct was to tell Snape and Schofield to "stuff it." Instead, he used his leverage to insist that the Europeans approach the Ryder Cup as professionally as the Americans had. He wanted no expense spared for the team. "Too many times in the past," he said, "the Ryder Cup has been run more for the officials than the players." He could point to the 1975 competition, when the plastic shoes he had been issued came apart during his match with Raymond Floyd.

Snape and Schofield agreed to give Jacklin *carte blanche*. The team could travel on the Concorde, stay in a first-class hotel and be outfitted with the best equipment. Now it was up to Jacklin—perhaps the only man then capable of reasoning with Ballesteros—to bring him in. After venting for the first part of his meeting with Jacklin, Seve liked the improvements Jacklin outlined, and Ryder Cup history was altered.

With Ballesteros, Cañizares and Langer representing the continent, Europe shocked the US by coming up just one point short. Wadkins cemented his Ryder Cup bonafides as a clutch player with a magnificent 80-yard pitch shot into the eighteenth to halve his match with Cañizares and provide the necessary half-point to clinch the tense affair. Captain Nicklaus, who called Wadkins' shot the best of its kind in Ryder Cup history, rushed onto the green to kiss the divot Wadkins' ball had kicked up, thanking the heavens for his team's narrow escape.

But Ballesteros was now firmly ensconced as Europe's leader. He had done yeoman work at PGA National. With his teammates unfamiliar with the thick Bermuda rough around the greens, he took it upon himself to demonstrate the proper shot. In what some interpreted as sacrificial, he agreed to shepherd rookie Paul Way around the course and won three of four matches. On singles day, he produced a shot for the ages with a 3-wood from a fairway bunker 250 yards out to defeat Fuzzy Zoeller. John Hopkins, the esteemed correspondent for the *Times of London*, called it "without question the most thrilling shot I have seen," adding, "I never expect to see another like it."

The defeat could have been crushing. Ballesteros turned it into a moral victory.

"We were all pretty glum in the dressing room afterwards because we felt we had let a golden opportunity slip away," teammate Ken Brown explained. "Everyone except Seve. We were all thinking about what might have been, but he was already looking into the future. He looked at us and then shouted, 'Why do you all sit there like that? What is the matter with all of you? This has been a great victory, a great, great victory. This proves we can beat them.'"

The entire atmosphere was different when the teams met two years later in what was being called the "Bell's Scotch" Ryder Cup at The Belfry resort, the British PGA's new headquarters in the English heartland near industrial Birmingham.

Hopes had been raised before, of course, but the Americans easily re-established superiority after their loss in the 1957 and the tie in 1969. This time, credible doubts surrounded the US chances, with the Europeans coming off their best-ever showing in America. They had built momentum out of defeat, and the odds were even money for the first time since Samuel Ryder was alive. Jacklin's return as captain created the belief that the ball would keep rolling, so to speak. Having achieved historic success at PGA National, he had more pull than any captain before. The PGA ceded him three wild card picks, for instance, and there was no three-man committee to challenge him.

That was more leeway than the PGA of America gave Lee Trevino. All twelve of his players were pre-selected, leaving him no flexibility. The first ten players came straight off the points list with automatic exemptions going to the winners of the US Open and PGA Championship, a change brought about when neither US Open champ Larry Nelson nor PGA Championship winner Hal Sutton qualified for the team in 1983. Andy North, the US Open champ, was having a comeback season and would have made it anyway. Hubert Green made the squad with his surprising win at the PGA, where Tom Watson fell short on points after missing a short par putt on the final hole, allowing Fuzzy Zoeller to claim the final spot. Obviously, Trevino would have selected Watson if he had any captain's picks. But he didn't. Again, the PGA of America got it wrong, and, unlike many times in the past, it mattered.

Trevino would be bringing a strong team that, in addition to North, Green and Sutton, included past major winners Wadkins, Fuzzy Zoeller, Raymond Floyd and Craig Stadler, plus future winners Mark O'Meara, Curtis Strange and Tom Kite. But without Watson, Nicklaus (who would have had to finish second at the PGA), Nelson and himself, the roster seemed less formidable.

Europe, meanwhile, boasted three of the top five players in the world rankings in Ballesteros, Langer (that year's Masters champ) and Sandy Lyle (that year's winner of The Open Championship). Nick Faldo was just two years away from winning the first of his six majors and Ian Woosnam six years away from his Masters championship. Nine players returned from the 1983 team. What's more, the home crowds could sense the tide turning and turned out twenty-five thousand strong each day—louder, rowdier and even more partisan than ever before. Faldo suggested that the Americans weren't prepared for the turnout and were shaken by it.

Indeed, traffic backed up eight miles on the first day of competition, compounded by the morning commute into Birmingham. Some sat in their cars for two hours. Soon, however, nearby fields were converted into makeshift parking lots to ease the massive snarl. Few complained.

Trevino, however, looked forward to the enthusiasm of the big crowds. He had always connected with British golf fans, whom he admired for their knowledge of the game As the 1971 and 1972 Open champ, he loved playing in the British Isles, and he insisted that, if offered the captaincy of the American team, it would have to be in the UK, where the Ryder Cup was truly cherished and where a win would mean much more.

"I'd love to be the captain when the matches are played in Britain," he said. "But Lord, I wouldn't want to be the captain of the team that loses."

Of course, the born hustler never expected to lose. The matches seemed to him, perhaps, an extension of the '72 Open at Muirfield, where Supermex broke Jacklin's heart with his short game magic. They were tied playing the par-five seventeenth, where Trevino put himself up against the face of a bunker with his tee shot and was off the green in four. Jacklin was in control, waiting to attempt an 18-foot birdie putt. Trevino, who had tossed his club in disgust after his third shot, remarked as they walked up the fairway: "It's your Open, Tony." But if Trevino were playing mind games, imagine Jacklin's astonishment as he watched Trevino, acting as if he had already given up and wasting little time over his difficult chip, send it on its way trundling down the slope and into the hole for five. The shot rattled the Englishman. He three-putted for six and bogeyed the last hole to finish third behind Jack Nicklaus. He said he was never the same again.

Thirteen years later, Trevino was hoping he'd still have the edge on Jacklin—and he was talking a good game.

"I keep hearing all this talk about being beaten for the first time since 1957. Forget it," he said. "This is no chicken liver I've brought over. My team is as strong as a garlic milkshake. There are no prizes for coming second. I don't make losing speeches. I do make certain that someone else has to."

Trevino even went on to claim that his team was "a little stronger" than it was in 1983. But the born hustler was having a very hard time finding any takers.

"I have all current money winners, tournament winners, and the ones that are playing extremely well. So, I'm very confident in winning this championship. I mean, I would be kind of silly to say no, that I'm not confident of winning," he claimed. "I may not have the twelve best players in the world, because I have high regard for Seve Ballesteros and Bernhard Langer. But when you take the whole team, as a team of twelve players, yes, I think my team is extremely strong."

Nevertheless, the fog of inferiority that had long hovered over the Brits in so many other previous Cup matches was about to lift. One of the first questions Sandy Lyle was asked after he raised the claret jug that July was what his win would do for Europe's Ryder Cup chances?

"This could definitely be our year," he said with aplomb. "Seve is still the best golfer in the world—my win here doesn't change that—and Langer is playing really well week after week. And we have so many other good men in Europe now. The gap has been closing for some time now."

Ron Wills of the *Daily Mirror* put it bluntly.

"If Europe's golfers don't beat the Yanks at The Belfry this weekend, they may never beat them," he wrote. "Everything is right for a European triumph. Europe has players of world class caliber in Severiano Ballesteros, Sandy Lyle and Bernhard Langer, men who have taken on the Americans, beaten them on their own soil and beaten them in the events that matter."

America's Andy North recognized that.

"The American team used to slide through this match, sometimes without needing to play its best golf. Not anymore," he admitted. "Now we know we've got to play our butts off to beat the Europeans."

In 1957, the last time the US lost, British captain Dai Rees had to beg the press not to talk up the Americans as supermen. This time Jacklin had to caution against "over-enthusiasm." He later wrote in his book, *Tony Jacklin: My Ryder Cup Journey* that his team was "overflowing with self-belief." Ballesteros did all he could to temper that supreme confidence when discussing his team's chances.

"Two years ago in Florida, I cried when we lost the last hole," he said. "It was an unjust result–a tied match would have been fairer. In my opinion, both teams this year are as close as they can be. It will be very even, and it is difficult to say who is the favorites. If I have to choose one, I'll choose my team–but I have a lot of respect for America."

As Ballesteros went into his third Ryder Cup, he had become a sort of lightning rod for the US team. Eric Brown may not have wanted the Spaniard and his ilk to represent his side, but they were kindred spirits. No one matched Brown's bloodlust for sticking it to the Americans more than Seve Ballesteros–and vice versa.

As Larry Nelson said after Seve's first Ryder Cup in 1979, "I think everybody played their best against him this week because everyone wanted to beat him."

No previous American opponent could rouse that sort of ardor. Indeed, the best British players had come at the US as feisty underdogs. Even Jacklin. As good as he was in 1969, he was still punching up against the Nicklaus mystique. But Ballesteros was different. He antagonized the Americans with shots they wouldn't even dream of attempting. And, he had a chip on his shoulder as massive as the Pyrenees. As Jacklin wrote in his book, "He liked beating them because they had the best of everything, and we didn't."

In his biography, *Seve*, Alistair Tait pointed out Ballesteros had, at best, "ambiguous" feelings toward America from the time of his first experience attempting to get through PGA Tour Qualifying School in 1985. On the verge of making it, he basically gave up on the final day when he realized it meant he'd have to play full-time in the States. Later, when he did play several events in the US, he sensed what Tait termed "cold indifference" from the American pros.

Furthermore, Ballesteros felt that the American press didn't give him enough credit when he broke through with his first major victory at Royal Lytham in 1979. He was certainly appreciated for his wins at Augusta National, but he was never fully embraced by the American public, as British golf fans had embraced their Open's American winners of the past—Walter Hagen, Bobby Jones, Ben Hogan, Arnold Palmer, Nicklaus and Watson, for example.

Seve was respected in America. He was worshipped in Europe. And that included The Belfry's Brabazon Course, which was hosting the Ryder Cup for the first of four times. The resort, with its three hundred hotel rooms and three golf courses, was the headquarters of the British PGA since 1977, thanks to a meeting Peter Alliss and Colin Snape had over a pint a few years earlier. The PGA was looking to leave its cramped offices in London. Alliss and Dave Thomas were co-designing the Brabazon Course and Alliss thought it the perfect location.

The site was steeped in history. It was part of the hamlet of Moxhull, site of the Knights Templar manor house before they were expelled from England in 1277. The later manor house built there in 1900 was eventually converted into a hotel, Moxhull Hall. The fifteen potato fields surrounding the place served as an outdoor concert venue for the Moody Blues, Led Zeppelin and most every other English band other than the Beatles and Rolling Stones. When the British PGA signed a ninety-nine-year lease on the property, it envisioned making The Belfry a permanent home course for the Ryder Cup. The Brabazon Course opened to great fanfare in 1977 with a challenge match pitting Ballesteros and Johnny Miller against Jacklin and Brian Barnes. The course was scheduled to host the 1981 matches but, even though it hosted a European Tour event every year since 1979, it wasn't deemed mature enough for the Ryder Cup that year and it was put off until four years later.

It was still a controversial choice. Alliss and Thomas designed the Brabazon Course as a championship test that was more American in nature. It was tree-lined with flared, American-style bunkers and water on eight holes. It was feared that American players would have an edge, but the turf had more bounce than the fairways back home and the Euros were more familiar with The Belfry as a regular tour stop. Jacklin also utilized his home captain's privilege to make certain the area around the greens was shaved to discourage flop shots, an American specialty, and to keep the greens slower than the Americans preferred. Ironically, things had changed since 1957 when captain Dai Rees set up Lindrick with thick grass around the greens and faster green speeds.

Wadkins, in detailing the Brabazon for *Sports Illustrated* prior to the 2002 Ryder Cup, called it the "world's best" match play course: "straightforward with no blind shots or hidden obstacles and so flat that you feel as though you're playing down a runway."

Two par-four holes stood out, the tenth and the eighteenth, one short, one long, with water playing a crucial part in the way each was played.

The tenth was originally planned as a long par four with the tee near the clubhouse. Instead, they opted to locate the practice green there, and that fortuitously led to the design of one of the most classic risk-reward holes in the history of the Ryder Cup.

Alliss and Thomas made the best use of the 310 yards available by placing the narrow green in the right-hand crook of the hole amid what the British call a "spinney" of trees over water. The safe play was to hit a 4-iron off the tee and a flip wedge across from 110 yards, an easy birdie chance. But the really bold players could pull out a wood and either cut it in or aggressively attempt to soar it onto the green over the trees—leading to anything from eagle to double bogey.

Seve Ballesteros, of course, was among the bold. He was playing against Nick Faldo in the 1978 Hennessy Cognac Cup between continental Europe and Britain and Ireland when Faldo had the honors and hit the "proper" iron shot down the fairway. Gasps could be heard when Ballesteros dramatically ripped the head cover off his driver as a matador would. With today's equipment, the required 280-yard carry is routine. But Ballesteros' clubhead was persimmon and his shaft was steel. Designer Thomas, a former Ryder Cupper himself, was a long hitter who had tried driving the green and got close. But no one had dared try it in competition until Ballesteros' ball flew onto the green and stopped ten feet from the hole. The event was televised, immediately creating anticipation for what would happen when the Ryder Cup got there. To add to the drama and temptation of that week, they shortened the hole to 280 yards by using the front tee. But every player that stepped onto the tee box was able to see the plaque that marked Seve's feat.

The 440-yard eighteenth, a magnificent stage for the final act of any match, was more about courage than risk and reward. Any match that got that far placed intense pressure on a tee shot that had to be carried over a lake, which then extended along the left side and back across the hole a second time in front of the green. The drive had to be drilled up the left side but, if pulled, it was wet. Anything hit right required a very nervy long iron shot in. If the ball found the bunker or deep rough, a layup was the only option. The hole could be won off the tee.

As he headed into the first day's matches, Jacklin was aware of the controversy surrounding his three captain's picks. The same man who felt so disrespected when passed over in 1981, left Christy O'Connor Jr. with the same feelings in 1985. O'Connor's uncle, Christy Sr., was an Irish icon who played a hero's role at Lindrick and the nephew was confident that he'd be a part of this victorious squad after finishing third at The Open Championship that year. But with nine automatic spots off the European Order of Merit, he fell to tenth by missing the cut in the final tournament that counted for Ryder Cup points. Jacklin poured salt on the wound when he bypassed him for Spaniard Jose Rivero.

Jacklin was blasted in Ireland for leaving the roster without a single Irishman. O'Connor was sure Ballesteros was behind the decision. Jacklin admitted that he had consulted Ballesteros before picking Rivero but only to confirm his own opinions. Jacklin said he couldn't leave out Nick Faldo and Ken Brown, his other two picks, and chose Rivero after seeing him win at The Belfry earlier that year with a long putt on the final hole.

"He impresses me very much when he is under pressure," Jacklin said. "He can hole putts when he has to, and at the end of the day, that's what you have to do."

O'Connor, who would return to The Belfry in 1989 to hit one of the Ryder Cup's greatest shots (a 2-iron into eighteen to beat Fred Couples) said he was "disgusted and totally shattered." He never forgave Jacklin for it.

"I expect to feel the pain and anger for a long time," he said later that year. "I felt I'd earned my place on merit and the fact that we won the Cup doesn't change anything. I'm convinced I would not have fared worse than some of those who played."

But Jacklin would not waver from his gut feelings.

"It is not my job to be a nice guy. I've got to get the best men for the Ryder Cup. I don't want it to become the Third World War, but it's winning that matters and, my God, it would be nice to win," he said.

Jacklin, for the most part, was able to avoid such dustups the week of the matches. He tried hard to build teamwork and keep his players eating and relaxing together at the hotel, building what Faldo called "an imaginary wall" to keep the media hype at bay. That deep camaraderie of European teams would come to be one of the chief reasons they took over the rivalry. And this was where it started, with stark contrast to the US side.

"It was noticeable they didn't behave like a team: they ate in twos and threes, then maybe disappeared to the movies," Faldo observed of the opponents. "It was though they still hadn't realized they were going to have to work really hard to keep the Cup."

Faldo was also unimpressed with Trevino's stewardship. He said as much in his autobiography, *Life Swings*.

"I don't think Trevino was a good captain," claimed the man who would be torn apart for his captaincy at Valhalla in 2008. "He is a great character and a fine player, but the psychological intricacies of captaincy weren't for him. I remember hearing he allowed arguments to develop who would play with whom, and when and how the team should practice foursomes."

In reality, any disputes over practicing foursomes were settled by Trevino who insisted on practicing alternate shot. To prove he was serious, he even put up $1,000 of his own money to go to the low pair. Naturally, Kite, known as a human cash register on the PGA Tour, took the pot with Calvin Peete.

As well as things turned out for Jacklin's captaincy, he initially experienced a bit of choppy water, mostly regarding his three wild card picks. He had intended to pair Ballesteros and Rivero together in the opening foursomes session, but Rivero couldn't find a fairway in the final practice session. To Jacklin's eye, he looked "overawed" playing with Seve, so the captain went to the bullpen. He pulled Rivero off the course after the fourteenth hole–he might as well have dragged him off by the ear–and had the more experienced Manuel Piñero play the final four practice holes with Seve. They would form the new pairing when the matches began the next morning.

"If he had played, it would have put Ballesteros under too much pressure," Jacklin explained to the press, which, naturally, took him to task. "Jacko's Blunder," read the back page headline in the *Daily Mirror,* which blasted Rivero as a "flop."

Luckily, Jacklin still had Ballesteros in that leadoff match, and it didn't take long for Seve to get things going against Curtis Strange and Mark O'Meara. He immediately dropped a 10-foot birdie putt on the first hole as he and Piñero jumped to a four-hole lead. The Americans sliced it in half by the turn, but the dramatic tenth was next. Trevino ordered his players not to try reaching the green in alternate shot and Strange obliged with an iron off the tee. Ballesteros, of course, obliged the excited crowd by hitting the green and winning the hole to restore a three-hole lead. The Americans made a nice birdie on sixteen to extend the match, but the day's first point went up for Europe, 2-and-1, when the US couldn't beat the Europeans' birdie.

Jacklin was clearly wise to sit Rivero, especially since Ballesteros and Piñero had won the 1976 World Cup together. But he wasn't off the hook completely, and his other two picks bombed.

First, Brown and Open champion Lyle made six straight bogeys and were thrashed, 4-and-3, by Wadkins and Floyd. It wasn't all Brown's fault. He didn't get any of the help he needed from Lyle, one of Europe's top guns. Lyle's longtime caddie, Dave Musgrove, told Lewine Mair of *The Scotsman* it was the worst he had seen his boss play in two years. The "indicator," Musgrove said, was when Lyle began to leak his drives out to the right, and it spread to the rest of his game. With 100 yards to the pin on nine, he came up 20 yards short in the water, and, when Brown did the same on the next hole, it was all but over.

Faldo was even more disappointing than his Scottish teammate. *Evening Mail* golf writer Derek Lawrenson called him "a lead weight" around Langer's shoulders and their partnership, so strong at PGA National, fell flat with a 3-and-2 defeat against the cash-rich Peete and Kite. Howard Clark and Sam Torrance didn't fare any better, falling by the same 3-and-2 score to Craig Stadler and Hal Sutton. The US had a 3-1 lead and Jacklin had a problem.

Faldo had a lot to manage both personally and professionally, as detailed in his autobiography. His first marriage to Melanie Rockall was ending in divorce. ("We were happily married for six months," he wrote. "Unfortunately, we were married for four and a half.") He was also badly off form on the links while going through a swing change with new coach David Leadbetter. But Faldo was the heir apparent to Jacklin as England's greatest player, and Jacklin was sure he would snap out of his slump— "an act of faith on his part," Faldo wrote.

"Nick, you're going to be my chameleon. I know you can change colors this week," he told him.

After Friday's first match, both knew that wasn't going to happen. Some pride had to be swallowed by each man. Jacklin gently pulled Faldo aside.

"Nick, I've got a job to do," he told him. "Do I send you out this afternoon, or do I sit you down?"

"Sorry mate, but I haven't got it. Sit me down," Faldo said softly. He wouldn't play again until the singles. Brown also took a seat, although unlike Faldo, he'd return for the Saturday afternoon foursomes. Lyle sat as well and furiously mouthed off to the press.

"Tony didn't play me in the fourballs in Florida two years ago, so I was sick when he dropped me again," he said. "He didn't give me an explanation. The way I see it the fourballs provide you with the chances to get your momentum going with a few birdies. My game is shooting birdies and I'm better equipped to do that when I'm playing my own ball. If I'm not playing in tomorrow's fourballs, I really will have something to scream about."

Jacklin didn't care. He was trying to find the eight players with the best form that day. He'd call on Lyle again–after the Open champion worked on his game on the range all afternoon–but, for now, Jacklin had to stop the American onslaught. To do so, Jacklin kept together his dynamic Spaniards, Ballesteros and Piñero, but played them in the second slot, something Trevino could not anticipate. Instead, he led off with the diminutive pair of Welshman Ian Woosnam and Paul Way, soon to be tagged the "Tiny Tots." Jacklin activated Cañizares to play with Langer and anchored his squad with Torrance and Clark, who he felt were somewhat unlucky in their morning loss.

Trevino wanted to make certain all his players got a game in before the singles, but his first two pairings didn't make much sense. He had rested Zoeller and Green in the morning–Zoeller's back was acting up, and Green was bothered by a sore knee. Now he paired his injured players in the first match facing Way and Woosnam. North and Jacobsen were both making their Ryder Cup debuts and, making their task even more daunting, were being matched against Ballesteros and Piñero. Trevino was confident, though, that Stadler and Sutton and Floyd and Watson could repeat their morning victories. Instead, it was Jacklin who got the start he needed.

With Woosnam off his game, Way drew a clear line in the sand by winning the first three holes against Fuzzy Zoeller and Hubert Green, a lead they maintained with eight to play. Then the Americans got hot. They would birdie five of the next six holes to square the match, only to lose in agonizing fashion on eighteen. There, the blonde, boyish-looking Way drilled a 2-iron 220 yards over the water and off the bank and, after both Americans barely missed their long birdie efforts, sank a 12-foot putt to win the match, 1-up. The two Brits shot 64, the Americans, 65. Jacklin planted a big kiss on Way's mug to thank him, while Way thanked divine intervention.

"Not many people realize it but that two-iron shot at the last got a lucky bounce." Way admitted. "I can't remember a more marvelous feeling than when that putt went in."

"We cogged it up perfectly," Woosnam said. "If I could just putt like Paul, we'd thrash anybody."

Unsurprisingly, North and Jacobsen were unable to break through the Spanish bulwark of Ballesteros and Piñero, although they fought mightily. The tenth was again the turning point with the match all square. Ballesteros almost routinely drove green for the second time, an accomplishment only teammate Sam Torrance managed, and won the hole with a birdie. The Americans couldn't match his power or touch on seventeen, where he hit a prodigious drive into the wind, another wood to within 60 yards of the green and a wedge to six feet to set up the birdie that won the match.

"Manuel played steady all day and that was the key," Ballesteros said, sheepishly underplaying his part. "But I did have a very good day myself with the putter."

It was all tied up at 3-3. Trevino feared an unprecedented European sweep of the fourballs. But Stadler and Sutton rallied to even their match with a birdie on thirteen and were unlucky not to have won the full point on eighteen, where Stadler's birdie putt missed by a hair. The final match of the day featured twelve birdies and became the third of the four fourball matches to reach the final hole. Wadkins, playing with Floyd, tormented the Europeans once more. After Torrance, partnered with Clark, had driven the tenth, Wadkins matched him by making his putt from 15 feet to remain all square. When Torrance hit an iron to six feet on sixteen, the Europeans looked as if they would easily take the hole. But Wadkins turned the screws by draining a swinging 25-footer for birdie. The "deceptively cherubic killer," as Mair called him, looked back toward Clark and Torrance with a wry smile. Neither was up to the moment. Clark's 12-footer never had a chance, and Torrance pushed his putt to the right in disbelief. The two teams halved the last two holes, and the 1-up win gave the US a 4 ½-3 ½ lead at the end of the day.

"I don't have any fingernails left and I felt much better at noon than I do now," Trevino said. "But I'm just as confident that we'll win as when I brought the team over."

Jacklin was breathing easier. He felt he'd weathered a storm, not just from the US but from all the pre-match expectations.

"The foursomes were a rude awakening," he said. "After all the enthusiasm, all the patriotism, all the getting carried away, I'm glad the first day is behind us, that we're into the matches and have a feeling of just how tough these guys really are."

It was just another example of how quickly perceptions turn in a Ryder Cup. After being criticized at the break for his underwhelming captain's picks, Jacklin was being hailed for his leadership.

"The European comeback only happened because non-playing skipper Tony Jacklin was brave enough to make a near-humiliating decision–admit he had picked the wrong men for the job," Wills wrote in the *Daily Mirror.*

No such thing, Jacklin said.

"Once the players assemble for the match, they are a team, and it doesn't matter a damn whether you are the Open champion or one of the captain's personal selections. That aspect of it never entered my mind," he said.

Some thought Jacklin had lost his mind when, having just watched Torrance and Clark lose for the second time, he sent them out again to lead off Saturday morning fourballs. He backed them up with the Tiny Tots and put his strongest pairing, Ballesteros and Piñero, third. Then, confident that the angry Lyle would regain his form after his poor Friday showing, he partnered him with Langer, a pairing of that year's Masters and Open Championship winners.

Trevino didn't make much of a fuss over who played with whom.

He thought his players could play with anyone else on the team. But he did have three injuries to manage. In addition to Zoeller and Green, Peete had a sore shoulder, and Trevino was careful not to play them twice the first two days.

Trevino needed Peete for the afternoon foursomes. He and Kite had clicked so well in the alternate shot format, beating Faldo and Langer, 3-and-2, after winning the cash the captain had put on the table in his practice challenge. So, he rested Peete and paired Kite with North, then put his other two injured men, Zoeller and Green, together to face Way and Woosnam for the second straight day. Wadkins, his toughest competitor, was 2-0 with Floyd Friday but Trevino needed to rest Floyd in at least one session, so he sent Wadkins out with O'Meara in a showdown against Ballesteros and Piñero. Stadler and Strange then took up the rear.

The weather was miserable, but, again, the crowds turned out *en masse.* And they would witness one of the biggest one-putt swings in Ryder Cup history. First, Europe regained the lead in the first two matches with Torrance and Clark finally coming through against Kite and North, and Way and Woosnam dispatching Zoeller and Green again without the need for final-hole heroics from Way. Clark was the difference in the first match, where his birdies on three and five opened a two-hole lead. The Americans used birdies on twelve and thirteen to square the match, but Clark rammed in a 55-foot putt over two tiers on the fifteenth green (he and Torrance celebrated with an impromptu jig) before chipping in on sixteen to restore the two-hole lead. Way had led the way Friday, but it was Woosnam on Saturday. He rolled in a 30-foot birdie on the first and added two more on four and five. The Americans were five down after only eight holes and never recovered.

Wadkins once again proved to be Europe's nemesis by standing up to Ballesteros in the third match. He holed three long putts on the first nine holes as the US took went 4-up in a match that ended on the fourteenth green. Everything now hung on the final match, and when Strange hit a beauty into sixteen to put Lyle and Langer dormie with two holes left, it appeared as if the Americans would hold serve—even after Lyle kept the match alive with a 25-foot putt for eagle on seventeen.

The wind was into the players' faces on eighteen, where Strange left Stadler on his own with an awful tee shot with both Europeans in the fairway. The Walrus responded with a 1-iron to a slick 30 feet, which he lagged 18 inches past the cup. Neither Lyle nor Langer made birdie. Stadler shot his eyes at them, expecting his putt to be conceded. They stood as silent and stolid as Stonehenge. "It was the sort we would have conceded if it had been for a halved match, but we had to see it in as it was for a win," Lyle would explain. Clearly irritated, Stadler swiped at the putt and missed the hole. He left it there as he walked away, reaching his hand back down his collar in despair as the European team room erupted in glorious disbelief.

"There was bedlam in the European team room," Alistair Tait reported in his biography of Ballesteros. "Seve leapt out of his chair when the ball missed the hole. The chair went tumbling and Seve came down with a bang and landed on his back. His teammates were hammering on the wall to the American team dressing room. The dream was alive. The Europeans had halted the American juggernaut. It was game on."

To the Europeans, it spelled both affirmation and validation. As Faldo noted, "It was probably the first time in the history of the matches that an American had so obviously buckled under pressure."

"I'm convinced Stadler missing that putt was the turning point," Jacklin said years later. "Our team seemed to take it as meaning the Americans weren't supermen after all, that they were as susceptible to pressure as we were—in other words, human. It's a cruel game. It was an example of what pressure can do. In all my years I don't think I ever saw anything that changed a Ryder Cup quite like that putt."

Strange agreed: "At that moment, you don't say anything. You certainly don't say, 'that's all right.' He might slap you inside the head, because it's not all right. You shake hands and go about your business. Recoup in a hurry because you have to play more golf in a few minutes. But it gave them such momentum. Half a point can mean a great deal, and it just changed the course of the matches. I don't mean anything against Craig but that's just the way it worked."

Stadler would have to hear about the "tiddler" for the rest of his life.

"Every time the Ryder Cup comes round, I've got to watch that all over again on telecast," he said in a 2002 interview with *The Telegraph.* "What they don't show is my partner whipping it into the water leaving me alone with a driver and one iron to the hole. Up ahead, Andy North had also hit it in the water, so did Peter Jacobsen . . . I was just about the only guy to finish the hole. I'll never understand the reaction—like I never three-putted before in my entire life? The putt that lost the Ryder Cup? Yeah, I've heard that a lot over the past seventeen years, but I've never bought that particular story. What was it, the Saturday morning? There was still a lot of golf to be played."

And the Europeans couldn't wait to play it.

"We took that and ran with it," Jacklin said. "As a team, we knew that was a sign, a chink in the armor, a weakness, and you have got to pounce on it."

Trevino didn't want his team to dwell on it. "As long as the game of golf is played, short putts will be missed," he said. But he also asked for a one-hour delay before handing in the afternoon lineups. It seemed he was only delaying the inevitable. And it didn't seem to matter who was playing in them.

Even Rivero, the man Jacklin so emphatically benched, came through. Paired with his countryman Cañizares, they blew away Kite and Peete, Trevino's best alternate shot duo, 7-and-5, in the first match. It was the largest American defeat since eighteen-hole matches began in 1961. Trevino was determined to play Stadler in all five matches and sent him out with Sutton second against Ballesteros and Piñero. Stadler "often looked at war with himself," wrote Jack Magowan of the *Belfast Telegraph,* and played miserably. The revived Ballesteros and Piñero won six of the first eight holes and locked up a 5-and-4 win when Ballesteros hit one within inches on the 194-yard par-three fourteenth. Even Wadkins failed to deliver, as he and Floyd were defeated by Langer and Brown, 3-and-2. Only Strange and Jacobsen prevented a 4-0 sweep when Way and Woosnam ran out of gas, 4-and-2.

The Americans had lost both fourball sessions for the first time since the format was included in 1963 and trailed going into the singles for the first time since 1949. History turned on its ear. "Two points is a lot to make up," Trevino conceded.

"I dare not think of tomorrow because I was so disappointed two years ago," Jacklin said. "I am determined not to be that disappointed again and I am sure we are ready. In your own backyard and with about twenty-five thousand pulling for you, it's a pretty good lead."

Trevino predictably front-loaded his lineup with Wadkins, Stadler, Floyd and Kite. "I want those two points back quickly," he said, adding, If I don't get some points from those first four matches, we're in trouble."

In anticipation, Jacklin put his strongest players in the middle of the lineup to fight off any opening charge. That still left open who to put up against Wadkins, the self-described "junkyard dog" against whom the Euros assumed they would be leading off. According to a *CNN* interview with Torrance years later, there was silence in the European team room when that question came up.

"Virtually none of us wanted to play against Lanny Wadkins, who was the best in the singles," Torrance recalled. "Piñero got up from his seat and shouted, 'I want to play against him.'"

In his book, Faldo remembered Piñero "hopping around like the proverbial cat on a hot tin roof." As Faldo recalled, Piñero's voice became increasingly strident as he chanted: 'I wan' Wadkins I wan' Wadkins. I wan' Wadkins.'"

Jacklin didn't hesitate. Wadkins may have made more money in his three appearances on the European Tour than Piñero did playing full-time, but that just provided the Spaniard with more motivation. Jacklin knew Piñero was juiced up after playing four matches with

Ballesteros, and he knew he would be hungry for revenge after Wadkins helped inflict their only loss. He also knew the effect on the US team if the man Trevino considered his "gutsiest" player, fell first.

"Wadkins was the cockiest member of the American team," he explained. "He looked at opponents on the first tee as if to say, 'I eat people like you for lunch.'"

But Piñero was tenacious, with as much of a canine mentality as his opponent.

"You wouldn't back Manuel in medal play, but he was a terrier in the Ryder Cup," Jacklin wrote in his book. "Manuel was almost born to play in the Ryder Cup. He was like a dog snapping at your ankles, he was so determined, and you just couldn't shake him off if you were up against him.

"When the draw came out half an hour later, we saw Wadkins at the top of the order, Manuel jumped about four feet in the air fists pumping. It was fantastic."

"The only match Seve and I had lost was to Wadkins. That was why I wanted to play against him," Piñero explained. "And it went like a dream."

It was the perfect match to kick off play with the Sunday atmosphere off the charts. "It was all theatre, burlesque at times," Magowan wrote. "The first fairway was teeming with people, six-deep along both flanks."

"It made the hair stand up on the back of your neck when you stood on the first tee and all you could see was an ocean of home fans," said Jacklin.

As Jacklin expected, Piñero wouldn't let Wadkins get away from him. A little man with what *Sports Illustrated*'s Barry McDermott described as a whiplash swing, Piñero defied buffeting winds and scrappily scrambled, unbowed by Wadkins' reputation. To the contrary, it was Wadkins who seemed on the back of his heels; immediately following both wins on the front side, Piñero answered with his own and they arrived at the pivotal tenth all square. As usual, the hole favored Europe. Piñero was off the green with his second shot and Wadkins was lining up a birdie putt. But Piñero's short-game wizardry struck again. He thrashed out of the fluffy greenside rough with a perfect chip that dropped into the cup. It was reminiscent of Wadkins' usual heroics and, when the American failed to make his birdie, a wave of momentum spread across the course like a seismic boom.

"Wadkins was the megastar of the moment and Piñero beat him," Torrance said. "Imagine what it meant for the other eleven of us who had to play next. It was magnificent."

Roars reverberated when Piñero sank three 15-footers to run away to a 3-and-2 win. While Stadler shook off his Saturday misfortune by defeating Woosnam in the poorly played second match, the dominos fell. Derek Lawrenson called it a "golden hour in which the home side could do nothing wrong." The forty-three-year-old Floyd almost shot his age with a front side 41 and couldn't complete a comeback against Way. That gave the Europeans four of the first six points against Trevino's top guys, and they would end up winning five of the first seven matches to America's one. Even the one halve felt like a European win with Ballesteros roaring back from three down with five to play. Seve was possessed, hitting what Kite called, "shots I never even dream about."

At that point, the only question was who would get the clinching point for Europe. England's Howard Clarke squandered his opportunity by missing a four-foot putt on seventeen. It then fell to Torrance, who had completed a comeback from three holes down against North, and who was told by Jacklin, while playing the seventeenth, that the team needed just one more point.

Torrance actually handed his driver over to Jacklin on the last tee box as if to say, "you hit it." "Go on son, you can do it," Jacklin replied, and Torrance hit what he called the tee shot of his life, over the trees and into the middle of the fairway. North tried to respond but couldn't. He skied his tee shot dead left, into the lake.

"When North hit his tee shot into the water at the last, I knew I could win the Ryder Cup for us," Torrance said afterwards. "That's when I began to cry. And I cried all the way up the eighteenth fairway. I never have felt as wonderful as I feel today. And never will I feel as wonderful."

North could have conceded the hole, but he allowed Torrance his moment, which the Scot recognized as a classy move. The stage provided by the eighteenth hole was perfect. Torrance promptly sealed the Cup by making his 22-foot putt and threw his arms skyward. He was immediately mobbed by Jacklin and the teammates who had finished their matches.

"Twenty-eight years," Langer mused. "That's my age."

The final score, 16 ½-11 ½, was America's biggest Ryder Cup loss up to that point and would remain so until Europe's stunning nine-point road victory at Oakland Hills in 2004. The Concorde, which would take the American team home, did a fly-by in honor of the European victory as, below, they popped the Bollinger champagne that had been on ice since 1957—when Dai Rees had set it aside for the next team to beat the US. They climbed through a window and guzzled it atop The Belfry roof. It was a shame Rees didn't live to see it; sadly, he had died in a car crash just two years earlier.

The Europeans' partying lasted past daybreak and included tossing Faldo into the hotel pool fully clothed. All the players, and a few of their wives joined him by plunging in.

Meanwhile, the Americans, Hall Sutton in particular, were left grousing about the behavior of the crowds, "muttering," as McDermott wrote, "about innumerable imagined transgressions: opponents tramping into their putting line, hostile fans stepping on their balls in the rough, match officials prejudiced against them, and, yes, fans hissing at their wives." To be sure, there was some truth to it. At one point, Jacklin's wife Vivienne, turned back toward the taunters and chided: "Sssshhh. Isn't it enough that they've missed their shot?"

Shaun Custis of the *Evening Telegraph* noted that Sutton "whinged" in "marvelously sulky fashion."

"It was more like a football game than a golf match. The fans were disgraceful," the future American captain had charged. "If crowds back in America behaved like yours, I'd never hit another golf ball."

Jacklin fired back, putting aside the conciliation he and Nicklaus enjoyed at Royal Birkdale.

"It's chaps like Mr. Sutton who make problems for Europeans going to America. I'm sure he cannot wait to get home, step on American soil and put his feet under a stool at his local McDonalds. All I know is that those fans shared in this win with us—they gave us everything they had and cheered us all the way to the finish. They were an influence on the result," he said.

Trevino, always a competitor, never a whiner, had to defer to Jacklin on this one. He called his players "crybabies" and noted: "You might as well ask the crowd at the Super Bowl to stay silent, not to take sides."

Trevino, of course, had become what he had dreaded: "the captain of the team that loses." Afterwards, some of his players felt they hadn't received enough support from him.

"Without trying to be negative, I really don't think Lee embraced the whole thing of being captain," Stadler said some years later. "He wasn't keen on having a big part in making the pairings. We rarely saw him on the course, he was out there somewhere, I don't know where. I love Lee to death, he is a very, very dear friend of mine, and I don't mean to be bad-mouthing him, I'm not. He agreed to be captain, but I think he'll tell you; it probably wasn't his cup of tea."

But Trevino was satisfied that he did everything possible.

"I teamed my guys the best I could, but I couldn't play for them. They criticized me afterwards, but I wasn't the one who lost the matches," he said. Above all, he questioned the squad's thin-skinned reaction to the fans. "My players weren't prepared to handle the galleries."

Jacklin, meanwhile, wished he'd have given his former nemesis more of the needle: "He shouldn't feel too bad about being the first losing American captain for twenty-eight years, because he is certain to have company in the next six to eight years."

Years later, he wrote in his book that he had "put one over" on Trevino and that out-captaining him brought him a degree of personal satisfaction,

"Victory tasted a little sweeter because we achieved it against Trevino," he confessed. "I had to take it very much in the solar plexus in The Open at Muirfield in 1972, where I was beaten into third place, and I was a bit disappointed he never came over to congratulate me when victory was clinched at The Belfry.

"I would have thought so much more of him had he had. Trevino doesn't like losing, although it has to be said that probably stems from the fact that he spent more time winning than losing in his playing career. Of course, we all react differently, but if you can't look your opponent in the eye at the end of it all and say, 'well done,' then we're all wasting our time. I think it's important to do the right thing at these moments."

Trevino was nevertheless gracious in his remarks to the press. He understood the consequences of a European win and called the result the "dawn of a new era.

"The sport over here will now take off more than ever. It is going to be unbelievable, what it will do," he said. "There have always been half-a-dozen good players in Europe but now there are many times that number, and it will continue to get stronger. More sponsors will take an interest in the sport, and the prize money will go through the roof."

The *Herald Express,* typical of the reaction in the British press, took it a step further when it editorialized: "Europe's Ryder Cup victory was more than just a glorious achievement. It was also the moment when the last remnants of the great American golfing myth were shattered."

Jacklin obviously agreed.

"It has gone up my nose for a long time that just because you have USA after your name you can get telephone numbers in appearance money while the Europeans are considered second best. Now perhaps people will sit up and take notice of us," he said.

Certainly, the impact of the continental players could not be denied. The four-person Spanish Armada lost only two matches all week. Combined with Langer, they went 12-4-4 and were in on nine and a half of the team's 19 ½ points.

"In a few years' time we will not just have the Spanish players and Bernhard Langer, we will have the Swedes coming through as well," Jacklin added. "This is now Europe. This result shows just how strong our tour really is. It has taken something like this to open people's eyes."

That's if anyone in America was shifting their eyes from the football and baseball being played. While Europe was enraptured by the result, American sports fans reacted with a yawn, partly because the US television networks didn't bother to cover it. *The New York Times* had been the only US newspaper to staff the Cup, with John Radosta limited to a five-hundred-word recap shoved to the back of the section. *Sports Illustrated* was there. *Golf Digest* wasn't.

That would all change, of course. The Ryder Cup would become as big a deal in the States as it always had been overseas. Europe's continued success made that possible. Jacklin may have been onto something, when he looked back at Stadler's 18-incher.

"You could say his failure to hole that putt changed the whole course of Ryder Cup history," he said.

At the time, the Americans weren't looking that far into the future.

"Wait 'til next time," Wadkins said.

The 1987 matches would arrive soon enough at the home of Jack Nicklaus.

DAY 1
FOURSOMES
Seve Ballesteros/Miguel Pinero (E) defeated Curtis Strange/Mark O'Meara (US) 2-and-1
Calvin Peete/Tom Kite (US) defeated Bernhard Langer/Nick Faldo (E) 3-and-2
Lanny Wadkins/Raymond Floyd (US) defeated Sandy Lyle/Ken Brown (E) 4-and-3
Craig Stadler/Hal Sutton (US) defeated Howard Clark/Sam Torrance (E) 3-and-2
United States wins session, 3-1

FOURBALLS

Paul Way/Ian Woosnam (E) defeated Fuzzy Zoeller/Hubert Green (US) 1-up
Seve Ballestero/Miguel Pinero (E) defeated Andy North/Peter Jacobsen (US) 2-and-1
Bernhard Langer/Jose Maria Canizares (E) halved with Craig Stadler/Hal Sutton (US)
Raymond Floyd/Lanny Wadkins (US) defeated Sam Torrance/Howard Clark (E) 1-up
Europe wins session, 2 ½-1 ½
United States 4 ½, Europe 3 ½

DAY 2

FOURBALLS

Sam Torrance/Howard Clark (E) defeated Tom Kite/Andy North (US) 2-and-1
Paul Way/Ian Woosnam (E) defeated Hubert Green/Fuzzy Zoeller (US) 4-and-3
Mark O'Meara/Lanny Wadkins (US) defeated Seve Ballesteros/Miguel Pinero (E) 3-and-2
Bernhard Langer/Sandy Lyle (E) halved with Craig Stadler/Curtis Strange (US)
Europe wins session, 2 ½-1 ½
United States 6, Europe 6

FOURSOMES

Jose Maria Canizares/Jose Rivero (E) defeated Tom Kite/Calvin Peete (US) 4-and-3
Seve Ballesteros/Miguel Pinero (E) defeated Craig Stadler/Hal Sutton (US) 5-and-4
Curtis Strange/Peter Jacobsen (US) defeated Paul Way/Ian Woosnam (E) 4-and-2
Bernhard Langer/Ken Brown (E) defeated Raymond Floyd/Lanny Wadkins (US) 3-and-2
Europe wins session, 3-1
Europe 9, United States 7

DAY 3

SINGLES

Miguel Pinero (E) defeated Lanny Wadkins (US) 3-and-1
Craig Stadler (US) defeated Ian Woosnam (E) 2-and-1
Paul Way (E) defeated Raymond Floyd (US) 2-up
Seve Ballesteros (E) halved with Tom Kite (US)
Sandy Lyle (E) defeated Peter Jacobsen (US) 3-and-2
Bernhard Langer (E) defeated Hal Sutton (US) 5-and-4
Sam Torrance (E) defeated Andy North (US) 1-up
Howard Clark (E) defeated Mark O'Meara (US) 1-up
Calvin Peete (US) defeated Jose Rivero (E) 1-up
Hubert Green (US) defeated Nick Faldo (E) 3-and-1
Jose Maria Canizares (E) defeated Fuzzy Zoeller (US) 2-up
Curtis Strange (US) defeated Ken Brown (E) 4-and-2
Europe wins session, 7 ½-4 ½

EUROPE WINS RYDER CUP, 16 ½-11 ½

1987

Poking the Bear

MUIRFIELD VILLAGE
EUROPE 15, UNITED STATES 13

There was a whiff of arrogance on the Concorde as the 1987 European team swooped down to Columbus, Ohio carrying the Ryder Cup with it. Biennial punching bags no longer, they were embarking on a history-making journey fortified by the delicious expectation of dealing the US its first-ever loss on home soil.

Love was literally in the air when Sam Torrance proposed to his girlfriend, actress Suzanne Danielle, somewhere over the Atlantic and the contingent, most of whom beat the Americans at The Belfry two years earlier, was in a jovial mood. According to Nick Faldo in his biography *Life Swings,* British Airways captain John Cook was playing along.

"Frightfully unaccommodating these Americans. They won't give us permission to stage a fly-past so I'm afraid we're going to have to land," he announced over the intercom. But as Cook counted off the descent, he suddenly pulled out of it at full thrust. "Shall we find the golf course?" he asked, followed by an enthusiastic affirmative from the team. A steep bank took the supersonic jet over the wrong course. Another steep bank and Muirfield Village was off to the left. The same aircraft that dipped its wings in salute to the European team at The Belfry before whisking the defeated Americans home, buzzed the course that Jack built, as if to say: "Even Paul Revere couldn't save you this time."

"We were going up and down like a jo-jo," complained Seve Ballesteros, who had always struggled with pronouncing the English letter "y." But, despite their top player's frayed nerves, the Europeans arrived at Port Columbus Airport with stylish bravado. My, how things had changed from the days when British Ryder Cup teams pulled sheepishly into American venues, with avoiding embarrassment by the powerful home team the only hope they harbored. Not even the sight of US captain Jack Nicklaus on the tarmac could dissuade them that they were the better team.

Tony Jacklin, in his third consecutive stint as captain, had barely stepped off the aircraft's airstair when a reporter shoved a microphone in his face and asked for his prediction.

"Oh, we'll win," he said without hesitation.

"Why?"

"Because," he blithely responded in a clipped tone.

Because. That snarky rejoinder became a battle cry.

"Simple as that. I meant it," Jacklin said years later. "It wasn't a boast. It wasn't a challenge I wasn't trying to anger the Americans or motivate my team. It was just what I thought, what I felt. Question. Answer. Next?"

If the tide had been turned at the 1985 Ryder Cup, 1987 would allow the Europeans to open the floodgates. They reminded one observer of the old TV commercial in which Robert Conrad dared anyone to knock the Eveready battery off his shoulder. They were going to win (just because). The Americans just didn't know it yet. Of course, how could anyone really anticipate the coming sea change?

Golf was in its pre-Tiger era. For generations, American had been turning out the world's preeminent players with a succession of greats from Walter Hagen, Gene Sarazen and Bobby Jones to Sam Snead, Byron Nelson and Ben Hogan to Arnold Palmer, Jack Nicklaus, Lee Trevino and Tom Watson. If incursions were made by non-Americans, they were by non-Europeans such as Bobby Locke, Gary Player and Greg Norman. Henry Cotton and Jacklin were the best of the Brits, great players but never at the top of the hill. Now came golf's European Renaissance with Ballesteros and Bernhard Langer as their DaVinci and Michelangelo.

There were no dominant Americans in the late 1980s. Norman was at the top of the World Golf Rankings, followed by Ballesteros, Langer and Sandy Lyle. Curtis Strange was the top-ranked American at No. 5, but he had yet to win his back-to-back US Open titles. Furthermore, before Woods burst onto the world scene at the 1997 Masters, Europeans had won eight of the previous twelve green jackets and ten of the previous twelve. Euros would also snatch six of the nine claret jugs awarded between 1984 and 1992. Clearly, if America were to turn back Europe in the Ryder Cup, it would have to come from depth, not dominance.

Nicklaus acknowledged as much months before the competition, when he described his team as "a bunch of guys who get the most out of their games, but we just don't have the kind of player with the game that can be dominant. And I don't see him emerging right away."

Understandably, the American team took umbrage. Through their perspective, they were sleeping dogs in 1985, beaten by what they considered an inferior team. The World Rankings were also a sticking point and a major topic of conversation after Jacklin casually but brashly pointed to them as proof of his boys' superiority.

"Day in and day out I don't think there is an American golfer who's as good as Severiano Ballesteros, Greg Norman and Bernhard Langer," Jacklin argued. "Head-to-head, one on one, over the course of a week or a month, I think those three would come out on top of any three you'd pick from America. Some Americans might be tired of listening to that but it's a fact."

Not to the US team. At least not yet. One by one, they sounded off about Jacklin's bravado.

"Well, it gets a bit frustrating," noted American firebrand Lanny Wadkins. "Langer and Ballesteros haven't won over here in two years. If they're the best, why can't they come over against the best fields and win? I've always felt if you're going to be the best in the world, maybe you ought to be playing against the best all the time. And there's no question we have the best tour."

"I'm sick and tired of reading that stuff, that Ballesteros is the best player in the game," groused the normally mild-mannered Larry Nelson. "Maybe he doesn't play over here as often because he can't win as often. I've got a 4-0 record against him in the Ryder Cup. It has all been team stuff, but it's still 4-0."

"We've got the best tour in the world and the best players in the world," said Payne Stewart, who topped the US Ryder Cup points standings. "One foreigner, Sandy Lyle, has won one tournament on our tour this year. Then they say we're not the best anymore. I don't see where they get off. How do they prove it?"

Mark Calcavecchia, playing in the Ryder Cup for the first time just as was Stewart, required proof.

"We've heard some over here on our tour that they think they are going to come over here and beat us," he said. "That sort of thing doesn't sit too good with any of us. They're coming over here pretty confident, which is fine. I wouldn't expect anything less from them. But the best team will win and that's going to be us. It's not even close. Their tour can't even sniff our tour."

"The fact that they talk about them being the 1-2-3 players in the world will have no bearing this week," said Hal Sutton. "The Europeans are certainly great players, but I don't think anybody on our team is scared of playing them. Any of our players is capable of beating them."

"I think we're going to kick their ass and I know that's how the other guys feel," Stewart added.

"What separates this thing now is the home turf," Sutton noted.

Ah, yes. The Europeans couldn't dare win in the lair of the Golden Bear, could they? As Peter Alliss, who described the action for the *BBC* that week, wrote, "I almost expected Jack to arrive on a white charger bedecked in a full suit of armor, gallantly leading his troops into battle. The setting was perfect . . . how could they fail?"

That point had been goring the sides of the Euros for some time. Indeed, a few months earlier, Jacklin was the main attraction at a press conference at Manhattan's swanky Four Seasons restaurant, to drum up American interest in the Ryder Cup and, hopefully, a first-ever American television deal. A waiter had been instructed to keep Jacklin's glass full during the cocktail hour before the official program began and he, as well as some of the organizers, were feeling a bit wonky at the podium. Martin Davis, the moderator who was friendly with Jacklin, began by extolling his virtues before a conspicuously long pregnant pause. He then looked straight at Jacklin and said in a most sardonically affectionate manner, "There's no fucking way that you're going to go into Columbus, Jack's hometown, and beat Jack, on his own territory. You guys have never won on American soil. What the fuck makes you think you can do that?"

Jacklin shot his bleary eyes at Davis and launched into a hysterical defense of his team's strengths that had the audience of golf writers in stitches. He'd save his final rebuttal for September.

Muirfield Village, as it would turn out, was less hostile to the Europeans than expected. Nicklaus played the gracious host, escorting the Europeans from the airport in a fleet of Cadillacs and hosting Jacklin and his team in on-site villas. More importantly, they also found the course to their liking. Nicklaus, as a six-time Masters champion, was a great admirer of Augusta National and the way things were done there. So, when it came time to design a course in his hometown, he named it after the original Muirfield, where he won his first claret jug, and created the course and his Memorial tournament almost as an homage to Augusta National and the Masters. It was even dubbed the Augusta of the North.

Cut out of Ohio farmland in the town of Dublin, where Jack had hunted wild turkey as a kid, Muirfield Village had seventy white sand bunkers and water on nine holes. Like Augusta, it was a second shot golf course where hitting the right part of the green was paramount. It was perfectly manicured with lush fairways and lightning-fast greens. Perhaps the Americans were more familiar with the layout, because the Memorial tournament was played there each year. However, if you're going to be playing golf on a course that so closely resembles Augusta National, you're going to make players like Ballesteros, Langer, Lyle, Woosnam and Jose Maria Olazábal—who would combine for ten Masters titles—very comfortable.

As Woosnam matter-of-factly said: "We can handle the shots Jack is trying to put up for us."

Muirfield Village resembled Augusta National's hospitality in another way. Its galleries behaved more like proper Masters patrons than the student section at the Ohio State Horseshoe. They poured through the gates to blow away US Ryder Cup attendance records with twenty thousand per day (and twenty-seven thousand on Sunday), but they hardly provided the kind of partisan noise that the Americans found so annoying, if not intimidating, at The Belfry. In fact, European tour groups brought over between two and three thousand leather-lunged supporters who booked twelve hundred hotel rooms and were often louder than the home fans. It was almost like a home game for the visitors.

Sutton had complained the most forcibly about the conduct of the galleries at The Belfry, but the European side dithered about whether the crowds were truly vile or simply vociferous. Now, Sutton had a new claim hung over from 1985: that while Andy North was teeing off on the eighteenth hole in his crucial match against Sam Torrance, British fans rattled a wooden fence during his backswing. "Disgraceful," Sutton called it.

"And so it would have been if it had happened," *The Guardian's* Dai Davies wrote of Sutton's "fertile" imagination. "But it didn't, and it is time that Sutton grew up."

Nevertheless, the future captain of the ill-fated US team of 2004 typified the attitudes of those teammates who suffered ignominious defeat in 1985, specifically Lanny Wadkins, Tom Kite, Curtis Strange and himself.

"I set a goal when I boarded the plane to come back here: I wanted to be on the 1987 team," he said. "Of the four of us, I'm the only guy who has not played on a Ryder Cup winner. So, this is a little bit special to me this year."

It just added to the charged atmosphere, as did a syndicated column by the *London Observer's* Peter Dobereiner, dean of British golf writers. It appeared in the *Columbus Dispatch* with details of how the Europeans would retain the Cup. Tom Kite tacked it up on the bulletin board in the US team room and, according to Dobereiner, four American players "buttonholed" *Associated Press* correspondent Bob Green and demanded he write a "stern rebuttal to the limey 'risshole's' ravings."

"At least I think the word was risshole," Dobereiner wrote in his account for his British audience. "Can they be getting jittery already?"

In fact, Dobereiner's theory was that the Americans would be undone by the tightness of their sphincters.

"Here we come to the crux of the matter. American pride, nurtured from the cradle into a state of mind bordering on master race fixation, could be their undoing," he wrote. "The real threat to America's chances is not so much the European challenge as the gung-ho factor, the temptation to try too hard."

In Dobereiner's opinion, the whole thing could be settled if the Euros gave the Americans "an early thump" right out of the box.

"My belief is that the Ryder Cup could and probably will be decided on the first day. If the Europeans could amass a substantial lead in the opening series of foursomes and fourballs, then I believe a whiff of desperation would infect the American camp. The Europeans would be in the position of needing only to play for par while the Americans, forced to go for birdies, would press and destroy themselves," Dobereiner reasoned.

"On the other hand, if the Americans get off to a fast start, it would settle the jitters of the novices and reassure the old hands of the eternal verities of the American way, of seventy-five years of golfing dominance and mom's apple pie."

Nicklaus hinted at how stinging a loss would be for his troops.

"We are determined to win," he said. "I think our guys would be very depressed if they lost again. They have a great sense of pride in wanting to win back the Cup and they still feel American golf is dominant as a force, so to be defeated again would really hurt."

Nicklaus, of course, was in danger of becoming the first American captain to lose on home soil. It was a captains rematch against his good friend Jacklin, whose putt he conceded to leave the 1969 Ryder Cup in a tie and who served as his opposing captain in 1983 when Wadkins saved the day at Palm Beach National.

The four Americans who played at The Belfry were hoping Nicklaus would do a better job of strategizing than Trevino had. Sutton, for instance, pointed to Trevino pairing him and Craig Stadler, two long hitters and the short-hitting Kite and Calvin Peete in alternate shot. Neither Kite nor Peete could carry that hazard on the fifth hole Sutton noted. "It's the little things like that that make the difference," he said.

However, just as Trevino and every American captain before him, Nicklaus was handcuffed shaping this team. The twelve players came straight off the Ryder Cup points standings, accumulated over two years, with the 1987 US Open and PGA champions granted automatic berths. Without any captain's picks, Nicklaus could be stuck in the unenviable position of having some of the hottest golfers excluded from his squad. It would take until 2008 and Paul Azinger's captaincy for the PGA to settle on a system that truly worked.

The system did bring Larry Nelson and his sterling Ryder Cup record back on the squad for the first time since 1991 by dint of his playoff win over Wadkins at the PGA a month earlier. Nelson, who would not have made the team otherwise, was seen as a welcome addition. But the team, in general, was regarded as a weak one–"lacking in quality," as one British newspaper described it. Although the roster included three of the year's four major champions, two (US Open champ Scott Simpson and Masters champ Larry Mize) would be making their Ryder Cup debuts along with Calcavecchia (the youngest member of the quad), Stewart and Dan Pohl. With Europe returning nine of its twelve men from the victorious 1985 team, Wadkins, Sutton, Kite and Strange returned from

America's 1985 team, while Ben Crenshaw brought experience from the '81 and '83 teams and Andy Bean from '79.

Jacklin was once again granted three captain's picks, which he spent on Olazábal, Lyle and Ken Brown. Olazábal and Gordan Brand Jr. were the only rookies on the roster, which was filled out by Eamonn Darcy, a veteran of three previous Cup teams and considered the weak link.

Jacklin's problems were bureaucratic in nature but demonstrated just how much power he held in his third successive stint as captain. First, he settled a clash between the British PGA and European Tour over the split of revenues. The two organizations had begun to share the auspices of their Ryder Cup team with the introduction of continental players. Jacklin advocated for a 60-40 split in favor of the Tour, which would eventually assume total control. Meanwhile, the PGA Tour committed the egregiously shortsighted miscalculation of declining to assume management of the Ryder Cup from the PGA of America, which has profited handsomely from the event to this day.

Next, Jacklin balked at a request from the PGA of America–some say instigated by Nicklaus–to add a fourth day to the competition with another round of singles. The Ryder Cup was being televised live in the States for the first time by *ABC* and *ESPN*, which considered the singles matches more popular to US audiences. Jacklin knew tacking on another singles round would only favor the US, which had all twelve of its players ranked in the World Rankings top forty, as opposed to six Euros. He told the Americans if they changed the format, he'd resign as captain.

There were other brushfires, once the European team arrived stateside. Oddly, their golf bags were too small and had to be replaced. Then, logo-gate. The Glenmuir company had been contracted to provide the team's apparel; however, team members sponsored by other sportswear brands refused to wear the Glenmuir logo. In the end, it was blackened out. Finally, representatives of the European Tour invited to meet with the team after Thursday's opening ceremonies were assaulted by a salvo of grievances from angry players over everything from practice balls to course conditioning. According to David Feherty in his *Totally Subjective History of the Ryder Cup,* European Tour chief Ken Schofield later said, "If the players were in that sort of mood, God help the Americans."

Nicklaus, a proud Buckeye, saw to it that his boys felt very much the home team at the opening ceremonies. As the teams marched in, they were welcomed by the plaintive bleating of four bag pipers. Shortly thereafter—and to the utter bemusement of the Europeans—the two hundred forty-member Ohio State marching band strutted up the eighteenth fairway, blaring out *LaBamba* and *Hang on Sloopy* at an amped-up 130 decibels. "The Best Damn Band in the Land," as it is known, blasted Buckeye fight songs, followed by the five national anthems representing all players.

Dobereiner's assertion of the importance of Day One would now be tested. Jacklin seldom made an error with his pairings in '83 and '85, and his gut feelings at Muirfield Village preserved his reputation for ingenuity. Two stood out.

At Ballesteros' suggestion, he once again used Seve in the mentor's role, pairing him with twenty-one-year-old countryman Olazábal, whom he had first encouraged as a sixteen-year-old. It would become a partnership for the ages with twelve points in their record fifteen appearances together.

"We knew the night before that we would be paired together," Olazábal explained. "Tony didn't know what to do with me. I was a rookie, I played well in 1986 when I was second behind Seve on the money list, but I didn't play that well in 1987. But Seve told Tony that we would be OK. I had never seen the Ryder Cup before, it was a totally new experience. I was used to playing in front of crowds but not like this. But playing alongside Seve I felt very comfortable, the pressure was there but I felt calm."

The new Spanish Armada would be his anchors in the Friday morning foursomes, just behind another powerful duo of Ian Woosnam and Nick Faldo. They certainly appeared to be an odd couple (Jacklin called them his David and Goliath) with Woosnam standing at 5-foot-4 and Faldo at 6-foot-3. Then there was Faldo's aloofness contrasted with Woosnam's animation, Faldo the methodical and stylish one, Woosnam aggressive and gritty.

Faldo was seen as the emergent European golfer, inspired by watching Jack Nicklaus on his parents' new color TV and, therefore, molded in the American style. "Woosie" was the throwback and would come to be seen as the embodiment of everything the American golfer was not: a throw-'em-down brawler, hard drinking and unapologetic–emblematic traits that, in fact, helped Europe thrive in these competitions. When *Golf Digest* previewed the Ryder Cup in its August issue, it featured a profile of Woosnam.

"There could hardly be a more complete opposite to the all exempt, all-college, all-mollycoddled American tour pro than Woosnam, a farmer's son whose earliest childhood memories are of shoveling out the cowsheds," Dai Davies wrote.

Indeed, Woosnam may have been wee, but he was a fireplug who developed a powerful swing from all those hay bales he threw around on the farm. He launched every ounce of his 146-pound frame into a swing that made him one of golf's longest drivers. That explosiveness meshed perfectly with Faldo's even keeled style. The chemistry was evident when Faldo and Woosnam rushed onto the course to discuss strategy as soon as they arrived.

"When Tony offered me the chance of partnering Ian Woosnam, I leapt at the opportunity," Faldo wrote in *Life Swings*. "Off the fairway, you could not find two more diverse personalities but on it our styles of play dovetailed perfectly."

Both came to Ohio at the top of their games. Faldo had won the first of his six majors two months earlier at The Open Championship at Muirfield. Woosnam was enjoying a marvelous season–his best to date–at the top of the European Order of Merit and the European Tour's money list with over £1 million in earnings.

Each was motivated, as well. Faldo had part of his reputation to redeem. Woosnam had an ax to grind.

Perhaps Jacklin's worst-ever decision as a Ryder Cup captain (and he didn't make many) was to choose Faldo as one of his three wild card picks in 1985. The ending of his marriage and the beginning of his swing change had culminated in a slump that Faldo was unable to shake at The Belfry. He was benched after his first match and played poorly in his last. As his teammates rollicked after the victory, he sulked.

"I could not find it in my heart to join in all those joyous celebrations," he recalled in *Life Swings*. "As far as I was concerned, the eleven other fellas had won the trophy. I simply did not feel part of the team, having failed to do my bit. And so, while Tony and the lads stood on the balcony at The Belfry spraying the jubilant spectators with champagne and Concorde flew overhead dipping its wings, I sat alone at a corner table in the clubhouse. One of the greatest moments in European golf and there was I, Little Jack Horner sitting in a corner."

Two years of the kind of hard work for which Faldo was known had him back at an elite level, more in line with the Ryder Cup record he enjoyed in the first four of his record eleven consecutive appearances.

Woosnam, meanwhile, was determined to shove it in the face of American golf. While he was becoming a folk hero in Great Britain, having finished in the Order of Merit's top ten for five uninterrupted years, he could barely scrape together sponsors' exemptions to play in a few PGA Tour events. He resented the stodgy officials of Augusta National for not inviting him to the Masters (which he would win in 1991) and the directors of the USGA for not widening paths for Europeans to qualify for the US Open. His aim was simple: to get to World No. 1 "so they can't ignore me."

Woosnam's one American major that year–the PGA Championship–had been a disaster. He couldn't deal with the oppressive Florida heat or the clingy Bermuda rough and missed the cut by a mile. He'd have to settle for making his mark in the US this week.

Woosnam, of course, had been a big part of the 1985 victory, teaming with Paul Way to form the successful Tiny Tots partnership. Way didn't make the '87 squad but the Welsh bantamweight was confident he could repeat his success with Faldo.

Jacklin opened play with Sam Torrance and Howard Clark with Langer teamed with Brown, who had been playing most of his golf in the US. Noticeably absent from the foursomes lineup was Lyle, Jacklin's other heavy hitter. Jacklin had famously left Lyle out of his fourball pairs in 1985, when he went 0-2 in alternate shot, influencing Jacklin's decision.

Nicklaus, looking for the early edge, led off with his strongest pairing of Kite and Strange, the PGA Tour's leading money winner with $714,974, followed by the fired-up Sutton and Pohl. Curiously, he broke up the historically unbeatable partnership of Nelson and Wadkins, pairing Wadkins with Mize third "on a hunch" and Nelson with Stewart last. Nelson said he could not have been "more delighted" by the pairing. Nicklaus, who was determined to play all twelve of his men before Sunday, said he paired by personality: the aggressive Wadkins fit with the laid-back Mize, Kite and Strange had requested to play together while Pohl and Sutton were both long hitters.

"Good for him," Jacklin said of Nicklaus' everyone-plays strategy. "I'm into winning points, not anything else. If somebody doesn't play until Sunday, you balance that against what you did earlier. You can outsmart yourself doing all this. I'm just flesh and blood, and so are my players. In the end, you just do it—and worry like hell you didn't do the wrong thing."

That's exactly what Jacklin must have been thinking as the matches got underway and exactly what Nicklaus must have been thinking when they ended. At one point, Jacklin's team trailed in all four foursomes matches (three down in the first match, three down in the second, four down in the third and two down in the last) and looking at an American sweep. At the close of play, Europe had its first-ever sweep of the fourball matches and a 6-2 lead.

Jacklin called it a "day of superior European golf" that left Nicklaus grousing that his team wasn't "tough" enough. Ballesteros played more brilliantly in a Ryder Cup than anyone before or since. Too few Americans were able to produce in the clutch.

Tim Rosaforte, writing for the *Palm Beach Post,* called the fourball session arguably "the worst afternoon in American golf history. If George Steinbrenner captained this team of Yankees instead of Jack Nicklaus," he wrote, "he'd trade them all."

Nicklaus got what he wanted out of his first two alternate shot pairings as the day dawned chilly under a cloudy sky. Strange and Kite handily defeated Torrance and Clark, 4-and-2, while making just birdies. "Nothing incredible," was the way Kite described the win. Sutton and Pohl then finished off Langer and Brown, 2-and-1, "playing smart and capitalizing on their mistakes," according to Sutton.

But as the day unfolded, the Americans couldn't match the great golf being played by the Europeans. Jacklin admitted "not feeling too swift" after eight holes of play, but everything started to turn his way in the match between Wadkins and Mize and Faldo and Woosnam. With the Americans four holes up at the turn, it seemed the best Europe could manage in the morning was a 3-1 deficit. That was until Wadkins, 12-4-1 in his previous Ryder Cups, got a bad case of the hooks. He and Mize dropped six of the last nine holes, two to European birdies, four because of their own bogeys.

Faldo, relishing his matchup as Open champion versus Masters champ, began the comeback by striping a 3-iron to within five feet on ten. Then, on the eleventh tee, a middle-aged man in a folding chair took one look at Woosnam and exclaimed, "Oh my! He's only a boy!" Woosnam said he sensed a "barely suppressed snigger" from the gallery before he outdrove Mize by 40 yards. "Yes," he said as he bent to pick up his tee. "But think what I'll be like when I grow up and become a man." Faldo laughed out loud, and, according to Woosnam's book *Woosie My Autobiography*, that's when the two men bonded.

A hole later, Wadkins found a bunker on the par-three twelfth then drove into a creek on fourteen. Faldo could sense the pressure reversing itself as Mize, a short hitter, felt he needed to draw the ball around the trees on the 490-yard, par-five fifteenth. When the drive clipped a branch and fell straight down, it left Wadkins 100 yards behind Faldo's drive. Wadkins had to lay up, and Woosnam wouldn't let the Americans off the hook. He produced a smashing 1-iron shot that carried 250 yards from an uphill lie into the wind and onto the green, leading to a birdie that evened the match. Another poor tee shot by Mize led to a bogey that forfeited the lead, and the match was sealed, 2-up, for Europe on eighteen, where the Americans three-putted from fifteen feet, trying for the winning birdie.

Wadkins got into shoving match with a TV cameraman on eighteen, storming off and shouting, "Get out of my fucking way." He then asked Nicklaus to bench him in the afternoon. "If I hadn't hit those bad shots on the front, we would have been 6-up at the end of nine," he said. "If I'd played anywhere close to my normal game, we win easily. I was fighting it all day."

That left Ballesteros and Olazábal against Nelson and Stewart in a match for which Seve could not have been more motivated. He came into the week with his usual grudge against the Americans, deepened further by being barred from the PGA Tour by Commissioner Deane Beman for all of 1986 following a dispute over the required number of tournaments played. Then, after hearing Nelson boast about his 4-0 Ryder Cup mark against him, Ballesteros had to contain himself after the first day's pairings were announced, staring down at his shoes and mumbling something to Jacklin, which the captain later paraphrased as, "I like this very much."

Still, there were questions surrounding Seve. He had only one win all year, and that was back in April. At the PGA Championship, he took himself out of the lead in the third round with two water balls on the last three holes, then shot 78 in the final round to fall into a tie for tenth.

"I'm trying to convince myself I'm a happy man," he said afterwards.

Fortunately, he had discovered one of the reasons for his choppy play the week before the Ryder Cup—a small muscle tear in his back. He had brought his own chiropractor with him to Ohio to tend to it. There was little doubt he would play through it.

Olazábal was feeling the jitters before that first Ryder Cup match when Ballesteros grabbed him. "I will never forget that little walk from the outing green to the first tee," he recalled years later. "I was shaking like a leaf. The crowds were huge. Very loud. So, I kept my head down, and Seve approached me as we were walking onto the first tee. He looked at me and said, 'Jose Maria, you play your game, I'll take care of the rest.' And he did."

The match was extremely well-played on both sides, beginning with Stewart's first-ever Ryder Cup putt for an eight-foot birdie winner on the first hole. But Ballesteros pulled off a brilliant shot from the bunker on seven, then drained a fast-moving 30-foot birdie putt on eight to even the match after being down two three holes before. He hit a great shot from the fairway bunker on ten and what Nelson called "as good a chip as I've ever seen" from thick grass on fifteen to set up a go-ahead birdie. Finally, protecting a 1-up lead, he turned things around on eighteen, when it appeared the Americans could pull out a halve.

Ollie had put his partner in a bunker to the right of the fairway 195 yards out with Stewart 35 yards closer on the fairway. Ballesteros was looking at an uphill shot with his ball sitting in a rut and the heels of his shoes flush against the lip. "No problema," he thought before sending a 3-iron soaring onto the green.

Understandably stunned, Stewart tried to cut his approach shot and watched in disbelief as it flew over the green to the rough on the hill behind it. Walking toward the green, Ballesteros raised his partner's hand in premature triumph as the pro-European gallery erupted. Nelson made a fantastic chip from there to nearly gimme range, but, after Olazábal masterfully eased his slick downhill putt four feet past the cup, Ballesteros finished off the amazing round for the par and the win.

"What we needed to do on the hole was get it close and we didn't get it close," Nelson explained afterwards. "I hit one of the best chip shots I ever hit in my life. I thought a four might win the hole. But Seve's partner made a great putt and Seve made a good one too."

Nelson wasn't disparaging Ballesteros now.

"That's about the best I've ever seen Seve play. He didn't miss a shot," he said." You could see a little bit of youth in Seve's partner but Seve more than made up for it. When you get beat 1-up by such a great player, you're disappointed but not depressed."

The British press, which had seen Seve at his best, asked him if it was his best round ever. He said it was difficult to choose but it was definitely among them. He should have been asked if it was his most satisfying. After all, he played as if he were carrying out a personal vendetta.

"It's nice to beat Larry Nelson after all these years," he said.

The scoreboard said it was 2-2, but the teams hit the lunch buffet in entirely different moods. Europe had won the morning by taking away the momentum and, if there were any doubt they would keep it, it soon lifted when Ballesteros chipped in from 10 feet on the first hole of his anchor match in fourballs. Taunting roars from the European fans on hand foretold the Americans their misery would only worsen. In fact, it took forty-two holes of golf before any American made a birdie and, by that time, the Europeans were off and running.

Nicklaus played everyone who sat out the morning, pairing four of them together in the first two games but getting nothing out of the Crenshaw-Simpson or Bean-Calcavecchia tandems. He then sent out the two pairings that won their morning matches—right into Jacklin's bear trap. The European captain had ruthlessly dropped three of his four players who had lost in the morning but kept together his powerhouse pairings at the bottom of his lineup. Faldo and Woosnam, Ballesteros and Olazábal obliged him by disposing of Sutton-Pohl and Strange-Kite, respectively. Worse yet for the Americans, Jacklin's hunch pairing of Gordan Brand Jr. and Jose Rivero dusted major champions Crenshaw and Simpson, 3-and-2, in the one match the US seemed certain to win. Bean and Calcavecchia blew their chances for a similar upset against Langer and Lyle, both major champions. They had had a 2-up lead with five to play, only to lose on the last hole. "That's like stealing a point there," Jim MacKay exclaimed on *ABC's* telecast.

Bean and Calcavecchia had even battled back from a two-hole deficit through six to go 2-up when Calc birdied thirteen from 13 feet. It was the lone glimmer of American hope at the time, and it quickly vanished. At fourteen, Calcavecchia missed a four-footer after Langer sank a 12-footer. At sixteen, Lyle's 25-footer earned a halve and the Americans could do no better than bogey on the last two holes. The match ended ingloriously when Calc topped a chip shot and Bean missed a shortie. You can't lose holes to pars in fourball.

Nicklaus rued that result but couldn't have been disappointed with the play of his bottom two pairings. Sutton and Pohl were 5-under. Faldo and Woosnam were 7-under. Strange and Kite were 6-under, Ballesteros and Olazábal 8-under. Sutton could have been speaking for both US pairings when he said, "Dan and I played well enough to win. We just played the wrong guys. We played good. They played perfect."

They were also unable to catch a break. The match was locked up at all square when, on the par-five eleventh, Woosnam and Pohl both went for the green in two. Pohl blocked his into the trees short and right of the narrow green. Woosnam blocked his shot on the same line, but the golf gods spit it out and it bounced down the slope onto the green 12 feet from the cup. Woosnam capitalized by sinking his putt for an eagle, then strutted away with a puckered grin. Faldo's 4-iron into the par-three twelfth barely made it onto the green after clearing the water and Sutton felt good about winning the hole after playing a marvelous shot five feet past the cup. But Faldo rattled his uphill 25-footer in for his birdie and Sutton, not the best putter, caught the edge of the cup and stayed out. "A body blow," Peter Alliss said on the shared telecast. And it was. The two Euros held on the rest of the way.

Ballesteros once again assumed his matador role with six birdies in his round, including a 16-footer on six, a 45-footer on ten, a 12-footer to halve fourteen, and a 22-footer to end the match on seventeen, leaving he and Olazábal 11-under for the day. He really couldn't do anything wrong, not even with gamesmanship on the opening hole. Strange had come up against Ballesteros before and knew he was a master of the art. Strange had a long putt, and Olazábal had just left his putt short on Strange's through line, the line of his putt past the hole. At the rules meeting the previous day, the teams agreed that no one could putt on an opponent's through line because, as Strange explained in *Us Against Them* by Robin McMillan, "you don't want people walking around on your through line as you could be putting on it if you miss the previous putt long." Olazábal wanted to putt out but Strange stopped him. "I said, 'Well, wait a minute, you can't do that. You're right on my through line,'" Strange later explained. "Then Seve came charging up. 'That bother you?' he said. 'That bother you?' I said, 'Yes, that *does* bother me.'

"And so, Seve stomped over to his chip and chipped it right into the back of the hole–then walked off the green pumping his fist at me!" Strange went on. "And I almost had to applaud him. More power to him. Goddamn, I was so mad I wanted to kill him."

Nicklaus had to applaud him as well. He marveled at how Ballesteros was able to concentrate on his own game while helping Olazábal.

"He not only hit his ball but Jose Maria's, too," he said. "He was so tied up in making Jose Maria relax, he was not worrying about himself. He was absolutely beautiful. He putted so well, it didn't matter how fast the greens were. He invented shots today. We do not have a Seve Ballesteros on our team, and we know it. He and Greg Norman are head and heels above everyone else in the world."

Jacklin concurred.

"I find Seve to be one of the most incredible human beings I've ever met," he said. "He becomes almost superhuman when it comes to these matches."

There were several takeaways from the day, beginning with the enormity of what Europe had accomplished. The fourballs session was the first time an American team had been swept in any session, and it led to Europe's biggest first-day lead anywhere, let alone on American soil, where US teams had outscored their opponents, 182-86, in the previous thirteen competitions.

It was also striking that the Europeans expertly handled the super-fast greens, which ran at 12.5 on the stimpmeter. Ballesteros had been lobbying the European Tour to keep the green speeds up as preparation for the Ryder Cup. It didn't happen, yet it didn't matter. Ballesteros called them the best he'd ever played.

Perhaps Faldo provided a clue in *Life Swings,* where he revealed that the Muirfield Village grounds crew had watered sections of the greens differently and had provided Nicklaus with that information, so his team knew where the soft spots were. Faldo also said Howard Clarke had overheard that discussion and was able to give the Europeans the same information.

Nicklaus noted, too, that it might have been a disadvantage for the Americans to be so familiar with the greens from the Memorial Tournament. They played entirely differently in September than they had in May. Nicklaus also couldn't help thinking about the matches that appeared locked up.

"The match that hurt this morning was Lanny and Larry. This afternoon, the way they were up, it was Bean and Calcavechhia. Those were two matches we gave away," he said, blaming those losses and others on the US PGA Tour, which he said was responsible for having made the players "soft."

"The European players are tougher," he said. "American golf is so competitive now, our guys rarely get themselves into position to win a tournament. They don't get the taste of winning like the Europeans do. When you get down to the last few holes of match play, we aren't as tough as the Europeans are."

Jack couldn't do anything about that now. He said he'd have to divert from his original plan and play his eight best players as much as possible on Day 2.

"There are twelve guys sitting in my house now who are very upset with themselves. It's not my job to kick them in the rear end. They have a lot of pride and we still have a chance of winning."

Dobereiner would have to be wrong about Day 1, however, and Langer knew it.

"If we continue to play like this, the more pressure they're going to feel," he said. "They can't afford to lose many more matches."

Nicklaus had another distressing problem. He noticed that every time he heard loud cheering Friday, he knew which side made a birdie, and that it wasn't his. The European fans, most of them British, may have been outnumbered ten to one but they were shouting down their mom-and-apple-pie-loving Ohio counterparts.

"I didn't see a lot of intensity by the American spectators," he bemoaned. "It sounded like we were in Britain. I'd like to see a more vocal American gallery. I don't want to see anything unsportsmanlike but we're trying to win the matches and it seemed like they were trying to be too polite. Our players need some encouragement. We're being overwhelmed."

So, to drum up enthusiasm, American officials pulled out the thousands of little American flags they intended to hand out on Sunday a day early, turning Muirfield Village into a Fourth of July parade without the fireworks. The Europeans found it amusing rather than off-putting.

"Even less pleasing to the eye," Faldo scoffed in *Life Swings*, "the wives of the US PGA officials had been dragged kicking and screaming from the beauty parlor to be dolled up like senior citizen cheerleaders, resplendent in more rhinestones than Dolly Parton. Having no idea who these ladies were, Woosie took one look at them on the first tee and enquired, 'Who the hell are those old birds?'"

Needless to say, it was for naught. Most of the attendees were still more concerned with Ohio State's football game at LSU that afternoon. Many brought portable radios and televisions to keep track of it. Sure, they were pulling for the old red, white and blue, but no one was going to lose any sleep over any of Andy Bean's bogeys. There may have been some half-hearted "USA, USA," chants but this was a long way from Lake Placid and the Miracle on Ice. Maybe the volume was turned up slightly. Not that there was much to cheer. The Europeans were at it again.

Bob Baptist of the *Columbus Dispatch* put it well:

"The sun was setting in the west and the Ryder Cup was disappearing as inexorably to the east when, finally, the United States began to play some good golf yesterday. But the long shadows at Muirfield Village Golf Club revealed it was late. Maybe too late."

Dawn's early light brought with it a half-hour frost delay and a temporary reprieve as the European team went right back to work making birdies. There wasn't much for the American galleries to so proudly hail. When long shadows ushered in dusk, the US deficit had only widened from the first day, 10 ½-5 ½. It would require what Nicklaus said would be "one of the most unbelievable comebacks in golf" to stop Europe from riding into Sunday's sunset holding onto Sam Ryder's Cup in Uncle Sam's backyard. Even the Americans' best golf might not be enough to stop the onslaught.

"I never thought I'd live to see golf played like I saw today. You run out of superlatives. It was incredible . . . incredible isn't good enough to describe it," Jacklin said in amazement. "This is why this event is so fantastic, players giving their all with no money at stake."

What Nicklaus saw, he didn't like.

"I've seen superior golf played by the European team. It's surprised me to see as much as I've seen," he said, exhausted by the spectacle. "This golf course wears down our fellas. I expected to see the Europeans wear down more. But they've worn down our players. They've worn down the course."

And they were having such a good time doing it.

Take Jacklin's "David and Goliath" pairing. Woosie had celebrated Friday's two victories with Faldo in typical Woosie fashion by knocking down a couple of beers and six glasses of wine, by Faldo's count.

"Although I am strictly a one beer and one glass of wine man, I had no fears on Woosie's behalf," Faldo wrote in *Life Swings.*" As I used to say to him, 'As long as you've got the mix right, I ain't worried, partner.'"

Just slightly more worried, Jacklin began the day by sending out the same four teams in foursomes that swept the fourball matches the previous afternoon. Nicklaus had only two teams who had won matches Friday, so he didn't have that luxury. He led off with Strange and Kite, who went 1-1 Friday (they'd be the only American pair to play all four times) and split up Sutton and Pohl, pairing Sutton with Mize and sitting Pohl the entire day. He attempted to rekindle old sparks, by pairing Nelson and Wadkins for the first time all week and went with Crenshaw and Stewart in the anchor match, in which Jacklin had ensconced Ballesteros and Olazábal for the third consecutive time.

The net result was another gain for Europe, a point added to its lead. As they did Friday morning, Strange and Kite once again got the US off to an early start by handling the weakest Euro partnership, Rivero and Brand Jr., 3-and-1. Sutton and Mize finally cracked the Faldo-Woosnam nut by fighting back from 2-down to secure a halve. But for the third straight time, Europe won the last two points of the session.

Nelson and Wadkins, who had won a still-unprecedented four points together in 1979, lost for the first time, 2-and-1, to Lyle and Langer in the first of two head-to-head matches that day. The teams traded spectacular shots, but the Europeans came away with more of them, like the two-iron Lyle hit three feet from the pin for an eagle on eleven or the 40-foot putt Langer raced into the cup on thirteen.

Ballesteros and Olazábal had to work a little harder for their third straight point. They lost the fourteenth hole to a birdie and the seventeenth to a par to allow Stewart and Crenshaw to close within one hole but pulled out the match by matching the Americans' bogey on the last hole. It would be a test of Olazábal's nerve. After he splashed out of a difficult lie that Ballesteros had left him in the bunker, they needed only to two-putt from 10 feet. Ballesteros asked his young partner for help reading the putt and Ollie told him, "Be careful, the green is fast, very fast." Ballesteros could hardly believe it when his putt kept rolling past the hole, leaving Olazábal with a five-foot comebacker. "That's really fast, isn't it?" he said. Olazábal then calmly made the putt that sealed the match.

It would be the last session won outright by the Europeans, but their five-point lead meant they could milk the sixteen remaining matches. The Americans calculated that they needed at least three points out of the afternoon fourballs and got only two. A desperate Nicklaus had switched out only one player from the morning, replacing Crenshaw with Bean to play with Stewart, leaving the other three pairings intact. The way the Europeans played, it wouldn't have mattered. Jack finally saw his men play some great golf, but he could have reached back fifteen years and paired himself with Tom Watson, and they still may not have beaten Faldo and Woosnam or Lyle and Langer on this afternoon.

Kite and Strange were 5-under par for fourteen holes in the lead-off match. Nelson and Wadkins were eight-under in the anchor match. Both lost. It was small consolation that the Americans finally took down Ballesteros and Olazábal, clearly gassed, thanks to Sutton and Mize, with Europe also able to absorb Brand Jr. and Eamonn Darcy's 3-and-2 loss to Stewart and Bean, after the Yanks made things comfortable for themselves with birdies on the first five holes. On the afternoon, the Europeans were collectively 25-under par, led by Faldo and Woosnam at 10-under and Lyle and Langer at nine-under.

"We just ran into a buzz saw all day. Every time I looked up, one of those guys was making a birdie or an eagle," Nelson said.

Strange later said that Nicklaus made a mistake by playing him and Kite in every session. "I thought Tom and I were an excellent foursomes pair but not fourball," he said in *Us Against Them*. "Tom and I played the same type of game, but we didn't make enough birdies for fourballs."

That was borne out by their records. Strange and Kite won their two matches in alternate shot and lost their two fourball matches. It wasn't for lack of fine play, however. They simply went up against Ballesteros and Olazábal, shooting six-under only to lose, 2-and-1. then Faldo and Woosnam. Then they shot 5-under in Friday's fourballs against Woosnam and Faldo and never had a chance.

"They got hit by the blitz both days," Nicklaus shrugged.

Woosnam and Faldo were determined to make up for the

half-point they felt they lost in the morning. They were a perfect fourball team and, as Woosnam wrote in *Woosie*, they took advantage of it.

"This was the Ryder Cup; this was America. There was no point in being cautious," he explained. "We had to go out there and seize control. It was resolved Nick would get into his groove and roll out the pars. I would attack Muirfield Village at every turn, taking every tiger line after tiger line, chasing every putt."

They were the definition of ham and egg. They never birdied the same hole, but they seemed to make a birdie on every one of them, including the first five and seven of the first eight. The match ended mercifully on the fourteenth green with Woosnam's 10-foot birdie putt. News of the 5-and-4 trouncing in the opening match sent shock waves around the course. Still, the Americans had a chance to get the three points they needed if they could somehow pull out the final match, a rematch of Langer and Lye against Wadkins and Nelson. The quality of golf was off the charts, including what Langer called the shot of his life, a chip-in from the deep rough on the tenth as he collapsed onto his back to ear-splitting roars from the visiting fans.

"If I fly it, it's in the bunker and I take five or six. It came out perfect and went in," he explained.

Perfection followed once more on eighteen. Langer and Lye were clinging to a 1-up lead, and it seemed that most of the 25,000 spectators were in the amphitheater surrounding the green. All four players, Langer and Lyle, Wadkins and Nelson, found the fairway. Lyle hit first, to six feet. Nelson made the green. The indefatigable Wadkins was coming off two straight birdies that kept the match alive after being dormie three. He was accustomed to hitting hero shots. He drew this one in and it landed a foot from the cup but didn't stick, leaving him inside 10 feet. After Lyle had hit his shot, he told his partner, "Knock it inside me and you'll be all right." Langer couldn't see where Wadkins' ball had finished, but he figured from the roar of the crowd that three would win the hole. He had 150 yards in and an 8-iron in his hands. The shot was perfect, falling out of the pink, late afternoon sky, almost directly into the hole. Unlike Wadkins' ball, it stuck, a foot away. Wadkins walked to the green, picked up Langer's ball, and the match was over.

"Larry hit a good shot. I hit a very good shot. Sandy hit a very, very good shot and Bernhard hit an even better shot," Wadkins said. "He almost holed that sucker on the fly. Win, lose or draw, anyone is happy to be involved in something like that. Do you realize I played those last five holes in five-under, and we lost ground?"

The Europeans had eight birdies, an eagle and the only bogey of the match. The Americans had seven birdies. Together on the afternoon, the teams combined for fifty-eight birdies and an eagle. But it seemed that anything the Americans did, the Euros did better.

"Our guys feel they haven't played that badly. They've just been beaten, and they know it.," Nicklaus said. "Yesterday we gave away a couple of matches. Today we fought to the end."

Trailing, 10 ½-5 ½, the United States would need to take 8 ½ points out of the twelve singles matches to reclaim the trophy. Crenshaw, who would face similar odds as US captain twelve years later, said, "We are going to have to play our natural asses off."

"They can do it," Nicklaus said. "They know it and I know it."

So did Jacklin. He knew from Muirfield in 1972 when Lee Trevino chased him down for the claret jug.

"The pundits thought it was all over. I never entertained those sort of thoughts–I'd been in the game too long," he wrote in *My Ryder Cup Journey.* "You never think it's all wrapped up. The Americans had produced several phenomenal last-day performances and I knew golf far too well to believe that the Fat Lady was clearing her throat just yet. I certainly felt comfortable with the lead, but you always have to wait and see what happens. That guy Murphy is never far away. Murphy's Law can take care of a helluva lot."

"Emotion in golf is fantastic when you're playing well, and so far, the Europeans have drowned us with it," Nicklaus added. "But it can work against you, too."

Especially on Ryder Cup Sundays. Although Europe captured the singles session to capture the Cup two years earlier, it was traditionally the province of the Americans, who usually exposed the opponents' lack of depth. The visitors had three impenetrable pairings the first two days. Used in eleven of the sixteen matches, Ballesteros-Olazábal, Faldo-Woosnam and Langer-Lyle went a combined 9-1-1 for 9 ½ of Europe's 15 ½ points. Now the big five accounted for a smaller percentage of the European whole. At least the US would have a chance to pick off the most vulnerable and create momentum.

Nicklaus employed a far different strategy than captain Crenshaw would during the historic US comeback in 1999. Expected to front-load his lineup, Nicklaus sent the least experienced players out early and hoped that his veterans still had a chance to win it late. And it nearly worked.

Jacklin spaced out his strongest players throughout his lineup, beginning with the eager Woosnam, who hadn't lost in the four matches he played with Faldo. Nicklaus threw out Bean first and the twelve-inch height difference between them was almost comical. Woosnam, though, gave away nothing when it came to length of the tee, leading Bean to wonder how the "little bitty fellow" outdrove him. It was Bean, however, who prevailed by taking advantage of the par threes. Woosnam, "out of gas" and "making a few too many mistakes," missed a chance to tie the match on seventeen when he couldn't get up and down from nine feet. They halved again on eighteen with pars, and the US had thrown the critical first blow of the day thanks to arguably its weakest link. Bean hadn't won a tournament since the previous May and had been battling tendinitis. Yet, he emerged from the week with an admirable 2-1 record.

Then it got interesting. Five of the first seven matches would go to the Americans. It could have been all seven. Pohl, all-square with Clark through seventeen, went from fairway bunker to deep rough to greenside bunker on eighteen and lost with a sloppy double bogey as Clark got a favorable line of sight ruling from the TV tower. Mize, 1-up through seventeen on Torrance, drove it the back of the hazard near where Clark was on eighteen and was forced to take a penalty drop after officials deliberated for several minutes.

He ultimately lost the hole to halve the match. That put Europe halfway to the three points it needed to retain.

In the end, the one match the US seemed certain to win doomed them. Irish journeyman Eamonn Darcy had never won a Ryder Cup match. He was staking an 0-8-2 record up against Crenshaw and anyone who watched Darcy swing that week probably thought they knew why he was 0-8-2. Dobereiner once described his swing as that of a man "picking a five-pound note from a grate with tongs." He went at the ball hard, but he had an extremely weak left-hand grip that forced his right hand to overcompensate so that his right elbow flew out wickedly, only to be slapped back into the correct position just before impact. It wasn't a swing made for pressure.

Crenshaw started off with a birdie to win the first hole, but Darcy responded with birdies on four and five to take the lead. Then, on six, Crenshaw, considered America's best putter, three-putted from 30 feet for bogey to fall two behind. Crenshaw might have been nicknamed Gentle Ben, but he had a temper, particularly with himself. Looking downward as he walked off the green, he spotted a buckeye–the shiny nut from the official state tree of Ohio.

"I just tapped it," Crenshaw bashfully claimed, like a kid downplaying hitting a baseball through a window. The blow missed the buckeye, hit the ground, and snapped the shaft of Crenshaw's iconic 1964 Wilson 8802 putter, the one he called "Little Ben," six inches above the head. "A fit of pique," Peter Alliss said on the telly. He'd have to spend the last twelve holes putting with the leading edge of his sand wedge and one-iron.

Two holes later, captain Nicklaus stopped by to check on proceedings.

"How's it going?" he asked Crenshaw.

"Not so good," Crenshaw replied, almost under his breath.

"What do you mean?" Nicklaus said.

Crenshaw covered his mouth and muttered, "I snapped my putter," which sounded more like, "I shnaptmaputr."

"You what? "I snapped my putter," he said more clearly.

Nicklaus couldn't believe it.

"What else could go wrong?" he asked.

"Psychologically I was shot," Crenshaw admitted after the round. "I've had that putter since I was fifteen. I felt like someone had taken a gun and shot me. It took me four holes to get over it."

Crenshaw was 3-down at that point. He was so good on the greens, however, that he fought his way back, even while standing eighteen inches behind his putts to compensate for the longer shafts. Darcy's nerves started to kick in, and he fell one behind with two to play after a bogey on sixteen. Putting wasn't Crenshaw's problem anymore. He faced a difficult chip out of the rough on seventeen, where he needed to land just over the bunker. It didn't make it, and he could only watch Darcy pull even with a brilliant birdie. Eighteen wasn't any better. He drove it into the left creek, took a penalty stroke and made bogey. Darcy left himself with a five-foot putt out of the sand to win the hole. But it was no ordinary five-footer. It was a downhill runner that easily could have raced past the hole, necessitating a pressure-filled comebacker of perhaps as long as ten feet. The Irishman took forever surveying it.

"All I could think was, 'Don't fucking miss,'" he revealed years later. "It was the hardest putt I ever stood over. It was all downhill and oh, so fast. I thought I could hole it, but if I didn't, I didn't think I would be able to get the one back, there would be just nothing to stop it. There was a little break to the left and I just kissed it."

The ball fell in through the side door.

"When old Darce sank that putt . . . well what could you say?" Jacklin exclaimed. "It was a dream come true for us—a victory that we felt could change the entire course of world golf."

Just minutes later, Simpson finished off Rivero, handing the US its fifth win in seven matches. Shockingly, big guns Faldo and Lyle, both previously unbeaten, joined Woosnam among the early victims, to Calcavecchia and Kite, respectively, while Stewart thumped Olazábal. After Crenshaw's loss, however, Europe needed just one more point to retain the Cup and another half to win it outright—and it still had its other two big guns, Langer and Ballesteros, on the course. As it turned out, they'd be the ones to administer the *coup de gras*.

Langer was matched with Nelson for the third time. It was a see-saw battle that got to the last hole all-square. They each had a putt of two feet and looked at each other as if to say, "good, good?" Nelson answered Langer's quizzical look by picking up both balls. They didn't realize it at the time, but by halving the match, it gave Europe its critical half point with three matches left. The agreement was detrimental to the US, which needed every half point it could get. Ironically, Nicklaus later told Nelson he should have made Langer putt it.

"Jack, I remember you giving Jacklin a putt on the last hole in 1969," Nelson reminded him. "I thought we were out here to have a good time."

Fittingly, Ballesteros now had the chance to pick up the winning point against Strange. The match, Ballesteros later wrote, was played in a "charged, tense atmosphere." According to Strange, Ballesteros immediately resorted to gamesmanship on the first hole, when the Spaniard, with an obviously longer bunker shot, asked Strange who was away—before holing his, of course. Ballesteros later claimed that Strange played his third shot out of turn on ten. By then, Ballesteros had a two-hole lead, which Strange reduced to one by the twelfth.

"I realized I couldn't afford any loss of concentration: the way things were going in my game was crucial. We had to forget any idea that the lead we'd built up over the first two days would give us a comfortable victory. That was wishful thinking."

When they got to seventeen, Ballesteros had regained his two-hole lead. After Ballesteros hit an easy 8-iron from 160 yards onto the green and lagged the first putt nicely, Alliss set the scene for the TV audience:

"They've been saying 'Seve's not good enough. They've been saying Seve's lost it. They've been saying Seve's finished . . . and here we have Severiano Ballesteros with a two-foot putt to win the Ryder Cup."

It found the heart of the cup for the Cup.

"How appropriate that it was Seve who should earn the historic point and cinch our first victory on American soil in the sixty-year history of the Ryder Cup," Derek Lawrenson wrote in the *Daily Mail.* "For he, more than any European, has done much to enhance the image of golf on this continent and raise our status. Now he has players fit to stand alongside him and do justice to his genius. An unforgettable player, Seve. An unforgettable weekend in Ohio."

Jacklin choked up as he told a TV interviewer, "This is the greatest week of my life." Nicklaus returned to his "toughness" theory and pointed out that the matches were lost on the eighteenth hole, which his team failed to win any of the seven times the singles matches got that far. Indeed, Ballesteros was the only European winner whose match ended before it reached the final hole. Had Crenshaw, Pohl and Mize simply parred the last hole, the United States would have won back the Cup, 14 ½ to 13 ½.

Furman Bisher, the venerable columnist for the *Atlanta Journal* was blunt: "Some had come to the eighteenth playing not for a fat purse but for a flag, and discovered they could choke on behalf of patriotism, and it hurt."

As if to claim the green as their own, the Europeans danced all over it in an impromptu can-can line. Olazábal started it by with an awkward impersonartion of a Flamenco dancer. If the figure of old Abe Mitchell could have leapt from the trophy's crest, he doubtlessly would have joined them. Nicklaus came over and told them not to worry, he was digging up the green on Monday. Langer unfurled a German flag, Torrance waved Scotland's.

"It will be a different world from now on," Jacklin said.

The Americans watched the celebration from the hillside. Some had tears in their eyes. Crenshaw, 0-3 for the week with his wife expecting a daughter any day, was devastated. "I'd just like to say one thing and that's that I was not any help to my team all week and I'm very disappointed," he said.

The European party ended only after the revelers reached a point of exhaustion.

"The Ryder Cup was fast becoming renowned among European golfers not only as an event of intense pressure and world class golf, but also as the time and place of the best parties in the game," Woosnam wrote in *Woosie.*

"To retain the Ryder Cup by triumphing on American soil for the first time in the 58-year history of the contest was a feeling like no other," Faldo wrote in *Life Swings.* "Tony insisted each and every player make his way to the beer tent where all two thousand European fans had assembled and were calling our names. Supporters and players danced, sang and generally made merry—I even danced on a table—as the Americans slunk away to lick their wounds. Whether it was the beer or the sense of jubilation, armed with a penknife the entire European team reassembled in the car park where we unscrewed the number plates from the courtesy Cadillacs—they read 'Ryder Cup '87'"

At one point, Faldo and Woosnam stripped off their tee shirts and tossed them into the rollicking mob of well-quaffed supporters. Not that the Americans begrudged the Euros their fun. They understood the history that was being made.

"They had all the right in the world to be excited," Strange said. "All you can do is shake their hands and applaud them, because they came over to America and beat us. It was a hell of a win."

"You can speculate and second-guess all you want, but the fact remains they just played better. I'm not happy about it, but I accept it and congratulate them," Nicklaus said, saving his disappointment for a team meeting before the official closing dinner.

"Muirfield was not nice, and Jack let us know about it when we finished," Payne Stewart disclosed. "Jack just wore us out. He told us, "You guys just don't know how to win. How many matches were we leading going into eighteen and didn't win them? Look at you, Payne Stewart. You make all this money on tour but how many tournaments have you won? Why don't you win more?' He said, 'you guys need to learn how to win or you're going to continue getting beaten in this thing.' There wasn't any sugarcoating it. I'll tell you, that speech was good for me."

Jack had become a victim of his own initiative in urging Lord Derby to bring continental players into the mix. Not that he fretted over it. Instead, he urged the PGA Tour to change its "archaic" membership requirements for foreign players, which demanded that someone play in a minimum fifteen events or be limited to five exemptions. It's why he was unable to invite Seve Ballesteros to the Memorial.

Most of the post-match talk in America centered around fixing the selection process. As Nicklaus suggested, Ray Floyd would be the first US captain to have wild card picks for the 1989 Ryder Cup at The Belfry.

The Europeans, meanwhile, didn't have to change a thing.

They zipped home on the Concorde, receiving a congratulatory message from prime minister Margaret Thatcher before they landed at Heathrow to a heroes' welcome, "although," Woosnam wrote, "not everyone was impressed, notably the policeman who pursued me for thirty-five miles on the M1, M6, and M54 . . . it was 1:30 am when the police clocked me at 112 mph. After an appeal, I was banned from driving for six months."

His driving of the golf ball had done enough.

"Against the odds, against America . . . we had won, at home and away; and, in victory, we had demonstrated that European golfers could hold their own on both sides of the Atlantic," Woosnam wrote.

As Jacklin said, "It will be a different world from now on."

It wasn't just that the Europeans had cracked the American mystique. It was that, from that point on, it was the Americans who had to prove themselves, and often didn't.

"A lot of Americans actually fell by the wayside when the real heat was on," Jacklin said. "That was interesting because through the years we'd always seen the Americans coming through and always holing those putts when they had to hole them. We sort of humanized them that week. All of a sudden, under real pressure, they realized they're human like everybody else. They make mistakes."

Perhaps, one had to go back to Friday afternoon to find the correct metaphor when Strange had to step back from a shot three times. "European bee," Ballesteros quipped.

And that bee has been vexing the Americans ever since.

DAY 1
FOURSOMES
Curtis Strange/Tom Kite (US)) defeated Sam Torrance/Howard Clark (E) 4-and-2 Hal Sutton/Dan Pohl (US) defeated Ken Brown/Bernhard Langer (E) 2-and-1 Nick Faldo/Ian Woosnam (E) defeated Lanny Wadkins/Larry Mize (US) 2-up Seve Ballesteros/Jose Maria Olazábal (E) defeated Larry Nelson/Payne Stewart (US) 1-up **Session tied, 2–2**
FOURBALLS
Gordon Brand Jr./Jose Rivero (E) defeated Ben Crenshaw/Scott Simpson (US) 3-and-2 Sandy Lyle/Bernhard Langer (E) defeated Andy Bean/Mark Calcavecchia (US) 1-up Nick Faldo/Ian Woosnam (E) defeated Hal Sutton/Dan Pohl (US) 2-and-1 Seve Ballesteros/Jose Maria Olazábal (E) defeated Curtis Strange/Tom Kite (US) 2-and-1 **Europe wins session 4–0** **Europe 6, United States 2**
DAY 2
FOURSOMES
Curtis Strange/Tom Kite (US) defeated Jose Rivero/Gordon Brand Jr. (E) 3-and-1 Nick Faldo/Ian Woosnam (E) halved with Hal Sutton/Larry Mize (US) Sandy Lyle/Bernhard Langer (E) defeated Lanny Wadkins/Larry Nelson (US) 2-and-1 Seve Ballesteros/Jose Maria Olazábal (E) defeated Ben Crenshaw/Payne Stewart (US) 1-up **Europe wins session 2 ½–1 ½** **Europe 8 ½, United States 3 ½**
FOURBALLS
Nick Faldo/Ian Woosnam (E) defeated Curtis Strange/Tom Kite (US) 5-and-4 Andy Bean/Payne Stewart (US) defeated Eamonn Darcy/Gordon Brand Jr. (E) 3-and-2 Hal Sutton/Larry Mize (US) defeated Seve Ballesteros/Jose Maria Olazábal, 2-and-1 Sandy Lyle/Bernhard Langer (E) defeated Lanny Wadkins/Larry Nelson (US) 1-up **Session tied 2–2** **Europe 10 ½, United States 5 ½**

DAY 3
SINGLES
Andy Bean (US) defeated Ian Woosnam (E) 1-up
Howard Clark (E) defeated Dan Pohl (US) 1-up
Sam Torrance (E) halved with Larry Mize (US)
Mark Calcavecchia (US) defeated Nick Faldo (E) 1-up
Payne Stewart (US) defeated Jose Maria Olazábal, 2-up
Scott Simpson (US) defeated Jose Rivero, 2-and-1
Tom Kite (US) defeated Sandy Lyle (E) 3-and-2
Eamonn Darcy (E) defeated Ben Crenshaw (US) 1-up
Bernhard Langer (E) halved with Larry Nelson (US)
Seve Ballesteros (E) defeated Curtis Strange (US) 2-and-1
Lanny Wadkins (US) defeated Ken Brown (E) 3-and-2
Gordon Brand Jr. (E) halved with Hal Sutton (US)
United States wins session 7 ½–4 ½
EUROPE WINS RYDER CUP 15–13

1991

The War by the Shore

OCEAN COURSE, KIAWAH ISLAND
UNITED STATES 14 ½, EUROPE 13 ½

The editors at *Golf World* likely had the faintest notion of how prophetic and accurate their September 20, 1991 magazine cover would become. Riffing off Operation Desert Storm, which had occurred nine months previously, they dubbed the upcoming Ryder Cup on the South Carolina coast the "War by the Shore."

The Gulf War had become the Golf War, and, while the Europeans chafed at the language, this transformational confrontation between the United States and Europe suited the metaphor. That one week turned the Ryder Cup into a veritable battleground, spiking emotions of both teams and supporters into a fever pitch that has not abated since. It had all the elements: revenge and revilement, raw nerves and heroism, patriotism and pathos, controversy and conceit, a treacherous golf course and a spellbound international television audience.

In fewer than fifteen years, Jack Nicklaus' 1977 initiative to even the sides had achieved much more than that. Gone were the days when the golfing sons of Great Britain and Ireland gallantly threw themselves at the Americans as a sacrificial Charge of the Light Brigade. While destined to lose, those teams gallantly held the flag high, as they hurtled toward their valley of death. No more. Europe was now the bully on the beach, kicking sand into American faces. The Ryder Cup had been tilted on its axis, and the US team had had enough of it.

The Americans begrudgingly accepted that continental Europe's first victory in 1985 was for the good of golf. Then came the stinging first home loss in 1987. When, two years later, their mission to bring the Cup home from The Belfry ended in the bitterest of ties, the Americans were seized by frustration. The Ryder Cup had become a vendetta.

Perhaps it was an omen when the Concorde, having swept over Kiawah Island's Ocean Course before approaching Charleston's airport, was forced to manually crank down the landing gear. This ride could be far bumpier than the Europeans' last trip to Muirfield Village. The opposition was roused this time, and so was the American public. The stars and stripes flapped on nearly every front lawn on Kiawah Island, while visors and sweatshirts in the merchandise tent displayed an emphatic message: "The Cup belongs here."

There was undoubtedly a swell of patriotism after the US military decimated Saddam Hussein's army in the Gulf War. Yet, the nation's gung-ho chest-thumping appeared as peculiar and in-your-face jingoism to the Europeans, who pointed out that their troops were also part of the allied coalition. But the Americans, too, had reason to be perturbed. The galleries two years earlier at The Belfry, as David Feherty wrote in his *"Totally Subjective History of the Ryder Cup,"* were "juiced up and in full, knob-waving, gloat mode. It was very loud, and a tough place to be an American." Jack Whitaker of *ABC TV* fame attended as an observer and called the "fractious" behavior of the British galleries the worst he'd ever seen.

US captain Dave Stockton was just as determined to make Kiawah Island a tough place to be a European. Certainly, no previous American captain had worked as hard at it as Stockton, as he turned his captaincy into a two-year, fulltime job. If Lee Trevino was too laid back, Nicklaus too domineering and Raymond Floyd too overwhelmed, the competitive Stockton seemed to strike the right balance in bringing his team together. "He was the first modern (American) captain," future captain Corey Pavin noted. His emphasis was on preparedness and motivation. He sought to gain an edge on the opposition by bringing his players to the newly minted

Ocean Course as often as possible before the matches. He sought to use every motivational tool at his disposal and, if that meant handing out camouflage-patterned caps, so be it.

As Stockton told *Golf Digest*, "I'll take full responsibility for that. We'd just finished the Gulf War. Patriotism was running high, and I wanted to take advantage of that. I wanted my team to bond."

Stockton would have his war. Originally, though, it was to be waged not on the shore but in the desert, at the Players Stadium Course at PGA West in LaQuinta, California. Fabled—and feared—architect Pete Dye was carving that course out of sand and rock when the 1991 venue was announced six years ahead of time at the 1985 PGA Championship. True to his reputation, Dye intended to turn it into the Ryder Cup's most difficult course ever.

As it turned out, the man who had earned the nickname, "The Marquis de Sod," would indeed provide a test in 1991, but across the continent at the newly created Ocean Course, which would become almost as big a story as the competition itself. It existed only as beachfront property when, in 1987, Jim Awtrey, the newly appointed executive director of the PGA of America, began to have doubts about staging the competition at PGA West. For starters, the PGA Tour pros who sampled Dye's work at the 1987 Bob Hope Classic didn't share the architect's philosophy. He wanted to throw into sharp relief the true talent gap existing between hacker and Hall of Famer.

As Dye wrote in his memoir, *Bury Me in a Pot Bunker*: "With its confrontational design, angled water hazards, monster bunker and desert aura, I felt I had created not only the hardest golf course in the world but a showcase for the talent of the PGA Tour. I couldn't wait for the professionals to show their stuff against the Players Stadium Course."

Instead, he incited a rebellion. The course was too hard, those pros said, and they presented a petition to Commissioner Deane Beman that it be dropped from the four-course lineup that made up the Hope.

Raymond Floyd called Dye's design "spiteful" and "belligerent" while a "sick and tired" Tom Watson bemoaned that the course "requires you to execute shots that no sane golfer should be expected to play."

With that already in mind, Awtrey fretted over typical September conditions in the California desert, when temperatures could very well break 100 degrees without a drop of rain. Excessive heat at PGA National in Florida nearly destroyed the greens at the 1987 PGA Championship. And there were also television considerations surrounding the western time zone. The PGA was receiving a rights fee for the first time from *NBC,* and the *BBC* objected to the eight-hour time-zone difference. With the '87 Ryder Cup having been such a success at Muirfield Village, there was talk of the '91 Cup being played there once again.

It wasn't that easy. The PGA had a licensing deal with Landmark Development Corporation, which operated PGA West. Awtrey hoped to persuade Landmark's co-founder, Joe Walser, the man who gave him his first job in golf, to let the PGA out of his contract. Walser immediately declined but lobbed back an alternative idea. Landmark, Walser explained, had acquired the Kiawah Resort on the South Carolina coast south of Charleston, and was planning to build a new course on a virgin strip of beachfront to be designed by none other than Pete Dye and his capable partner, his wife Alice. Awtrey didn't have any other options, so he agreed to the half-baked plan. Pete and Alice, with an unlimited budget and a clean canvas, were presented with an architect's dream.

It was love at first sight for Pete when he first laid eyes on the dunes, the ocean, the Stono River, the marshes and scrub oaks and wax myrtles sculpted into gnarly shapes by the wind. "I would have bent down on my knees and begged (perhaps even traded in for Alice) for the opportunity to build a course on such a magnificent property," he wrote. He was, he said, "like a kid with a lollipop," calling the site, "the best piece of land that I have worked on in the Northern Hemisphere."

Now, when it came to the Ryder Cup, Dye believed that European success came, in part, from the greater experience of coping with varying conditions. PGA Tour pros were being spoon-fed perfectly manicured layouts where they held onto their tour cards with conservative game plans, safe fairways and greens approaches that consistently produced low scores. Meanwhile, European Tour players were accustomed to a wide range of challenging conditions and course design features that required imaginative shot making. Dye built risk factors into his layouts. To him, simple wasn't sublime. He differed from his contemporaries by using preliminary plans only as a rough outline. The real work came on site in heavy machinery, used as a sculptor would wield a chisel, and he could be aggressive in altering the topography. He not only tested a player's skills but also his mind and endurance. He applied visual intimidation and optical illusions and made a point of making the finishing holes among the most challenging.

Dye had the ocean, the salt marshes and the elements. As the Scots say, 'No wind, no golf" and he had plenty of that. The only thing he lacked was time. The change in venue came in May of 1989, and the first shovel pierced the ground in July. Two months later, whatever prep work they'd put in was obliterated by Hurricane Hugo, with winds of up to 140 miles per hour. It was the largest loss-producing hurricane (to date) in US history, and it essentially denuded Kiawah Island.

The disaster cut both ways. The hurricane destroyed centuries-old oak trees and forced Dye's team to invent novel ways of replanting sea oats in the dunes. It made an exceedingly-tight timeframe even tighter, raising doubts over whether the project could be completed on time. But, with road access to the island blocked and authorities fixed solely on emergency clean-up operations, Dye was left alone to do his work, unnoticed and unsupervised, eighteen hours at a time. Today, environmental oversight would most likely not have permitted his heavy hand on the tiller. And, we would not have had one of America's great golf courses–or one of the most dramatic Ryder Cups of all time.

For instance, Alice Dye desired an ocean view for each hole, but that required some fairways to be elevated six feet, so that every hole would be exposed to the wind. Similarly, she favored a drama-filled par-three seventeenth hole, as the Dyes had built at TPC Sawgrass, the home of The Players Championship. They then carved out an eight-acre lake that ran along the entire 197-yard length of the hole with nothing but sea oats and dunes to swallow any bail-out shots that ran left or long of the huge offset green. Thrashing ocean winds would only rachet up the hole's tension.

"When this course opens, it can't be just any old golf course," project director Chris Cole said. "It's got to be born Miss America." And it was.

The team Europe brought to court Miss America featured four of the top five players in the World Rankings, led by World No. 1 Ian Woosnam and including No. 2 Jose Maria Olazábal, No. 3 Nick Faldo and No. 5 Seve Ballesteros. With Aussie Greg Norman holding down the fourth spot, the top-ranked Americans fell in at Nos. 6 through 8: Payne Stewart, Paul Azinger and Fred Couples, the vanguard of a new generation of US stars.

Depth, as always, favored the US, however, with an average world ranking of 19 compared to Europe's 34. The Americans also had the edge in experience. Seven players (including Lanny Wadkins, Mark Calcavecchia, Mark O'Meara and captain's pick Chip Beck) returned from the 1989 matches to join their captain, Ray Floyd (Stockton's interesting wild card pick) and Hale Irwin, who qualified for the first time since 1981. Steve Pate, Wayne Levi and Pavin rounded out the squad as rookies. By contrast, five Europeans would make their Ryder Cup debuts, starting with Colin Montgomerie, a cub who would grow into a Ryder Cup lion. The aforementioned Feherty was making his only Cup appearance, along with fellow newbies Steven Richardson, Paul Broadhurst and David Gilford. Savvy veterans Bernhard Langer, Mark James, Sam Torrance rounded out the squad.

The biggest difference on the European side was the man in charge. Tony Jacklin had stepped aside after guiding Europe to two wins and a tie in his four captaincies. He and Ballesteros were like a Bill Belichick-Tom Brady combination that made Europe's resurgence possible. While Ballesteros set an example of resolve and courage on the course, it was Jacklin who convinced his players they could beat the Americans and who shrewdly devised the tactics and strategy to do so.

Jacklin's replacement, Bernhard Gallacher, was more qualified than anyone to take over. He was a veteran of nine Ryder Cups as a player and was Jacklin's right hand man at The Belfry in '89. But he was far less intense than his predecessor. *The Telegraph's* Michael Calvin perfectly described Jacklin as "an urgent, emotional figure whose suntanned face reflected the state of play with far greater clarity than the scoreboard." Gallacher was a tough cookie, but he wasn't meant for monuments.

As it was, the hangover of hostilities from 1989 was revived even before the Europeans boarded the Concorde for the speedy hop over, when Faldo fanned the flames with a few parting comments.

"The disappointing thing is that even though we've won on the last three occasions, the Americans still won't recognize we're number one," he griped. "Perhaps if we can hit them again, they might accept the truth."

It was Stockton who returned the fighting words on behalf of his players.

"It doesn't take an Einstein to understand what Faldo's comments meant to my team," he fired back. "They read the reports where he said we're number two–I don't think any American is ever going to get used to being second in anything."

Deepening the animosity was a stunt by a local radio disc jockey, Michael D. Forcier, who specialized in crank phone calls. The guy thought it would be a clever idea to wage a "Wake Up the Enemy" campaign by urging listeners to ring European rooms in the middle in of the night. *Damn Yankees Dirty Tricks*, trumpeted a headline in Britain's *Post* tabloid. When Faldo's wife Gill received an obscene phone call Gallacher threatened to call the FBI. The *BBC* retaliated by rousing Forcier with a call to his home at 4 a.m.

The battle lines were even more firmly drawn that evening at the big Wednesday banquet, where the seating arrangements cast the Europeans off to the side and situated the Americans front and center. Both teams viewed a screening of a twenty-minute film, *History of the Ryder Cup,* produced by the PGA of America. If it were meant to peeve the Euros, it succeeded, for it should have been entitled *A One-sided History of the Ryder Cup.*

"Of course, we figured that would be good, see a bit of the old boys playing," Faldo recalled a few years later. "And we're sitting there and watching this and the only European person we saw was (when) Jack Nicklaus put his arm around Tony on the last green in '69. It didn't show one European player hit a shot."

Seve was furious, as was Ken Schofield, executive director of the European Tour. "Shameful," he cried out.

"Bernard was too diplomatic. Ken Schofield was seething, and I think most of the some of the old school—we were seeing as well as well," Faldo said. "Really, we should have got up and walked out fine. If it's gonna be like that, let's have it like that."

To the Euros, it was as if the PGA of America were symbolically sticking a knife through Samuel Ryder's heart, not unlike the actual pain Steve Pate was feeling at the moment, back in a Charleston hospital. A caravan of limousines had ferried the teams to the banquet, and, as Feherty wrote in his history of the Ryder Cup, his then-wife Carolyn had set off a chain reaction by distracting their driver just as their car was nearing a stoplight. The driver slammed on the brakes, and the car carrying Pate and Pavin slammed into them and was rear-ended by the car carrying Azinger and Beck. Pate wasn't wearing a seatbelt and, as Feherty put it, "parked his ribs into a decanter of Jack Daniels." His availability for the entire week was in question. After blistering the course with a 65 that day, he had been very much in Stockton's plans as a partner for the bulldog Wadkins.

The final practices came and went. Langer made a hole-in-one in more favorable conditions on the brutal seventeenth, followed by more militaristic displays at the opening ceremony—a fighter jet flyover, a Marine honor guard and a drill team from the Citadel. It all played out in brilliant sunshine, but the warming fall weather wasn't as benign as it seemed. All week, the two teams enjoyed a mild, southeasterly wind. Overnight, however, it switched direction and gained intensity. The difficult stretch of closing holes would play into its teeth for the remainder of the competition.

"Diabolical," Hale Irwin said, pun intended. "It is a typical Pete Dye course, built for low, raking drives and high, flying approach shots. But how do you play those kind of approach shots in this wind?"

They were about to find out. Gallacher and Stockton matched wits for the first time in the morning foursomes with the lineups boomed out by ring announcer Michael Buffer. Two of Gallacher's pairings were automatic, and he sent out Ballesteros and Olazábal first and Faldo and Woosnam last. He placed veterans Langer and James in the two-hole but gambled by pairing rookies Montgomerie and Gilford in the third match. Stockton, with Pate unavailable, led off with Azinger and Beck, followed by Floyd and Couples, Wadkins and Irwin, Stewart and Calcavecchia.

Zinger and Beck were unbeaten as rookie partners at The Belfry, while the crusty Floyd had been picked specifically to pair with the young Couples. Although preferred in Stockton's poll of his players, Floyd was a somewhat controversial selection, because it meant bypassing John Daly, who had emerged from oblivion to power his way to the PGA Championship crown. Daly didn't grouse about it. He sent Stockton a FAX, "Good luck and Kick butt," which Stockton pinned to the American team's bulletin board. Irwin, like Floyd, was a throwback to the old days, but both O'Meara and Stewart declined to play with him given Irwin's intimidating persona. According to Curt Sampson's book, *"The War by the Shore,"* it seemed Wadkins was the only guy who wanted to play with him.

"What wimps," Wadkins said. "I told them, 'He'll be on *your* team.' So I said, 'I'll take him.' Shit, who wouldn't want Hale Irwin?"

Stockton, meanwhile, had guessed that Gallacher would place Ballesteros and Olazábal in the anchor spot, their usual place whenever Jacklin was filling out the lineup card. He didn't want Azinger up against Seve, considering their histrionics of two years previously. Instead, they were hooking antlers again and bringing the contentious tone from *off* the course *on* to it as what Dermott Gilleece of the *Irish Independent* ranked the two most implacable rivals in Cup history. Their competitive intensity extended even into their captaincies: Ballesteros in '97, Azinger in '08..

Their relationship had actually begun on a good note. Partnered with Azinger in the final rounds of the 1987 PGA and 1988 US Open, Ballesteros generously offered Zinger encouragement and to stay relaxed. However, that rapport all changed when they were competitors in the first singles match at The Belfry. After halving the first hole, Azinger wedged in to three feet, Ballesteros to 12. When they got to the green, Ballesteros surprised Azinger by telling him his ball was damaged and that he wanted to take it out of play. When Zinger asked to look at the ball, he discovered groove marks but no visible cuts.

According to his autobiography, *Zinger,* he told Ballesteros that in the US, the ball needs to be visibly cut. "European rules say this ball is unfit for play," Seve countered, before the referee was called over, agreeing with Azinger.

"This is the way you want to play today, we can play this way," Ballesteros said smugly.

As he so often did in these situations, Ballesteros drained his 12-footer while Azinger missed his three-footer. But, undeterred, the American would somehow get the best of the Spaniard with a 1-up victory, even as Ballesteros contested two of Azinger's drops on ten and eighteen. Although it was the first match of the day, it eventually meant that the Europeans wouldn't win outright. Ballesteros was distraught over the loss.

It didn't take long for tensions to return–and escalate–at Kiawah, when Ballesteros asked for–and got–a drop from a bad lie on No. 2 and another favorable ruling after a lost ball on four.

"By the ninth hole I was livid," Azinger related in his autobiography. "When Jose hit his drive off to the right, I was right there to spot the drop. The referee was intimidated by Seve and Jose, so he simply stood there and waited to see how we would settle things. Seve and Jose wanted to drop the ball much farther up the fairway from where I thought the ball had gone into the water. 'You need to drop it back here,' I said, as I pointed to the original position I had indicated. Reluctantly, Seve dropped the ball at that spot."

The Americans were 3-up at the turn when the Euros charged that they had switched to a different compression ball two holes earlier. Olazábal had noticed it at the seventh but didn't say anything. When Gallacher became aware of it, he told Ballesteros to appeal. Nothing came of it, because the infraction had occurred two holes earlier.

Zinger told Ballesteros he wasn't trying to cheat.

"I did not accuse you of cheating," Ballesteros said. "Cheating and ignorance of the rules are two different things."

They continued to vex one another the rest of the match. Azinger noted that Ballesteros had somehow developed a cough and later dubbed him "The King of Gamesmanship." Ballesteros said he had the flu (in reality, he had allergies) and accused Azinger of crowding him. Azinger and Beck, who missed a four-footer for par immediately after the dustup, were rattled, and so, apparently, was Ballesteros, who needed Olazábal to do most of the heavy lifting. The Americans ended up losing their lead and the match, but it was the only match they lost that morning.

Couples, with his sublime, effortless swing, hit a superb shot into seventeen that sealed a 2-and-1 victory for him and Floyd over Langer and James, while the all-rookie pairing of Gilford and Montgomerie were schooled by Wadkins and Irwin, as Pate sat out the session. Irwin later said he was inspired by rumors that Montgomerie had said, "too bad it didn't kill him," when Pate was injured. He never did. Still, Irwin reveled in his play: "I wanted Monty and I got him. I threw some darts in there that were pretty spectacular." Even Montgomerie was impressed with what he called "Godlike shots" from his opponent. It was a clear backfiring of Gallacher's opening gambit. So, too, was counting on the previously indomitable partnership of Faldo and Woosnam to repeat their magic. They may have been ranked as the top two players in the world, but both men were struggling coming into the week. Stewart and Calcavecchia took them down in the anchor match, 1-up, as the two Brits griped about the Bermuda greens.

With the US up, 3-1, the mood around the course was euphoric, observed Ken Burger of the *Charleston Post Courier*: "one that football fans associate with having a three-touchdown lead at halftime. The high-powered offense of the opposition had obviously been overrated. A good old-fashioned butt-kicking was at the top of the mental menu. It was, however, far from over."

Most surprising was the result of the opening afternoon fourballs match, where American's traditional horse, Wadkins, was up against Torrance and Feherty, who admitted to being a "nervous wreck," but happily paired up with his good buddy. The future broadcaster scuffed the putter behind his first 20-foot effort on one, leaving the putt "four feet wide and six feet short," as he recounted in his book.

"Sam took me aside on the second tee and said, 'If you don't pull yourself together, I'm going to join them and you can play all three of us, you useless bastard,'" Feherty wrote. When they fell three holes down at the turn, Feherty went on, "I forced my gonads out of my throat" to hole a long chip for a win at ten, followed by a birdie at fourteen to pull within one. But it was at eighteen where Feherty produced the shining moment of his career. He was the last man with a chance at par, looking at a 12-foot putt to pull out a halve.

"The Almighty was clearly a total bastard—why me?" he wrote. He read left edge, Torrance read right edge, and he accidentally hit it straight, then watched it disappear into the hole. It was such an impressive show of nerve that Stockton immediately walked out to congratulate his adversary. Of course, had Stockton not assumed Gallacher would send out his Spanish Armada first, Feherty and Torrance would have been up against Azinger and Beck. As it was, while trying to keep them apart, Stockton inadvertently sent them out against Ballesteros and Olazábal again, for another 2-and-1 defeat (Gallacher wanted to give his star pairing a little extra rest).

Zinger called it the match of his life with eight birdies, but the Spaniards "ham-and-egged" it beautifully. When both Americans fired their tee balls into the water on the treacherous seventeenth, it was over.

By that time, James and the long-hitting Richardson had put a 5-and-4 hurting on Calcavecchia and Pavin, in his camouflage cap. Gallacher had learned his lesson from the morning by pairing Richardson with a Ryder Cup veteran. He had also stuck with Woosnam and Faldo one more time, but, after they were destroyed, 5-and-4, by Couples and Floyd, they would not be paired again.

Floyd, who was one year from the start of his Senior Tour career, was hailed as the hero of the day, with Bob Verdi of the *Chicago Tribune* calling him "the best draft choice this side of Michael Jordan to the Chicago Bulls." Floyd had been through seven previous Ryder Cup wars and had racked up more losses than any US player. But he was a rock on the tricky greens all day, and his mentorship of Couples was exemplary. As US captain two years earlier, Floyd consoled Couples immediately after he bogeyed the last hole to drop a pivotal match to Christy O'Connor. He told him the experience would make him a better player. Couples, earning the nickname "Boom Boom," would win three times in 1991 and his bond with Floyd at Kiawah was stronger for it.

By winning the session, 2 ½-1 ½, Europe crawled to within a point of the US. Stockton, calling it "a brutal day for the players" because of the unrelenting winds, remarked, "I don't believe either side is satisfied." Still, it was America's first first-day lead since 1985. The US, in fact, had failed to win a single point in the first-day afternoon matches of the previous two competitions.

With the first day in the books, the charged atmosphere it produced had even extended to the media center, bursting with seven hundred occupants. Liz Kahn of the *Sunday Mail*, who moonlit with a daily column for the *Charleston Post Courier*, admitted to what Americans might call the homer-ism of the European "journalists" as they cheered every good shot from their side. She also noted how Hubert Mizell, the grizzled columnist for the *St. Petersburg*

Times, chided such partisanship, informing her curtly that "we don't do that here." Kahn did not relent. However, she did compliment the US wives for the flair of their patriotic wardrobes.

"I had forgotten what a great job the American wives do with their clothing and additional paraphernalia of adornment," she wrote. "Toni Azinger, delightful and gasping with nerves for her man, had sparkling shoes. Karen Beck sported amazing sparkly American flags dangling from her ears, and when I saw a heron gracefully fly overhead, I was surprised that no one had sprayed it to carry the colors."

The Saturday crowds were even more immense, the winds evermore menacing. It made for one of the longest and most exhausting Ryder Cup days ever, only to leave teams where they started, all even with singles forebodingly ahead. Once again, the Americans owned the morning foursomes, and the Europeans dominated the afternoon fourballs. As dusk fell, the momentum slid to the visitors' side, where they sensed what Johnny Miller, working his first Ryder Cup for *NBC*, would have called an American "choke."

As Tim Rosaforte described the European team's trailer in the *Palm Beach Post*, "It sounded like a looting party by a bunch of pirates who had just stole gold. Ian Woosnam and Sam Torrance were drinking beer from long neck bottles and whooping it up, not caring that they were being heard by the downtrodden American team. You would have thought they won the Ryder Cup Saturday. Maybe they had."

Both captains had issues to negotiate. Gallacher's came first. His two best players—the two best players in the world, in fact—were in a funk, and he had to decide whether to send them out again. Woosnam made it easy by asking out. Gallacher obliged. Faldo then made it convenient to sideline him for the afternoon, when he and Gilford were on the wrong end of a record 7-and-6 thumping from O'Meara and Azinger, finally free of Ballesteros.

Critics blasted Gallacher for the Faldo-Gilford pairing. Every headline in the British tabs followed Faldo's name with "Flop." Gilford was quiet and as nervous as a cat playing with the World

No. 2. He needed support from Faldo, who was instead swamped in his own misery and uttered not a peep to his struggling partner. Faldo disclosed in his autobiography *Life Swings* that he was offered the choice of Gilford or Montgomerie and chose Gilford after asking which player was in better form. "I daresay I could have offered David more support and a friendly word of advice," he admitted. "But in the cauldron of Ryder Cup, when you are fighting your demons on the course as I was, it is difficult to provide your equally despondent partner with a stout shoulder."

That was the first morning match to end only to be followed in short order by Irwin and Wadkins' 4-and-2 beating of Friday's heroes, Torrance and Feherty. Calcavecchia and Stewart hung on for a 1-up win over Richardson and James after Richardson's four-footer grazed by the right edge of the cup on eighteen. Naturally, it took Ballesteros and Olazábal to avoid a morning shutout by handing Couples and Floyd their first loss, 3-and-2.

That extended the Spaniards' Ryder Cup record to 9-1-1, and, at that point, they had accounted for three of Europe's four wins. Clearly, Gallacher needed someone else to step up, but with many of his veterans faltering, who would that be? In a risky move, he turned to three of his rookies, Broadhurst, Montgomerie and Richardson, and paired them with veterans Woosnam, Langer and James, as he had Gilford with Faldo, Feherty with Torrance and Richardson with James in the morning. He'd also benefit from a US misfortune. O'Meara had played only twelve holes in the morning but was stricken by back spasms. Stockton had intended to use him with Azinger again, but he was now forced to play the forty-six-year-old Irwin instead of resting him. Pate declared himself ready for action, so Stockton reverted to his original strategy and paired him with Pavin in an all-UCLA duo. He also gave Levi his first action of the week. The 1990 PGA Tour Player of the Year had suffered through a terrible slump in 1991 but made the team anyway because the US awarded points on a two-year basis. Floyd needed a breather, so Stockton paired Couples with Stewart to take on the Spanish leviathan in the anchor match. Suddenly, Europe had hope.

"We said at lunch, we have to win three matches in the afternoon," Ballesteros said. "When we saw those three matches ahead, it was certainly a boost for us."

So was recent history. The fourball format should have been an American strength. The Yanks were far more familiar with it than they were with alternate shot. Yet, incongruously, they had dropped twelve of those sixteen points available in the last two competitions. It would be even worse this time. Europe claimed all but one-half point as Stewart and Couples finally shattered invincibility of Ballesteros and Olazábal in an unbearably tense match that played out in near darkness.

As they hit the turn, it looked good for the Americans, who trailed in only the Wadkins/Levi-Richardson/James match. Then came the inevitable European response, accompanied by that infernal, throbbing *Ole, Ole, Ole, Ole* sing-song from their fans. Most surprisingly, perhaps, was Azinger and Irwin squandering their one-hole lead against Broadhurst and Woosnam. Even more surprisingly, it was Broadhurst, whose only previous action on US soil was in the BC Open, picking up that year's Masters champ, who had been vexed by the Bermuda greens and benched that morning. Broadhurst was making his first appearance of the week in a pressure spot in the tone-setting first match. But, unlike the unfortunate Gilford with Faldo, Broadhurst had one thing going for him. He was good friends with Woosnam and hardly in awe of him. Like Woosnam, he was a working man. He'd driven a truck, worked as a gardener and in a glass factory before his golf career took off. Always among the steadiest players on the European Tour, he birdied thirteen and fifteen for the lead, then stood by as Woosnam got up and down from the bunker on seventeen, sealing the win with a nervous three-footer.

Pate and Pavin, wearing the camo hats so despised by the Europeans, probably shouldn't have been playing together, and Pate not at all. According to Sampson's *The War by the Sore,* Brett Fisher, physiotherapist for the American team, walked with Pate the entire match, applying heat packs. Pavin wasn't at full strength, either. He had suffered a mild case of whiplash in the limo crash. Pate, playing through the pain, won the only two holes for the Americans, at eight and nine, pulling the Americans even. Pavin, though, was MIA. When they both missed short putts, they fell behind by two, then trudged to the intimidating seventeenth. Monty hit first and found the green, then two-putted for the first Euro point.

Even Wadkins, one of America's most fierce Ryder Cuppers, couldn't pull Levi out of his funk. He watched as Levi started with two bogeys and a double. Levi hadn't broken 80 in a practice round all week, but Stockton didn't want to send him into his singles match without having played. Wadkins would wonder: why didn't Stockton pair him with Irwin after they had gone 2-0? Wasn't it more prudent to let Levi gain experience playing with Pate in a sacrificial pairing? The 3-and-1 loss, he felt, could have been avoided.

An afternoon that began in relative comfort now loomed as a total disaster for the US. If Ballesteros and Olazábal could win for the tenth time in twelve Ryder Cup matches, Europe would take the lead going into Sunday.

"In the pm, the red, white and blue began fading to a frightened, almost deathly gray," Verdi penned. "Whether Uncle Sam's boys were emotionally choking, or simply athletically breaking, they muffed one afternoon match, then another, and, also, a third.

"Pressure," Verdi wrote, "kept escalating."

Couples, however, proved unflappable. On the par-five seventh, for instance, Ballesteros had already stuffed his third shot to two feet. Couples was just off the green in two, 40 feet away with a putter in his hands, but Olazábal, in what many interpreted as an attempt to "freeze" Couples, took forever to locate his ball in some scrub, then replace it because it was cut. After the excruciatingly drawn-out performance, he finally executed the shot. Freddie wholly ignored the conspicuous gamesmanship and promptly drained his double-breaking putt to win the hole, punctuated with a fist-jab.

On the broadcast, Johnny Miller made note of Couples' abnormal animation, quipping "Normally, he's yawning." Indeed, the networks would soon discover that all this emotion and all this drama was made for TV. In a fortunate bit of happenstance, *NBC* had lost the rights to major league baseball and needed something big to fill that void. The Ryder Cup had never been broadcast on such a grand scale by an American network before, and network executives rolled the dice. The gamble paid off on this Saturday, when the action continued well beyond *NBC's* planned sign-off time. The decision was made to stick with it, commercial-free. With no prime-time baseball or college football airing, *NBC* had the full attention of America's sports fans. They soaked up the remainder of the compelling final match. They were hooked.

The back-and-forth action was dizzying. Each hole appeared more enthralling than the last. Couples dropped a clutch 15-footer for a winning birdie on No. 11 to put the US 2-up. Stewart agonizingly missed an eight-foot putt on twelve that would have put the US 3-up. Ballesteros summarily cut the lead in half with a 15-foot birdie putt on thirteen. Olazábal made birdie with a 10-foot putt on fourteen, only to see Stewart drop his 10-foot putt on top of him. Fifteen upped the emotional ante, as Ballesteros answered Couples in emphatic fashion, teaching his partner a lesson in the process. Seve was on the green in two, ten feet away. Couples, meanwhile, was stranded in the sand in three. As they approached the green, Olazábal turned to Ballesteros and said, "This is looking good for us."

Seve was "not at all pleased," Olazábal recalled. "He looked at me and said, 'hang on a minute, let's see what happens.'"

Sure enough, Couples heroically holed out for par, rousing the gallery with a gyrating celebration, one that turned out to be premature. An undaunted Ballesteros still had a putt to win, and the cheers of the US crowd only made him more determined. The ball fell into the heart of the hole. Ballesteros shook his fists in his trademark fashion. The match was tied.

"Seve wasn't surprised," Olazábal said. "He was ready and prepared."

Couples was left wanting. He could only walk off to the next tee.

With two Europeans and Couples safely on the green, the TV cameras captured Olazábal backing off his putt after being distracted by a stray noisemaker. Ballesteros gestured menacingly at the offender. Nothing was settled, though, as everyone failed to birdie. They marched to the dreaded seventeenth, with its green ringed by most of the twelve thousand fans who stuck out the long day, now casting golden hues and elongated shadows. Pete Dye was undoubtedly smiling, having provided such a stage for both angst and celebration. Neither Stewart or Seve found the putting surface and, when Couples came up five feet short on his lag putt, Olazábal had a 10-footer to win the hole. He missed, and Couples kept the match all square with his knee-knocker.

Those golden rays of the early evening swiftly succumbed to incipient darkness on eighteen, where enthusiastic fans were circling the green waving a Union Jack. There, Olazábal matched Couples' grit. On the same green that would exert even more pressure in twenty-four hours, Seve's intrepid partner sank a six-footer to halve one of the most dramatic matches ever played.

"I think Jose and I may have a heart attack," Ballesteros managed. "Jose and I played eleven hours yesterday and ten hours today. I think we should be in the Guinness Book of Records."

Stockton sang Couples' praises for saving the day: "It didn't look good, but Freddie wouldn't let us lose. He was magnificent with the pressure of the entire team on his back."

Each side tried to spin the tie in their favor, the Europeans because their top pair had rallied from two holes down to keep them undefeated, the Americans because they avoided the afternoon sweep and at least challenged the Spanish mystique. Even so, Stockton admitted to waking up in the middle of the night to the possibility, for the first time, that his team might "actually lose."

"We got something out of this match, which was important," Stewart said. "Now we go into tomorrow all even. We haven't been in this position for a long time. Now we'll see who has the best players. It's show-and-tell time. It doesn't matter who plays who."

Ah, but it did. When the captains submitted their singles lineups that evening, the Europeans could anticipate two victories: Gilford, who was eager to redeem his 0-2 record, against the hapless Levi in the sixth match, and Ballesteros against the sore-ribbed Pate in the seventh. Pate, however, had suspected during his Saturday afternoon match that he was finished. The bruises to his abdominal muscles had turned from blue to black and a minor slip during the match brought intense pain. He tried to hit a few balls under Stockton's watchful gaze, but his fears were confirmed. He couldn't hit his sand wedge more than 40 yards. The US captain would have to tell Gallacher that Pate was a no-go.

Ryder Cup rules covered such an occurrence. Rather than forfeit the match, each side would receive half a point. Each captain had submitted the name of one player who would sit out the singles, should a player on the other team be unable to compete. Gallacher had stuffed Gilford's name in the envelope.

Levi would now drop down to play Ballesteros, but the chances of Europe picking up two easy points were gone. As it turned out, another full point would have been just enough for Europe to retain the Cup.

As Nick Callow wrote in *The Complete History of the Ryder Cup,* the Europeans "smelled a rat." To them, Pate looked perfectly fine the day before, "hitting the ball a country mile," said Gallacher. The distraught Gilford said: "They obviously did it to get half a point," and Montgomerie added, "We thought it was fishy. Pate played on Saturday and injuries don't get worse overnight."

"To this day, I wonder how hurt Pate actually was," Torrance wrote in *Sam,* his 2010 autobiography. "I was in one of the cars that bashed into each other, and it wasn't much of a concertina effect at all."

Gallacher would have preferred Ballesteros against one of America's top guns. As Torrance pointed out, "It was a real waste of Seve's point. I reckon anyone on our team could have beaten Levi. We felt it was the Americans who got half a point out of the affair."

"Considering how things were going, it was hard not to think something underhanded was going on," Ballesteros asserted. "And the Americans were right to be afraid of me for I was playing at my best."

Although Pate would win three more PGA Tour events and make the 1999 Ryder Cup team, he has always maintained that the injury affected the rest of his career. His hip never worked the same way again, and he was forced to adjust his swing to one less dependent on his lower body. The accusations of '91 were unfounded.

As it was, Gallacher was taking a chance that Ballesteros would be up against one of the weaker American players by putting both Spanish stars in the middle of the lineup, where Olazábal drew Azinger in what loomed as a pivotal fourth match. Stockton, who later said he was "blown away" by Gallacher's unorthodox strategy, was expecting Ballesteros to lead off, so he sent Floyd out first. Instead, Floyd drew Faldo. Critics wondered why the European captain would send out a slumping player to set the tone. Ben Wright, commentating on *USA Network's* share of the coverage, had damnably called Faldo, "a spent force," and Faldo seemed inclined to agree. "I've lost my touch," he admitted, on greens that had him "petrified." But the draw was a fortunate one for Faldo. The previous year, he had defeated Floyd in a playoff for his second straight Masters victory. Floyd, who would have become the oldest major winner at the time, beat himself with a stray shot into the pond on eleven. "You cannot imagine, just *cannot* imagine how this feels," he said at the time. "I have never felt like this. I have never had anything affect me the way this is affecting me."

Faldo may not have been feeling much better himself at the moment, but at least he could take solace in that he had Floyd's number. Outside of the Ballesteros-Levi draw, the rest of the match-ups didn't provide any clear favorites. Stockton, though, had more players playing well than did Gallacher, who had gotten little from anyone apart from his Spaniards the previous session. Stockton stacked Couples, Wadkins and Irwin at the bottom of his lineup. Couples was having a great week, Wadkins was a Ryder Cup warrior and Irwin a three-time US Open champ. They'd face Torrance,

James and Langer, who finally recovered his form Saturday with Montgomerie as his partner.

The wind was at twenty miles per hour when the first match teed off, and the Europeans were in what Woosnam called a "siege mentality." Faldo had kept himself up with worry for most of the night. It didn't help that Gallacher put him out first. But, as he wrote in *Life Swings,* "I knew I could beat (Floyd) in a strong coastal wind." Floyd, who looked out of gas, proved him right with two bogeys on the first three holes to go 3-down. Faldo went 4-up with eight to play and held on for a 2-up victory.

"I hated every moment of it," he said. "I didn't want the pressure of going out No. 1 and trying to put up a point to help out the guys."

Feherty soon extended the Euro lead to two points by overcoming a shanked 2-iron on fifteen with a 2-and-1 win over a struggling Stewart, followed by a match that cast ominous overtones for the US. Calcavecchia had been cruising along against Montgomerie with a five-hole lead at the turn. He was still 4-up with four to play, needing just to halve one of the closing holes. Easy? Not so much, considering the Ryder Cup pressure and howling left-to-right wind. Calc was a left-to-right player, and he was nagged by a dread that all his shots would be blown into the ocean. Those fears were indeed realized with a triple bogey on fifteen. Johnny Miller suggested he was getting rid of all his bad shots on one hole. After all, the match was still dormy with three holes left. Calc nearly ended it on sixteen, where his 15-foot putt for par grazed the left side of the hole. Frustrated, he took off his visor and wiped his brow with his forearms. He knew what awaited him: the devilish seventeenth with Alice Dye's man-made lake on the right. While measuring 197 yards, the hole was playing at least 210 with the wind. Monty was also a fader, and he had the honors. With a 2-iron in his hands, he backed off the shot twice. When he finally pulled the trigger, his ball came up short and right into reeds hugging the shore.

"I would say Mr. Calcavecchia has to aim left a little," Miller told his TV audience.

"Way left," said Charlie Jones, his broadcast partner. "Just make sure you stay out of the water."

Miller surmised that Calcavecchia would fade it off the left waste bunker. He'd still be in command if he found the sand. Calc would later admit to feeling "tension and panic" as he inexplicably decided to try to hit a low hook into the wind rather than his customary fade. Instead, the ball left the clubface with a direction and trajectory most familiar to a 20-handicapper in a member guest shootout—a skulled half-shank thwacked some twenty feet to the right. It skipped mockingly a few times over the lake's surface before laying rest in the watery grave. It was an epic meltdown for the ages. The British writers in the media center went nuts.

"Are you kidding me?" Jones bellowed incredulously.

"That might have been the strangest shot by a pro I've ever seen right there," Miller added.

Both men headed to the drop area. Neither man had been there before, which made the choice of club total guesswork. Monty guessed correctly with a 6-iron and found the green 20 feet from the hole. Calcavecchia hit 7-iron, assuming that was what Monty had used. But Montgomerie's caddie had concealed the top of the club from the American's view, so there was no way to be sure. He came up 30 feet short and, after making a nice lag putt two feet past, he conceded Monty his one-footer. Montgomerie thought about returning the favor but, being a rookie, thought better of it. Half expecting the concession, Calcavecchia jabbed at the putt and missed it.

It seemed almost inevitable that Calcavecchia would also lose the eighteenth. And he did. As they teed off, Miller said Ryder Cup pressure puts you "over your red line." Calcavecchia seemed to steady himself when he outdrove the Scot and had the door opened to him again when Montgomerie misjudged the wind and left himself with a 35-foot putt. As Calc swung his 3-iron, teammate Ray Floyd yelled, "what a shot," but it came in hot, hit a few yards behind the flagstick and bounced down the slope. From there, needing to land his chip just where the fringe met the green, he missed his spot and left himself 12 feet. Montgomerie made a brilliant effort at birdie, leaving it on the lip. Calcavecchia had one last chance, but he missed badly on what is called "the amateur side."

The half-point felt like two to the Europeans. Calcavecchia was inconsolable. It was worse than the shot he put into the water on eighteen two years earlier to lose his singles match at The Belfry. He wandered off to the beach without a word, physically ill and mentally distraught.

"I just sat there in the sand and shook my head. All I wanted was my daughter Brittany. I just wanted to see her smile," he would explain. "I cried. I lost it, mainly because I thought of the circumstances–that it might cause a loss for those other eleven guys who worked so hard. If we had lost, I wouldn't have played for a long time. I would have gone into hibernation."

Calc's collapse was a classic example of the intensity of Ryder Cup pressure, and that pressure would exert itself again hours later. For now, though, it was up to seven of those other guys to make up a three-point deficit, beginning with Azinger in his match against Olazábal. Ballesteros would not be there to embolden his fellow countryman. That didn't make Olazábal any less formidable. He was purpose-built for the Ryder Cup, but so was Azinger. His competitive fire would make him the perfect US captain in 2008, with his bonafides stemming from moments like this.

Zinger's 1991 season had been interrupted by an inflamed right shoulder that became so severe at the US Open, that he enlisted famed orthopedic surgeon Dr. Frank Jobe. Jobe extracted some bone matter for a biopsy while performing surgery to remove the bursa sac he felt was causing the inflammation. The diagnosis from bone specialists at the time was negative, but Jobe was advised to monitor it. Two years later, they found cancer. Azinger missed six weeks of the '91 season, including the PGA Championship, and arrived at Kiawah with scant recovery time but with the same tough attitude.

Bob Verdi's description of him is apt: "Azinger is not a golfer who fell out of the textbooks. He started playing late in life. He uses a funky grip that makes him look like he's trying to pull the cork from a wine bottle. His head tilts upon address, as if to keep a bug off his nose. He has the body of a 2-iron. But he's the leader in the clubhouse for spirit. He probably even sleeps enthusiastically."

That made Azinger the perfect man to be in this spot, trying to stem the bleeding after Europe's early onslaught. Although he was 1-3 in his four matches before the singles, he knew he had been playing well, particularly from a shot-making perspective. Two of those losses came against Ballesteros and Olazábal and the chance for revenge against the junior Spaniard provded the perfect motivation. As he noted in his autobiography, Zinger, he and Olazábal didn't say a word to each other on the first tee. "Words were not necessary," he wrote. "This was war. It was the most incredible match I have ever played in Ryder Cup competition."

Azinger called Olazábal's play "brilliant," adding "I never felt as though I had him beaten." From nine to fourteen, they took turns winning holes, Ollie answering Azinger each time to bring the match back to all square. Neither seized fifteen or sixteen, where Zinger blasted out of the sand and saved par with a 12-footer. With Calcavecchia faltering in the group ahead, Azinger felt his burden even more. "Looking at the board, I felt I had to win for us to have a chance," he said.

Yet again, seventeen loomed ominously. The previous night, Zinger had given the US players' wives a wise directive: "Listen, I'm not going to say anything to the players, but tell your guys to play seventeen tonight in their minds, just visualize hitting it right onto the green."

Perhaps Mrs. Calcavecchia didn't relay those instructions, but Azinger had certainly followed his own advice, "all night long . . . about fifty times." Olazábal was first to play the hole for real. He tried to play a cut 1-iron, but it stayed left, into an awkward lie atop a sandhill. Now, it was Zinger's turn. He went through an interminable pre-shot routine, tossing tufts of grass into the air, until he was in synch with the situation. His 2-iron cut shot through the wind as if on angels' wings, which perhaps it was. A devoutly religious man, he told *NBC's* Mark McCumber that his arms seemed to relax for some reason, thanks to the Lord granting him peace of mind.

Despite ending 50 feet from the hole, it was nevertheless a magnificent shot under the circumstances. With his Spanish foe unable to execute his difficult up-and-down, Zinger finished him off by making his tricky six-footer with surprising aplomb. Each missed the green on eighteen, but, after Olazábal came out of the sand to 10 feet, Azinger chipped to four. Ollie missed his putt, then conceded Azinger's.

The American point was massive. Azinger had survived the toughest match of the day against a superb opponent. Had another blue square gone up on the board, the momentum may have been too much. As it was, Pavin, thanks to a fantastic shot out of the sand on seventeen, beat Richardson, 2-and-1, before Ballesteros' expected victory over Levi, 3-and-2.

The US, however, won three of the next four matches. Chip Beck was eager for redemption after sitting out all of Saturday. Boosted by holing a wedge shot for an eagle on eleven and a chip-in for birdie on fourteen, he defeated Woosnam, 3-and-1, and dropped the World No. 1 to 0-5 in Ryder Cup singles. O'Meara dunked two balls in the water on seventeen and conceded to Broadhurst, 3-and-1, prompting critics to wonder why Gallacher hadn't played the 2-0 Broadhurst more than twice? Couples and Wadkins each then moved to a team-best 3-1-1 for the week with 3-and-2 wins over Torrance and James. Wadkins, in putting the US up, 14-13, broke down crying on the green and then in front of the TV cameras saying, "I don't know if I've ever worked harder."

One match remained. The US couldn't lose, but the Europeans could still return home with the cup, if Langer could take down Irwin and leave the matches as deadlocked as they were two years earlier. As each match finished, all but the distressed Calcavecchia joined their teammates in following the final three holes, each one ratcheting up the intensity.

"This literally was coming down to who was going to crack," Irwin said a few years later. "With maybe two or three holes left, you start to count faces and you see the whole team is there. And the whole European team is there. When I heard that crowd chanting, 'USA, USA,' I couldn't breathe, I couldn't swallow. The sphincter factor was high."

Wadkins would say there was nobody he'd want in that position other than Irwin. Stockton agreed.

"I wanted to have somebody at the back who had a cool mind and a good putter to come in and finish the job," the captain explained. "Hale was it, because anybody who has won three US Opens has to be able to withstand pressure."

Langer obviously fit that bill as well, except for his Achilles heel. Over his entire Hall of Fame career, he could be a shaky putter. His woes on the green even drove him to using the broomstick. At Kiawah, he was employing what he called the "split cross-handed forearm grip," which he developed after a severe case of the yips in 1989. He was anchoring the putter against the inside of his left arm before gripping the club and left arm with his right hand. It looked weird but boosted his confidence.

Given the fierce wind, Irwin, who was a fader of the golf ball, figured that Langer, with his ability to keep the ball down with a low hook, would have the advantage on the starting and finishing holes. Irwin was a very smart course manager, however, and he thought he'd be able to gain ground over the middle part of the golf course. After holding serve early, he did just that, for a 2-up lead through fourteen, which he'd luckily won with a bogey. Glancing at the scoreboard, however, it was beginning to look to Irwin like what he called, "a fight to the finish.

"And you talk about a guy who will fight to the finish—Bernhard Langer was that kind of player," he said.

Irwin's assessment that he'd be at a disadvantage over the closing holes now proved correct. With his Teutonic stoicism, Langer marched away from his double bogey on fourteen and hit two stinging hooks onto the fifteenth green while Irwin was all over the golf course. His par, finished off by a six-foot putt poured into the heart of the cup, cut the lead to one.

The par-five sixteenth was halved, but not without drama. The wind treated Irwin's drive rudely, pushing it left and into the sand. Irwin did his best to get back in play in the middle of the fairway, but he was still a windblown 188 yards out. Meanwhile, Langer had laid up to a comfortable 135 yards. Irwin hit first and sliced it off a TV tower into the gallery, where it charitably bounced back onto grass. Woosnam, sitting back near where Irwin was hitting, later claimed foul play, that someone in the gallery had tossed it back to safety, a charge that was first levied by the Americans at Southport & Ainsdale in 1937.

In any case, Langer still had a chance to stick one close to the flag. Instead, he hit into a huge sand pit to the left of the green, a mistake that left him muttering to himself in German. Irwin summoned all his short game might and spun his chip to three feet. He never thought Langer could pull off his shot, but he did so magnificently and, once more, he stroked his par putt into the back of the cup.

More drama ensued on seventeen, where the crowd was at least fifteen deep and one guy clung to the top of the waste bunker, peering through spectators' legs. Langer finished hole high, just off the green to the left. Irwin conquered his nerve in the left-to-right gusts and put a 3-wood shot safely near where Langer's shot finished, although the TV audiences were fooled when a prankster from the gallery tossed a Top Flite to fifteen feet from the cup. After order was restored, both men used putters for their downhill shots. Langer judged it well to four feet. Irwin did not. His putt was too strong, and it raced eight feet past. That putt, which would have clinched the Cup, didn't fall. Langer's did—again, dead center into the cup. He was stroking it beautifully.

The match was all square with one hole to decide it all.

Langer's nerves were high-grade steel on the tee, and his drive soared down the middle of the fairway, guarded by wide walls of spectators. Now Irwin. To quote Mark Rolfing, who was following the match for *NBC:* "Oh, this ball's way left. This ball is headed into the crowd. It'll need to spit out."

Irwin had double-crossed himself and hit a pull hook. Neither Irwin nor Langer could see the final resting place. But, after they finally waded through the masses, they discovered Irwin's ball sitting, suspiciously, on the edge of the fairway. Irwin had gotten away with a snap hook that probably should have plunged into an alligator pond, save for the thick galleries. Suspicions flared that an American partisan had intervened and kicked it to safety. In reality, the PGA of America had saved the day—unwittingly. Kathy Jorden, a member of the PGA's media staff, had been on the course for the first time all week. Her job? To escort PGA president Dick Smith, as he carried the Ryder Cup to the green for the presentation. She still had her back turned when she heard, "Fore!" She froze. Irwin's pill caromed off the small of her back and down to the short grass.

Although Langer didn't mention it in his 2002 book *Bernhard Langer: My Autobiography*, he was later adamant that something other than Jordan's back intentionally redirected the shot. Irwin still wasn't in an admirable position. He was about 225 yards from the center of the green. He ended up hitting a defensive fairway wood that drifted right and was halted by the wind well short of the green. Langer's shot exploded off the clubface of his 3-iron, hit the front of the green, and kicked about a yard off, but still puttable. If Irwin could pitch it close—something he'd done thousands of times—it would probably suffice. To his astonishment and dismay, he fluffed the run-up shot about halfway to the hole, leaving himself 35 feet for par.

Langer asked for relief from a sprinkler head. All he needed was a good lag. The rollout got him. He was six feet past. It wasn't all bad, considering that there is typically an advantage to a putt going long, because it affords the opportunity to reverse read the break. Langer thought he had it. Irwin had to putt first, though, and his came up a foot and a half short. Langer, in shades of The Concession between Jack Nicklaus and Tony Jacklin, told him to pick it up. As with Nicklaus in 1969, several of Langer's teammates questioned his generosity in giving an obviously shaky Irwin anything longer than a tap-in.

"They said that as Hale was really struggling over the last few holes, there must have been a chance he would have missed the putt," Langer recalled in his book. "I said I just thought it was the right thing to do. I didn't want him to lose it, I wanted to win it. I wouldn't have conceded it if I thought it was long enough for me reasonably to ask him to putt it."

As Langer went on to explain, he was putting well and had made several longer putts under the pressure of the back nine, including on the previous three holes, where he had absolutely poured them in. Irwin's day was done. He sat with his teammates and told them, "this putt will break from the back to the front more than you think.

"I could hardly watch," he'd say. "But in my mind, I'm saying to myself, 'he's made two of these in the last two holes. Can he make three in a row?'"

As he always did, Langer consulted with his caddie, Peter Coleman.

"Where do you see it?" he asked him.

"Left edge," Coleman said, firmly.

"I agreed with him," Langer wrote in his autobiography. "The problem was that there were two spike marks directly on the line, about halfway to the hole. And on Bermuda grass, they get very crusty and crunchy—unlike the soft bent grass that we are used to in Europe."

Langer asked him about the spike marks.

"Yes, I see them," Coleman said.

Langer wrote he was concerned that if he hit the spike marks, the ball could "go anywhere." They looked at it one more time and decided against the left edge. He would hit it firm, taking out the break.

Langer could not have felt lonelier. The only sound was the roar of the waves, an ocean away from Europe. Thousands fixed their gaze upon him, including his teammates and opponents alike, each one thankful it wasn't he over that putt.

As religious as Azinger—whose arms relaxed on his clutch shot earlier—Langer sought divine intervention. Not to make the putt.

He would have to do that himself. "I prayed for courage, strength and a quiet hand," he wrote, and his stroke had all those qualities. He sent the ball on its way, hitting it firm. The moment took an eternity as the golf ball slipped past the right edge of the waiting hole.

Langer's knees buckled, and he let out a cry. Photos of that moment capture the agony. The United States had won, perhaps by a spike mark. The celebration was on, full throttle. The home crowds let out a full throated, "USA, USA, USA." Stewart poured champagne over the head of Calcavecchia, who finally had left the beach behind him (as well as his funk). And, amid the hysteria, Irwin immediately consoled the man with whom he had just halved an epic match.

"It was one of those times you didn't want to see anybody to have to face. And it was almost a sad time," he would say in retrospect. "But of all the players in the world that could have handled that, very few could have handled as well as he did."

Everyone felt for Langer, starting with Seve Ballesteros, who promptly leapt to his teammate's defense.

"Nobody in the world could have made that putt under that pressure," he said. "Not even Jack Nicklaus in his prime. I certainly would not have made it. It was too much for anyone."

Said Stockton: "One, I was mad that there was a chance we might not win this thing, and two, if we did win, it would be because Langer missed the putt, and that just didn't seem fair."

The US captain recalled the low-country cookout, where the teams had mingled earlier in the week.

"I'd found out that his daughter had a serious illness, which they thought was possibly terminal (it was not), and here the poor guy was facing this last putt. I was still thinking about his daughter and felt sorry for him."

"As I walked off the green, I felt bad for my team," Langer wrote in his autobiography. "I could handle that I missed the putt, and I might be blamed for it. But I didn't want the other guys to suffer. Then as I walked into the team room there was Seve giving me a hug and crying. He set me off.

"At first, I wanted to say, 'Don't cry, it's not that serious,' but I guess, for some, it was. And of course, some people are more emotional than others. So I felt bad for the captain and the team because it was such a crucial thing. But as I got my perspective in order, I got it into context."

Langer would find comfort in his intense faith.

"Looking at the Ryder Cup from a Christian point of view, there had been only one perfect man, the Lord Jesus Christ, and we killed him. I only missed a putt," he wrote.

As it was, John O'Leary of the European Tour knew Langer needed some cheering up and shepherded him to a huge tent where two thousand mostly British fans were drinking their sorrows away. A huge roar erupted when Langer entered. According to Dai Davies of the *Guardian,* Langer was "at first dazed, then visibly moved." He climbed to a table to acknowledge the tribute, but it collapsed under his weight.

"It was that kind of day," Davies wrote.

The Europeans retreated to their trailer. According to Curt Sampson's book, Langer's wife, Vikki, turned on a TV while the US celebration was being aired. It was eventually turned off, possibly by a well-tossed iron. The Euros, though, regained their composure before the presentation, where Gallacher reminded US vice president Dan Quayle that British troops had also died in the Gulf War.

"Personally, I think they showed much greater class when we beat them than I think my team would have if we would have lost," Stockton admitted.

Promptly, the American team, dressed in pale blue blazers and grey slacks, ushered Stockton to the beach and threw him into the surf. They changed into dry clothes for the closing dinner, where the Europeans showed no hint of defeat. And so ended a week that was as much hailed as it was criticized.

"No Masters, no US Open, no British Open, no tournament these eyes have ever seen—and few sports events of any kind—could rival this for emotion, drama, thrills spectacle," wrote veteran *Charlotte Observer* columnist Ron Green. "It was golf stripped of some of its traditional starchiness and played with the gritty intensity of a street fight and the noisy, colorful spectacle of football."

Yet, as *Sports Illustrated*'s John Gerrity noted, Sam Ryder's homely little trophy had been forever turned into a blood prize. Everything would now be ratcheted up, including the sponsorship money and the problems that would come in its wake. "Everything changed," Gallacher would one day reflect, "and not for the better."

"As a sporting contest, the Ryder Cup surrendered its dignity and unique charm that September when winning became the be and end all of everything," Faldo wrote in his book, capturing the European attitude.

For his part, Gallacher harbored an interminable grudge. In a 2018 interview with *Bunkered,* a British golf magazine, he revealed that he had not spoken to Stockton since that Sunday at Kiawah.

"He sent me a Christmas card featuring a picture of himself and the winning US team, which I threw in the fire," he said.

He had been more descriptive in an interview with *The Observer* in 2004, in which he claimed that the American team and fans had, "exceeded the bounds of sporting ethics.

"What happened at Kiawah was deplorable," Gallacher charged. "The level of aggression was something I'd never experienced before in any previous outing in the Ryder Cup.

"It was like that World Wrestling Federation stuff on television, where you have bad guys and good guys. We were the bad guys. When the Americans apply themselves to winning something as seriously as they have the Ryder Cup, you know you have to cope with a very ruthless animal."

Gallacher claimed that he'd received notes from American players who were upset about their team's "antics" that week. Perhaps one was Ray Floyd, who called the week "a blemish of sorts" on the competition.

"I was not for it," he said. "It was not in the spirit of the Ryder Cup and how it was started and what it was meant to be."

As for what it was about to become . . . .

DAY 1

FOURSOMES

Seve Ballesteros/Jose Maria Olazábal (E) defeated Paul Azinger/Chip Beck (US) 2-and-1

Raymond Floyd/Fred Couples (US) defeated Bernard Langer/Mark James (E) 2-and-1

Lanny Wadkins/Hale Irwin (US) defeated David Gilford/Colin Montgomerie (E) 4-and-2

Payne Stewart/Mark Calcavecchia (US) defeated Nick Faldo/Ian Woosnam (E) 1-up

United States wins session 3–1

FOURBALLS

Sam Torrance/David Feherty (E) halved with Lanny Wadkins/Mark O'Meara, USA

Seve Ballesteros/Jose Maria Olazábal (E) defeated Paul Azinger/Chip Beck (US) 2-and-1

Steven Richardson/Mark James (E) defeated Corey Pavin/Mark Calcavecchia(US) 5-and-4

Raymond Floyd/Fred Couples (US) defeated Nick Faldo/Ian Woosnam (E) 5-and-3

Europe wins session 2 ½–1 ½

United States 4 ½, Europe 3 ½

DAY 2

FOURSOMES

Hale Irwin/Lanny Wadkins (US) defeated David Feherty/Sam Torrance (E) 4-and-2

Mark Calcavecchia/Payne Stewart (US) defeated Mark James/Steven Richardson (E) 1-up

Paul Azinger/Mark O'Meara (US) defeated Nick Faldo/David Gilford (E) 7-and-6

Seve Ballesteros/Jose Maria Olazábal (E) defeated Fred Couples/Raymond Floyd (US) 3-and-2

United States wins session 3–1

United States 7 ½, Europe 4 ½

FOURBALLS

Ian Woosnam/Paul Broadhurst (E) defeated Paul Azinger/Hale Irwin (US) 2-and-1

Bernhard Langer/Colin Montgomerie (E) defeated Corey Pavin/Steve Pate (US) 2-and-1

Mark James/Steven Richardson (E) defeated Lanny Wadkins/Wayne Levi (US) 3-and-1

Seve Ballesteros/Jose Maria Olazábal (E) halved with Payne Stewart/Fred Couples (US)

Europe wins session 3 ½–½

United States 8, Europe 8

DAY 3
SINGLES
David Gilford (E) halved with Steve Pate (US)
David Feherty (E) defeated Payne Stewart (US) 2-and-1
Nick Faldo (E) defeated Raymond Floyd (US) 2-up
Colin Montgomerie (E) halved with Mark Calcavecchia (US)
Corey Pavin (US) defeated Steven Richardson (E) 2-and-1
Seve Ballesteros (E) defeated Wayne Levi (US) 3-and-2
Paul Azinger (US) defeated Jose Maria Olazábal (E) 2-up
Chip Beck (US) defeated Ian Woosnam (E) 3-and-1
Paul Broadhurst (E) defeated Mark O'Meara (US) 3-and-1
Fred Couples (US) defeated Sam Torrance (E) 3-and-2
Lanny Wadkins (US) defeated Mark James (E) 3-and-2
Hale Irwin (US) halved with Bernhard Langer (E)
United States wins session 6 ½–5 ½
UNITED STATES WINS RYDER CUP, 14 ½–13 ½

1997

The Seve Show

VALDERRAMA, SOTOGRANDE, SPAIN
EUROPE 14 ½, UNITED STATES 13 ½

So long as the Ryder Cup is played, Europe will surely pay homage to one man: Seve Ballesteros. As a player, he heroically took on the colossus that was American golf with a new, heightened level of competitive fire. Outdoing himself, the ultimate Ryder Cup player then became the ultimate Ryder Cup captain; indeed, the eternal Ryder Cup captain. Twelve years after his death, Ballesteros was still inspiring the European team at the 2023 matches in Rome.

As they cruised to a rout of the Americans, Ballesteros' fellow Europeans stayed true to his words they'd tacked up in the team room: "If you ever feel sorry for someone on a golf course you better go home. If you don't kill them, they'll kill you."

In that spirit, the 1997 Ryder Cup at Valderrama was the Spaniard's final masterwork, where he turned slaying his opponents into both an art and a science. Ballesteros took control of the event by demand. His incredible omnipresence was perfectly described by Rick Reilly of *Sports Illustrated:*

It was Seve all the way. It was Seve's Ryder Cup, in Seve's Spain, on Seve's trap-sprung course, won by Seve's hand-wrangled team, played under Seve's terms, for Seve's honor. It was Seve everywhere you looked, Seve in the world's only Formula One golf cart, driving rings around US captain Tom Kite, cutting through bunkers, sending sand flying and separating them from their disposable cameras, showing up wherever Seve was needed and showing up wherever he wasn't, lining up putts, arguing over club selection, handing out advice and quite often, a sandwich. It was Seve driving his players out of their minds and straight into the most flawless golf some of them had ever played. It was Seve and the only result he could have lived with, a win by Europe at the soggy Valderrama Golf Club in Sotogrande, Spain. Yeah, Seve won the Ryder Cup and never fired a shot.

To this day, Ballesteros remains the only man to have truly upstaged Tiger Woods. As a twenty-three-year-old, Woods was making his Ryder Cup debut in Seve's homeland, six months after his win at the Masters, where he was a transcendent force. In Spain, he was totally eclipsed by the force of nature that was Seve Ballesteros.

The Ryder Cup was at a pivotal stage in 1997 with each side poised to take control. After the US proved it was serious about the Cup by prevailing at the 1991 War by the Shore, visiting teams absconded with the Cup on the next two occasions: the Americans, captained by Tom Watson, at The Belfry in 1993, and the Europeans, captained by Bernard Gallacher, at Oak Hill in 1995. Both were narrowly won. Davis Love III's 1-up win over Costantino Rocca capped off an American comeback on the final day to clinch a 15-13 squeaker in '93. Two years later, Europe, trailing by two points heading into the singles, overcame a Sunday deficit for the first time, 14 ½-13 ½, when the unsung Phillip Walton secured a 1-up victory over Jay Haas.

On paper, the US figured to continue the trend at Valderrama. Three of the four majors that year went to Americans (Woods, Justin Leonard and Love III) and none to a European. Eight of the top thirteen spots in the World Ranking were held down by Americans. Only one Euro–Colin Montgomerie–was ranked as high (fifth) but, Monty had performed miserably in the majors, including a flop at his home course, Royal Troon, in The Open Championship. Perhaps Ballesteros had the Americans just where he wanted them: fat, sassy and overconfident.

"The American team isn't possibly as strong as we think it is, and a lot of their guys are beatable and have been beaten," Monty offered, perhaps aware that his side would be relying more on grit and comraderie over the Americans' steady metronomic approach, typical of their captain, Tom Kite. To that end, Gordon Simpson of *The Record* likened the captain's matchup to "a matador against a tax inspector."

Yet, it is important to note that the European road to Valderrama wasn't as wide and smooth as Germany's Autobahn. As was often the case, the British press had been rankled by some of Ballesteros' typical political maneuvering with the European Tour, so much so that just a year before the first ball was struck in Spain, Alister Nicol of the *Daily Record* lobbed an insulting assessment: "The Spanish Man o' War's reputation as flagship of European golf is sadly running aground on a beach of bitterness. This season the Spaniard has been at his bitchiest."

What's more, as much as Ballesteros will be forever linked with what unfolded at Valderrama, he staunchly opposed holding it there once Spain was awarded the '97 Ryder Cup in 1993. As always with Seve, the road to Sotogrande was paved with intrigue. It started in 1990, when Ballesteros lobbied hard for the 1993 matches to be played in his home country. At the time, the British PGA and the European Tour, which shared control of their half of the Ryder Cup, were embroiled in a power struggle. The Ryder Cup had turned into a revenue jackpot, and each organization had its own interests in determining the venue.

Ballesteros was acutely aware that his game was waning. Despite this, he wanted Spain's contributions to the Ryder Cup to be recognized, and he wanted the opportunity to represent Europe in front of his home fans, "before I have to hit a 1-iron over the water and not a wedge," he quipped. At the time, however, the best Spanish course available was Club de Campo, near Madrid, although many, including Nick Faldo, considered it unsuitable. Faldo preferred Portmarnock in Ireland, feeling that the Emerald Isle's contributions to the Cup outweighed and predated those of Spain. Seve naturally scoffed at such a suggestion.

"The British PGA have to remember that perhaps there would be no Ryder Cup without the Europeans," he argued, adding:

"Faldo is just another player in the Cup, and all he has to do is play and shut up."

When it came time to vote, the three European Tour members of the six-man selection committee agreed with Ballesteros. The three PGA members did not—although they disagreed with Faldo as well. Their vote went not to Ireland but (for a third time) to The Belfry in the heart of England. Lord Derby, who headed both organizations and was the man most responsible for bringing continental players into the event on Jack Nicklaus' urging, cast the deciding vote.

Spain would have to wait until 1997, and Ireland would sit out even longer, until 2006. Ballesteros rued the announcement. "I feel disillusioned," he said. "My motivation as a player will not be the same. I feel sorry for Spain and Spanish golf because they deserved better than this."

Those remarks drew an immediate backlash, foremost from legendary Ryder Cupper and TV commentator Peter Alliss: "Seve's a star of his time. But he should remember he is just a player, and you can't build the Ryder Cup around one player. And when he says you don't have a team without Spanish players, it's a form of blackmail. It's the tail wagging the dog—player power gone crazy."

Three years later, the sulking Ballesteros got his wish. Spain received the 1997 bid. Now, the controversy centered on where in Spain to host it.

Bolivian-born billionaire Jaime Ortiz Patino had built Valderrama as a brilliant showpiece on the Costa del Sol. His deep pockets had gone a long way in awarding the Cup to Spain. As it was, Valderrama had been hosting the Volvo Masters for many years and was considered one of the toughest courses in Europe. Ballesteros had designed its most famous hole, the par-five seventeenth. But when the European Tour invited Spanish courses to offer bids, Seve, who had not yet been named captain, came out in favor of Novi Sancti Petri, a public course he had designed near Cadiz. His reasoning? Valderrama was too elitist.

"It's against my principles," he asserted. "It must be played on a public course reachable by everybody. It would be contradictory if the match went to a private club. The Ryder Cup is supposed to help spread the game to everyone. Augusta and Valderrama are the two most exclusive clubs in the world."

On the eve of the selection announcement, Ballesteros pulled a trump card. He claimed Patino enticed him with a $1 million "bribe" to throw his support to Valderrama. Dai Davies of *The Guardian* would later report that Patino, in April of 1993, had sent Ballesteros a letter offering him a cut of all greens fees as compensation for his work on the seventeenth hole for which he was never paid and "for your agreement to support our candidacy for the Ryder Cup."

"I felt honestly that, knowing politics in Spain, it could become very nasty, as it did in the end, and that I could avoid all this nonsense," Patino told Davies. "I knew we had the best course, and if we had Seve on my side there would be no opposition. You want Jack Nicklaus on your team you give him $2 million. There's nothing wrong with making someone a business proposal."

Valderrama ultimately won the bid, and Ballesteros resigned from the Ryder Cup Committee in a snit. He remained, however, the obvious choice to captain the team and was finally offered the position in February of 1996—but only after leaking the news two weeks earlier, further annoying the committee. The offer came with one condition: that he drop his request for more than the two captain's picks and accept the current selection process. Ballesteros, meanwhile, hoped he could qualify to become the first playing captain since Arnold Palmer in 1963. But he reserved the right to decline the spot and replace himself, if he felt he wasn't in form and promised he would not pick himself if he didn't qualify on points.

As Tim Glover of *The Independent* put it: "Nobody will expect a smooth ride with Ballesteros at the wheel. A buccaneer on the course, he is prone to blasting a battery of loose cannon off of it."

Of course, he did just that.

Miguel Angel Martin, Seve's compatriot, was in the process of earning the tenth and final automatic spot on the Euro roster. With just two wins in fifteen years on the European Tour, he was considered the weak link on the team. That presented Ballesteros with a problem. He wanted Nick Faldo, Jesper Parnevik and his long-time partner Jose Maria Olazábal on the squad but all had failed to qualify, requiring an odd man out. Then, as fate would have it, Martin injured his wrist at the Loch Lomond tournament and further aggravated it the following week at The Open Championship, requiring surgery on August 5.

Seve had hoped that Olazábal would sneak past the idle Martin and snatch the tenth automatic spot in the last tournament where points were awarded: the BMW Open in Munich, held in late August. When he didn't, the wily Ballesteros schemed to circumvent the problem. European Tour director Ken Schofield (perhaps at Ballesteros' insistence, although Seve denied such meddling) demanded that Martin prove his fitness to a European Tour physician by playing eighteen holes. Martin refused. He had not swung a club since the surgery and said he was under doctors' orders to even avoid chipping. He called the request "sheer stupidity." With the Ryder Cup three weeks away, he wanted more time to recuperate, a courtesy accorded Olazábal two years earlier. He wrote to Schofield assuring him he would participate only if he was "in the best physical condition." Ballesteros answered Martin by booting him off the team, with Olazábal sliding into the tenth automatic spot and Faldo and Parnevik aboard as wild card picks. He had the three men he wanted.

Martin threatened legal action.

"Seve Ballesteros is responsible for this," he fumed at a packed press conference. "If Olazábal had been No. 17, this would not have happened."

At first, Ballesteros tried to beg off, claiming he had asked the committee to give Martin more time: "No, No, No. It was not me. I don't make the rules here. I only have so much power. Please don't implicate me in this. I am not trying to excuse myself or defend myself, but I am in a very difficult position."

But the fiery Seve could contain himself for only so long. Martin's lawyers filed for an appeal and Ballesteros came back swinging the next day: "Do you think Martin can stop the Ryder Cup? That little man! You are crazy! Lawyers can only do so much. Martin is only thinking of himself. He is like a kamikaze pilot flying towards the ship. I thought Miguel was more intelligent than this. He must have a square head. He has had very bad advice. It's just too bad. He's making things worse and worse. You think he wasn't welcome before, what about now?"

Many thought the last part of his tirade was a giveaway. He never wanted Martin on his team. Many European Tour players felt that Martin had been wronged, and when Garrido—who had won an automatic spot on the roster—came to his defense, Ballesteros was not pleased. Public opinion, though, held that Martin should do the right thing and get behind the team. Eventually, a financial settlement was reached. Martin hung around Valderrama for a couple of days, shook Seve's hand and posed for the team picture before departing on his own, tired of playing the third wheel. "I don't feel like being here," he explained deflatedly. Alistair Tait, in his otherwise adoring biography, *Seve,* called it "one of the most shameful episodes in European Tour history."

Seve, of course, persisted in seizing total control of every possible aspect of his captainship. For several years, home captains were given free rein to set up the golf course as they saw fit, a practice first put to partisan use by Dai Rees at Lindrick in 1957. Ballesteros took advantage of his prerogative like Rommel at Normandy. He would be the first to engage in what would later be called "Tiger-proofing" a golf course by tightening the landing areas of the fairways to take the driver out of the hands of Woods and many of other big-hitting Americans. The quirky par-five seventeenth, which he designed in 1993, was an example of his cunning ways.

Dubbed "Los Gabiones" after the gabion wall that hugs the right side near the green, the hole measured only 511 yards, sixty yards shorter than the original version. But Ballesteros ensured it was 511 yards of treachery. He placed veritable camel humps to the fairway to knock good drives offline, followed by a strip of rough across the fairway to snare the 300-yard drives Woods could unleash. A pond guarded the front and left sides of the green, requiring a dangerous pitch and three bunkers behind the green that sloped downward. A steep bank in front of the green sloped down toward the water hazard.

Even Monty called the hole "hideous," though it probably played to his team's advantage. Tom Lehman played it driver, sand wedge, sand wedge during a practice round. "I don't know how to play it," said a befuddled Kite. "I don't think Seve even knows how to play it." "If the Americans are not comfortable," Seve sneered, "they should win 3-and-2."

Ballesteros, for reasons he did not disclose, also changed the order of play. The competition had always opened with the alternate shot format. However, Ballesteros, with Kite's acquiescence (he should have known Seve had something up his sleeve), set up fourball play for the morning rounds. He cryptically announced to the press: "It's a risk but I don't want to tell you why I did it." Most likely, the move was intended to build momentum heading out of Friday and Saturday, given his confidence in his squad's strong tee-to-green play.

By 1997, Ballesteros had fomented a full-bore hostility toward the Americans. As Montgomerie put it, "I'd hate to imagine the sight of him passing the Cup over to Tom Kite. It would turn him into a bumbling wreck. I'd rather see him become a bumbling wreck because we'd won the Cup again. Seve has a pure hatred of losing in America and to Americans."

The brewing of that contempt was well documented in Tait's 2007 biography of Ballesteros. He felt wholly ostracized when he first played in America, and that led to a burning personal desire for redemption. Raymond Floyd intensified those sentiments when, as the US captain in 1985, he invoked Ben Hogan and introduced his team as the "twelve best players in the world." Tom Kite didn't help matters when—after teeing off in a foursomes match at those heated 1985 matches—he turned to Ballesteros and cracked wise, "Remember the Alamo."

"I thought perhaps he was wrongly informed about the Alamo and had gotten his Mexicans mixed up with his Spaniards,"

Ballesteros gibed. “Well, like the Mexicans, we beat them when I sank a two-meter putt for par at the last hole.”

Kite seemed far less combative as the US captain. He had assumed more of the low-key, steady-as-she goes approach he had as a player, relying on organization, thoroughness and planning. Seve, meanwhile, had already injected his piss and vinegar into his team’s veins. The American team had barely hit the ground, when they were hit with the first blasts of European defiance. Montgomerie had granted the Scottish writers an exclusive interview in which he cast doubt on Woods and the rest of the US team. Brad Faxon, he lectured, was too inaccurate for Valderrama and bound to be distracted by his divorce. He claimed that Jeff Maggert wasn’t going to intimidate anyone and added that his team would love to see Scott Hoch look down a pressure putt. He debunked Tom Lehman’s reputation as a “world beater” and questioned Jim Furyk’s ability to cope with pressure. The derision didn’t stop there. Phil Mickelson “can hit it anywhere,” he scoffed.

At the same time, Europe’s No. 1 player was puffing out his own chest, even comparing himself to Woods in terms of managing the pressure of expectations.

“People now expect me to win and that’s a very difficult place to be. When you’re expected to beat people sometimes you feel as if you can’t lose,” he said. “That will also be Tiger’s problem. Let’s say he plays four times–people will expect him to win all four points. My feeling is that if you’re a European player and you’re drawn against Tiger then you can’t lose.”

He further explained: “If you get beaten by him then that’s only what people expect to happen anyway. But if you beat him, then you’ve done really well. If I played Tiger at Augusta then, yes, I would feel as if I was in a bit of trouble. But at Valderrama, I fancy my chances and feel as if I’ve got as good a chance as anyone of defeating him. Apart from the Masters, if you look at the other majors this season, I’ve beaten him in two and finished on the same mark in another.”

That was true, but it wasn't quite that simple. Monty was the runner-up to Ernie Els at the US Open at Congressional, seventeen spots better than Woods, who blew up over the weekend. But it was a devastating second with victory having slipped through his hands on the closing holes. They were a joint twenty-fourth in The Open Championship at Troon, but Monty was the pre-tournament favorite at the course where he grew up. Instead, he face-planted with an opening 76, with US Ryder Cupper Justin Leonard claiming the claret jug. Finally, Monty tied for thirteenth and Tiger twenty-ninth in the PGA Championship at Winged Foot, where US Ryder Cupper Davis Love III would win his only major.

The Masters, however, was the only major where Montgomerie and Woods went head-to-head. Monty played the peacock there, too, and was fairly plucked in the end. He was three behind the phenom heading into the weekend, when he tried to put some mental heat on him before playing together in the final group.

"There's more to it than hitting the ball a long way, and the pressure's mounting," he crowed. "And I have a lot more experience in major championships than he has."

That tune went major to minor after Montgomerie's vaunted experience helped him to a 75 with Tiger shooting 65 to build a nine-shot lead over Costantino Rocco. He was twelve better than Montgomerie, who offered a humble-pie concession speech afterwards.

"All I have to say is one brief comment today: There is no chance," he said. "We're all human beings here. There's no chance humanly possible that Tiger is going to lose this tournament. No way."

A reporter asked, "What makes you say that?" noting that Tom Kite, eleven strokes behind, had reminded the media that Greg Norman had been considered a lock the year before, only to blow a six-shot lead over Faldo. Montgomerie stared back incredulously.

"Have you just come in, or have you been away?" he asked. "Have you been on holiday or something, or have you just arrived? Sorry. This is very different. Faldo's not lying second, for a start. And Greg Norman's not Tiger Woods. I appreciate that he hit the ball long and straight, and I appreciate his iron shots were very accurate. I did not appreciate (until witnessing it firsthand) how he putted. When you add it all together, he's nine shots clear, and I'm sure that will be higher tomorrow."

It was. Woods won by twelve. Montgomerie shot 81 and finished twenty-four back.

At the Ryder Cup, however, they don't count the strokes, only the number of holes won, and the Europeans were quite adept at winning holes. In fact, Montgomerie wasn't the only one with Tiger in his crosshairs. Every word from Team Euro appeared calculated to heap pressure upon him.

"Any of my twelve men are willing to compete with Tiger Woods and can beat Tiger Woods," Ballesteros said emphatically.

"Give me Tiger in the last match on the last day and I'll whip his butt, as the Americans say," added Ian Woosnam.

To them, Woods encapsulated the entire American team: arguably the strongest ever on paper, but impossible to forecast because the Ryder Cup was a different animal. As Brad Faxon said, "it's really become something beyond the boundaries of golf." The Europeans thrived on it and while Seve had five rookies, they were balanced out by vets such as Montgomerie, Langer, Woosnam, Faldo and Olazábal, all of whom had played big roles in prior victories. Only Fred Couples, Mark O'Meara and Davis Love III had played more than two Ryder Cups. Woods, Leonard, Jim Furyk and Scott Hoch were rookies. Faxon, Tom Lehman, Phil Mickelson, Jeff Maggert and Lee Janzen were playing in their second, and that was a home loss at Oak Hill. As Ballesteros said of his squad, "It's a very good combination. I don't think I could have a better team."

What's more, the Europeans knew every quirky detail of the course, with a Euro Tour event being played there every year. If the Americans dropped in for a quick look, as Woods had done in July, it was a lot. With Robert Trent Jones as the original designer, it had the look of an American course. Greg Norman even gave the US the advantage on it. But, while it was called the "Augusta of Europe" for its immaculate conditions, it was hardly that. Augusta

National's wide fairways encouraged aggressiveness. Valderrama's cramped fairways forced uneasy thoughts off the tee. Its small greens demanded accuracy and a pinpoint short game.

The beauty of its setting, however, belied its danger. It could lull a player into a false sense of security. It was a veritable nature preserve, with magnificent copses of olive and cork trees, birds of myriad species and the azure waters of the Mediterranean and the imposing Rock of Gibraltar as a backdrop. Even its bunkers, filled with pulverized marble, were resplendent.

And so, the week steamed toward the first shots to be struck in anger. Ballesteros rose on Thursday at 4:30 a.m. and roused his vice-captain, Miguel Angel Jimenez, with a phone call.

"Come over to my room; we have to make the pairings," he ordered. Jimenez, a man who savors fine wine, cigars—and sleep, groggily replied, "Are you crazy (actually 'loco' in Spanish)?"

"Well, this is very important," Seve explained. "And I think this is a good time because in the morning I am more sharp."

Those pairings were announced prior to an Iberian-themed opening ceremony featuring King Juan Carlos and Queen Sofia. Kite's biggest surprise was leaving British Open champ Justin Leonard on the bench. "Everyone will play," he explained, while opening with Mickelson and Love III, followed by Couples and Faxon and Lehman and Furyk. Seve's early morning skull session turned out Olazábal and Rocca first, then Faldo and Westwood and Parnevik with his fellow Swede Per-Ulrik Johansson.

Unsurprisingly, Montgomerie would immediately get the chance to test his Tiger theory in the anchor match, where he and Langer would challenge Woods and his pal and mentor Mark O'Meara. Fate would match them up in the afternoon as well.

Ballesteros explained sending out Monty and Langer out last by joking about Langer's notoriously slow play: "I thought if we put him in the first match, we'd probably all miss lunch." Naturally, there had to be a bit of gamesmanship in that choice as well, a way to off-put Woods, who, even at twenty-one, had an unbreakable mental game hardened by his father, Earl.

Woods had done well in responding to Montgomerie's mulling. "It's true. They can beat me," he said. "But vice versa, we've got twelve guys on this side who can beat any of their guys. I've played enough match play. I should be OK. I always prefer match play over medal, any day. Match play is the epitome, one-on-one. Anyone can win in match play. That's what makes it so great. There's so much emotion, you ride the wave . . . it's neat."

But Butch Harmon, Tiger's coach, may have betrayed his true emotions.

"I think that Tiger is very happy to get Monty," he said. "I feel really good about it. I find it rather strange how they all keep saying they want to play Tiger Woods. This all goes back to Augusta and those things Monty said. I don't think Tiger has forgotten about that. That fired him up. You remember how that played out over the weekend. Tiger beat the hell out of him."

All that would have to be put on hold. The area hadn't seen any significant rain since May, until a storm front moved in from North Africa and hit Sotogrande around 5:30 a.m. The rain in Spain fell not mainly on the plain but rather as a deluge rendering the course unplayable. Violent lightning lit up the Rock of Gibraltar like a laser light show. In the morning, American golf writers accomodated near the shore hastily bailed out their condos with buckets. Not since 1947 in Portland had weather so badly affected the competition. Headline writers loved it: Ryder on the storm.

The delay only made Ballesteros more antsy. As soon as the session got underway, after the grounds crew somehow wrung things out, Seve traversed the course to wherever he figured a crisis could arise. He appeared omnipresent.

In his autobiography *"Life Swings"* Nick Faldo noted that that no one brought more passion to the role of non-playing captain: "Armed with only a buggy, I think Seve must have been using an illusionist's magic mirrors, so repeatedly did he pop up to hiss, "Six-iron Monty, three-iron Nick." I remember his assistant, Miguel Angel Jimenez, coming down for breakfast one morning looking for all the world as if he had been up all night fighting a deranged gorilla; his eyes were red, his hair was all over the place, he was unshaven."

Seve's wife Carmen complained of nights with two hours sleep and threatened to file for divorce if it were to continue.

Not everyone appreciated that "*Hermano Mayor*" was watching, however. Ian Woosnam confided to the British press that, "Europe has a captain who goes around as if he were playing blind man's bluff." He said Ballesteros was "running around like a headless chicken."

Montgomerie recoiled when Ballesteros moved in to offer advice on how to play seventeen. He stopped him before he could speak. "Seve, I know what to do! I really do!"

"Colin, I know you do," Ballesteros replied just as forcefully. "I only wanted to remind you."

When play finally started, Montgomerie needn't be reminded about his Tiger musings. His prediction didn't pan out at first. He and Langer achieved a split with Woods and O'Meara—a 3-and-2 fourball win for the Americans followed by a 5-and-3 European rout in alternate shot. When Monty missed a putt that would have won the first hole of the day, his expressive countenance turned simply to pursed lips, as if he'd bitten into a lemon. Noting his sour mood throughout the match, Tim Dwyer of the *Philadelphia inquirer* wrote he "played all morning as if in a fog."

When Tiger birdied the par-five fourth, the US took its first lead and when he added another on the par-four tenth the lead increased to three holes. When his wayward drive on sixteen took a fortuitous bounce off a cork branch back into the fairway, it was apparent the match was over. The Euros had not made a single birdie.

Ballesteros could have broken up the pairing, but he instinctively gambled on their resurgence. Monty had a quick lesson with his former putting coach, Bill Ferguson, and Langer changed putters. And, suddenly, tides turned dramatically. Now, it was Tiger missing everything.

"I was cutting across the ball. Bill sorted it," Montgomerie explained. "It was a wonderful, wonderful afternoon, a great way to leave the course at the end of the day."

Woods instinctively blamed the rains. "They screwed up my feel for the greens," he alibied. "Some were kind of fast, some were kind of slow."

Kite, however, expressed more than a degree of concern about his superstar's performance beyond just putting. "Tiger was not even right in the morning," he fretted. "He struggled with it and wasn't as sharp as he wanted to be. Mark O'Meara played flawlessly this morning. He played super and Tiger contributed a little bit."

It wasn't the only ominous sign.

With the course setup taking away any American edge in length, the short game became a premium around the small greens. As such, Mickelson, who had gone 3-0 as a rookie in '95, was considered key. But, partnering Love III in the morning, the lefthander missed a five-foot putt on the last hole that allowed Olazábal and Rocca to escape with a 1-up win. Mickelson was left standing in disbelief. The match had rewarded Seve's faith in Olazábal who, after trailing by two holes early, shifted momentum with the shot of the day, holing out a pitching wedge from 131 yards for an eagle on fourteen.

If that wasn't enough of a surprise, Europe pulled off the biggest upset of the day, with the Swedish fourball pair of rookies Jesper Parnevik and Per-Ulrik Johansson defeating Tom Lehman and Jim Furyk, 1-up. Parnevik, in a preview of what would be an outstanding Ryder Cup career, drained clutch putts of fourteen and eighteen feet for wins on the two closing holes. Mark Cannizzaro of the *New York Post* had noted how the Swedes appeared "white as ghosts on the first tee" but they didn't play that way.

At least there was some redemption for two Americans. Six weeks before the Cup, Faxon was hit with a divorce suit by his wife Bonnie, the mother of his three daughters. Three weeks later, one of his best friends was killed in an automobile accident. Understandably, this all took a toll on his game. But, as his fourball match with Fred Couples against Faldo and Westwood reached the final hole, something good finally happened. For two years, he had shouldered the burden of missing a seven-foot putt at Oak Hill that would have kept the Cup in America. It came after he had blasted out of a bunker. Incredibly, he faced a similar bunker shot on eighteen at Valderrama which he left six feet away. This time, the Americans' best putter didn't miss. He was able to get a read from Faldo as the Englishman missed from a foot behind him before draining it—as well as a bit of inspiration from his partner—just before he struck it.

"He told me he loved me," Faxon joked. In reality, Couples reminded him that he was "the best putter in the world."

"Oak Hill is going to hurt forever but this feels awfully good," Faxon said later.

Scott Hoch, of course, did not share Faxon's reputation on the greens as the world's best putter. Quite the opposite. *Sports Illustrated* had described him with as nasty an invective as there ever was. After he missed a three-foot putt that would have won the 1989 Masters, the magazine reminded the world that "Hoch" rhymed with "choke." It may have taken ten years for Hoch to answer that slur, but it couldn't have come any more sweetly. This time, after Lee Janzen dropped a soaring 6-iron shot six feet from the hole on eighteen, Hoch drained the putt that lifted the US into a 3-3 tie.

That left two foursomes matches on the course in the impending darkness, including Faldo and Westwood against Jeff Maggert and Justin Leonard. Naturally, it wouldn't be a Ryder Cup if the day had ended without controversy. The Euros were up by two, when Faldo hit his second to six feet at sixteen with the Americans 25 feet away. A Westwood make would ice the match, but Maggert claimed it was too dark to see his line. Faldo threw up his arms in disgust as the match was carried over until Saturday. Maggert would admit he had an ulterior motive.

"It surprised them that we didn't want to finish and frankly, that was our intent," he said. "There was a little strategy involved. They had momentum and we didn't want them to take it to the clubhouse."

The ploy also forced Faldo to wait a day until he could become the Ryder Cup's all-time leading scorer, passing Billy Casper with twenty-four points (he'd end his career at 23-19-4). Seve had tasked Faldo, who'd experienced a down year in '97, with mentoring the rookie Westwood, "to shield him from all the bullets and let him play," Faldo explained. Faldo had failed in a similar role with David Gilford at Kiawah. He didn't do so here, and Westwood would go on to build a sterling Ryder Cup resume of his own.

Did it really matter? As the teams slept on the results of the protracted first day, they knew that a Faldo and Westwood win was a mere formality. Westwood made his six-footer to secure the point when Saturday play resumed after more rain came and went. Parnevik and Ignacio Garrido earned another half-point in their carry-over match against Mickelson and Lehman. At that point, the only criticism directed at Ballesteros was his decision to sit Ian Woosnam, Darren Clarke and Thomas Bjorn over the first two sessions, to which he responded, "This is the way I see the situation, obviously."

No one was criticizing Seve by the time darkness halted play again—mercifully for the US. For the first time in Ryder Cup history, the Americans failed to win a match all day. They went 0-5-2 to fall behind 9-4 with three matches yet to be completed Sunday morning. They'd have to win all three, it seemed, to have a reasonable chance in the singles. They were up in one, down in one and even in the other.

As Ed Sherman of the Chicago Tribune wrote, "The anatomy of the disaster wasn't hard to understand. It happened because Europe's unheralded young players—Westwood, Bjorn and Ignacio Garrido—are outplaying young American superstars Tiger Woods, Justin Leonard and Phil Mickelson. It happened because the Europeans made their putts and the US didn't. It happened because the Europeans made pars from the trees, while the US made bogeys from the fairway: in two days of fourball matches Brad Faxon never had a birdie in thirty-five holes."

Excuses ran rampant. Kite claimed his team was at a disadvantage with not having experienced the course play wet after so many perfectly dry practice days. Lehman complained that the course was "claustrophobic," and later moaned that the disjointed sessions never gave the Americans time to regroup. Woods' frustrating play stood out the most; he even putted into the water from the back of the seventeenth green. And, even when the Americans did something great, it wasn't great enough—as when Mickelson hit one of the best shots of his life, a 240-yard 2-iron from out of the rough on seventeen. Garrido, facing an almost impossible bunker shot, somehow got up and down and when Mickelson missed his five-foot eagle putt, the home team escaped with a halve.

Meanwhile, being benched didn't affect Clarke, Woosnam or Bjornas, who won their fourball matches. When the three matches carrying over to Sunday ended, Hoch and Maggert had provided the US with its only outright win. The Euros won the two sessions, 6-2, to carry a 10 ½-5 ½ lead into the singles.

Kite had called on President Bush to deliver an unplanned pep talk on Saturday night (as Ben Crenshaw would do with the younger President Bush when the US faced a 10-6 deficit heading in the singles two years later). This one fell just short. As Kite top-loaded his lineup, the Americans caused considerable angst, starting with Couples' 8-and-7 thrashing of a rusty Woosnam, but the hole was too deep—and arguably the top US players were to blame.

For the week, Woods, Leonard and Love, winners of three of the four majors, were a combined 1-9-3. Love was 0-4 by himself. Of the four points Europe won on Sunday 2 ½ came against that threesome. Of the first six matches, Love and Woods were the only Americans to lose. Had either won their singles matches, the US would have pulled off a miracle comeback.

Tiger took the brunt of the media assault, starting with Joe Posnanski of the *Kansas City Star:* "Trouble is, Woods is not ready to be king of the world, not yet. He played positively bland golf this weekend . . . and the United States team followed his lead."

Dave Sheinin of the *Miami Herald* piled on: "The United States would have won the Ryder Cup if its legendary twenty-one-year-old trained assassin had beat a stock forty-year-old Italian who was working in a box factory when he was twenty-one."

Rocca, of course, was along for the Sunday ride as Tiger swept to victory at the Masters, shooting 75 to Woods' 69. But he was in control of this one from the start, winning the first four holes. The deficit was still four when they got to nine, but Woods missed a three-footer for birdie after Rocca drained a 20-footer for par. The match would end, 4-and-2.

When Ballesteros asked Rocca whom he wanted that morning, the Italian replied, "Tiger," without hesitation.

Woods was the only American to play in all five sessions. He finished 1-3-1 with his only win due more to his partner O'Meara's play than his own. On the week, he won only eleven of the eighty-two holes he played.

"Tiger Woods was intimidated," Posnanski posited, noting that Michael Jordan, walking alongside him, had to urge him to smile and that Butch Harmon said, "I've never seen him this nervous."

"It's called golf," Woods shrugged afterwards. Nevertheless, his dismal 13-21-3 record in the Ryder Cup fell woefully short of his nearly incomparable PGA Tour mark. "He proved me correct," crowed Montgomerie, whose 20-9-7 Ryder Cup record gave him license to brag.

Rocca's win moved the Euros to within a point and a half of retaining the Cup, within two points of winning it outright. Then Leonard blew a 4-up lead against Bjorn and escaped with a half. Fittingly, it was Bernhard Langer, to whom fate was so cruel at Kiawah, who earned the magic fourteenth point. Faxon bogeyed thirteen and fourteen after birdying twelve to pull even with Langer. This time, the German needed only to two-putt seventeen to win. The US reeled off three more victories, leaving Montgomerie and Hoch to determine the final outcome. Hoch made a nice birdie on seventeen to close within a hole; but, with Hoch on eighteen in three and Monty on in two, Seve ordered his man to give Hoch his longer putt, shouting "Concede it, concede it," as he approached the green. Monty didn't seem pleased, yet he did as his captain wished.

The match ended all square. Europe won, 14 ½-13 ½. It would be a different story in two years when Payne Stewart conceded Montgomerie the final match of the week at The Country Club.

The rains had already returned by the time the match ended and continued in earnest through the presentation ceremony, drenching the US team and adding insult to injury.

"If you're asking me what it's like to be standing there in the rain when they're giving them the Cup, it sucks," Faxon said. "It was like asking the Yankees to watch the Red Sox celebrate after they've clinched. I'm glad we didn't understand anything they said."

Like many of his teammates, Faxon also couldn't grasp how they lost.

"We've won more tournaments. We had higher-ranked players, we had a captain we love and respect, we had the pairings we wanted. There's no rhyme or reason," he said.

But Lehman knew why.

"I'm still totally convinced we have the twelve best players. Today proved that," he claimed. "But put their guys together, and they have magic at their fingertips. The sum is greater than the parts."

Or, as the victorious Faldo boasted, "The dollars are far, far bigger in the States. But there's a lot more character in Europe."

For Seve Ballesteros, it was a perfect week, one that cemented his Ryder Cup legacy.

"I have won the Masters. I have won the British Open. I have won championships around the world. But there is nothing like the Ryder Cup."

In the aftermath, Ballesteros was hailed for outcoaching Kite. Even Kite had to admit, "When Seve gets it going, it's like trying to catch a Ferrari with a Chevy pickup."

Having completed his crusade, Ballesteros immediately announced that he would not return as captain for the next Ryder Cup in Brookline. He wanted to work on rehabilitating his game. Indeed, it was his final Ryder Cup as captain or player. He would succumb to brain cancer just fourteen years later, his passionate contributions forever inextricably tied to the event—and never to be forgotten.

DAY 1

FOURSOMES

Jose Maria Olazábal/Costantino Rocca (E) defeated Davis Love III/Phil Mickelson (US) 1-up

Fred Couples/Brad Faxon (US) defeated Nick Faldo/Lee Westwood (E) 1-up

Jesper Parnevik/Per-Ulrik Johansson (E) defeated Tom Lehman/Jim Furyk (US) 1-up

Tiger Woods/Mark O'Meara (US) defeated Colin Montgomerie/Bernhard Langer (E) 3-and-2

Session halved 2–2

FOURBALLS

Scott Hoch/Lee Janzen (US) defeated Costantino Rocca/Jose Maria Olazábal (E) 1-up

Bernhard Langer/Colin Montgomerie (E) defeated Mark O'Meara/Tiger Woods (US) 5-and-3

Nick Faldo/Lee Westwood (E) defeated Justin Leonard/Jeff Maggert (US) 3-and-2

Jesper Parnevik/Ignacio Garrido (E) halved with Tom Lehman/Phil Mickelson (US)

Europe wins session 2 ½–1 ½

Europe 4 ½, United States 3 ½

DAY 2

FOURSOMES

Colin Montgomerie/Darren Clarke (E) defeated Fred Couples/Davis Love III (US) 1-up

Ian Woosnam/Thomas Bjorn (E) defeated Justin Leonard/Brad Faxon (US) 2-and-1

Nick Faldo/Lee Westwood (E) defeated Tiger Woods/Mark O'Meara (US) 2-and-1

Jose Maria Olazábal/Ignacio Garrido (E) halved with Phil Mickelson/Tom Lehman (US)

Europe wins session 3 ½–½

Europe 8, United States 4

FOURBALLS

Colin Montgomerie/Bernhard Langer (E) defeated Lee Janzen/Jim Furyk (US) 1-up

Scott Hoch/Jeff Maggert (US) defeated Nick Faldo/Lee Westwood (E) 2-and-1

Jesper Parnevik/Ignacio Garrido (E) halved with Justin Leonard/Tiger Woods (US)

Jose Maria Olazábal/Costantino Rocca (E) defeated Davis Love III/Fred Couples (US) 5 -and-4

Europe wins session 2 ½–1 ½

Europe 10 ½, United States 5 ½

DAY 3

SINGLES

Fred Couples (US) defeated Ian Woosnam (E) 8-and-7
Per-Ulrik Johansson (E) defeated Davis Love III (US) 3-and-2
Mark O'Meara (US) defeated Jesper Parnevik (E) 5-and-4
Phil Mickelson (US) defeated Darren Clarke (E) 2-and-1
Costantino Rocca (E) defeated Tiger Woods (US) 4-and-2
Thomas Bjorn (E) halved with Justin Leonard, (US)
Tom Lehman (US) defeated Ignacio Garrido (E) 7-and-6
Bernhard Langer (E) defeated Brad Faxon (US) 2-and-1
Jeff Maggert (US) defeated Lee Westwood (E) 3-and-2
Lee Janzen (US) defeated Jose Maria Olazábal (E) 1-up
Jim Furyk (US) defeated Nick Faldo (E) 3-and-2
Colin Montgomerie (E) halved with Scott Hoch (US)
United States wins session 8–4.

EUROPE WINS RYDER CUP, 14 ½–13 ½

1999

A Date with Fate

THE COUNTRY CLUB
UNITED STATES 14 ½, EUROPE 13 ½

Two defining images compete as the most lasting memory of the 1999 Ryder Cup, depending upon which side of the Atlantic they are remembered. There was Ben Crenshaw's wagging finger, which foretold an epic American victory. But that gesture, the Europeans insisted, was spoiled by an unedifying celebration on The Country Club's seventeenth green. Both incidents demonstrate the wild emotional swings that the Ryder Cup generates above any other golf tournament and why there is a limit to the fellowship between teams that is supposed by many as the foundation of the competition.

Known as the Battle of Brookline, the '99 Ryder Cup was almost as contentious as the 1991 War by the Shore–with a comeback for the ages and a comedown for decorum. It simultaneously tore down and reinforced stereotypes of the United States team while affirming that there was no golf tournament as dramatic, tumultuous or emotionally draining as the Ryder Cup.

It was ironic that Crenshaw found himself at the center of all the tumult. Golf was a sacred thing to "Gentle Ben." When Crenshaw won the Masters four years earlier, he was certain that Harvey Penick–his longtime mentor whose funeral he attended that week–was placing his hands on the club as he had when he first taught the tow-headed boy in Texas. Poignantly, Crenshaw had visited him on his deathbed, where the great old man insisted on one last lesson. Having doubled over in exhaustive emotion after sealing victory on the eighteenth green, Crenshaw slipped on the green jacket and declared Penick's omnipresence. "I believe in fate. He was with me all week."

Fate then followed him to Brookline after the death of his father, Charlie, that May. A prolonged slump prompted him to suspend his own playing career to focus on his captaincy. "He has the weight of the world on his shoulders," recalled his wife, Julie. And he showed it. He acted as if he were personally beholden to the spirit of Francis Ouimet, the teenaged caddie from across the road who shocked the world by beating Harry Vardon and Ted Ray on the same ground at the 1913 US Open. But the pedestrian approach of some of his best players seemed to rub him the wrong way. Crenshaw had an emotional attachment to the Ryder Cup–and to the fiercely competitive spirits of the legendary players of the past. The American team was coming off two straight defeats, most recently a crushing loss to Seve Ballesteros' squad at Valderrama. But its foremost stars seemed more concerned with receipts than revenge in the weeks leading up the Cup. "And they wonder why they can't win this event," scoffed Nick Faldo.

"It's only the Americans who claim money should be involved," Colin Montgomerie gibed." Not one European I have spoken to wants to be paid. We should play for flags, not money."

A month earlier, an agonized Crenshaw was forced to stamp out a brushfire at the PGA Championship at Medinah. That's where Tiger Woods won his second major, fending off the irrepressible youth of Sergio Garcia, who skipped his way into the galleries' hearts. All wasn't so carefree, however. The Nos. 1- and 2-ranked players in the world, Woods and David Duval, had derided the Ryder Cup, with Duval calling it "a pretty large corporate outing" and Woods dismissing it as "pros on parade." Phil Mickelson and Mark O'Meara (a two-time major winner the previous year) added to the discontent by raising the issue of player compensation, which Crenshaw feared was eroding the team's chemistry, pride and patriotism he had been hoping to build.

O'Meara had started the chatter before the '97 Ryder Cup when he griped about the requirements the PGA of America made of the team, specifically corporate functions that handsomely profited the PGA while players were handed a meager $5,000 stipend for their time and effort. The sight of PGA officials parading around in team gear had to rankle, when it was the players who put themselves on the line and took the heat if they didn't perform.

"I wish I could tell you exactly what I think of the Ryder Cup, but I won't," O'Meara told *Sports Illustrated*'s Gary Van Sickle. "Unfortunately, players on both sides have been lambasted in the press for losing matches. I don't think that's fair. You win or lose as a team. I mean, the players aren't getting paid, and a lot of people are paying a lot of money to watch."

The media saw it as an ignoble stance, and the matter simmered for another two years until *Golf Digest's* Ryder Cup preview issue, which reported that the PGA of America would gross $63 million for the week, splitting the net profits (excluding television broadcast revenue) with The Country Club. Duval blew up in a Q&A in that same issue. While he later denied he was threatening a boycott, it certainly seemed that way.

"The Ryder Cup is an exhibition. The whole thing has become a little overcooked, but it's probably going to stay that way until players choose not to play," Duval said.

"Could that happen?"

"I think it could."

"Would you be among them?"

"I don't know. It's hard for me to say. But it goes back to where we were before. Where do you draw the line? There are the four majors every year, plus the four World Championships, plus the Players Championship, the Tour Championship. That's ten. And they're basically saying to a guy like Tiger that, for the next ten or twenty years, he will play either a Ryder or Presidents Cup every autumn. And you have no choice. Imagine the outcry if Tiger Woods chose not to play in a Ryder Cup."

"Or David Duval."

"Or David Duval."

Reading that, Crenshaw must have felt a pang in his heart, as he strode into an emergency closed-door meeting on Tuesday of PGA Championship week along with PGA of America CEO Jim Awtrey, PGA Tour Commissioner Tim Finchem and the top sixteen players in the Ryder Cup standings (the final roster would be set with Crenshaw's two captain's picks the next Monday). Just that morning, he had to listen to Woods, undoubtedly under the influence of his good buddy O'Meara, add to the discord at his press conference, where he told a packed room: "It's an exhibition. It always has been."

That was before the meeting in which Awtrey and Finchem attempted to assuage the rising rancor and explain all the good things the PGA was doing to "grow the game" with Ryder Cup profits. Not surprisingly, they emerged to announce that everyone was on the "same page."

"We're going to be talking to the players about the charitable contributions and what we can do that lets everybody feel good about our support of the game," Awtrey said. "The players right now are focused on the Ryder Cup, winning the Ryder Cup, and there is no issue between the PGA of America and players."

That could have been the end of it. Even O'Meara parroted the "same page" message. But not so fast. Crenshaw was still tormented by the entire thing. When questioned at his press conference the next day, it was apparent that there wasn't as much goodwill and understanding as Awtrey and Finchem purported there was. And that, at best, only a temporary truce had been reached. Without naming names, Crenshaw named names.

"I'm personally disappointed by a couple of people in that meeting," he said. "I mean that. And they know who they are. Whether some players like it or not, there are some people who came before them who meant a lot to this game. And it burns the hell out me to listen to some of their viewpoints."

Crenshaw admitted he was unable to hold his tongue even though he intended to do so.

"If playing for your country is not a reward, I don't know what is," he said. "I cherish my times in it. And every player who has ever played in a Ryder Cup on both sides thanks the good Lord for their chance to play in something that means so much. You cannot ask for a purer form of competition. I get emotional talking about golf. Golf has meant so much to our lives. To be part of playing for your country, I can't imagine any more than that. It's an honor in itself. It's a duty."

The public scolding revived the controversy, and, by Thursday of that week, some players were accusing others of greed. Meanwhile, Crenshaw attempted to apologize to players with the players not readily accepting the apology. Duval had watched Crenshaw's press conference live on the *Golf Channel* and immediately called him. He asked Crenshaw if he had been talking about him. Crenshaw said he was. Meanwhile, Mickelson, who was said to be the most vocal player at the meeting, claimed he was unaware of Crenshaw's disappointment but added: "I'm disappointed he decided to use the media as a forum."

It was too late to keep the lid on things as more details leaked out. Ryder Cup veteran Brad Faxon, who wasn't part of the meeting, disclosed how Davis Love III, a future US captain, felt about the malcontents, quoting Love's alleged charge: "Let's be honest, this isn't about charity. It's about putting money in your pockets."

"This talk about the money going to charity is a crock," Faxon fumed. "I know a lot of guys at eleven, twelve, thirteen (in the Ryder Cup points standings) who would pay to play on that team. I think we would be better having them than the guys who are complaining about how much they're getting."

There were also players in the middle like Tom Lehman, who would be one of the two captain's picks announced the next week. "The whole thing makes me want to throw up. We should be ashamed of ourselves," he sighed.

Realizing how much worse he'd made things, Crenshaw tried to walk back (or at least contextualize) his criticism when he was approached after his first PGA round on Thursday.

"I know I'm from a different generation. I'm trying to understand their side," he explained. "I don't care who it is, we've got to be focused as a team. I told them I'm very frustrated. I've spent a long time thinking and worrying about this."

Crenshaw's counterpart, European captain Mark James, must have enjoyed the dustup as another example of American greed. "We're not going into the Ryder Cup for money, never have been," he scoffed. "We're losing touch with reality, people."

The money flap simply fueled stereotypes that had been forming since Jack Nicklaus left the Ryder Cup arena. To many, the difference between the US and European players was spelled out on the hats they wore. The Americans had each player's name stitched into them, while the backs of the Euro hats read simply "European Team."

Through the European perspective, Americans were a bunch of uptight, entitled and arrogant individuals coddled by their parents' country club memberships. They performed well on singles day yet struggled when playing—and sharing the limelight—with partners. The Euros were fun-loving lads who loved sharing a pint and had each other's backs while unselfishly and perfectly blending with their partners. They played for the love of the game. The Americans played for the almighty greenback. Such perceptions, in fact, went back to British papers of the 1920s. What's more, many American fans (and media) agreed with the "spoiled millionaires" theory.

To add to Europe's motivation, the Americans seemed rather cocky about their chances. "On paper, they shouldn't be caddying for us," Payne Stewart said, while Jeff Maggert added: "Let's face it, we've got the twelve best players in the world."

Almost. Ten Americans resided among the top sixteen of the World Rankings, including three of the top four. Europe had only three because stalwarts Faldo, Ian Woosnam and, most surprisingly, Bernhard Langer, didn't make the team, leaving seven European players to play in their first Ryder Cup matches. It was a problem James would have to face as the week went on but, for now, he and his team embraced the underdog role as if it were a comfy blanket. Colin Montgomerie must have reveled in the psychological advantage as he remarked blithely: "The pressure's clearly on the Americans." Even O'Meara noted that the Europeans had nothing to lose and everything to gain.

Mostly, James seemed above it all with his wry smiles and quick wit. This was a man who had been fined by the tournament players committee of the British PGA for conduct unbecoming at the 1979 Ryder Cup where his infractions were listed as "arriving improperly dressed when the team departed from London, failure to attend rules and team meetings and writing an offensive remark on a menu when asked to autograph it." James, to put it mildly, was a non-conformist. Yet it was as if he felt no need to say anything controversial, because the Americans were doing such a good job of messing things up by themselves. His dry, clipped one-liners contrasted with–and even appeared to mock–Crenshaw's wistful discursiveness.

James could also take some comfort in the golf course, a superb one for match play. It may have been one of the cradles of American golf, but The Country Club had an English flair. According to golf architecture guru Ron Witten, The Country Club was an example of steeplechase golf design more prevalent in Britain's inland courses such as Sunningdale. Rocky and wild in some spots, its twisting, tumbling fairways, tiny greens, blind shots, mounds and pot bunkers would make the visitors feel right at home, no matter how much Crenshaw set up the course to favor his team.

At least Crenshaw could rest more easily with the compensation issue having died down; however, it did pop up again early in the week at Awtrey's press conference and it didn't make the PGA of America CEO look too good. Jimmy Roberts, then early in his career at *ESPN*, asked Awtrey why, if the PGA were making tens of millions of dollars, the players shouldn't have a piece of the pie? Instead of answering, Awtrey shouted down and belittled Roberts, who shrunk back down into his seat. Awtrey then called on Dave Anderson, the esteemed columnist from the *New York Times,* who he undoubtedly assumed would steer the conversation away from money and back to golf.

Anderson rose and, in his inimitably easy manner said plainly: "Yes. I'd like you to answer Jimmy's question."

In any event, Crenshaw had ultimately managed to put the thorny issue behind his team. It also seemed as if he was finally striking a chord with the players (in a way Tom Kite, the previous captain, could not) and, in doing so, getting them invested in the cause. To promote camaraderie, Crenshaw arranged for his players to stay in a cluster of rooms surrounding a large team suite at the Boston Four Seasons hotel. Knowing Woods' obsession with video games, he had a Nintendo 64 hooked up. Blowup photos of past Ryder Cup teams decorated the walls, and an inspirational video of Arnold Palmer's life played in a loop. The Crenshaws based the welcome dinner menu on that of the first Ryder Cup in 1927. And, while somewhat gaudy, the burgundy shirts to be worn on Sunday featured silk-screened images of victorious American squads. They even got team haircuts, and everyone–including the recalcitrant O'Meara–was talking about team unity. The rhetoric couldn't have been further removed from the grumbling that had gone on that summer.

"I think there's more of a calmness, a maturity that I see in our team," O'Meara said. "I see twelve guys plus a captain who want to go out and give it one hundred and ten per cent."

"This team, with Ben as the leader, is maybe a little more respectful of what the Ryder Cup means," Love said. "We're a little more determined. There a few of us who have been through some losing teams."

"There's a very strong sense of urgency for this team to win," added Lehman, who worked harder than anyone to earn a captain's pick along with Steve Pate. "I think we need to win. That's all there is to it."

"We've all put it behind us," Justin Leonard summed up. "As a team, we're in a good position. We're comfortable with what's going on, and now it's let's go ahead and play and get the Cup back."

The British press guffawed over this newfound *esprit de corps* as same old, same old. Tony Stenson, reporting for the *Daily Mirror,* scoffed that the Americans usually arrive at the Ryder Cup together "then promptly play for themselves."

Maybe that's why Crenshaw described figuring out the right combinations for the opening foursomes matches as "agony", while James said he simply listened to his players. "It's an easy team to pair," he deadpanned. "None of the countries are at war with each other, which is a big help."

Then Day One happened, leaving Crenshaw still in agony, James in control and Tony Stenson channeling Nostradamus. Dawn's early light had the red, white and blue in the lead in three of the four foursomes matches. Lehman, paired with Woods, chipped in for birdie on the first hole, and Love showed no ill effects of a recent shoulder injury by sticking one close on the third where his partner Payne Stewart, clad in his signature plus fours and Hogan-style cap, cleaned up the birdie.

Then the sweaters came off, along with the gloves of the Europeans. Their fast start stalled, and the Euros never relented until they built a startling 6-2 lead. It was, until then, the worst opening day in America's Ryder Cup history, and it ended ingloriously with Crenshaw's super pairing of Duval and Woods losing 1-up in the gloaming to Lee Westwood and Darren Clarke and their spectacular six-birdie performance. The European pair reveled in the theatre. When Woods, in trademark fashion, walked a rare birdie putt into the hole on eight, Clarke responded with a birdie of his own, embellished by returning an imaginary saber back into its scabbard. Touché.

On the day, the top two-ranked players in the world were a combined 0-4. And, meanwhile, the four rookies James put into action didn't lose a match, Crenshaw didn't get one win from Woods, Duval, Mickelson or Love (Hal Sutton and Jeff Maggert provided the only full point). Love, at least, showed some guts. If not for two clutch putts to halve both of his matches, Europe would already have been halfway to the fourteen points it needed to take the Cup home on the Concorde. Love's forty-foot putt on his final hole of the day prevented a European sweep of the fourball matches.

Afterwards, Crenshaw sounded like a punch-drunk fighter who didn't know what hit him. He wasn't even sure about the score. "I can't believe we're looking at a four-point difference here," he offered, calling the difference in play "infinitesimal.

"I just don't think, at least from my position, that it indicates how people played," he said. "It's what I've been saying for a long time, that holing out is the name of the game in match play. It gets you into the frame of mind where you're a little more bullet-proof. You're ready to take on the next little crisis. Gosh, they do a good job of that."

To prove that point, Europe one-putted forty greens on the day. Meanwhile, Mickelson, who was eleven-under par with Jim Furyk in their spectacular fourball match against Garcia and captain's pick Jesper Parnevik (the Swede shot a blistering 29 on the front nine), threw away a half-point by yanking a three-footer after a great shot into the par-three sixteenth, then missing a five-footer on eighteen. Garcia and Parnevik, an unlikely pairing of the exuberant Spaniard and eccentric Swede, were the stars of the day, with Garcia calling it the most enjoyable day of golf he'd ever had.

It began with the second match of the morning alternate shot session against Woods and Tom Lehman in what amounted to a super-hyped Medinah rematch seemingly aligned by fate.

Tiger was still stinging from his first encounter with the Ryder Cup two years earlier in Spain. Handcuffed by a golf course that took driver out of his hands, he secured just one and a half points out of a possible five. Garcia, the youngest player in Ryder Cup history at nineteen, had been too young to be a part of that European victory in his home country. But, of the seven rookies on the visiting side, more was expected from him than of any other. He was their golden boy. The youthful Garcia had even won over the American crowds during the practice rounds and while he, along with Woods, downplayed the showdown, it was evident that whoever took down the other would give their team a huge morale boost.

The Americans jumped out early when Lehman chipped in from off the green at four, with Woods fist-pumping in his most emotional outburst of the day. When Parnevik, who otherwise stole the match, botched a chip on five, Woods and Lehman had a 2-up lead. But the lead lasted only two holes after the Swede, with upturned brim flashing the Ryder Cup logo, played a brilliant shot to the 197-yard, par-three seventh. On twelve, the match turned for good. The hole was rated the toughest on the course, a 486-yard par four with a blind approach. Although Woods found the fairway and Garcia the rough off the tee, Parnevik got lucky by skidding a shot that somehow avoided the greenside bunkers while Lehman pulled a 3-iron slightly to the back fringe. It was still advantage US, but the Americans three-putted from there. Garcia, meanwhile, hit a marvelous bump-and-run to four feet. The Americans had been thinking par, the Europeans were looking at bogey, and both got the reverse.

Woods consistently outdrove Garcia as they both teed off on the even holes. However, when El Nino finally got Woods by a few feet on fourteen, he walked over to Parnevik's caddie, Lance Ten Broeck, and broke out into a huge grin that summed up the match and the day. "All I do is feed him chocolate and let him go," James said of his wonder kid.

James' stoicism contrasted with Crenshaw's angst. "Good day for us–only one out of three though," he said in his understated fashion. "But a day's job well done. I would say they are somewhat chuffed."

Asked about the psychological impact of Clarke and Westwood's win over Woods and the particularly struggling Duval, James added: "I don't think they're ones to suffer lasting psychological damage."

Yes, it was all good fun for James, as he headed back to the team room. Yet, he shouldered one lingering problem: what to do with the three rookies–Jarmo Sandelin, Andrew Coltart and John Van de Velde –he'd left out of action the entire day. He'd already decided to sit them in the Saturday morning foursomes. Could he risk hiding them until Sunday's singles? While he could be flippant about how easy it was to pick his teams, the depth of his roster had yet to be tested against a solid, one-to-twelve, American squad.

"I'm going to do whatever it takes with my team to get the most points possible at every stage of the match," James asserted. "And if that means resting guys, I'll rest them. There are no egos to be bruised."

Rest or rust? That was the real question. But James probably had settled on his game plan before he had arrived in Boston. It was part of the European playbook. The "Fab Five" of Ballesteros, Langer, Woosnam, Faldo and Sandy Lyle were what Europeans liked to call their talismans and, ever since, European captains relied on a core of studs to run up the team points before holding on Sunday.

James, undoubtedly, was counting on winning the day to open an insurmountable lead and not fret over the holes in his singles lineup. Crenshaw hoped to at least chip away at the deficit. Neither got explicitly what he wanted. Europe held serve, leaving the US with a sliver of hope and not much more. The day began in hazy sunshine, then a steady drizzle that reflected the Americans' mood and ended with Garcia gyrating and hugging Parnevik after sinking a nine-foot birdie putt to win the hole and halve a great match with Duval and Love. That left teams splitting the day's eight points and the Europeans in a 10-6 lead, needing to win just four of the available twelve Sunday points.

Crenshaw had tried to mix things up. In the morning foursomes, he paired Woods with captain's pick Steve Pate, who was kept out of the Friday matches. The pair took a combined 1-5-1 Ryder Cup record into the match but clicked to produce Woods' first Ryder Cup win, 1-up , over Padraig Harrington and Miguel Angel Jimenez in the last match remaining on the course. The Europeans had erased an early three-hole deficit to tie the match on the eleventh hole but Woods' 15-foot putt for eagle on fourteen provided the slim winning margin and a point the Americans desperately needed.

Hal Sutton and Jeff Maggert had provided the first point of the day with a 1-up victory over Montgomerie and Paul Lawrie. However, thanks to Maggert's iron shot to within inches of the cup on eighteen, Europe would convincingly win the other two matches. Garcia-Parnevik pairing continued to dominate, 3-and-2, over Payne Stewart and Justin Leonard, and Padraig Harrington and Miguel Angel Jimenez edged out (also 3-and-2) Jim Furyk and Mark O'Meara, playing his first match of the week.

With his traditional advantage in alternate shot now achieved, James went for the kill in the afternoon, sitting Sandelin, Van de Velde and Coltart once again. He didn't get it exactly, but was what he did get enough? It was the best-played of the team sessions with brilliance on both sides, but the second stalemated session of the day left things as they were on Friday. Needing to win the afternoon, the Woods-Pate magic fizzled out in the anchor match, losing to Monty and Lawrie, 2-and-1 with Tiger fighting his putter. Mickelson changed his putter after Friday's mishaps, and he and Lehman, who both sat out the morning, started the afternoon well for the US by knocking off Clarke and Westwood, 2-and-1. The middle two matches were halved, thanks to Garcia's final clutch putt. That match produced the most drama of the day as well as the best shot after Love's tee shot on the par-five ninth came to rest in trampled down fescue on top of a rock outcropping, 231 yards from the green. He nearly holed out with a tap-in left for eagle. Three holes later, Parnevik pitched in from 50 yards away to save par, sending Sergio into another wild, ecstatic celebration.

"No matter what we do, it seems they do a little better," fretted Love, who missed a putt on seventeen that would have ended the match. "We're trying to hang in there but it's getting tougher and tougher."

It would now take the greatest comeback in Ryder Cup history to prevent the greatest upset.

Crenshaw's somber press conference addressed a disbelieving crowd. He tried to convince the room that his players were doing everything in their power to win the thing. However, after two days of excuses, his act was getting stale. His answers wandered, as he increasingly found questions tediously dispiriting. Suddenly, in a pique of frustration, he lashed out at the negativity, a display that would go down in the annals of Ryder Cup captaincies.

"I'm gonna leave y'all with one thought then I'm gonna leave," he said firmly. "I'm a big believer in fate," he continued, wagging his right index finger. Then he wagged his other index finger, winked and looked sideways at his inquisitors.

"I have a good feeling about this. That's all I'm gonna tell you," he abruptly concluded, once more wagging his right index finger for emphasis. Clearly wanting the last word, he summarily walked off the podium, carrying both his water bottle and his prophecy.

Fate was one thing, but it wasn't all wings and prayers. James had given Crenshaw the narrowest of openings–but an opening nonetheless–and the American team knew it. James could no longer hide his three weakest players. He had to play them, and he had to play them early. After all, if it went down to the wire, he couldn't ask them to hold up in one of the last matches with everything on the line. But what James didn't have to do is what he did. He set them up like bowling pins in the third, fourth and fifth matches which put them up against three of the most talented Americans–Sandelin against Mickelson, Van de Velde against Love and Coltart against Woods. Those points were nearly automatic, and if the Americans could pull out wins in the first two matches, with Lehman facing Westwood and Sutton facing Clarke, it would create a tidal wave of red.

Crenshaw would later admit he couldn't believe James sent them out three in a row. In fact, at an intense team meeting to figure out the Sunday lineup, most figured James would try to play his strongest players early to sew things up. That's why some of the strongest American players ended up in those lopsided matchups.

Some members of the team were back at the hotel watching Crenshaw's press conference and were now genuinely inspired by his closing remarks. Then they saw the pairings and realized they could win the first six matches.

Years later, Furyk told *Golf Digest* that he went from "being really upset to thinking maybe we've got a strategy. We went up to the team room and that's when I really started to believe." Love added that the turning point didn't occur on the golf course, "it occurred Saturday night."

Despair transformed into determination as the night played out.

When Crenshaw reunited with his team, he projected a nearly palpable, and apparently quite infectious, certitude. "The course will take care of us," he said, aware that an American had never lost at Brookline through two Walker Cups and three US Opens, including Curtis Strange's 1988 playoff win over Faldo. Then he shared a note that had just been handed to him. It claimed that Montgomerie had boasted: "You know it's over, don't you?" Monty later called it rubbish. At that point, it didn't matter.

Crenshaw put up a motivational video that included inspirational quotes, and the clip from Animal House in where John Belushi asked "Was it over when the Germans bombed Pearl Harbor? Hell no!" along with footage of cheerleaders from each players' alma mater before introducing a special guest, Texas governor George W. Bush, the future president.

Bush had planned his presentation months earlier but couldn't have known how appropriate it would be. He started to read the letter commander William Barret Travis sent to the people of Texas from The Alamo. It began with the line, "I am besieged" and ended with the famous quotation, "victory or death." Bush told them the entire nation was pulling for them. "Godspeed," he said as he left the room to silence. Gifts and shared stories with the wives present ensued.

Then, one by one, Crenshaw had the teammates share what the Ryder Cup meant to them. "Every night I go to bed with a smile on my face," Woods said. There was actually an air of confidence when they hit the sacks. The team could not have been in a better frame of mind under the circumstances.

Of course, those circumstances appeared dire to most outside those rooms. The introduction to *NBC's* coverage the next morning drove that point home, warning of "the indignity of losing on your own turf–again." For sure, one member of the *NBC* broadcast crew, veteran Ryder Cupper Johnny Miller, was providing more motivational material as they read his quotes in the morning paper. In what he later said was the one moment of his career he'd want back, he ripped Crenshaw's hunch for playing Leonard with Sutton over the steady Maggert Saturday afternoon. "I have a feeling he should've stayed home and sat on the couch, because he's not doing any good out there," Miller said as Leonard missed putts. Leonard, of course, would have his response in a few hours.

Now, the Europeans were becoming nervous. If they had harbored any notions that they'd locked it up, they could no longer do so now that James had provided the US with a clear path to a comeback victory. The scoreboard displayed the roadmap. When Parnevik, who had partnered so brilliantly with Garcia, checked the lineup on the practice range that morning, it gave him a bad feeling. He was overheard saying he couldn't see where the four European points were going to come from. He also understood that, playing in the sixth match against World No. 2 David Duval, he might have to stop the bleeding.

Of course, for the dominos to fall, the US had to win the two challenging leadoff matches. For those, Crenshaw sent out two of his "horses," Lehman and Sutton. As Lehman was on the table being stretched out in the clubhouse, the captain told him he was in the leadoff spot because "we believe in you." Lehman craned his neck and replied simply. "I can do the job." And he meant it.

While the Americans, sporting their garish shirts, seemed to have had a shot of adrenaline, the Europeans were battling fatigue, beginning in the opening two matches where Westwood and Clarke were among the seven Europeans who had played in all four matches over the first two days. Together, the pair won a total of three holes all day. Lehman took the lead for good on the fourth hole, hit all sixteen greens and would win, 3-and-2. Sutton lost the first hole when Clarke chipped in but didn't lose his next until fourteen, when the match was all but locked up. He won, 4-and-3. Before either of those matches ended, the US already had its first point from Love's 6-and-5 defeat of the overmatched Van de Velde, the first of James' weak cards.

As the avalanche gathered momentum, the American fans were getting riled up—too much so, perhaps. James might have made one major miscalculation preparing his team. The matches were being played in Boston and, as any American sports fan knows, Boston has some of the rowdiest and rudest fans in the nation, especially when overserved. James assumed there would be a degree of civility from the home galleries, especially after encouraging his team to reach out to fans and accommodate autograph requests. He would have been better off taking them to Fenway Park and sitting them in the bleachers with the Yankees in town. These were Boston fanatics, not Augusta patrons. It may have been unsportsmanlike and uncalled for, but that's the kind of treatment he could have expected. The Europeans seemed to be caught by surprise when they got it. And they got it good, once those fans could go full throat about something.

There had already been no shortage of boorish behavior directed toward the visitors before Sunday. Again, Montgomerie was razzed for his resemblance to Robin William's Mrs. Doubtfire, and in one instance, Jimenez was put off by some intentional chatter during his backswing. Not that the Americans escaped unscathed. The same crowd that seemed to embrace Sergio were so frustrated that they resorted to heckling the American wives in their cute outfits. Duval caught an earful from one hometown fan who screamed: "What do you think of the exhibition now? This is a long way for you to come for a whipping."

But hometown fans can be fickle as well. By the end of the final day, they had turned all of their hostility toward the Europeans. The distinguished Sir Michael Bonallack of the Royal and Ancient Golf Club called it a "bear pit," and James used that as the title of his book. Frank Hannigan, the former USGA executive, was so put off he wrote an op-ed for the *New York Times* on the rise of the golf hooligan.

Someone spat at Mark James' wife, while a marshal who was supposed to be neutral purposefully sent Coltart in the wrong direction in search of his ball in his match against Woods. "They wanted to win at all cost—and that cost was their dignity," said Jimenez, heckled throughout. But the hecklers saved most of their scorn for and hurled most of their abuse at Montgomerie, who had been playing near-flawless golf all week.

To the hometown fans, Monty was the embodiment of British golf–a bit too proper, somewhat haughty, and prone to strutting like a peacock when he was playing well, which he was. His body shape made for easy fodder. But the Scot was also known for his rabbit ears and for staring back into the gallery after responding with a good shot. There was plenty to pick up on this day and much more than ribbing. It was vitriolic.

Much of it occurred during Montgomerie's pre-shot routine and when he was over the ball.

"Choke, Monty!" someone cried. "Shank it, you fat pig!" jeered another. Someone on the ninth tee shockingly crossed the line by calling him a "cunt." Montgomerie's father couldn't take it. He left the course midway through the match. Stewart was appalled at the treatment Monty was receiving and assured him that if he had a problem, he would take care of the perpetrators. When one lout howled during Montgomerie's backswing on the fifth tee, Stewart had the guy thrown out.

"I was disgusted with some of the actions and some of the name calling that goes on with Colin," Stewart said. "What's he got–a big bullseye on his back? He doesn't deserve that. That's not what this event is about."

While abuse was wholly uncalled for, the roars were not. What started as plaintive pleas of "USA, USA" turned into a deafening din resounding throughout the course informing all, especially the Euro players, of what was unfolding. The Country Club's grounds aren't big. The galleries' reverberations swelled to a decibel (and animosity) level that genuinely alarmed and intimidated the European players.

Indeed, the rout was on. The Europeans just weren't losing. They were getting hammered with one match feeding the next. James' gamble failed spectacularly. Love destroyed Van de Velde. Mickelson took advantage of Sandelin's double bogey at ten and won,

4-and-3. Coltart hung with Woods for a while but Tiger's chip-in birdie on seven led to a 3-and-2 win.

Mickelson must have taken particular delight in throttling Sandelin, Europe's resident bad boy, free spirit and loner. Take your pick. The lefthander lost to the Finnish-born Swede at the 1996 Dunhill Cup at St. Andrews where Sandelin celebrated every birdie putt by firing an imaginary rifle. Mickelson believed the feigned gunfire was aimed at him and took umbrage. Walking off the thirteenth green, they came nose-to-nose and had words.

"I told him to fuck off," Sandelin explained in an interview with *Sports Illustrated* just before coming to Brookline. "I haven't spoken to him since and have no desire to do so."

"I feel sorry for Mickelson and O'Meara," he remarked with mocked concern. "Think about the pressure on them! They really have to kick my ass. If they lose, at home? My god, imagine the shame. For me, to lose is expected. It's no big deal because no one is rooting for me."

No one who wasn't European, at least. Heckled throughout, Sandelin lost and lost big, self-destructing after the turn, although none of the bad blood boiled over. "I was expecting gamesmanship and he showed nothing but class," Mickelson said. But there was one amusing incident on the second hole. Sandelin had hit his shot to three feet and was expecting Mickelson to concede the putt. As Sandelin fumbled in his pocket for a marker, a fan yelled, "Jarmo, do you need a coin?" When Sandelin nodded yes, he was greeted with a shower of dimes, nickels and quarters.

Woods, meanwhile, said he was fired up when he matched Coltart's shot to within three feet on four. "Let's go to the next," Coltart said. "No," Woods replied. "Let's putt 'em."

While hoping he could squeeze a half point out of his over-matched trio, James was counting on Westwood and Parnevik to win their matches. But after carrying Garcia most of the week, Parnevik had nothing left. Ten Broeck, his caddy, later recalled the blank look on his face and how he couldn't focus, that he was worn out. The same guy who shot 29 on the front nine Friday shot 38

Sunday, losing 6-and-5, to Duval. The same guy who said the Ryder Cup was "an exhibition" then exhibited something else. With his shirt untucked, Duval revved up the crowd with double fist-pumps and later admitted, "as many people have told me, it's something you can't explain or appreciate until you're part of it."

That victory gave the Americans a sweep of the first six matches, the exact outcome they had hoped for Saturday night. Pate made it seven straight by finishing off Jimenez. Four and a half hours in, the US had its first lead of the week. At the same time, things were not looking good for Europe in the Furyk-Garcia match where Sergio appeared nearly as burned out as Parnevik had become. Furyk noted that, despite his record, Garcia had been relying too much on Parnevik and wasn't at the top of his game. So, he kept the pressure on by doing what he does best–hitting fairways–and walked off with a 4-and-3 win. Garcia was in tears at the end of the day.

After Harrington and Lawrie managed to secure points for Europe, there were two matches remaining on the course–Leonard-Olazábal and Stewart-Montgomerie. If the Americans got a half point out of either match, they'd pull it off. Both matches were at all-square, Monty and Stewart with three to play and Leonard and Olazábal with two to play. The defiant Montgomerie would still present a tough halve but Leonard had totally shifted the momentum against his Spanish foe.

Leonard was struggling when Love's match ended so quickly and, with Leonard in the rough again, Crenshaw sent Love out to lend his teammate some moral support. Love found him nearly in tears. Leonard made his fifth bogey in eleven holes and considered shooing Love away. With Olazábal four up at that point, the match looked like a certain European point.

"I kept telling him, 'Win a hole. He's going to give you a hole. He's due to hook one. Look how low he's teeing the ball,'" Love told *Golf Digest* years later. "I was trying to tell him anything to give him some confidence. Then, all of a sudden, he did win a hole. And then Olazábal did give him a hole. And then he made a putt. And then he birdied fourteen (with a 12-footer). Then, all of a sudden, his eyes were getting real big and he was starting to believe that he could win."

"We talked about a lot last night," Leonard said afterwards. "Not thinking about the result or the outcome but playing each shot one at a time. When you win one or two holes in a row, the momentum shifts. And even though I was two down going up fourteen I felt like I was in the driver's seat."

Leonard caught him on fifteen when he drained a 25-footer with confidence. Now most of his teammates were following his match as it reached seventeen. Olazábal hit his approach shot first, finding the green 25 feet from the hole. He kept pointing to a gallery member who had let out a dramatically loud yawn during his backswing. His caddie, Brendan McCartain, snapped at the offender: "If you need to win the Ryder Cup that bad, then you can have it." Leonard had a wedge left into the green, and it looked like a superb shot until it spun back past Olazábal's ball to 45 feet. The crowd murmured. Michael Jordan was watching the action from inside the ropes. Love passed by and told him he was too nervous to talk to him. There was no telling about Leonard's nerves.

But confidence is everything on the greens. Leonard had relied on his putter while winning the 1997 Open Championship at Royal Troon and, after struggling all week, that feeling returned with each ball that went into the cup during his comeback. As he eyed the uphill putt, he had a good idea what it would do.

"I didn't know if I could make it," he admitted. "But let's say this–I was trying to make it but I was also trying to get the ball close. It's a putt we hit as a team during practice rounds. Everybody knew it went right up to the top of the hill. It was just one of those things."

The entire world seemed congregated around the seventeenth green, including the wives, the caddies, the media, PGA officials and Crenshaw. As he squatted, he knew that just over the wall was Ouimet's boyhood home, and the seventeenth was the very green where Ouimet sank two critical twenty-footers to force the playoff against Vardon and Ray. He reflected again about Penick, his father and the fate that had delivered him and his team to this most perfect of places. And then Leonard swung back his putter, stroked through smoothly, and the ball rolled and rolled as if the green were a bowling alley. And then the ball, and fate, fell into place. It was "destined to go in," Leonard said.

Now, if there were ever a moment to hit the reset button, this would have been it. Leonard, understandably, lifted both arms, danced clumsily and leapt into the air as high as he could, which set off a wild stampede of those wives, caddies—and even a cameraman—over the expanse of the green. It was as if a gasket had blown, releasing a week's worth of pent-up frustrations and emotions. But the celebration was premature. The hole had not yet been won. Olazábal still had a putt for the halve. Lehman was blamed by most of the Europeans for being a prime instigator of the over-the-top display, and he was certainly part of the charge. But the whole scene seemed to be touched off by a few wives who were kneeling directly in the path of Leonard's putt. While the players skirted the green on the way to Leonard, who had made his way over to the left corner, the wives' path sent them trampling directly over Olazábal's line as he stood there stunned. At last, order was restored as Leonard, aware of Olazábal's predicament, pleaded with everyone, "Off the green!"

Olazábal finally got his read and stepped over the putt only to back off when a siren went off in the distance. The gallery hooted. At least they managed to remain silent as Olazábal sent the putt on its way. When it rolled wide of the hole by two inches on the low side, the Americans had clinched, but in a way that would live in infamy, so far as the Europeans were concerned.

"I thought it was very sad to see . . . very ugly to see," Olazábal said. "Cheer for your team all you want. Just show some respect for your opponent."

Assistant captain Sam Torrance called the episode, "about the most disgusting thing I've seen in my life.

"This is not sour grapes," he said. "The whole American team and spectators ran right across the green over Ollie's line. He still has a putt to tie the hole and we could still take the Ryder Cup home. It was disgusting and Tom Lehman calls himself a man of God. His behavior was disgusting."

Montgomerie couldn't believe the scene as he walked up seventeen. He saw TV commentator David Feherty, a former European Ryder Cupper, but no friend, and told him, "I don't know how you live here."

Crenshaw later apologized for everyone's conduct but, for now, he was overwhelmed. He immediately fell over and kissed the ground three times, then started asking for Lanny Wadkins, the 1995 captain whose team had collapsed in the singles that year. He started mumbling something about Ouimet's horseshoe, thinking back to a photo of the young caddy carrying a horseshoe while being held aloft after his playoff win over Vardon and Ray. Another image emerged: his father accompanying him around the course as a sixteen-year-old at the 1968 US Junior Amateur, when The Country Club provided him with his first national stage.

"They had a beautiful horse racing track that crossed just to the right on number one and came right in front of number eighteen. I can see my father walking across there. And this is for him, too," he said.

Leonard later blamed himself for the sorry scene. "I should have calmly walked off the side of the green, which would have been very hard to do. But if I hadn't displayed so much emotion maybe some of the other guys (would not have). So, if you're looking to point a finger at somebody, please point it at me. I do apologize for that."

Lehman wasn't as remorseful.

"What happened on seventeen was unfortunate. We all got excited," he said. "There was never any ill intent on anybody's part whatsoever. We probably wish we all would have jumped up and down in place instead of running down the side of the green. But I'm not going to apologize for being excited. It was a great day for the American team. I guess memories are somewhat short. Valderamma wasn't exactly a cakewalk for us. Their fans were pretty interesting, too."

It was left to Stewart to demonstrate some semblance of sportsmanship. He and Montgomerie needed to finish out their match if only for the final score. On eighteen, he hit out the greenside bunker to twenty feet. Monty was on in two, twenty feet out. Had Stewart made his putt and Montgomerie two-putted, the match would have ended up all square. Instead, Stewart conceded for a 1-up loss. Final score: US 14 ½, Europe 13 ½.

Less than a month later, Stewart was among six people killed in a Learjet crash in South Dakota. The night of the US victory, Stewart and Sutton discussed how honored they would be to be named Ryder Cup captains one day. Sutton got his chance in 2004.

Montgomerie, whose Ryder Cup record improved to 6-0-2 at Brookline, wouldn't forget Stewart's gesture.

"When he won the US Open at Pinehurst, the first thing he said was he was in the Ryder Cup team, and he was thrilled to be in the Ryder Cup team—even more than he was winning the US Open," Montgomerie remembered at the time of Stewart's death. "It meant so much to him to represent his country. And to have drawn against me, of all people, in the singles match—I'm sure that it hurt his game, as well as it did my own. And it was a shame the way it finished. He'd had enough, I'd had enough, and he picked my ball up at the last. I'll never forget that. Not all the memories (from Brookline) are fond. But that match I will always think of with fond memories of that game with him."

Fan behavior and the scene at the seventeenth green aside, there was no denying it was an incredible performance by the home team. Sutton called it "a display of American firepower," a red wave, said James, that the Europeans were powerless against.

"The putts were just going in from all angles. And the chips," he said, sardonic until the end. "We couldn't do anything to stop it. Perhaps I could have rung up a bomb scare. Maybe that would have stopped it." At the same time, James didn't regret his lineup decisions. He insisted the Europeans were "outplayed," not "outmaneuvered" and said he'd do it all over again.

Olazábal felt worse than anyone. Angry with his inability to hit more fairways in his critical match against Leonard, he tossed two drivers off the European balcony. Garcia, who was found crying after the American victory, spilled over two dozen golf balls.

Meanwhile, the Americans mixed it up with their equally delirious fans from the balcony over the men's grill. No one was complaining about compensation. Stewart and Sutton sprayed champagne from above on revelers who waved American flags and chanted, "USA, USA" Woods had a bottle of champagne in one hand and the other around his caddie, Mike "Fluff " Cowan. Stewart hugged and kissed Leonard as the crowd below chanted, "Jus-tin. Just-tin, Jus-tin" and then, in unison, "Jus-tin-Leonard, Jus-tin-Leonard."

In emerging as the unlikely hero, Leonard ironically didn't win a match all week. But Miller owed him an apology. When he arrived at the course in the morning, Leonard's caddie, Bob Riefke, found his boss sulking. "It's Johnny Miller, right?" he asked him. "Don't worry about it," he said, slapping him on the back. "Let's go prove him wrong."

After Leonard did just that, he said simply: "I guess it's a good thing I didn't go home."

While American newspapers regaled readers with details of the miracle comeback, British papers launched into scathing criticism of the overzealous celebration and fan behavior, some overreacting to the overreaction. It was jingoism, they claimed.

The staid *Times of London* went relatively easy with its headline: "Americans grab tainted triumph."

But others were not as reserved.

The *London Evening Standard*: "How to win a Cup but lose all dignity."

The Express: "A horror show."

The Daily Mail: "Utter disgrace."

Sport: "Disgusting"

The Daily Mirror: "Crenshaw won it by controlling a bag of weasels."

"Let us be painfully honest about it," Matthew Norman wrote in the *Evening Standard.* "Yes, they are repulsive people, charmless, rude, cocky, mercenary, humorless, ugly, full of nauseatingly fake religiosity and as odious in victory as they are unsporting in defeat."

The *Daily Telegraph* quoted British analyst Peter Alliss, a former Ryder Cup star declaring, "I think Americans are bad winners. Their exuberance seems to be less gracious than our exuberance and I have no idea why. Americans are totally different to us; they might as well be Chinese. In their eyes, pretty much everything in Europe is rubbish."

"Ben Crenshaw and American golfers stand accused this morning of trampling over the fine traditions of golf. Football hooligans act better than the way the Americans have treated the Ryder Cup over the last three days," wrote Tony Stenson.

"Crenshaw calls himself a traditionalist owning a vast library of books and golf memorabilia. When he reads the story of the thirty third Ryder Cup, he should feel shame. He cared nothing for others when he dug his size ten heels into the green and acted like a demented teenager."

Meanwhile, Kate Battersby of the *Evening Standard* tore into the Americans for, of all things, winning.

"So the Americans love themselves again. What a relief to us all," she wrote. "For one brief shining moment—or rather, since the row over money erupted at the PGA—their abiding self-adoration was dimmed a little and dimmed a lot over the first two days of the Ryder Cup . . . The US triumphed here because they managed to do separately what they could not do together. Only in America could the inability to work as a unit be hailed as a triumph of teamwork."

Not that Crenshaw, who was too busy kissing the ground to have charged onto the green, immediately concerned himself with those recriminating slings and arrows from abroad.

Afterwards, the American caddies presented Crenshaw with a gift. They had chipped in on a $6,500, twenty-three-inch replica of the statue of Ouimet and caddie Eddie Lowery that stands at The

Country Club's first tee. They also placed a tiny American flag in Lowery's bag. It could not have been a more fitting commemoration of what Crenshaw called a "spooky" victory.

"I've never seen such an indomitable spirit," he said. "They did not ever lose sight of what they were doing.

"Today . . . I'll tell you, it's up in the trees." he said, glancing up to the heavens. "It's fate."

Whatever it was, it was not soon forgotten.

DAY 1

FOURSOMES

Paul Lawrie/Colin Montgomerie (E) defeated David Duval/Phil Mickelson (US) 3-and-2

Sergio Garcia/Jesper Parnevik (E) defeated Tom Lehman/Tiger Woods (US) 2-and-1

Davis Love III/Payne Stewart (US) halved with Padraig Harrington/Miguel Angel Jimenez (E)

Jeff Maggert/Hal Sutton (US) defeated Darren Clarke/Lee Westwood (E) 3-and-2

Europe wins session 2 ½–1 ½

FOURBALLS

Sergio Garcia/Jesper Parnevik (E) defeated Jim Furyk/Phil Mickelson (US) 1-up

Justin Leonard/Davis Love III (US) halved with Colin Montgomerie/Paul Lawrie (E)

Miguel Angel Jimenez/Jose Maria Olazábal (E) defeated Jeff Maggert/Hal Sutton (US) 2-and-1

Darren Clarke/Lee Westwood (E) defeated David Duval/Tiger Woods (US) 1-up

Europe wins session, 3 ½–½

Europe 6, United States 2

DAY 2

FOURSOMES

Jeff Maggert/Hal Sutton (US) defeated Colin Montgomerie/Paul Lawrie (E) 1-up

Darren Clarke/Lee Westwood (E) defeated Jim Furyk/Mark O'Meara (US) 3-and-2

Steve Pate/Tiger Woods (US) defeated Miguel Angel Jimenez/Padraig Harrington (E) 1-up

Sergio Garcia/Jesper Parnevik (E) defeated Justin Leonard/Payne Stewart (US) 3-and-2

Session is halved, 2–2

Europe 8, United States 4

FOURBALLS

Phil Mickelson/Tom Lehman (US) defeated Darren Clarke/Lee Westwood (E) 2-and-1
Sergio Garcia/Jesper Parnevik (E) halved with Davis Love III/David Duval (US)
Justin Leonard/Hal Sutton (US) halved with Miguel Angel Jimenez/Jose Maria Olazábal (E)
Paul Lawrie/Colin Montgomerie (E) defeated Steve Pate/Tiger Woods (US) 2-and-1

Session is halved, 2–2

Europe 10, United States 6

DAY 3

SINGLES

Tom Lehman (US) defeated Lee Westwood (E) 3-and-2
Hal Sutton (US) defeated Darren Clarke (E) 4-and-2
Phil Mickelson (US) defeated Jarmo Sandelin (E) 4-and-3
Davis Love III (US) defeated Jean Van de Velde (E) 6-and-5
Tiger Woods (US) defeated Andrew Coltart (E) 3-and-2
David Duval (US) defeated Jesper Parnevik (E) 5-and-4
Padraig Harrington (E) defeated Mark O'Meara (US) 1-up
Steve Pate (US) defeated Miguel Angel Jimenez (E) 2-and-1
Justin Leonard (US) halved with Jose Maria Olazábal (E)
Colin Montgomerie (E) defeated Payne Stewart (US) 1-up
Jim Furyk (US) defeated Sergio Garcia (E) 4-and-3
Paul Lawrie (E) defeated Jeff Maggert (US) 4-and-3

United States wins session, 8 ½–3 ½

UNITED STATES WINS RYDER CUP, 14 ½–13 ½

2008

Zinging 'Em

VALHALLA GOLF CLUB

UNITED STATES 16 ½, EUROPE 11 ½

To understand how the 2008 Ryder Cup was won, start at the 2007 Open Championship.

It took place in Scotland at a sinister and torturous place known as Carnoustie—"Carnasty" to its countless victims—where US captain Paul Azinger, on hand as a TV commentator, had a eureka moment while forming his strategy to pry the diminutive but prized Cup from Europe's stubborn grasp.

The day after Padraig Harrington's victory, Azinger relaxed in the Edinburgh Airport lounge, shooting the Scottish breeze with a group of American golf writers. But it wasn't Harrington who was occupying his thoughts. Sergio Garcia, the volatile Spaniard who'd been spending his Ryder Cups inside the heads and under the skins of his American opponents, had laid bare the dark side of his psyche. "Zinger" sensed an opening.

Garcia, twenty-seven at the time and still seeking his first major victory, was close to fulfilling the enormous promise expected of him since he exploded onto the golf scene as the perky nineteen-year-old dubbed "El Nino." Playing his best golf, he had led from the opening round and had built his third-round lead to three shots, eight clear of nemesis Tiger Woods. With a 0-for-34 record in majors, Garcia sensed that the first of those championships was "there for the taking."

But, midway through that press conference, it was apparent that Garcia's demons still loomed. A reporter began his question with a caveat: "I don't want to rekindle any bad memories . . ." Sergio could have laughed it off. Instead, he stopped him in mid-sentence: "Okay, don't."

The next day, Garcia created a fresh string of memories–and the worst yet. After adding a stroke to his lead early on, he shot a nervy 38 on the front side and fell two back. Ultimately, a sloppy double bogey on eighteen by Padraig Harrington re-opened the door. Just a simple par and Garcia would be quaffing sangria from the claret jug. But nothing was that simple with Garcia. Playing safe with an iron off the tee, he found the greenside bunker with his longer approach shot and was agonizingly left begging as a 10-footer for par curled around the cup in the rottenest of breaks. Garcia threw back his head in disbelief and headed for a four-hole playoff where more bad luck–and a loss to Harrington, no great friend–awaited him.

Later, Garcia blamed everybody but the vendor selling Arbroath Smokies–and himself. He whined over three lip-outs on the last four holes of regulation and groused how workmen were too slow with their rake jobs on eighteen, forcing him to wait what he cynically claimed was "fifteen minutes" to hit his final approach shot. He couldn't fathom the depths of his misfortune when he hit the flagstick in the playoff, only to watch the ball bound pitiably twenty feet away.

In an attempt to console the Spaniard, the R&A's press conference moderator gently began the session. "I know you're bitterly disappointed." Before he could continue, Garcia shot back.

"No, I'm thrilled."

He proceeded to allow his emotions to spill over the packed interview room. He was a quivering mess. Some saw it as self-indulgent, self-absorbed and nearly paranoid. Whatever it was, it wasn't pretty.

"It's funny how some guys hit the pin and go a foot. It's tough but to tell the truth I didn't do anything wrong. I guess it's not news in my life. I should write a book on how to not miss a shot in the playoff and shoot one-over. You know what's the saddest thing about it? It's not the first time. It's not the first time unfortunately. So, I don't know. I'm playing against a lot of guys out there, more than the field."

Garcia's display of what appeared as whiny self-pity—and how to exploit it—quickly became the topic of conversation in the airport lounge. Azinger knew that the Ryder Cup always brought out the best in Garcia, and that his best was as good as anyone's. He also knew that Garcia got the Americans' goat more than anyone on the European team. In 2002, he taunted David Toms by dancing a jig in front of him after Europe clinched the Cup at The Belfry. After winning the 2006 Ryder Cup at the K Club he crowed: "There's nothing sweeter than beating the Americans."

Now Azinger's mind was churning with ideas, consumed by a Bill Belichick-like quest for victory. Just as the mastermind of the Patriots would home in on neutralizing the opposition's best player, Azinger began to think of ways to transform Europe's energetic, cocky spark plug from asset to hindrance.

"Sergio is the key," he said. "Take down Sergio and the dominos will fall."

That thought certainly wasn't part of the sporting, gentlemanly tradition of Ryder Cup play exemplified by Jack Nicklaus and The Concession in 1969. But Azinger, after all, played the villain in the 1991 War by the Shore where Seve Ballesteros described the American team as "Eleven nice guys . . . and Paul Azinger." The man who kicked cancer's butt wasn't about to change his pugilistic nature. Now, after years of being kicked around, the US team needed a healthy shot of chippiness. Azinger was the right captain at the right time.

He was named to the position in November of 2006, six weeks after America's embarrassing defeat at the K Club, where the Europeans became the first squad to capture all five sessions. Europe had won two straight Cups by identical record 18 ½-9 ½ margins and eight of the past eleven Cups in all. Azinger was determined to change nearly everything about how the team was put together and how it would stick together.

First, he instituted a qualifying process that used money earnings as the barometer with more value placed on the bigger events, reflecting his personality (as a player, Azinger often said he only got nervous when cash was on the line). That displaced the previous system that awarded points for top ten finishes, making a ninth-place finish in an opposite field event on the PGA Tour worth more than an eleventh-place finish in the major played the same week. He also emphasized most-recent play by awarding 2007 points in the four majors alone. He also gave himself greater latitude by increasing the number of captain's picks from two to four.

"I'm going to get the blame if it doesn't work," he said at his introductory press conference. "I would like some of the credit if it does."

Azinger hadn't yet devised his clever pods system, but he was already thinking outside the box that held every Cup for Europe since the Americans' rousing victory at Brookline. He might have had nothing to lose but just as an incoming coach can change the culture of a losing NFL franchise, Azinger knew that bold ideas would be required. The European team was strong but perhaps less united as it had been in the past, Captain Nick Faldo could be somewhat of a polarizing figure, even though his playing record of 23-19-4 accounted for (and still accounts for, at the time of this writing) the most points in Ryder Cup history. Here was a chance for the Americans, for once, to be the team that bonded more easily. That was probably truer with the best American player unavailable. Tiger Woods, whose Ryder Cup record was the only part of his resume that wasn't brilliant, was sitting this one out. He'd given everything he had to win the US Open on one good leg but sacrificed the remainder of the golf schedule to do so. There had been suggestions that Woods be brought into the team room as a vice captain, but he'd remain at his Florida home, "a text away" as he put it.

In what some saw as a risky decision, Azinger stocked half his roster with Ryder Cup "rookies," players, unscarred by the drubbing of Euro wins. Azinger instead hoped the newbies would bring a refreshing boost of enthusiasm to the team. All of it led to Azinger's ability to play up the underdog role and, for once, exert pressure on the Europeans. His next challenge was the perception, right or wrong, that the Europeans cared more about the Ryder Cup than the Americans. He also sought to dispel the conventional wisdom that Europeans were a team greater than the sum of its parts, and that the Americans were merely a team of individuals. So, he divided his twelve-man team into three four-man teams or pods.

He'd gotten the idea four years earlier, purely by chance.

"Lying on my couch with my shoes off, I sipped sweet, iced tea and watched a show about Gibson guitars on the Discovery Channel," he explained. "When the show ended, I was too lazy to hunt for the remote, so I started watching a documentary on how the Navy turns raw recruits into SEALs, the most effective and feared fighting force ever assembled. Between segments on special weapons and tactics training and 'drown-proofing' the recruits, one of the officers said, 'We break the men into small groups. That's the core. Those guys eat, sleep and train together until they know what the others are thinking. Every man knows what his fellow SEAL is going to do before he does it. They bond with each other in a way you can't understand if you've never been there.'"

He didn't leave it there, however. He made more use of his vice-captains than anyone ever had, naming the uber-competitive Raymond Floyd and Dave Stockton as two of his three assistants. Floyd, he said, was one of the best Ryder Cup players he'd ever seen. "Raymond would cut a hole through you with his eyes," he recalled of the contentious 1991 Cup. Stockton, of course, captained that team to victory, adopting a win at all costs mentality. Azinger then named fellow Floridian Olin Browne as the third captain. At age forty-eight, he'd be closer to the players than the sixty-four-year-old Floyd and the sixty-five-year-old Stockton. Each was to be the hands-on coach of one of his own pod with Azinger's supervision.

By contrast, Faldo had just one vice-captain, Jose Maria Olazábal, who had a brilliant Ryder Cup record as a player. And he wasn't shy about questioning Zinger's choice of three.

"I think he already regrets it," he proffered. "I don't think those guys have brought to his team what he wanted. Jack Nicklaus made a few comments to him. Yeah, I think he isn't too sure about that one now. Too many cooks."

"Interesting, this, isn't it?" John Hopkins of the *Times of London* noted. "A bit of subtlety from Faldo, who is not known for it. He has stuck a knife between Azinger's ribs so quietly that Azinger probably hasn't even noticed it."

Azinger laughed it off. Certainly, the opposing captains didn't enjoy a cozy relationship despite sharing a TV booth as commentators in 2006. The rift dated back to the 1987 Open where Azinger, among the best bunker players in the world, botched a shot out of the sand on the last hole. He took a double as the pro-Faldo crowd hooted and hollered, giving the Englishman the first of his six majors. Azinger was devastated. Faldo was condescending.

"Hard luck, old boy," Faldo said as they shook hands. Azinger confessed he was a little "hurt" after grinding all week and from that point on, he vowed to "repay the compliment."

Then, two years later at the Ryder Cup at The Belfry, Azinger and Chip Beck were facing Faldo and Ian Woosnam. Faldo seemed to be crowding Beck as he lined up a putt, and Azinger didn't appreciate it. "I'll read my partner's putt if, you don't mind," he snapped. Four years after that, back at The Belfry, the final day matched up Azinger, the best player in America, and Faldo, the best player in the world, in the anchor singles match. Faldo, who had aced the fourteenth hole, took a one-hole lead to eighteen but the drama fell flat when Ray Floyd's point clinched the US win. With the matter settled, Azinger had a six-foot birdie putt to halve the match and expected Faldo to concede it. "That would have been the gracious gesture," he said. Faldo made him putt it.

As co-commentators, Faldo played the straight man to Azinger's caustic style, and the two appeared to have put their differences behind them. But, in the months leading up to the Ryder Cup, Zinger's lingering disdain for Faldo prompted him to say something he'd regret.

"Nick Faldo has tried to redefine himself," he said in an interview with the *Daily Mail.* "I'd say he is both who he is and who he was. Some people have bought it. Some have not. But if you're going to be a prick and everyone hates you, why do you think that just because you're trying to be cute and funny on air now that the same people are all going to start to like you?

"The bottom line is that the players from his generation and mine really don't want to have anything to do with him."

Azinger denied the quote until the audio tape was produced. The two captains enjoyed dinner together about a month before the matches and claimed everything was fine between them when they got to Valhalla. Still, Azinger sensed an edge over his old rival in the way the two captains would be perceived.

"I've got more of an everything-to-gain situation," Azinger said. "There's going to be a little more heat on Nick to get it right, and I think a little more of the microscope will be on Nick if he gets it wrong."

He could not have been more prescient. Faldo had a frosty relationship with the British tabloids. While they understood that his persona as a ruthless loner was one reason of many he climbed to World No. 1, they found him aloof and off-putting with a strange sense of humor and the skin of a banana. The European press is usually unabashed in its support of the European team. They typically cheer when every blue point goes up in the media center. But 2008 was different. Clearly, they felt conflicted: while they almost reveled in Faldo's failure, they were, at the same time, angered at the outcome.

Meanwhile, Azinger played up every advantage, including the golf course setup, the home captain's preference. The K Club had been set up with thick rough and narrow fairways to counter the Americans' length. Azinger reversed that to let his guys bomb away and take aim at the greens. To offset Europe's perceived edge in the short game, he grew the greenside rough and set the greens at a speedy twelve on the stimpmeter. Most Americans hate slow greens more than anything.

Valhalla Golf Club—carved out of a flood plain by Jack Nicklaus—in itself, wasn't the greatest test of golf. David Duval was quoted in John Feinstein's book, *The Majors,* that it was a "perfectly nice golf course–for a Nike Tour event." But they weren't playing a stroke play event this week. It was match play and it was suited for that with Nicklaus' unique design that included an alternate fairway par five, an island green par four and an eighteenth green shaped like a horseshoe. Valhalla had certainly provided enough drama when Woods beat Bob May in a playoff at the 2000 PGA Championship. That's the same year the PGA of America bought the course and made it its signature property with 438 acres holding 4000 spectators and twenty-two acres of corporate tents and merchandising. It also suited Azinger's intentions as a fantastic spectator venue with built-in amphitheaters perfect for amping up the roar of cheers he hoped would carry his team if they performed well enough to inspire it.

Azinger told his players they were on a "free roll" due to low expectations, especially with Woods on the shelf. Consider Boo Weekley, Woods' replacement. Weekley came out of the Florida panhandle, where he once worked as a hydroblaster at a Monsanto chemical plant and had to be lowered into big ammonia tanks to clean them. He had no trouble playing up the Redneck Riviera image. He said his tux for the pre-tournament gala felt like a strait-jacket, and that the team trousers he was issued were the most expensive thing he had ever owned. But the folksy humor couldn't conceal his confidence.

"It's time for a new era," he said. "We're the underdogs but that's all on paper. It's like getting a new pack of hounds when we were growing up and going deer hunting. You don't know what kind of dogs you've got until you run them so let's run them and we'll see."

Azinger joined the chorus.

"This team hasn't ever trailed. This team has never been put together," he said in his final pre-tournament presser. "This is not the same team. This is not the same time. What happened in the past happened in the past. It has no bearing on this."

Azinger and that team later left the stuffy opening ceremonies to crash a downtown pep rally sponsored by the city of Louisville that night. Azinger wanted his men to stay behind and get some rest. They went along anyway to see him rev up the crowd by handing out Thirteenth Man T-shirts while encouraging them to be as vocal as they might be for a University of Louisville basketball game. He even brought along Louisville coach Rick Pitino for effect. "It's okay to cheer missed putts," he said, an over-step for which he was lambasted in the European media. "The Gloves Are Off," a *Daily Mail* headline screamed atop a story lambasting the American captain. Azinger didn't back down. He said they cheer missed putts in Europe, and he had personal experience in that Open loss to Faldo.

Some took it further. Lee Westwood, for one, said he was "harassed from start to finish" all week. And, in a vacuous stunt by a local radio station, they attempted to awaken him at four in the morning before his Sunday singles match, only to mistakenly ring the wrong Westwood room, that of his parents.

Whether or not Zinger's approach was sportsmanlike, it worked. When it was time for the first tee shots Friday, the Europeans must have felt that the Thirteenth Man was putting them under a full court press.

"I'm a Southern boy and we got the Southern crowd and it played right into our hands," Weekley said.

Meanwhile, the British press was reporting on some odd behavior by the captain. Faldo was brought to tears when he met Louisville native Muhammad Ali. His rambling at the opening ceremony made him appear to the Fleet Street mob as a drunken uncle. He had also walked around the course on the last warmup day clutching a piece of paper with initials scribbled on it, which sparked speculation that he was giving away his opening day pairings.

"I just had the lunch list," he scoffed. "It had sandwich requests for the guys, just making sure who wants the tuna, what wants the beef, who wants the ham.

"So that's all it was, a sandwich list."

"Baloney," fumed the scribes, who felt as though they were being played throughout. They'd gotten a head start on their critique of Faldo when he bypassed mainstays Colin Montgomerie and Darren Clarke as captain's picks (even after Clarke had won two tournaments over five months). and they were looking for any opening, such as the silly sandwich flap, to pounce. Friday gave them plenty more material.

For sure, that first day of competition defied every pattern and every expectation since the Euros started their string of domination. It wasn't all Faldo's doing—perhaps none of it was—but circumstance also made Azinger look rather smart as the US chipped away at the European mystique. That thing about cutting off the head of the snake by taking down Garcia? It started on Friday. The absence of Montgomerie, who had never lost a singles match, and Clarke, who had been on only one losing team in five Ryder Cups, created a leadership vacuum. Ian Poulter would eventually grow into that role, but this was only his second Ryder Cup. The pressure was squarely on Sergio, and, to some degree, Lee Westwood, to assume the leadership mantle. But Garcia was a reluctant Napoleon.

"I'm not going to stick out my chest and say I'm a leader," he said somewhat surprisingly at the start of the week . . . but for good reason. Emotionally, his relationship with main squeeze Morgan Leigh Norman, Greg's daughter, was on the rocks. Physically, he was under the weather and on a course of antibiotics. Taken together, he looked disconnected from the one event he loved most. Faldo needed to play psychologist with his sparkplug, but that wasn't Faldo's thing. And, if it weren't going to be Sergio's week, it wasn't going to be Europe's. Azinger was lucking out.

The first salvo against Garcia came in the opening foursomes, which Azinger specifically picked to get the week going. The Spaniard had enjoyed an 8-0-0 Ryder Cup record in alternate shot but paired with Westwood, he suffered his first blemish, escaping with a fortunate halve when Kentucky favorite Kenny Perry, playing with Jim Furyk, dunked his approach shot into the drink on eighteen.

Elsewhere, no one picked up the slack. Oh, it started out grandly for Europe. For almost ninety minutes, the scoreboards were a sea of blue, as the US was down in all four morning matches. Azinger admitted that the start was so painful he wanted to go back to the hotel and get under the covers. But the tide turned suddenly as Stewart Cink and Chad Campbell came back from three holes down to win their match against Justin Rose and Ian Poulter and Phil Mickelson and the energetic Kim came back from 3-down to halve theirs with Padraig Harrington and Robert Karlsson for a 3-1 lunchtime lead.

Fueled by momentum and the home crowd, the positive vibes continued in the afternoon when the Americans erased deficits in two of the four matches. Faldo split up Garcia and Westwood this time, pairing Garcia with fellow Spaniard Miguel Angel Jimenez, but the kindred chemistry failed to produce a combustible effect. Garcia, 13-1-2 in partner play coming into the week, was handed his first loss since 2002 in a 4-and-3 throttling from Justin Leonard and Hunter Mahan. Meanwhile, in the first of the afternoon matches, the Mickelson-Kim combination continued to click against Harrington and McDowell, 2-up. Poulter got the first of his four points (the most on ether team) when he and Justin Rose dispatched Ben Curtis and Steve Stricker in their Ryder Cup debuts, 4-and-2. Weekley and Kentucky native J.B. Holmes gave away a half-point when each both found the water to allow Lee Westwood and Soren Hansen to halve them on the final hole of the final match.

"I suppose 5 ½-2 ½ sounds better than 6-2 at the end of the day," Westwood said. "The crowd had been pretty noisy all day long and on that last green they were pretty quiet. Hopefully, that's a trend."

But it was a day for trend-busting. The first-day lead was the Americans' first since 1991, which was also the last time they'd won the morning session. It was the first time both sessions went to the US since 1979, and the first time Europe had won only one full point since 1975.

Faldo maintained a stiff upper lip. "We are down in points but up in spirit," he said. That was debatable though, especially since he invited criticism by announcing his lineup for the next morning's alternate shot session, a lineup that excluded fixtures Westwood and Garcia, despite that Garcia had never lost in that format and Westwood was on a 7-0-2 streak in Ryder Cup play. But Faldo had a Sergio problem. There was speculation that Garcia, with his confidence waning, asked out of the Saturday morning round. Westwood certainly did not, even though Faldo claimed he had blisters.

"I would play in the Ryder Cup with my arm hanging off," Westwood noted.

But if the atmosphere in the Euro team room was chilly, the three American pods were positively giddy. Mahan was Exhibit A. A few months earlier, he'd complained in a magazine article that "you're just a slave" during Ryder Cup week. Now, he described the supercharged Friday as "the best day of my life man . . . this is an incredible event."

Saturday, then, was a day of extraordinary golf, raw emotion, intense pressure and clutch play on both sides. Of the eight matches, only one stopped short of the seventeenth hole. Ian Poulter and Graeme McDowell had a best ball 62 in their afternoon fourball match and won by only one hole. Mickelson, paired with Mahan, had five birdies and an eagle in the afternoon. Karlsson, paired with fellow Swede Henrik Stenson, had six birdies in seven holes, including four in a row, in the same halved match. Putts were being holed everywhere, and the roars and sighs of the Kentucky crowd resounded across the grounds of Valhalla signaling where matches stood.

"It was a roller coaster," Azinger said. "We could have lost 3 to 1 in the afternoon. We could have won 3 to 1. Adrenaline is a beautiful thing."

So are unlikely heroes. Stricker, for instance. Although he accounted for just half a point, it was a big one. He and Curtis played Paul Casey and the beaten-down Garcia, re-inserted into the afternoon fourball lineup, to a draw. With Curtis struggling, Stricker carried him. He got up and down for birdie from the heavy rough to the right of eighteen, finishing it off with a fifteen-foot uphill putt for the halve that brought the crowd to its feet and found the usually staid Stricker pumping his fist like Woods.

"I'm not the type of player you saw right there," Stricker said. "There I was fist-pumping. Me fist-pumping? This thing will make you crazy."

Earlier, he rolled in a 30-foot putt on top of Garcia's 40-footer, hoisting his arms to the heavens in uncharacteristic jubilation. "I'm telling Ben, 'We're going to put it right on top of him and we're going to keep applying the pressure," Stricker related. "Sure enough, I was able to make it."

Such momentum swings had been conspicuously absent for the Americans in so many previous Ryder Cups, although the Europeans, while trailing overall, still claimed they'd recaptured some impetus by winning the day. Faldo claimed the Americans "most definitely" were hearing footsteps. "It was America's day Friday. It was our day today," he asserted. "We clawed in there, hung in there. That was the goal to chip away at what they had. Obviously, we believe we have a great opportunity."

Azinger, though, wasn't conceding anything, and his team was non-plussed, needing just five points out of the twelve singles matches to win.

"Yeah, we took some blows today," he said. "They played great, and we only lost one point. We're happy about that. We were clearly underdogs. The greatest player in the world is sitting home watching and text messaging me ("Kick their ass," among other encouragements), and Europe comes in here with this just unbelievable team. And for us to be two points ahead is good."

Up to this point, everything Azinger had done turned out right. Now he was about to administer his *coup de gras*—a Spanish matador making the finishing blow to a suffering bull. Sergio Garcia, naturally the recipient, had been served up mercilessly by Faldo. Despite Garcia's rocky week and a not-too-sterling singles record, Faldo believed that the Spaniard was the one man who could kickstart the comeback, as Seve Ballesteros had in the leadoff spot at Oak

Hill thirteen years earlier. Azinger anticipated that and was ready with the one guy he had selected to take Sergio down. The strategy conceived in that airport lounge in Edinburgh was about to be put into action.

Anthony Kim's career would turn out to be star-crossed, but he will always be remembered for this Sunday match. He had already done splendid work by rejuvenating Mickelson, whose Ryder Cup record had been wanting. Now, it seemed as though the twenty-three-year-old was born for this mission.

Kim was the poster boy for the so-called Tiger effect—making golf "cool." A decade earlier, not too far from where Woods grew up, on the corner of Sixth and Kingsley in downtown Los Angeles, the eleven-year-old son of Korean immigrant store owners was doing what a lot of cool Angelino kids did: hitting the asphalt basketball courts with plenty of attitude. Soon, though, he fell under the influence of Woods' seminal win at the 1997 Masters. Kim hung up his kicks, picked up golf and, in some corners, was being hailed as the next Tiger, another wunderkind to emerge from an unlikely background.

As Kim was doing his thing on green Kentucky fairways, he might as well have been back on the LA macadam, challenging Sergio to a one-on-one hoops throwdown. Kim had been lobbying Azinger all week to be the one to face Garcia, not that the captain needed any convincing. Zinger called Kim his "off-the-course team leader.

"Everybody laughed at A.K. because he was a street kid, a chip-on-your shoulder kid," Azinger said later. "He wanted Sergio all week. I don't think he realized that we couldn't just match 'em up when we got there. He kept saying, 'I want to play Sergio, Zing. I want to play Sergio.' It never worked out until Sunday, and we got lucky. Anthony ate it up and responded. He said on the first tee, 'I'm gonna whup his ass for you today, captain.'"

Early in the week, Garcia laughed derisively when it was suggested how much of an irritant he had been to the US side. "In which way? Because I play well?" he posed. "Sorry, what can I say?"

But Kim, arguably, would have been the one guy Garcia wouldn't have wanted to face, because, as one member of the American team put it, "Anthony can out-Sergio Sergio. He won't take any bullshit from him." Garcia would have to bring his A-Game and his A-Mind.

The atmosphere on that first tee Sunday was supercharged, replete with combative chants from each side's supporters, organized flag waving and nervous energy from the captains. Faldo kept sending his players off, whispering "visualize victory," to them. But he had gambled with his order by stacking his best players at the bottom, hoping it would come to that. He absolutely needed Garcia to come through with the first point to set things into motion.

If Kim felt the pressure, he didn't show it, appearing at the match with an outsized USA belt buckle, more apt for a cocky heavyweight champ. The requisite gamesmanship commenced swiftly—on the very first green. Both hit great approach shots, Garcia inside three feet, Kim to two. Garcia smiled as he approached the two balls and said, "Good, good?"

"Let's putt 'em," Kim replied, establishing the tenor of the day. Garcia shot back a cold stare then tapped in his putt and picked up Kim's coin. If that was supposed to send a message back to Kim, it didn't register. Kim promptly birdied the second hole to take the lead. After halving the third, both players drove to within 40 yards of the 375-yard par-four fourth. This time, as soon as Garcia pitched to two feet, Kim told him it was good. Kim then stuck one to three feet. Garcia made him putt it, as the US fans erupted in a chorus of boos. A hole later, Kim wouldn't concede another three-foot putt. Off they went to the sixth and seventh, where the match turned decisively in Kim's favor.

Garcia, who was now slow-playing Kim, drove it into thick rough skirting the right side and asked referee John Paramor, a no-nonsense European, for relief, arguing that his back foot would abut cement stairs. Kim sauntered over to hear the deliberations. Ultimately, Paramor denied Garcia a free drop, claiming that Garcia would have to come out of his natural stance in order to be impeded by the stairs.

"Do what you gotta do," Kim said dismissively, irritating Garcia by piping up. The penalty drop led to a Garcia bogey followed by more trouble for the Spaniard on the par-five seventh. There, Garcia hit two balls in the water after Kim cleared the hazard just short of the green. The gallery serenaded Garcia's misery with those Azinger-approved roars as Kim doffed his cap in recognition. Garcia, rattled, missed a short putt on eight and, after finally winning the tenth, yipped another from eighteen inches on eleven. His old partner, vice-captain Jose Maria Olazábal, tried to console him with an arm around his shoulder on the twelfth tee. The apparently inconsolable Sergio reacted by kicking his bag over in anger.

Kim kept working the crowd between birdies—five in total–and, by the fourteenth hole, he had taken down the Spaniard, 5-and-4. Kim was so worked up, he had to be informed the match was over as he marched to the fifteenth tee.

"I wouldn't trade this for ten million dollars. This is the experience of a lifetime," he said.

With the Garcia match lost, Faldo's gameplan backfired. Azinger once again appeared a genius with what he called his "middle four" players whose job it was to get the galleries going. Weekley channeled Happy Gilmore's bull dance as he galloped off the first tee, his driver between his legs, riding an imaginary horse in horse country. Then, he went out and shot 29 on the front side to pull away early from Oliver Wilson. Kenny Perry kept popping Advils for the pinched nerve in his shoulder and embraced his eighty-five-year-old father after subduing Henrik Stenson. At the tail end of his career, Perry looked back and said this Cup match defined it. J.B. Holmes, the other Kentuckian on the team, pumped up the crowd with his 340-yard drives. He pulled a Babe Ruth on the practice range when he pointed to a building in the distance and hit one on its roof. Holmes pulled the team to the edge of victory with a gutty birdie-birdie finish to beat Soren Hanson. Then Jim Furyk, who had been on all those losing teams, secured the winning point after being conceded a short putt by Jimenez.

The final tally was 16 ½-11 ½, the biggest winning margin since 1981. Azinger's rookies were 9-4-8. Europe's big guns, Garcia, Westwood and Harrington, were a combined 0-7-5. Try blaming Faldo for that.

"We know what it's like to be on the other side of it. It's no fun," Mickelson said of he and his fellow veterans. "We had six guys who had not experienced that, who were determined to help turn the United States' performance in the Ryder Cup around. And they did that. Look at their record. It was phenomenal. They brought game, an attitude, an energy and it invigorated the team."

It had been a while since the Americans could rejoice on a balcony, spraying fans with champagne. And, as the crowd chanted, "We want the Cup," hockey-style, they responded with: "We got the Cup."

The Europeans had no excuses. "We got out-golfed," McDowell conceded. Naturally, the European press focused on them being out-captained. Faldo was pilloried in analysis after analysis.

"Witches got a fairer hearing in medieval Europe," Kevin Garside wrote in *The Independent.* "He is paying the price for a lifetime of self-serving, a leading figure in the cult of the individual."

The *Times of London* piled on. "Faldo's thin skin, the need to have his sports shrink by his side even on the course and his grating sense of humor had confirmed what we knew all along, which is that he is no natural leader. But what we had not expected was that a man who had dedicated himself so much to this job would make such a colossal mistake."

Ditto the *Daily Mail:* "Faldo, not the crowd, was America's thirteenth man." It panned his decision to bottom-load his Sunday lineup, likening it to "sending an aircraft carrier to a conflict that was already over. His list will go down as one of the great leadership howlers and it confirmed the sense we had of Faldo being swept away by instinct and whim."

The Telegraph concurred: "Faldo's gamble on the big finish left Ian Poulter, Lee Westwood and Padraig Harrington thrashing at thin air, their legs amputated by a hopelessly incontinent ego."

In a stinging report card, Lawrence Donegan of *The Guardian* dubbed him "Captain Cock-up."

"For the loser, there are no privileges, only duties, the most important of which is to take the ultimate responsibility for defeat," Donegan opined. "It was not surprising, although somehow appropriate, that Faldo failed miserably in this task, too."

Faldo, to the dismay of his critics, had quite enough of it all, when he headed home the day after. Confronted by the Fourth Estate a final time, he blew them off. "Officially, no more."

At first, the players rallied around their captain, although Donegan pointed out that "privately, the mere mention of Faldo's name in the presence of some of those in and around the 2008 European team is liable to produce eye-rolling on the scale of Marty Feldman in Young Frankenstein."

"We hold the golf clubs and we hit the shots, not the captain," was a typical reaction from Lee Westwood.

As time passed, though, Westwood and a few others became more candid—and critical—about their assessment of Faldo's captaincy. In 2010, Faldo admitted he was "scarred" by the experience, and, in 2014, decided he could not let sleeping dogs lie.

As a Golf Channel analyst at the Ryder Cup at Gleneagles, he ripped Garcia for a "bad attitude" and for making a "useless" contribution at Valhalla.

The remarks took Garcia by surprise. "Are you sure you didn't misquote him?" he asked and was told, "No."

"That's unfortunate. I guess he doesn't feel European," he said. "That's the only thing I can think of. You know, there's a lot of things I could say about Nick Faldo, but I'm not going to put myself down to that level."

Faldo would double down, however, when confronted by the Associated Press. "He was always labeled as the man who brings emotion and passion. We didn't have it that week," Faldo said. "That's, in my opinion, how it looked and felt."

Was 2008 an anomaly? It was the only recent example of a European team not pulling on the same rope. Meanwhile, the Americans were justified in thinking they had figured it out, that they had leveled out the intangibles. The next three Cups would test those theories.

DAY 1

FOURSOMES

Phil Mickelson/Anthony Kim (US) halved with Padraig Harrington/Robert Karlsson (E)
Justin Leonard/Hunter Mahan (US) defeated Henrik Stenson/Paul Casey (E) 3-and-2
Stewart Cink/Chad Campbell (US) defeated Justin Rose/Ian Poulter (E) 1-up
Kenny Perry/Jim Furyk (US) halved with Lee Westwood/Sergio Garcia (E)
United States wins session 3–1

FOURBALLS

Phil Mickelson/Anthony Kim (US) defeated Padraig Harrington/Graeme McDowell (E) 2-up
Ian Poulter/Justin Rose (E) defeated Steve Stricker/Ben Curtis (US) 3-and-2
Justin Leonard/Hunter Mahan (US) defeated Sergio Garcia/Miguel Angel Jiminez (E) 4-and-3
J.B. Holmes/Boo Weekley (US) halved with Lee Westwood/Soren Hansen (E)
United States wins session 2 ½–1 ½
United States 5 ½, Europe 2 ½

DAY 2

FOURSOMES

Ian Poulter/Justin Rose (E) defeated Stewart Cink/Chad Campbell (US) 4-and-3
Justin Leonard/Hunter Mahan (US) halved with Miguel Angel Jimenez/Graeme McDowell (E)
Henrik Stenson/Oliver Wilson (E) defeated Phil Mickelson/Anthony Kim (US) 2-and-1
Jim Furyk/Kenny Perry (US) defeated Padraig Harrington/Robert Karlsson (E) 3-and-1
Europe wins session 2 ½–1 ½
United States 7, Europe 5

FOURBALLS

Boo Weekley/J.B. Holmes (US) defeated Lee Westwood/Soren Hansen (E) 2-and-1
Ben Curtis/Steve Stricker (US) halved with Sergio Garcia/Paul Casey (E)
Ian Poulter/Graeme McDowell (E) defeated Kenny Perry/Jim Furyk (US) 1-up
Phil Mickelson/Hunter Mahan (US) halved with Henrik Stenson/Robert Karlsson (E)
Session tied 2–2
United States 9, Europe 7

DAY 3
SINGLES
Anthony Kim (US) defeated Sergio Garcia (E) 5-and-4
Hunter Mahan (US) halved with Paul Casey (E)
Robert Karlsson (E) defeated Justin Leonard (US) 5-and-3
Justin Rose (E) defeated Phil Mickelson (US) 3-and-2
Kenny Perry (US) defeated Henrik Stenson (E) 3-and-2
Boo Weekley (US) defeated Oliver Wilson (E) 4-and-2
J.B. Holmes (US) defeated Soren Hansen (E) 2-and-1
Jim Furyk (US) defeated Miguel Angel Jimenez (E) 2-and-1
Graeme McDowell (E) defeated Stewart Cink (US) 2-and-1
Ian Poulter (E) defeated Steve Stricker (US) 3-and-2
Ben Curtis (US) defeated Lee Westwood (E) 2-and-1
Chad Campbell (US) defeated Padraig Harrington (E) 2-and-1
United States wins session 7 ½–4 ½
UNITED STATES WINS RYDER CUP 16 ½–11 ½

2012

Miracle or Meltdown?

MEDINAH COUNTRY CLUB
EUROPE 14 ½, UNITED STATES 13 ½

In his 2010 book *Cracking the Code,* Paul Azinger chronicled his masterful captaincy at Valhalla in 2008, what seemed to many a turning point in America's uphill battle to regain traction against the dominant Europeans. The Europeans may have rebounded with a narrow one-point victory at Celtic Manor in 2010. Yet, many American supporters felt that, following Azinger's formula, the US would *likely* leverage home soil and a partisan crowd to regain the Cup when the rivalry returned to the States at Medinah Country Club on Chicago's outskirts.

For the first two days, that mindset held. But "likely" never reached "absolutely." The problem with the most encrypted codes is that they can be scrambled. And, so it was. The 2012 Ryder Cup was to become the most painful of them all for the United States. For the seventh time in the last nine meetings (and the second time in the last three at home), the Sunday press conference featured a long row of browbeaten Americans feeling sorry for themselves. Suddenly, the 2008 victory appeared as an outlier. Europe was back in charge, and it would take a drastic reengineering of the overall game plan to change that.

Miracle or meltdown? Europe's Sunday charge back from a four-point deficit equaled the American comeback at The Country Club in 1999. Back then, though, the US simply steamrolled to the win in a show of sheer force. Europe didn't have a chance. It was different at Medinah. All it would have taken was a few clutch putts to stem the European onslaught and bring what had been a week of revived American spirit to a happy conclusion. But the Americans had no backbone on this day. As it wore on, everyone began to expect their putts to stay above ground, forshoulders to slump, for countenances to turn to disbelief. The result was as inexorable as it was miraculous. It took on a feeling of inevitability that carried on to Gleneagles in Scotland two years later.

"I don't have a reaction yet," US Captain Davis Love III said as he stood among the celebrating Euros and their ecstatic fans after it was over. "We're all kind of stunned."

Love purposely took on much of the criticism. "It's my job to be second-guessed," he acknowledged. Yet, in the post-mortem analysis, the guys swinging the clubs had contributed most to the defeat. "Choke" is a harsh word, but it was thrown around a lot in America's sports pages on that Monday. The shocking part was how dominant the US had been for two days. It wasn't that the Euros were struggling. They were simply getting outplayed. As Love said, "We were playing so well. Everybody on our team was playing so well. We just figured it didn't matter how we sent them out there."

Perhaps the ultimate outcome shouldn't have been so surprising. Golf had entered the start of its post-Tiger Woods era with injury and scandal besetting the longtime World No. 1. The sport's landscape was experiencing a seismic shift. Eight of the twelve-man European squad were playing regularly on the PGA Tour and living in the States. Europeans were holding down four of the top five spots in the World Rankings with Rory McIlroy at No. 1, Luke Donald third, Lee Westwood fourth and Justin Rose fifth. Woods was still holding on at No. 2, but he had not won a major since his epic playoff victory over Rocco Mediate at Torrey Pines in the 2008 US Open.

Part of Europe's strategy had always been to target Woods. Beat Tiger Woods, and it would all fall into Europe's lap. It had been turning out as planned. Europe had won five of the six previous Ryder Cups when Woods was on the American team, with the loss at Brookline the sole exception. The other American win during that period came with Woods recuperating and sitting out 2008 at Valhalla. The most famous example of Tiger targeting came at Oakland Hills in 2004 when US captain Hal Sutton confidently paired together Woods and his rival Phil Mickelson. Sutton boasted they might "shoot 58," pausing to add, "if it gets that far."

It did not get that far, at least not in the way Sutton envisioned. Colin Montgomerie and Padraig Harrington, hand-picked by captain Bernhard Langer, dusted the powerful but ill-matched pair to launch a humbling 18 ½-9 ½ blowout on US soil. Few can forget the incredulous look on Woods' face when Mickelson put him up against a fence with a wild slice off the tee after Sutton stubbornly sent them out again in alternate shot. In fairness, however, finding a partner for Tiger (as well as Mickelson) had always been vexing. Woods' overall Ryder Cup record going into the 2012 Cup was a mediocre 13-14-1, 9-13 in fourball and foursomes, but an impressive 4-1-1 in singles, prompting teammate Jim Furyk to fire back: "That's probably the rest of our faults then. How's that? That's my theory."

The other theory was that every European playing against Woods had upped their game with nothing to lose. It had been the game plan of the European team in most every Ryder Cup since 1997, not unlike slashing the head to kill the snake. Ah, but by 2012, the snake had turned. Woods experienced a resurgence in 2012 with three PGA Tour wins, his first since his fall from grace in November of 2009. But there was less focus on Europe taking him down than the bullseye the Americans had on McIlroy's back. The 23-year-old Northern Irishman was the hottest player in the world, with three victories in the previous six weeks, including his second dominant major win in two years at the PGA Championship along with two FedEx Cup events. Greg Norman even noted that McIlroy had been intimidating the inveterate intimidator. Woods, with an apparent sense of relief, acknowledged that McIlroy was the man to beat this time.

"It's part of being No. 1. It's part of winning major championships," he said in the runup. "You're always going to want to take out their best player. That's just part of the deal. That's a fun challenge. I certainly have relished it over the years, and I'm sure he's going to relish it this week."

Love tried to follow the Azinger game plan as closely as possible. Zinger had whipped the Kentucky crowds into a frenzy, and Love was counting on the Chicago galleries to turn up the volume. British writers even fretted over the possibility of another Kiawah. Love also set up Medinah with generous landing areas and minimal rough. He had a team of aggressive players, and he wanted birdies. Like Azinger, Love had four captain's picks, which he used on the long-hitting Dustin Johnson, the hot-putting Brandt Snedeker and the calming presence of veterans Jim Furyk and Steve Stricker. Announcing his wild cards two weeks prior to the competition, he called his team the deepest ever, with every man winning at least one PGA Tour event that season.

"The European team is obviously great. I know they are going to be tough; they are every year. They are playing well," he acknowledged. "But I can tell you this. I love my team. I'm excited about my team, and I can't wait to see how it matches up."

Love left off two key members of the 2010 team, Hunter Mahan and Rickie Fowler. Mahan won twice in 2012, including the WGC Accenture Match Play Championship, where he soundly defeated McIlroy. A nod from Love would have given Mahan the chance to redeem himself for this heartbreaking loss to Graeme McDowell in the clinching singles match two years earlier. But Mahan was slumping late in the season, while both Johnson and Snedeker were charging.

"I look forward to getting to Medinah and making Davis look like a genius," said Snedeker, a player not prone to boasts.

The US roster included four rookies (Keegan Bradley, Jason Dufner, Webb Simpson and Snedeker) to Europe's one (Nicolas Colsaerts). Simpson, though, was that year's US Open champion, and Bradley had won the PGA Championship the previous year. It wasn't as if they hadn't been under the gun. And they lacked the scar tissue of a Ryder Cup defeat. In fact, rookies on both sides were very much the story of the first day, as the US moved out to a 5-3 lead, one made to seem larger than it was by Bradley's inspiring performance.

The Vermont native, a nephew of LPGA star Pat Bradley, was able to do what Woods and others before him could not – energize the other American superstar with a less-than-stellar record. Phil Mickelson was 11-17-6 in eight previous Ryder Cups, his swashbuckling play sometimes a detriment to his partners. When playing his own ball in a tournament, Phil could always thrill his followers by extricating himself from seemingly impossible situations. It's how he won his first Masters. However, at the Ryder Cup, he would sometimes land his alternate shot partners in those sticky spots. It was different with Bradley. Sixteen years Mickelson's junior, Bradley had an intense competitiveness, displayed though clenched teeth and with fist pumps whenever birdie putts fell, and it brought out the lefty's best. Considered underdogs in both of their Friday matches, they cruised to impressive wins. Sergio Garcia was long a Ryder Cup nuisance for the Americans. Luke Donald, a Northwestern University grad with an American wife, had settled in Chicago and had as much a home field advantage as any player on the opposing team. Yet, the Bradley-Mickelson juggernaut took them down, 4-and-3, to put the first American point on the board. It marked the first time either Garcia (8-0-1) or Donald (6-0-0) had a lost a foursomes match and they had been 4-0-0 when paired together. Then, for an encore in the afternoon fourball match, they KO'd the heavyweight pair of Graeme McDowell and the inimitable McIlroy, 2-and-1. It was the first time Mickelson had ever gone 2-0 on any day in his ten Ryder Cups to date.

Mickelson was euphoric. "He's got such great, positive energy," he said of Bradley. "When we were walking down the first hole and I'm fifty yards ahead of our playing partner in the middle of the fairway with a little wedge, I just knew that over the course of eighteen holes, if you keep giving me wedges in the fairway and having Keegan putt it, we are going to be really tough to beat. I just think that the odds are going to be in our favor."

Those odds seemed weighted in Europe's favor in the early going, as it led in three of the four morning matches. Donald then missed a six-footer on twelve and Mickelson-Bradley seized on the mistake by winning four straight holes to turn momentum of the entire session and bring the crowd to life. Their chest bumping increased with each hole won, as Bradley played to the crowd. For instance, Mickelson was about to hit to the fifteenth green with the match dormy. Bradley, spotting six fans who had unfurled an American flag, ran over to the ropes and high-fived each one. Mickelson would leave him with a 20-foot putt, which Bradley holed to seal the victory. It was the last of his four birdie putts in the morning with six more to come as he played his own ball in the afternoon against McDowell and McIlroy. When Mickelson finished off the Irishmen by sticking a 7-iron to two feet on seventeen, Bradley hyperbolically called it the greatest shot he'd ever seen.

"I wish I could go thirty-six more," he said afterwards. "It could be the best day of my life. We were running down the fairway, we had our arms around each other, we were screaming. It was like a Patriots game out there. I'm just having such a blast playing with Phil. Love every second of it."

"There is a reason why Keegan is perfect for the Ryder Cup," Mickelson said. "The more pressure the situation, the better he plays, the better he sees the shot, the better he focuses and the better the result. There's no higher pressure situation than the Ryder Cup. As a player, you feel more pressure and intensity during these matches than you do at any other event. And that's when he's at his best."

"I felt young," Mickelson went on, continuing to gush. "I would say to him a couple of times, "I need a little pep talk,' and he would give me something, get me boosted up and I would hit a good shot. He drives the ball as well as I've ever seen a person drive it. Alternate shot was my favorite format because I got to hit the next shot."

No one would have blamed Bradley's girlfriend, Jillian Stacey, if she were a bit jealous of the bromance.

"They couldn't stop talking about each other," she told *Sports Illustrated*. "It was like, 'Oh, that shot you hit was so great.' 'No, that putt of yours was even better.' 'But I couldn't have done it without your amazing read.' They're infatuated with each other. Every now and then they would stare into each other's eyes like they were a long-lost love. At some point Amy (Mickelson) was like, 'It's a good thing we're here or they might start talking about getting married!'"

Bradley's caddie, Steve "Pepsi" Hale, celebrated the rout by wildly waving the flagstick overhead, acting, as *Sports Illustrated's* Alan Shipnuck wrote, "like a deranged samurai." The enthusiasm was infectious . Bubba Watson, first off in the afternoon along with Webb Simpson, waved his arms and encouraged everyone in the grandstand behind him to make noise as he teed off. Then he pumped his drive down the middle of the fairway. He and his partner went out in 28—no Ryder Cup partnership had ever done that—and made ten birdies in a match that lasted only fourteen holes against Paul Lawrie and Pete Hanson. The 5-and-4 win started a 3-1 afternoon for the US, which made thirty-five birdies on the day, an average of nine per match. When Dustin Johnson and Matt Kuchar finished off Justin Rose and Martin Kaymer, 3-and-2, by making seven birdies in the last match of the day, the Americans' 5-3 lead seemed as if it would only grow.

"I've never been to a tournament where the crowd was so loud," said Simpson, unfazed by being a rookie. "We just had a blast. We got off to a good start and we did what we did best —we had fun. And luckily the birdies kept rolling."

The exception to all the revelry, however, was Woods, who played two matches with Steve Stricker and lost them both, 2-and-1 to Ian Poulter and Rose, 1-down against Lee Westwood and Colsaerts. Looking back, it wasn't as much of a disgrace as it seemed. Poulter would go on to post one of the best Ryder Cup records of all time, and Rose wouldn't be far behind him. Woods started out wild in the morning match, beginning with his opening tee shot, a snap hook that ended up against a fence amongst a group of trees. Later, a wayward tee shot drew blood from a gallery member. Woods then put together his best Ryder Cup round to date, making seven birdies while getting two more from Stricker. But even that effort wasn't enough. Colsaerts, a long-hitting Belgian, had perhaps the greatest Ryder Cup debut in history, going 10-under on his own ball. Woods could have halved the match with a 15-foot putt on the last hole, but he burned the edge. It was the type of putt Colsaerts had been draining all afternoon.

He could only shrug it off and call Colsaerts' performance, "one of the greatest putting rounds ever.

"I didn't hit it well warming up and it carried into my play," Woods explained. "Sean (Foley, his swing coach) talked about my swing basically at halftime. We made a few adjustments. I really hit it well this afternoon. But we ran into a guy who made everything. He was 7-under after ten. I quit counting after that."

"When somebody like Tiger Woods goes, 'Great playing, man,' you understand you've done something pretty good," Colsaerts said. "There are no tools you can use out there. You've just got to use what you have in your pants."

The Belgian likely meant to say he was flying by the seat of his pants. In any case, no other European would have a chance to beat Woods the next morning. Love was grounding him. Causing quite the stir among the otherwise positive American vibes, Love announced that he was putting in the red-hot Watson and Simpson in place of Woods and Stricker in Saturday's alternate shot session. It wasn't based on performance, Love claimed, but rather on providing them with rest.

"We just felt like we didn't want anybody to have to play five matches on this golf course," he explained. "I think Tiger needs a rest. I think Steve needs a rest. We need Tiger and Steve in the afternoon. We need Tiger and Steve on Sunday. It's a team effort and they're supportive friends of mine. They told me they'd do whatever I asked, but I guarantee you that neither one of them are very happy about it, not because they are sitting out, because they have to wait until Saturday afternoon to come back."

The way most of his team was playing, it didn't seem like a bad idea, and it wasn't the first time Woods had sat out a session. Corey Pavin left him out of the second session of fourballs at Celtic Manor in 2010, after Tiger went 2-1 with Stricker in their first three matches. Still, if Love didn't want anyone playing all five matches, did that mean he'd sit Bradley and Mickelson the next afternoon? He said that would depend on how many holes they went in the morning.

Olazábal, too, had been questioned by his media for benching Donald, Garcia and Poulter, all team leaders, Friday afternoon, but he wasn't giving his biggest gun a break. McIlroy, as well as Rose, would play all five matches. The captain did, however, deliver a message to his team after what he felt was an underachieving day by his stars.

"I'm going to make it clear to the boys that they need to step it up," he said. "There are no secrets to this game. You have to make more birdies than your opponent. And if you don't do that, you are going to struggle."

It would take until the shadows were at their longest before the captain's plea was answered. Until then, the American party continued almost unabated. As alternate shot began Saturday, a plane flew overhead, pulling a fluttering message: "Has Anybody Seen Tiger?" The answer could have been, "Who Cares?" as the American superstar spent the morning watching his teammates win three of the four matches to extend their lead to a commanding 8-4. Once again, it was the Bradley and Mickelson man-crush leading the charge by crushing Donald and Westwood, 7-and-6, with the Euros fittingly sporting raspberry golf shirts. It matched the most lopsided score in the history of foursomes play.

Left to marvel, Westwood said of Bradley, "He's obviously been a rock star this week and they've done nothing wrong."

Meanwhile, Mickelson's caddie, Jim "Bones" MacKay, noted that his man and Bradley play, "identical types of golf" and are "identically excitable.

"Keegan is a twenty-six-year-old Phil Mickelson. He reminds Phil of Phil," Mackay said. "There are all kinds of different golf brains and these two have the same type: 'Let's go after it, let's go get them.' I thought yesterday was good but today . . . alternate shot, my gosh. I've been around a little bit, I've certainly never seen alternate shot played like that, on a big golf course."

The same could be said, perhaps to a lesser extent, of Jason Dufner and Zach Johnson, who went to 2-0 in foursomes play by cooling off Colsaerts and Garcia, 2-and-1. "We have very similar games, very similar demeanors," Dufner said. "The only difference today is that Duf carried me," Johnson added. Colsaerts' Friday magic had worn off. This match ended after he dunked his tee shot into the lake on the par-three seventeenth. As it splashed, his mom, Daniele, covered her face and cried, "This is too much for an old lady to take."

Furyk and Snedeker closed out the session with a 1-up win over the stalwart McIlroy-McDowell tandem, which failed to make a birdie until the fourteenth hole. The match provided the reversal of a long-standing trend in which Europeans won the closing holes as McIlroy missed a short birdie putt on seventeen that would have evened the match. Furyk then made a superb approach shot from a fairway bunker to the heart of the eighteenth green. The Americans held on, as McIlroy's long birdie putt grazed the edge.

The only European point of the morning came out of the first match, a portent of what was to transpire. The American strategy may have been to take down McIlroy, but it was Ian Poulter providing the real inspiration. The Englishman gladly took on the role of the man the Americans most wanted to beat, and he did it with a combination of humor and defiance. Poulter and Rose were matched against Simpson and Watson, who had riled up the crowd on the first tee Friday by encouraging them to get loud as hit his first shot. Poulter had the honors and decided to match Watson's stunt. He'd literally steal Bubba's thunder.

"When I saw Bubba whooping everybody up (on TV), I said 'that won't happen tomorrow. If we get drawn together, I'm going to make sure I get in there first,'" Poulter promised. "That's exactly what I did. He's going to get some of his own medicine. It was insane. First tee of the Ryder Cup, your heart rate's up. But with 20,000 fans going absolutely bananas, it was at 180 for sure. I was going to make contact. It was just a case of where it would go."

With both fan bases bellowing—and Watson urging them on as well—Poulter hooked his shot into the left bunker. Then it was Watson's turn to tee off, to an even louder racket. His ball avoided the trap but found rough beyond it. "It was fun for a second. From that point on, it was game face on," Poulter said.

Poulter continued to hear it from the pro-American gallery, and he continued to answer them. He made a 20-foot putt from the fringe on twelve to put his team 2-up and, on seventeen, hit his tee shot to fourteen feet. Rose, struggling with the putter the entire match, left Poulter with a tricky four footer for par, but Poulter sank it to remain 1-up. Simpson had a chance to halve the match after Watson hit a nice approach to twelve feet on the difficult eighteenth, but his putt slid by.

Still, American fans could feel very good about the home team's four-point lead going into the afternoon. That is, until Love announced his fourball pairings. A manager or head coach has few cardinal rules: ride momentum, stay with the hot hand and go for the jugular. Sending the red-hot Bradley and Mickelson out again seemed like a no-brainer. But Love insisted on sticking with his game plan of not permitting anyone to play five matches.

"Phil gets his break, and he was asking for his break. After all that great golf. He wanted his break because he knows how important tomorrow is going to be," he said.

Still, it was odd. When he left Woods out of Saturday morning's session, explaining his decision not to play anyone in every match, Love was asked if that meant he'd be sitting Bradley and Mickelson for the same reason. He said it depended on how many holes their match would last. As it turned out, it lasted twelve holes—no team match had ever gone shorter. In fact, Bradley and Mickelson had played only forty-four holes in their three matches combined, which they won by a total of fourteen holes. What's more, two of those matches were in the alternate shot format, with each player hitting half the shots that he would have in a foursomes match.

And, if the forty-two-year-old Mickelson were tired, what about the twenty-six-year-old Bradley? Love could have gotten creative and paired him with Woods, sitting Stricker. A month earlier at the PGA Championship, Bradley's father Mark told reporters that Keegan hoped he'd be paired with Tiger so he could "pump him up." Love, however, stuck with his plan.

In the final press conference Sunday, Love was asked if he'd change anything in hindsight, specifically the Bradley-Mickelson benching.

"Well, in hindsight, we would have done a lot of things differently, I guess," he began. "No, these guys asked to do certain things during the week, and there are some guys that didn't want to sit out; but guys that felt like they needed to rest, we let them rest. I'm going to second-guess myself for a long time. I could have done a lot of things differently, but I'm proud of . . ."

Mickelson wouldn't let Love go any further.

"Hold on, Davis, hold on one sec, Davis," he interrupted. "As far as playing Keegan and I, you need to hear something. Keegan and I knew going in that we were not playing in the afternoon, and we said on the first tee, 'we are going to put everything we have into this one match, because we are not playing the afternoon.' And when we got to ten, I went to Davis and I said, 'listen, you're seeing our best; you cannot put us in the afternoon, because we emotionally and mentally are not prepared for it. And I know you're going to get pressure, because we're playing so good. But we have other guys that are dying to get out there, and we have mentally put everything into this match; we won't have anything later, and so you need to stay to our plan. So, you cannot put that on him; if anything, it was me."

"I'll add to that," Love then said. "One of my most special moments this week was some of the guys back in the team room and the guys on my radio were calling for Keegan and Phil. So, I rode out to ten and popped under the ropes and Phil came running over and started yelling at me, 'we are putting the most effort into this, we are giving you our all and we are going to win this match and do not play me in the afternoon.' And I thought that was the funniest thing I had ever heard. He was really adamant . . . that some of the other guys would have a lot more energy and would play well. It was a tough call. We had a lot of tough calls."

Certainly, as the first two matches played out, the point seemed moot. Simpson and Watson put the first red point on the board, recovering their form to trounce Rose and Molinari, 5-and-4, the identical margin by which they won their first fourball match against Lawrie and Hanson Friday. They were a perfect fourball pairing once more as they relied on Watson's length to birdie the par-five holes and Simpson's accuracy on the others. Simpson made seven birdies in this one, including four straight at one point, with Watson smoking a 222-yard seven-iron to seal the match on the par-five fourteenth. As they danced on the green, the margin was five points, shortly to balloon to six when Dustin Johnson and Kuchar edged Colsaerts and Lawrie, 1-up. The hot-putting Kuchar, with five birdies, carried Johnson until seventeen when Johnson won his only hole of the day by rolling in a 25-foot downhiller to the roars of the huge gallery. Colsaerts, so hot with the putter on Friday, never threatened the hole with a 14-footer that would have halved the match on eighteen.

As that match unfolded, Woods and Stricker were attempting a comeback against Donald and Garcia in a match that would have virtually clinched things for the US. Medinah roots ran deep in this one. Woods won his first PGA Championship at Medinah in 1999 (he'd win again in 2006) with Garcia nipping at his heels. Donald made his home in Chicago. Stricker was from just up I-94 in Wisconsin. Woods played poorly early, so poorly that Colin Montgomerie, commentating for *Sky Sports*, opined, "We are glad that Tiger Woods is out there playing because he's not playing very well at all. At four of the first five holes his ball might as well have been in his pocket." But with the Americans 4-down at the turn, something clicked in Tiger's game, and he started hitting clutch shots. His fourth birdie on the back side pulled the US within one with two to play. Woods hit first on seventeen, and stuck one to five feet, then Garcia put his to seven. Donald's was even better, to four feet, a distance he covered with the putt to keep the Europeans ahead. Dueling pars on eighteen gave Europe the crucial point.

"I've played well the last two afternoons and didn't get a point," sighed Woods, who was on his way to his worst Ryder Cup showing, a half point. "It's tough. Yesterday, I made a bunch of birdies and today I made five on the back nine and it just wasn't enough. Yesterday, I played terrible in the morning. Really, really struggled. I turned it around in the afternoon and unfortunately, we ran into a guy who made more putts than anyone I've ever seen."

One match remained with the thus-far unbeaten pairing of Dufner and Zach Johnson against the somewhat surprising tandem of Poulter and McIlroy, playing his first match without McDowell. The official count placed the day's attendance at 40,000, and it seemed most of them were scurrying to watch the closing match. Poulter—who had been hearing it since he teed off to the crowd noise in the first match of the day—seemed to be engaging in battle with the galleries, as he responded to their taunts with magnificent shot after magnificent shot, further stoking the crowds' frustration.

He was in his element. As John Hopkins, of the *Times of London*, wrote, Poulter "loves the limelight as a pig loves manure." He described the 36-year-old as "an anomaly, an Englishman with chutzpah, a man who likes to draw and designs clothes, a man who is not afraid to wear pink, a man with a big mouth, but someone who can back it up."

Said McIlroy, "When Poults get that look in his eyes, the week of the Ryder Cup, it's really impressive."

As it turned out, Poulter kept making birdies, until he ran out of holes on which to make them. He finished the match with five straight, including a magnificent up and down from the bunker on the par-five fourteenth and final 10-foot putt on eighteen that matched Dufner's four-foot birdie putt to secure the point. He single-handedly kept his team in it. Europe had come out of the doldrums and was now a back-slapping mob on the eighteenth green as Olazábal told the TV cameras, "I think the Ryder Cup should build a statue for him."

"It wasn't as if we gave it to them. That was just a buzz-saw at the end," a stunned Zach Johnson said. "Nothing you can do. Just tip your hat and shake his hand. The beauty of where we're at is we are up, 10-6. We were up two going into today, so we have doubled the lead if my math is correct."

But momentum doesn't work that way.

As the two teams headed off to their respective team rooms, the songs of "Ole, Ole, Ole" were drowning out the chants of "USA, USA, USA." It was clear who was feeling better about matters.

"Those last two matches were massive," Olazábal said, clinging to hope. "That gave us just a chance. It's been done before in the past. I believe that momentum will come our way and why not tomorrow?"

"To go in, all right, four points behind, but we won the last two points of the day . . . Sergio and Luke's point, huge. This point, absolutely crucial," Poulter said, looking back. "It just shows that little seed of doubt in the Americans' mind that, wow, we just lost the last two points. At 10-4, it's over. It looks dead and buried. Hang on a minute. It's 10-6. It's possible at 10-6 for there to be a comeback."

As Garcia gleefully noted, "It would be kind of nice to give it back the way they did to us in ninety-nine."

"It was a glimmer of hope, but it was huge," Rose offered. "We didn't need a big pep talk from Jose. For the first time, we felt inspired. When he handed out the singles (lineup), we liked what we saw. Golf does the talking at the end of the day, but we had a feeling. Ben Crenshaw said it can happen, so you never know."

Yes, 1999. Crenshaw had the same kind of "feeling" as put his faith in higher powers. There were indomitable spirits at work, he believed, that would prevent his team from defeat. After that miraculous Sunday at Brookline, he stumbled about in a daze, mumbling, "Fate," through glassy eyes. But this year, fate caught up to the Americans. Facing the same four-point deficit, but on foreign soil,

Olazábal had one ploy, to summon the spirit of his old partner, Seve Ballesteros. A year earlier, Seve lost his fight against brain cancer, the one thing he couldn't defeat by sheer will. The European team literally wore that spirit on their left sleeves Sunday in the form of Seve's silhouette in his trademark white and blue.

"Ollie said to us that the Ryder Cup is what memories and dreams are made of and last night that team room was buzzing," Poulter said. "We weren't four points down. We felt like we were all square. For some reason, everyone was calm. Everyone was cracking jokes. We just felt we had that tiny little chance."

While the seeds of the comeback had indeed been planted, the comeback was over almost before it began. Olazábal was front-loading his lineup, beginning with Donald, Poulter, McIlroy, Rose and Lawrie. McIlroy's match was huge. He was up against American sparkplug Keegan Bradley. But with his tee time approaching, McIlroy was nowhere to be found at Medinah. Back in the area where the official cars arrived, PGA transportation official Erica Stoll noticed that he hadn't yet arrived. According to *The Independent,* she urgently called her colleague, Maggie Budzar, at the European team hotel, about half an hour away from the course. Budzar had seen McIlroy's caddie, J.P. Fitzgerald, leave about an hour earlier. When she walked outside, a huge crowd that had been trying to land a few autographs and photos was asking about Rory.

"The crowd was getting antsy asking where he was, so I just lied and said he had already left," Budzar recalled. "And then I started getting worried that something had happened to him or that he had taken a different ride to the course. The hotel said he was maybe on the players' floor. There was only one room still in use when housekeeping checked, and a male voice said not to come in. We figured it had to be him because by now we knew he wasn't at the course. I called the European Tour officials to alert them. We then had someone go up to his room. He was in panic when he came down."

When hotel personnel got to McIlroy, he was just emerging from his room. It was 10:52. He had just taken a call from his manager, Conor Ridge, who had phoned to wish him luck. McIlroy had woken up at 9 am to call his tennis superstar girlfriend Caroline Wozniacki, who was competing in the China Open in Beijing. He said he had been "just hanging around" and had ignored a few calls to his cell phone because he didn't recognize the numbers. His picked this one up from Ridge, as *The Independent* described:

"Are you at the golf course yet?" Ridge asked.

"No, I'm not."

"But you're teeing off in twenty-five minutes."

"No, I'm not, it's an hour and twenty-five.

"You're taking the Mick (joking), you are at the golf course.

"No, I'm not."

At that point, McIlroy realized that he had seen the tee times listed in Eastern Time, an hour later.

"It's the most worried I've ever been," he would confess." If I was playing for myself, I'd be fine. It's my own fault. But to let down all the boys and the vice captains and captain – I would never have forgiven myself."

Budzar was on the phone with her superiors, who told her she'd have to grab a courtesy car and drive McIlroy herself, an impossible task through bumper-to-bumper traffic. That's when Pat Rollins, deputy chief of Lombard Police Department, saved the day for Europe. He had stopped by the hotel to chat with some colleagues and overheard Budzar's conversation. "I have my patrol car," he told her. McIlroy frantically appeared in the lobby. Rollins told him to jump into the front seat of his black Ford Interceptor, turned on its siren and flashing lights and delivered his passenger to the golf course in the nick of time, just as Donald and Watson were walking down the fairway in their opening match. Fitzgerald was there, waiting with his clubs along with McIlroy's parents. He sprinted to the locker room, put on his shoes, hit a few putts on the practice green and reported to the tee. "Is everything okay, no one's hurt or anything?" Bradley asked him. Everything was suddenly fine for Europe. Had Bradley teed off by himself, McIlroy would have had five more minutes to join him and the match would have been forfeited to the US. That point would have flipped the matches.

American fans, jeered, "Central Time Zone" as McIlroy got set to his opening tee shot, which he promptly drilled way to the right among some television cables. But, like most European fortunes, that would change. He'd shoot 32 on the front without a warmup. The Americans were defensive, just as they sounded when having the to face questions about Saturday's late flurry from the Euros the night before.

"We're not disappointed. We haven't lost a segment yet and we're just trying to keep that string going," Love said.

"We want to win and there are twelve points on the board, so we have to go out there and get them," Watson added. "Europe is not going to lie down. They are not going to give it to us. We have to play good golf and come out focused and ready to win some points."

It wasn't as if Love's lineup choices had set up his team for failure, as Mark James had done in 1999. Some criticized Love for putting the winless Stricker and Woods in the last two matches, but Tiger's 4-1-1 record in singles was among the best on the US team. Anticipating Olazábal's front-loading, Love opened with Watson, Simpson, Bradley and Mickelson, who were a combined 10-2 the first two days. He was counting on a fast start to put it away. As he said later, "we could have laid them out in any order and played like that. It really wouldn't have mattered."

Later, Tom Watson, upon being named captain of the 2014 team, summed it up: "There was a cloud on the horizon that was a harbinger for the next day. And when that happened, that cloud grew to a storm. And when those first five matches went blue midway through the matches, that storm was howling. That pressure was great. The momentum had changed."

At Brookline in 1999, the tumultuous echoes of the Boston crowd created that kind of momentum for the US. Here, it was the opposite. The European comeback was answered with a dead quiet. Noted Westwood, "We silenced the crowd by playing great golf early. It's not that the crowd turned on them, but the crowd went quiet and almost got desperate, saying, 'We need you, we need this point,' and that was a lot of pressure to put on their players."

Donald was 4-up on Watson through twelve, McIlroy 2-up on Bradley through nine, Rose 1-up on Mickelson through ten and Lawrie 3-up on Snedeker through nine. The only break in the early blue wave came from Simpson, who was 2-up through six and 1-up through eleven on Poulter. But Poulter was no easy mark. The Europeans had been taking their cue from him all week, and Poulter kept delivering, just as he had since his Ryder Cup debut at Valhalla four years earlier. In fact, he had stirred things up before play even started by saying his team wanted to "kill" the Americans, while admitting "The Americans want to kick my arse." The Americans didn't deny it. "When it comes down to playing Ian Poulter in the Ryder Cup, I don't want to lose to him. When he yells and screams, his eyes bug out," Stricker said. "That's why you want to beat him."

That was Simpson's task, and he couldn't pull it off. American fans had greeted the then-current US Open champ with chants of, "Major winner, major winner," as the two opponents got to the tee, a clever way of taunting the major-less Poulter. But it only fueled the cocky Englishman. He was a man possessed, finally playing a game to match his flashy attire. As *The Independent's* Kevin Garside wrote, "Poulter's face-distorting yells had kids, and adults, reaching for mummy's hand at greenside." It did no good to heckle him. Poulter twice had to step away from his curling 10-foot putt on twelve as a loutish fan jeered him. His celebration matched the moment after rolling it in and tying up the match. It stayed that way through sixteen, where Poulter saved par with a clutch up and down after noise from a nearby hole erupted in his backswing and forced him to clank his approach shot off a tree. With help from Simpson's nervously poor tee shot on seventeen, Poulter then closed it out with two birdies, including a masterful one on eighteen, after putting himself behind a tree. Initially, he planned to lob it over to a spot in front of the green. But his caddie, Terry Mundy, suggested that he had a bit of room to bend around it by hitting a cut. The wind calmed, and Poulter pulled off a spectacular shot inside 10 feet. His birdie putt was conceded when Simpson missed his long birdie try. The overall score was now tied, 10-10, but only for a short while.

One hole back on seventeen, more European heroics ensued. Mickelson was 1-up through sixteen, the only current American lead in the first five matches. Two holes earlier, he'd missed a short birdie putt that would have extended his lead, and it gave Rose a lifeline. The Englishman, having matched the lefty's 12-footer for par to keep the match from going dormie on sixteen, watched as Mickelson nearly holed out a chip from behind the green, celebrating prematurely. The Englishman then stood over a 35-footer and sent it across the green and into the hole. He stood there proudly with his head cocked, lips and fists clenched, still holding the putter. Mickelson laughed a "how did he do that?' laugh and applauded the effort. They walked to the eighteenth tee all square and left it with Europe having secured another huge point. Mickelson would airmail the green and chip it close before Rose's 14-footer for birdie disappeared into the hole.

That placed a finishing bow on the package of the first five matches. European's front-loaded lineup had been formidable. Despite Dustin Johnson temporarily stemming the bleeding by closing out Colsaerts just prior to Rose's win, the Americans were shaken. They still had their chances, but the score was now tied, 11-11, with the US up in the next three matches and Europe ahead in the last three. If those leads were to hold, Europe would retain the cup. As it turned out, Zach Johnson gave his squad its last lead of the week by defeating Graeme McDowell, 2-and-1, and Jason Dufner gave the Americans its last point over Peter Hanson, 2-up. Everything else fell to Europe, with two of the veteran captain's picks (Dufner was the only wild card to earn a singles point) stumbling the worst.

First, Furyk had his match flipped by Garcia after getting to 1-up with two to play. If he could have held on, it might have broken the European momentum and provided a red line in the sand. But the sand is exactly where Furyk put his tee shot on seventeen, blown into the worst possible spot in the back bunker by the wind coming off the right. Garcia hit safely onto the green to set up a routine two-putt as Furyk studied a sloping green that ran straight down toward the water. Before his shot, Furyk could hear the fainter European cheers that signaled Lee Westwood's 3-and-2 takedown of Matt Kuchar. The matches were tied again at 12-12. He did well to blast out, with the trundling golf ball running out eight feet past – but still on the green. Garcia putted to gimme range. Furyk, one of the steadiest putters in the world, would have to make the uphill comebacker. But he pushed it slightly. The match was even.

Garcia had the honors and found the eighteenth fairway off the tee. Furyk caught the right fairway bunker. Both hit the green from there, but Furyk had the more difficult putt, a long downhiller that he ran seven feet past the hole. With Garcia in the hole for par, Furyk took forever to get his read before sliding the putt past the hole on the left side. Garcia's stolen point meant that Europe would need one point out of the last two matches, Martin Kaymer against Stricker and Francesco Molinari against Woods.

Stricker was winless coming into the final day, but Kaymer was considered the weakest link on the European side. He'd slumped horribly all season just two years after winning the PGA Championship at Whistling Straits and had played once, a 3-and-2 loss with Rose in the Friday afternoon fourballs. He'd been sitting around all day Saturday and most of Sunday until his penultimate match teed off. But, as he was left out of Saturday's lineup, the German had made an emergency phone call to his compatriot, Bernhard Langer, who was well aware of the agony and ecstasy of Ryder Cup competition.

"I told him that I needed to talk because things were not going great for me, and I was feeling flat. We spent a couple of hours together, which was great," Kaymer elaborated.

Langer told Kaymer not to hide from the rest of the team, to relax, to get involved in team-room activities and to accept he was an equal member of the squad. He told him he was getting in his own way. Of course, there was nowhere to hide against Stricker on

Sunday but Langer's advice, Kaymer said, "gave me the confidence to go out and play on Sunday."

Stricker had no such haven. His partnership with Woods failed miserably. They never led in any of their three matches after the first three holes of the opening session. Their Friday afternoon fourball loss was the match that jump-started the European comeback from 10-4 down. When Love put them at the bottom of his singles lineup, he probably didn't think it would come down to them, although he said he still had confidence in them if it did. "I needed some stability in different spots," he explained at the time. "You needed guys like Tiger and Strick down towards the end."

The match was neck and neck, with neither Stricker nor Kaymer taking more than a one-hole lead. They halved the eleventh with bogeys and exchanged wins over the next four holes as Stricker bogeyed twelve by missing a four-footer, Kaymer doubled thirteen after finding the water and bogeyed fifteen—a miserable display of both players' short games. "Stricker has looked stricken over the last few holes," observed Sam Torrance on the Ryder Cup's world feed. Kaymer didn't seem much steadier. When they arrived at seventeen, after each bravely saving par from the same bunker on sixteen, each looked tight, with the fate of the entire week weighing on them, most heavily upon Stricker. If the US were to regain the cup, Stricker and Woods couldn't afford giving away more than a halve in their two matches—and both were now even. At least one of the Americans had to win his match, while the other needed at least a halve.

Stricker's shot into seventeen finished on the back fringe about fifteen feet behind the flag. Kaymer, who had driven into the water on the previous par-three, pulled his shot but safely made it across more than 50 feet from the hole—on the same line Rose had while dropping his bomb on Mickelson. Stricker held the advantage. He watched as Kaymer's putt drifted just past the hole to the left, but it was a good one from that distance, about five feet away. Now Stricker, needing a birdie, opted to chip it and, under tremendous pressure, hit it much too hard, running it down the sloping green six feet past.

"Sam," Dougie Donnelly said to Sam Torrance on the Ryder Cup's world feed. "Pressure, if you're playing in a major championship or a normal tournament, is one thing, but playing for your country is something completely different."

"There's no second prize here," Torrance replied.

Stricker, unquestionably the best putter on the American team, made the same mis-read everyone had been making on that putt. It slid past the right lip of the hole. Kaymer was able to complete his fine two-putt par and Europe was sure of 13 ½ points. Woods would have to win his match. But first, Stricker would need to capture the final hole.

Kaymer drove it into the left fairway bunker and Stricker followed with a drive into the fairway for the advantage. Meanwhile, roars echoed from seventeen, indicating that Woods had won the hole to go 1-up. Kaymer, a natural fader of the ball, hit his preferred cut shot out of the sand and stared at its flight path as it fortuitously kicked to the right onto the green instead of left into the bunker. That still left Stricker with an opening. If he could stick one close and win the hole, he could let Tiger do the rest. He couldn't. The approach shot ran to the back of the green, leaving him with a long putt that wasn't even close. Now, needing a two-putt from 25 feet to secure the cup for Europe, Kaymer rolled it almost five feet past. Stricker was able to make his eight-footer to force Kaymer to match his par. The comparisons to Langer's final putt at Kiawah were unavoidable and ran through his mind. Had he missed it, as Langer had done, it would leave the fate of the Cup in Tiger's hands–and Tiger had a 1-up lead with one to play.

"When I stood over that putt, I thought of him," Kaymer confessed later. "I remembered the putt he had at Kiawah Island to win the match for Europe."

With a spike mark in his way, Langer chose to play a different line and missed the putt. Kaymer had a similar issue.

"There was a footprint across the line of the putt," he explained. "So I thought, 'Okay, it's not going to happen again.' And to be honest with you, I didn't really think about missing. There was only one choice you have. You have to make it. I just chose the line and hit it. I can't even remember seeing the ball roll. All I know is it went in."

Kaymer threw his arms skyward and leaped into the arms of Sergio Garcia. Medinah exploded in European joy. Back on the eighteenth fairway, where they were with the Woods-Molinari match, Olazábal bear-hugged Poulter. Rose somehow had his nose bloodied in the mayhem. There was still one match left on the course, but it would only determine whether it would be an official tie or a European win. The visitors would be flying home with the chalice regardless. With the European revelry going on around them, many felt Molinari should have conceded Woods his four-foot putt in the spirit of Jack Nicklaus' concession. He didn't, and Woods made an indifferent stroke that left him with a bogey. He then told Molinaro to pick up his slightly shorter par putt to make it 15-13 Europe instead of a 14-14 tie. It left Woods with just a half-point for the entire week, his worst Ryder Cup performance.

"It was already over," explained Woods, likely tired of hearing the "Ole" song as they finished up. "We came here as a team. This is a team event, and the Cup had already been retained by Europe, so it was already over."

The Americans were dumbfounded, but the defeat was well-earned, and excuses rang hollow, as the twelve Americans and their captain assembled in the media center for the same funereal ritual, explaining away an inexplicable loss. For the first time, the US had lost more than a two-point advantage on the final day.

"We were four ahead. The plan worked the first two days. It just didn't work Sunday," Love told the media mob. "That's my job to get second-guessed. Those guys tried their hardest and we could have put out a whole bunch of different plans, but if we don't play well, none of them work. And when a team plays like Europe did, you're going to get beaten." He attributed the loss to his guys trying too hard.

"We came here as a team," offered Furyk, so often burdened with spokesman duties. "We wanted to win the Ryder Cup as a team, and we didn't do it. But we are going to leave here in the same fashion. I'm pretty sure Sergio would tell you that I out played him today, but I didn't win."

But Ryder Cups are usually decided by who plays better when it counts. And, when it counted, the Americans, as a team, simply did not show up. Back in 1987, after the Europeans stunned the US on captain Jack Nicklaus' home course, the Golden Bear lit into them for their inability to finish on seventeen and eighteen. He had chided them: "You guys need to learn how to win or you're going to continue getting beaten in this thing." His admonishment was fitting yet again. Woods' loss on eighteen can be forgiven. He would most certainly have protected his lead against Molinari if it counted. Nevertheless, three of Sunday's matches were decided when the Americans lost the last two holes. Another point was lost on seventeen. The Americans were 4-over par on those holes in those matches. The Euros played them in 3-under. That's a seven-shot difference.

ESPN's website ran a story two years later debating whether it was a miracle or meltdown. Brandt Snedeker was brutally honest.

"Scott Hoch had a great quote, and it applies to the Ryder Cup," Snedeker told them. "He said, 'Golf is just a game until you lose a major.' And I think golf is just a game until you're part of one of those epic collapses at a Ryder Cup. Right or wrong, I don't think it was a collapse, but it is. At the end of the day, we were up four points—one of the largest leads in Ryder Cup history—and we lost. You can spin it any way you want to, but we didn't get the job done. If that's not a collapse, I don't know what you would call a collapse."

The Europeans weren't the least bit concerned with what the US players thought went wrong. They were convinced that Seve Ballesteros' spirit had won the day for them. Olazábal, Seve's long-time partner, was naturally the most affected. He seemed to fight back tears as he bit his lip, then paused for a reflective moment with his hand over his mouth and looking toward the heavens where he was sure Ballesteros was watching.

"This one's for him," he'd tell a *BBC* camera crew.

"Seve will always be present for this team," he said later at the official press conference. "Last night, when we were having that meeting, I think the boys understood that believing was the most important thing. And they did."

McIlroy disclosed that Olazábal's speech "had a few of us in the team room in tears."

"Jose wanted to win it for Seve, and we wanted to win it for Jose and Seve," McDowell said. "We dug in and dug in deep today."

"I have no doubt in my mind he was with me today," Garcia said. "There's no chance I would have won if he wasn't."

It was also a redemption for Olazábal. He was not only a member of the 1999 European team that blew the same four-point lead but was also on the seventeenth green when Justin Leonard made what would be the Cup-winning putt.

"To the twelve men of Team Europe," he told his team at the closing ceremony, "You believed, and you delivered. All men die but not every man lives and you made me feel alive again this week."

Love, ultimately, wasn't blamed by the US camp. He'd be selected as captain just four years later.

Medinah, however, was maddening for the US cause.

The US team had looked certain to continue the home mojo from Valhalla in 2008. Through two days, Keegan Bradley had given it energy, Bubba Watson some good-natured fervor, Jason Dufner a steely disposition. Phil Mickelson had been rejuvenated. And, with the rookies playing so well, the future looked promising. But the week ended the way so many others had recently, with the Euros spraying champagne for the fifth time in the prior six meetings. The Americans would have to face the music—that same, taunting, bullfighting chant. And it would get a lot worse before it got better.

DAY 1

FOURSOMES

Rory McIlroy/Graeme McDowell (E) defeated Jim Furyk/Brad Snedeker (US) 1-up
Phil Mickelson/Keegan Bradley (US) defeated Luke Donald/Sergio Garcia (E) 4-and-3
Jason Dufner/Zach Johnson (US) defeated Lee Westwood/Francesco Molinari (E) 3-and-2
Ian Poulter/Justin Rose (E) defeated Steve Stricker/Tiger Woods (US) 2-and-1
Session tied, 2–2

FOURBALLS

Webb Simpson/Bubba Watson (US) defeated Paul Lawrie/Peter Hanson (E) 5-and-4
Phil Mickelson/Keegan Bradley (US) defeated Rory McIlroy/Graeme McDowell (E) 2-and-1
Lee Westwood/Nicolas Colsaerts (E) defeated Steve Stricker/Tiger Woods (US) 1-up
Matt Kuchar/Dustin Johnson (US) defeated Martin Kaymer/Justin Rose (E) 3-and-2
United States wins session 3–1
United States 5, Europe 3

DAY 2

FOURSOMES

Ian Poulter/Justin Rose (E) defeated Webb Simpson/Bubba Watson (US) 1-up
Phil Mickelson/Keegan Bradley (US) defeated Lee Westwood/Luke Donald (E) 7-and-6
Jason Dufner/Zach Johnson (US) defeated Nicolas Colsaerts/Sergio Garcia (E) 2-and-1
Jim Furyk/Brad Snedeker (US) defeated Rory McIlroy/Graeme McDowell (E) 1-up
United States wins session 3–1
United States 8, Europe 4

FOURBALLS

Matt Kuchar/Dustin Johnson (US) defeated Nicolas Colsaerts/Paul Lawrie (E) 1-up
Webb Simpson/Bubba Watson (US) defeated Lee Westwood/Francesco Molinari (E) 5-and-4
Luke Donald/Sergio Garcia (E) defeated Steve Stricker/Tiger Woods (US) 1-up
Rory McIlroy/Ian Poulter (E) defeated Jason Dufner/Zach Johnson (US) 1-up
Session tied, 2–2
United States 10, Europe 6

DAY 3

SINGLES

Luke Donald (E) defeated Bubba Watson (US) 2-and-1
Ian Poulter (E), defeated Webb Simpson (US) 1-up
Rory McIlroy (E) defeated Keegan Bradley (US) 2-and-1
Justin Rose (E) defeated Phil Mickelson (US) 1-up
Paul Lawrie (E) defeated Brandt Snedeker (US) 5-and-3
Dustin Johnson (US) defeated Nicolas Colsaerts (E) 3-and-2
Zach Johnson (US) defeated Graeme McDowell (E) 2-and-1
Sergio Garcia (E) defeated Jim Furyk (US) 1-up
Jason Dufner (US) defeated Peter Hanson (E) 2-up
Lee Westwood (E) defeated Matt Kuchar (US) 3-and-2
Martin Kaymer (E) defeated Steve Stricker (US) 1-up
Francesco Molinari (E) halved with Tiger Woods (US)
Europe wins session 8 ½-3 ½

EUROPE WINS RYDER CUP 14 ½–13 ½

2016

Task Masters

HAZELTINE NATIONAL GOLF CLUB
UNITED STATES 17, EUROPE 11

The United States' jarring collapse at Medinah left the PGA of America not only longing for the good old days but also desperate to recreate them. Had Davis Love III's team finished off the Europeans, the PGA would likely have gone the conventional route and named David Toms the captain for the 2014 matches at Gleneagles in Scotland. Desperate times, however, were calling for desperate measures. In the wake of Medinah, that meant handing the reins to the legendary Tom Watson, the last US captain to win on foreign soil at The Belfry in 1993. The throwback, it was hoped, would bring the necessary tough love to the American cause as a sort of Vince Lombardi in FootJoys. Watson spoke a lot about winning at his introductory press conference in December of 2012. And, for good reason. He had a 10-4-1 record as Ryder Cup player and had not been on a losing side (3-0-1) in four Cups. He'd won eight majors during his playing career, including five Open Championships, four of which were in Scotland, where, at Turnberry in 2009, he came within a seventy-second-hole bogey of winning again.

"We're tired of losing," he said with a twinkle in his eye suggesting he was up to task for the unenviable job. "I always said that early in my career. I learned to win by hating to lose. It's about time to start winning again."

The US had lost seven of their previous nine tussles with Europe, and the blame seemed to be directed at everything but the golf itself. The Europeans had more spirit and togetherness. The Americans weren't team players. They didn't care. Etcetera, etcetera, etcetera. Optimists hoped Watson would bring accountability to the team. After all, he had the guts to call out Tiger Woods with comments that Woods needed to "show some humility" when he returned to golf after sorting out his personal life in 2010. Yet, at sixty-five, could the old-school warrior relate to younger players?

"Why is Watson, being the old guy, being the captain?" he asked rhetorically. "I deflect that very simply by saying, 'We play the same game.'"

None other than Paul Azinger, the only winning US captain since 1999, endorsed the choice. He quickly noted on Twitter how he had relied on oldsters Dave Stockton and Ray Floyd as vice-captains at Valhalla.

"I saw tremendous value in having Dave and Raymond's no non-sense old school of thinking at our 2008 RC," Zinger tweeted. "Tom will bring those same intangibles."

Tangibly speaking, it couldn't have worked out any worse. Europe kicked the Americans from glen to glen in the Perthshire country-side. The 16 ½-11 ½ rout drove American fortunes to their nadir, with a 1-6 record since 2002. Three decades earlier, Jack Nicklaus saved the Ryder Cup by lobbying for the rest of Europe to join in the competition. Now it seemed as though the United States could use the rest of the world's help. Uncle Sam was pleading "uncle."

Worse yet, as Phil Mickelson dragged Watson and his leadership style through the mud at the climactic press conference, it seemed that the entire program had descended into chaos. The headstrong Mickelson and the temperamental Watson had been at loggerheads well before the first ball was struck. Reportedly, Watson had never returned Mickelson's phone calls to confer on strategy and the like—and that signaled to Mickelson that it was going to be Watson's way or the highway, the antithesis of Azinger's inclusive philosophy at Valhalla. In general, the players had been feeling that the event had become more about the executives at the PGA of America and less about them. Watson may have been a legend of the game, but a generation gap separated him from this team, a void the players felt he was disinterested in bridging. Watson's chumminess with PGA president Ted Bishop only deepened the players' apprehension.

When the week went sideways, the chilly relationship between captain and team went glacial. It wasn't just that Watson benched Mickelson in two sessions. It's *how* he benched him—via text. *ESPN* reported that he scolded the team during the Saturday night meeting—which is customarily an inspirational pep rally—by scoffing at the gift the team presented him—a replica of the Ryder Cup trophy signed by every player. An uninspired team proceeded to play out the string in the Sunday singles. Later, about a third of the way through another mopey post-match press conference, the question came: "Phil, and anyone else who was at Valhalla, can you put your finger on what worked in 2008 and what hasn't worked since?"

Mickelson must have felt as if he were free to speak his mind for the first time that week—and relished such opportunities to send such messages. Clearly, Watson was being shoved under the proverbial bus: however, in Mickelson's mind, his comments were less vindictive than constructive. He didn't refer to Watson or directly criticize his moves. Rather, he hailed Azinger's "winning" philosophy and how it had been "strayed" from. Zinger had everyone "invested" in the process, Mickelson said. He had a game plan (unlike Watson's admitted seat-of-his-pants approach). After Mickelson finished, a British reporter eagerly jumped in. "That felt like a pretty brutal destruction of the leadership that's gone on this week," he said.

"Oh, I'm sorry you're taking it that way," Mickelson replied blithely. "I'm just talking about what Paul Azinger did to help us play our best. I was asked what I thought we should do going forward to bring our best golf out and I go back to when we played our best golf and try to replicate that formula."

"That didn't happen this week?" "Uh, no," he stammered. "No, nobody here was in on any decision. So, no."

His teammates squirmed. No one volunteered a comment—whether in support of, or against, their captain. Another reporter probed for a reaction from Jim Furyk: "You've listened to the back and forth between Phil and Tom, and as the other veteran, I was curious for your opinion." "Gee, thanks," Furyk replied, as laughter lightened the mood a tad. "Just sitting over here minding my own business." And, so it went.

Mickelson was criticized in many corners of the golf media for skewering a legend. As Jaime Diaz of *Golf Digest* put it, Mickelson, "with captain Tom Watson sitting wincingly close, dialed passive aggression to eleven and poured his salty rebuke into the Hall of Fame icon's gaping wound." Caustic commentator Brandel Chamblee called it a "one-man mutiny"—but many of Mickelson's teammates agreed with Phil. A few years later, Keegan Bradley, Mickelson's partner in 2012 and the 2025 Ryder Cup captain, admitted as much.

"We all were pretty frustrated, so it could have come from anybody," he told *Golf Magazine*. "But again, Phil is our guy. Phil is the guy we look up to on that team."

The PGA of America found itself in a tough spot. It needed a phoenix-from-the-ashes moment of renewal. It had played its last trump card with Watson and was left with no option but to turn to Phil and his fellow players for answers. A "task force" was formed to come up with a new playbook. Eight active and former players, including Mickelson, Woods and Davis Love III, whose return as 2016 captain was yet to be announced, joined three PGA officials on the panel. Bishop explained that the idea was to "give the players a voice but not total control." Conspicuously absent from the group was Azinger, who chose not to get involved so soon after the Ryder Cup. Also conspicuous from the task force itself was the absence of anyone outside the golf world who could have offered a much-needed wider perspective.

The Europeans, quite naturally, guffawed. There was no secret to their success, they felt. They simply were outperforming the Americans. Lee Westwood quickly took to Twitter to mock the initiative: "What a massive pat on the back & confidence booster it is for Europe that team USA needs to create a Ryder Cup task force!!!"

Nor was every American on board. Billy Horschel called it "a lot of political BS." Jack Nicklaus called it, "overkill." "I don't think we need a task force," chimed in Fred Couples, who had captained the US to Presidents Cup victories in '09, '11 and '13. "I don't think we need the PGA of America straining about this."

Despite the mockery, the mission of the task force differed little from what Tony Jacklin accomplished in taking over decision-making from the British PGA and European Tour as a condition for accepting the captaincy for the 1983 matches. It also gave the players a chance to air their grievances and empower them for perhaps the first time. Love, for instance, noted that the size of the Ryder Cup contingent had gotten out of hand and that there were too many "strap hangers" in the room. The panel also attempted to begin a collaboration with the Presidents Cup teams that had been dominating the internationals in the years in between Ryder Cups. A system for the selection of captains and vice captains encouraged continuity by establishing a sort of apprentice system, with captains staying on as vice captains the following Cup. Timetables and points used in the selection process for both qualifying and wild card players were adjusted to add weight to the most recent results, affording hot players a better chance of making the team. In general, it sent the US team into the 2016 matches with a more positive attitude–albeit with increased pressure to win–especially Mickelson, who had thrust himself to the tip of the spear.

The selection of the 2016 captain was the task force's initial task, and for that, the gang of eleven went back to Love, absolving him of the 2012 failure. Couples and Steve Stricker were the other two names considered but Love, despite some reluctance on his part, got the eventual nod.

"He felt like he was taking somebody else's spot. He felt it wasn't his place to do that," Mickelson explained. "But when you look at the next ten Ryder Cups and trying to build a platform and a blueprint to follow, you want somebody who can look back on things that have been done well and things that could be improved upon. Davis in 2012 did a lot of things right."

"I'm here with the same goal I had in 2012 but not as the same captain," Love demurred. "The task force has been an open, honest, team-building experience. I don't think we have to make massive changes. We have to make some small changes that add up to half a point here or there."

One of those changes meant that Love could make his last wild card selection as close to the start of the Ryder Cup as ever before, right up to the week of the competition itself. It was to be announced with fanfare on national TV at halftime of the Bears-Cowboys Sunday night football game. That changed with the death of Arnold Palmer earlier in the day. Instead, Love issued a press release, naming rookie Ryan Moore over World No. 7 Bubba Watson. Moore had lost to Rory McIlroy in a four-hole playoff at the Tour Championship that afternoon, his ninth top ten finish of the season and his fourth in six weeks. Watson, the two-time Masters champ, had desperately wanted to make the team. Speculation, especially from the European press, was that he was unpopular with his teammates and that Love couldn't find a suitable partner for him, discounting how Watson had teamed quite well with Webb Simpson at Medinah. Ultimately, those rumors were squashed when Love brought Watson into the team room as the unprecedented fifth vice-captain, honoring Watson's request in the event he wasn't selected. He would join Woods, Furyk and Stricker and Minnesota native Tom Lehman.

In putting Moore on his first Ryder Cup team, Love followed task force's strategy to pick the player with the hottest game going into the week. It didn't matter that Watson was ninth–and Moore twentieth–on the points list.

"Ryan fits so well with what we have in place," he explained. "He's an easy-going, thoughtful guy but don't be fooled: Ryan's a great match play player. He has guts and determination, and everyone saw that today."

Before he made the selection, Love appeared on *Sirius XM Radio* and proclaimed that his squad was "the best golf team maybe ever assembled." It was a wild stretch of imagination, considering some of the teams that included Nicklaus, Palmer, Lee Trevino, Billy Casper, Tom Weiskopf, Tom Watson et al. Ironically, Bubba Watson would have made the team even stronger on paper by giving the US three of the seven top-ranked players in the world, with Dustin Johnson at No. 2 (behind Jason Day) and Jordan Spieth at No. 4. Still, the US was regarded as the clear favorite. Europe's inspirational star, Ian Poulter, was sitting this one out with a foot injury (he participated as a vice-captain), and half the roster was made up of rookies. Johnny Miller even called the collection "the worst team they've had in many years," despite the presence of three players in the World Rankings top ten, McIlroy at No. 3, Open champ Henrik Stenson at No. 5 and Masters champ Willett at tenth.

The Americans had just two rookies: Moore and the long-hitting Brooks Koepka. Only two Americans had played on a Ryder Cup-winning team (Mickelson and J.B. Holmes). However, they had a lot of young blood who had experienced Ryder Cup pressure, such as Spieth, Rickie Fowler, and firebrand Patrick Reed, a rare bright spot for the Americans two years earlier at Gleneagles where he compiled a 3-0-1 record. And, as Westwood noted, "it shows their strength if they can skip No. 7 in the world."

Palmer's passing kept things civilized at the start of the week with tributes from both sides. Everyone knew the King from his sponsorship of the Bay Hill Classic over the years. While Palmer played in an era dominated by the US, his Ryder Cup record stands out, nonetheless. He was 22-8-2 overall in six Ryder Cup appearances and captained two teams to victories, as the last playing captain in 1963 and as non-playing captain in 1975. "This team would beat the rest of the world combined," he boasted before the US crushed GBI, 23-9, in '63. In 1967, he took several members of the visiting team for a ride in his plane and scared the wits out of them by buzzing Champions Golf Club. Ben Hogan benched him for a session and the Federal Aviation Administration admonished him, but Arnie went 5-0 in the matches he played.

It was left to Peter Willett to introduce some traditional vitriol. Danny's brother, a golf instructor from the West Midlands, took sarcasm too far as he ripped American golf fans in an article in England's *National Club Golfer.* Peter, or "P.J.," had become something of a Twitter celebrity with a stream of amusing tweets as his brother was winning the Masters. His encore was less well-received. "For the Americans to stand a chance of winning, they need their baying mob of imbeciles to caress their egos every step of the way," he wrote, adding that Europe needs to "silence these cretins quickly" and "shut those groupies up.

"They need to silence the pudgy, basement-dwelling, irritants, stuffed on cookie dough and pissy beer, pausing between mouthfuls of hot dog so they can scream 'Baba booey' until their jelly faces turn red. They need to stun the angry, unwashed, Make America Great Again swarm, desperately gripping their concealed-carry compensators and belting out a mini-erection inducing 'mashed potato,' hoping to impress their cousin. They need to smash the obnoxious dads, with their shiny teeth, Lego man hair, medicated ex-wives, and resentful children. Squeezed into their cargo shorts and boating shoes, they'll bellow 'get in the hole' whilst high fiving all the other members of the Dentists' Big Game Hunt Society."

While Willett was making his clumsy attempt at humor, neither his brother nor European captain Darren Clarke were laughing once his remarks found their way to the States. Clarke addressed the matter with Danny, who spent Thursday trying to apologize for his brother's unhinged rant, which had placed him in the crosshairs of gallery hecklers, some of whom would live up to P.J.'s stereotypical caricatures.

"Yeah, it was tough to concentrate," he said. "As soon as I got done on the golf course, I went to see Davis and had a chat for a few minutes, and he took it very well. Hopefully everyone else can do the same, and we can get on and have a great tournament.

"I was obviously disappointed on what was written about the American fans that took me under their wing fantastically back in April (at the Masters)."

The same day the Willett story broke, so did some of the tension. McIlroy, Andy Sullivan, Justin Rose and Stenson were failing at repeated attempts to sink a tricky 12-foot putt on the eighth green when David Johnson, an insurance agent from Mayville, North Dakota, yelled out, "loud and obnoxiously" that even he could make the putt. Stenson obliged him, went into the crowd and pulled him onto the green. As Johnson, clad in baggy jeans, sneakers and a red pullover, lined up the putt, Rose, pulled out a $100 bill and placed it beside the ball. "No pressure," someone yelled. Apparently not. Johnson's putt steamed ramrod straight into the hole, although it would have gone at least twelve feet past had it not. Johnson, of course, went wild, danced on the green and did a double high-five with Rose's caddie, Mark "Fooch" Fulcher. There were hugs all around as the crowd erupted in "USA, USA." It was a cool moment.

When play finally started with foursomes in Friday's morning fog, Palmer's 1975 Ryder Cup bag was on the first tee, as, for once, the US stole the emotional edge away from Europe. It would seem Arnie had pushed Seve Ballesteros aside and interceded from above when, having passed that bag on the way toward their opening shots, the Americans swept the opening session for the first time since that same 1975 Cup. But the good karma could last only so long. The day ended with Rory McIlroy draining an eagle putt to win his match and pull the Europeans back within 5-3 for the day, before mockingly bowing twice to what he called the "hostile" American crowd.

Other story lines emerged, starting with Mickelson, who couldn't seem to avoid heaping needless pressure upon himself. Two years earlier, he had eviscerated captain Watson to spark the formation of the task force. Then, during a midweek press conference, he answered an open-ended question about the role of a captain by taking down 2004 captain Hal Sutton. Mickelson could not forgive him for the most embarrassing moment of his heretofore 16-19-2 Ryder Cup career, when he was disastrously paired with Tiger Woods at Oakland Hills. As *ESPN's* Ian O'Connor noted, "It seemed Lefty had ripped every American captain except Captain America." To his credit, Mickelson realized he'd inserted his Size 13 into his mouth yet again and quickly issued a personal apology to Sutton. To be sure, however, the week-long spotlight was squarely on the lefthander, and Mickelson knew it.

He said he'd felt it coming for two years before stepping on the first tee in the second match of the morning, teamed with Fowler, his fellow task-force member. He hadn't been able to sleep the night before the match against McIlroy and Sullivan, and, admittedly, his heart was pounding. Love had even asked him if he was "ready to go," thinking it might be best to leave him out.

"Given the buildup over the last couple years, the criticism, the comments, the pressure certainly was as great or greater than any I've ever felt. I could have copped out and asked to sit," Mickelson acknowledged. "That would have been a total weak move. I wanted to get out there. Put me out there. I enjoy that pressure."

Mickelson took little joy in his tee shot on the sixth hole, which he sailed out of bounds, nor Fowler's third shot along the fence line, forcing Mickelson to swing right-handed with an inverted clubface. But Fowler, who carried a dismal 0-3-5 Ryder Cup record into the week, came alive by chipping in on the ninth to cap a string of three straight winning holes. The Euros fought back to take a 2-up lead with four to play but Mickelson, admittedly "tight" at the start, won the fifteenth with a par putt. He followed that up with a sweet approach into the par-five sixteenth, after putting Fowler in trouble off the tee. Sullivan's shot into the water on seventeen handed the Americans the lead. Mickelson thankfully found the fairway on the final hole and when McIlroy missed a curling 10-footer for birdie, the Americans had a 1-up win, Fowler's first full point in a Ryder Cup.

"I didn't play the way I wanted to off the tee," Mickelson said. "But Rickie was able to get the best out of me and get me to hit some iron shots I needed to hit, and to get me to perform. We showed a lot of heart those last four holes to win that match."

It was the only close match in the morning session. Love had set up the course for birdies (Rose would later call the setup "incredibly weak" with "pro-am" pin placements), and the US team obliged with hot putters. In a preview of what was to come, Spieth and Reed took down Europe's No. 1 pair, Rose and Stenson, 3-and-2, handing that pair their first loss after a 3-0 record at Gleneagles. Zach Johnson and Jimmy Walker topped Sergio Garcia and Martin Kaymer by the same score, and Dustin Johnson and Matt Kuchar dusted Westwood and rookie Thomas Pieters, 5-and-4. It was an even more surprising sweep in that the US had lost six and halved two of the eight alternate shot matches two years earlier at Gleneagles.

After Medinah, Love wasn't taking anything for granted. Still, his afternoon fourball pairings allowed all twelve of his players to see first day action in keeping with his 2012 strategy to rest everyone. He stuck with two of his morning pairings, Spieth/Reed and Johnson/Kuchar but sent out two new pairings in Holmes and Moore and Brandt Snedeker and Koepka. It meant that all four of his captain's picks were in action. Clarke sent out six of the eight players he started in the morning, confident his horses would gallop back. Mostly, they did, except for one partnership that stumbled spectacularly.

After his brother's article had made news during the week, Willett was sure to catch it from the aggrieved US fans, who, by the afternoon, were well lubricated by $10 beers. Perhaps Clarke should have sent Willett out in the morning, before the alcohol had taken effect. Instead, he took the brunt of the fans' abuse in Europe's only afternoon loss, a 5-and-4 pounding from Koepka and Snedeker while paired with Kaymer. As the European pair left the fourth tee already 2-down in the match, they were hit with a salvo of "P.J., P.J." chants. And it only got worse. Meanwhile, Koepka was enjoying an outstanding Ryder Cup debut. The man who would go on to win five major championships over the next seven years slept throughout the morning until his afternoon tee time, hit a trademark booming drive off the first tee and staked the US to a lead it wouldn't relinquish–with birdies on one and three. Willett didn't play poorly. His scores were used on every hole on the front nine, but the rude treatment was just getting started. When he headed off to the practice range afterwards, he was followed by an inebriated spectator who taunted him from the grandstand. As it was, he made light of it.

"It was exactly what we thought it was going to be," he told the British media. "There were a few little shouts in there, and bits and bobs, but hopefully they are all following me around so the rest of the lads can do their business."

They did that quite well. In a rematch of their morning match, Rose and Stenson got their revenge over Spieth and Reed, 5-and-4, while Garcia teamed with fellow Spaniard Rafael Cabrera-Bello to handle Holmes and Moore, 3-and-2. It was left to McIlroy and Pieters to cool off Dustin Johnson and Kuchar, 3-and-2.

McIlroy had four birdies on the first ten holes, but Pieters did his part. He birdied the fourth to put Europe 1-up, the seventh to go 4-up and the thirteenth after McIlroy found the water. The match ended on sixteen with McIlroy's 15-foot eagle putt, animated by wild eyes and a fist pump. He then bowed twice in melodramatic fashion to the suddenly silent American crowd. Every European in sight got a high-five.

"Even before I hit that putt, I wanted to put an exclamation point on that session for us," he explained. "I actually thought about the celebration before I hit the putt. I just want everyone that's watching out there to know how much this means to me personally and obviously us as a team."

After running into what Love called a "buzzsaw," the US still had the lead, but the Euros had the momentum with recent history warning the Americans and their fans how this one might turn out.

"We were bitterly disappointed at lunchtime," Clarke said. "The guys just didn't play the way they can, and the Americans did. And then for the guys to come back after being as far back as we were is scintillating. Shoulder to shoulder. It shows how strong we are, to be able to do what we did in the afternoon. We find ourselves two points behind, but a very good two points behind."

Even Love admitted that "a little air went out of the balloon," creating a "letdown feeling" when everyone returned to the team hotel. But this time, the Americans would not crack. Day two provided several opportunities to do so, but when dusk fell on what had been a brilliant fall day, the US was very much in control at 9 ½-6 ½. Was this team made of "stronger stuff" as some suggested? Not judging by their collective amount of scar tissue. Instead, the results of the first two days showed that the US was simply the deeper team. Love was able to get everyone into action each day. Clark had to be more careful. He didn't want to pair two rookies together, but, with six on his squad, he was in a bit of a bind. After sitting Chris Wood and Matthew Fitzpatrick on Friday, he did the same to Sullivan Saturday. Five of his players—McIlroy, Rose, Stenson, Garcia and the rookie Pieters—would play five matches. Only Reed and Spieth played every match for the Americans.

Clarke, however, had found one indomitable partnership in McIlroy and Pieters, the best of the Euro rookie class. Pieters had been trounced while playing the Friday morning foursomes session with Lee Westwood. However, after his crucial, momentum-snatching win with Rory in the last Friday match it was a no-brainer to send them out first in the morning fourballs, and again in the afternoon. Opposing them was another heavyweight pairing, Mickelson and Fowler, who had fed off each other so well in their foursomes win the morning before. It was an extremely well-played match that the Europeans took over with a string of three birdies starting at the fourteenth. Their convincing 4-and-2 win, which pulled Europe within a point, turned up the home crowd's angst.

"It's huge," McIlroy said. "To go out and lead Team Europe and get that first point on the board is massive. Darren put a lot of faith in us sending us out first. We had not really practiced, had not chosen what golf ball to play, had not chosen even what tee to go off. We flipped for it on the first tee. But it seemed to work out pretty well."

The win was especially important to McIlroy, who had not beaten Mickelson in three previous Ryder Cup meetings, including a 1-up defeat the previous morning.

"Personally, I maybe wanted it a little bit more. Thankfully, I was able to get one back on him," the Irishman said, before heading out to watch the completion of the last three matches, the first two of which were split. Snedeker and Koepka, sparked by Snedeker's hot putter and despite a Koepka shank, came from 2-down to beat Stenson and Fitzpatrick, 3-and-2, before Rose and Wood nipped Walker and Zach Jonson, 1-up. That left Garcia and Cabrera-Bello against Spieth and Reed, a match that seemed over with the Americans 4-up with six to play. Reed and Spieth were 5-under through the first seven holes, while Garcia hit a ball of the fifth tee that landed in a marshal's hip pocket and missed a two-footer on eleven. But there has always been something about Spanish partnerships, exemplified by Seve Ballesteros and Jose Maria Olazábal. Garcia and Cabrera-Bello rekindled that spirit by fighting back to earn a half point. They were about to go 5-down on twelve where Reed chipped in for birdie, but Cabrera-Bello matched it with a brave 15-foot putt. The Americans handed over the next three holes with bogeys, the Euros claimed the seventeenth, and matching pars on eighteen (Reed, in true fashion, drained a clutch six-footer for the halve) left them all square.

"They kept throwing darts at us," Garcia said. "We made an amazing birdie on twelve to halve the hole, thanks to my partner's putt. And then we just saw that little window they gave, and we grabbed the momentum."

Such stolen points are often turning points. Instead of retaining a two-point lead, the Americans' advantage was a slim one point. The captains had one last session to figure out pairings. Love, of course, had been in this position before. Four years earlier, at Medinah, he had chosen to sit the scorchingly hot pairing of Mickelson and Bradley, who had cruised to three straight wins. It was arguably his biggest mistake that week. Now, he was considering sitting Spieth and Reed, the most solid US partnership since 2014 at Gleneagles. Here, Tiger Woods made one of his most valuable Ryder Cup contributions without even swinging a club.

Earlier in the week, when Woods told Reed he might be sitting out a session, Reed's reply was succinct: "you're not sitting me in any matches." So, when Love asked Woods whether to play them or sit them, he in effect made the final call, "No, you have to send them back out there.'"

Some questioned why Clarke wouldn't send out Garcia and Cabrera-Bello once more after their stirring back-nine comeback to halve Spieth and Reed. But Clarke stuck with his original plan to pair Garcia with Cabrera-Bello in fourballs and with Kaymer in foursomes. They would oppose longtime friends Mickelson and Kuchar, who had always wanted to pair up in a Ryder Cup but never got the chance.

First, McIlroy and Pieters did their thing once more, leading off against the bomber brothers, Koepka and Dustin Johnson for a 3-and-1 win, beating them at their own game. With McIlroy blasting 380-yard drives and Pieters driving the par four fifth hole for an eagle, the Euros combined to shoot 11-under for 17 holes. They never trailed through forty-nine holes, winning all three of their matches. That 4-0 lead the US enjoyed was entirely gone, thanks to McIlroy and his new ligntening rod role. With Ian Poulter's role reduced to vice-captain at Hazeltine, McIlroy was embracing the challenge. Like Poulter, and Colin Montgomerie before him, McIlroy had become the target of the most bellicose of the American supporters, a minority who were making Peter Willett's description look spot-on.

"Irrespective of the score, the US players are policing the fans as they are embarrassed by their behavior," Poulter noted. "Shame spoiling this."

This was the match where things became venomous. As McIlroy would say looking back at the week, it was the first time he had "played the villain.

"Even at Medinah in 2012, the crowd wasn't quite as vocal, quite as bad. But at Hazeltine, I felt as though you're out there pushing at me, I need to push back at you. So, it was tough. I mean, I enjoyed playing in it. I love the fact that you hold a putt to win a hole, and you might hear a couple of claps and that's it. I sort of like that."

When McIlroy drained a huge putt for a birdie on seven, he turned away from the gallery toward Lake Hazeltine and raised his fist in defiance before letting out a full-throated howl. A few nitwits in the crowd took it personally. The walk from the seventh green to the eighth tee was over 200 yards, lined by phalanxes of hostile fans. As McIlroy was making his way through, one leaned over into his face and screamed out an obscenity as loudly as McIlroy had yelled on the green, urging him to suck on something that was not a lollipop. With his Irish up, McIlroy stopped abruptly and called for security, all the while pointing at the offending fan, until they arrived to escort him off the premises. He then stepped onto the eighth tee and striped a 3-iron into the green. Europe won the hole.

There would be other moments. He was serenaded around the course with "Sweet Caroline," a reference to his breakup with tennis star Caroline Wozniaki, as his current fiancée, Erica Stoll, walked beside him. When he hooked a 4-iron shot into the water, trying to reach the par-five sixteenth, it brought on one of the biggest roars of the week. Pieters played so well down the stretch, it didn't matter. "He's a stud," McIlroy said after they combined to shoot 11-under through seventeen holes. But the boorish fans weren't helping their team any.

"It fueled me a lot," McIlroy said. "The more they shouted, the better we played. I hope they shout at us all day tomorrow."

With that, McIlroy popped a couple of Advils for the headache he'd been suffering all day and headed back to the course to bring his teammates down the stretch. The problem, however, was that his teammates didn't follow up. The US won each of the last three matches, all of them tightly contested. It might have been different had Westwood and Willett won the second match, having led through the first sixteen holes. Instead, Moore and Holmes rewarded Love's faith as wild card picks to win the last two holes for a 1-up win. For once, one of Europe's old lions let them down. Clarke had made Lee Westwood a captain's pick as Europe's most experienced player. But with his game suffering, Westwood asked out of the Friday afternoon session and spent hours on the putting green. Birdie putts on five, six and seven seemed to indicate he'd worked it out, until he missed three putts inside five feet over the last six holes. His final two-foot birdie on eighteen would have salvaged a half point but he wiped it, a common amateur lament. It turned out to be Europe's last best chance to rein in the Americans.

Garcia, the longtime US nemesis, couldn't find enough magic with Kaymer while Mickelson and Kuchar created all the mojo with their putters. Mickelson's birdie putt on three gave the US a lead it never surrendered. And, when Mickelson drained a long putt on ten to put the team 2-up, he responded with a curtsy to the crowd. "That was for the bow," he said, referring to McIlroy's salute the previous day. "They gave us a bow, so we gave them a curtsy." The celebrations continued on thirteen. Kuchar rolled in a putt from 50 feet, bringing about a cringe-worthy shimmy shake between the partners in homage to the Golden State Warriors' Steph Curry. The well-played match ended in a 2-and-1 win for the Yanks, with Mickelson's five birdies leading the way.

The momentum was solidly back on the American side, and that's where it remained, unlike Medinah, where Europe won the last two Saturday matches to give them hope heading into the singles. This time, Reed made sure it would be the Americans sleeping more soundly. The day before, he and Spieth had split with Rose and Stenson. They'd won in foursomes, 3-and-2, but lost in four-balls, 5-and-4, when Stenson got hot. It was Reed and Spieth's first loss as Ryder Cup partners, and they were determined not to have a second in the rubber match. Poulter was Europe's hero in the final Saturday match at Medinah. Here, it would be Reed.

"You felt like we, single handedly, got beat by Henrik Stenson, Friday afternoon. He just went on an absolute tear," Reed said. "The biggest thing was, 'how are you going to respond? How are you going to bounce back? Jordan was just like, 'All right, let me just make a lot of pars and have a chance at a birdie here and there, because Captain America is going to do something.'"

He sure did. In leading the way to a 2-and-1 win, the American catalyst reeled off six birdies and an eagle (for a front nine 30) in a magnificent show of inspirational golf, outdoing Stenson, who was nearly as good. The eagle on six was the perfect example. The

Euros went out in front on the first hole and Stenson was in tight for a guaranteed birdie. Spieth had no chance to match Stenson and Reed was looking at a 79-yard shot with a lob wedge in his hand and full confidence in his mind. "Perfect," he thought.

"I just had this kind of funny feeling that this one could get pretty close," he'd recall. "I saw where it landed, I could kind of see it come back, and I could see it kind of tracking towards the flag. I knew it had a chance at that point."

The shot, hit at ninety per cent, landed behind the hole and came back to it as if Reed were pulling a string, falling into the side of the cup. The place erupted. Reed watched the shot with his club tucked into an imaginary scabbard, repeatedly yelling, "C'mon" until the ball disappeared. He slapped hands with Spieth, nearly taking his arm off, then the two American caddies, and even Stenson at one point. It was an all-time Ryder Cup moment, especially given that it triggered a string of four consecutive holes won by the US while jolting an electric charge into every other match on the course. Rose and Stenson weren't through battling, however. They birdied twelve and thirteen to cut the lead to one hole, reviving memories of Reed and Spieth throwing away a half-point over the last stretch of holes in the morning. Not here. Reed responded yet again with birdies on the next two holes to restore the 3-up lead with three to play. As he reached the par-five sixteenth with a 269-yard 4-wood into the breeze, the galleries gushed with enthusiasm.

"Before it even reached its apex, with the scene around us—the most amount of people either one of us has seen on a golf hole—we were both screaming. That's how cool it was," Spieth related. "I was screaming, 'Let's go, Patrick!' and I don't know what he screamed at that point. That hole was so cool, walking up and just hearing the noise. He was getting what he deserved for what he did this afternoon."

The PGA of America had set up the sixteenth as a showcase, figuring that so many matches could very well be decided there, collaring the green with huge grandstands to create a stadium-like setting. The spectators seated there would spontaneously respond with a salute. Reed was lining up his putt when they began a chant of, "Pat-rick Reed." Reed paused from his geometrical calculating, smiled, then raised his putter, hoisting it up and down to beat of the cheers as Spieth shouted along. Stenson would actually win the hole by chipping in to extend the match, but it ended on seventeen with matching pars as Rose lipped out his birdie effort.

"I rode Patrick's back like nobody's ever ridden a partner before," admitted Spieth, who spent a lot of the day spraying it around the course. "He's as good as anybody on the big stage. I knew he has that in him. We've seen it all before. He's Captain America for us."

Although the US lead was three points (not four as it was at Medinah), the day had closed in a distinctly different mood than it had four years earlier, when Poulter ripped off those five straight birdies to save the day. Reed was the clear hero. Europe would have to manufacture its faith and belief. It didn't come naturally this time.

Clarke fell back on his shoulder-to-shoulder mantra, borrowed from rugby parlance. When he was asked what his message would be to his team, he said, "Same as what we've done all week. Believe in ourselves and go out and play. First and foremost, teams have overcome bigger deficits. There's that, and the guys, they won't need me to lift them up. They will be keen to go out and play well tomorrow."

The media, of course, salted the wound of Medinah at Love's press conference.

"This team never played together before. This is a new twelve. We're not looking at past records," Love shot back. "We are in a good position. The team bonded together. We always get criticized that we don't bond as a team and we don't have enough passion, and we do, but this time we've taken it personally."

Or, as Spieth put it, "We're tired of hearing people tell us we can't win one of these things."

Clarke's strategy was obvious. He had to front-load his lineup as Jose Maria Olazábal did in 2012 and as Ben Crenshaw did in 1999. McIlroy, as in 2012, when he almost missed his tee time, had to be the leadoff hitter. However, this time the Americans had the perfect counterthrust.

"I wanted Rory because he was playing, I felt, the best golf on their team," Reed recalled a few years later. "I felt like I was playing the best golf on our team. We didn't know exactly where (Clarke) was going to put them, but we knew they had to get off to a hot start. So, we knew that Rory, Stenson and a couple other guys were going go with the first couple of matches. And I told the captain, 'Hey, I want to go out first. Throw me out first. I'll go out and get that point early and get our team going.'"

No one objected. It set up, then, what would be one of the greatest matches in Ryder Cup history. Not that it was the only terrific matchup. If the prospects of Stenson against Spieth in the second match, Pieters against Holmes in the third and Rose against Fowler in the fourth were all exquisitely appetizing, Garcia against Mickelson in the six spot was a pièce de résistance.

It was easy to understand why McIlroy had assumed his role as the man. He was beloved in Europe, well-respected everywhere, a childhood prodigy who had risen to the top of the world. But Reed? He was a polarizing figure on the PGA Tour and sullied by rumors of sketchy character. But he thrived in the crucible. He was the NHL player who got under the opponents' skin, the cocky kid who always made the clutch three-pointer. In other words, the guy you wanted on your team. He couldn't be intimidated, given his unflappable belief that he was just as good as anyone. And that included McIlroy.

"I was made for this kind of stuff," he said. "Anytime I can get in front of a crowd, especially Americans, it fuels me. For some reason, getting hyped up doesn't affect me."

The grandstands were packed for the 11:04 tee time and the fairway ropes were lined 25-deep. European fans love to sing on the first tee, sometimes to the annoyance of the Americans present, changing the words to suit their purpose. This ditty went like this: "Patrick Reed is terrified, Rory's on fire. Patrick Reed is terrified, Rory's on fire." McIlroy must have heard them as he performed a bit of an Irish jig to the beat. Reed utterly ignored it. He'd heard similar taunts when he went 3-0-1 at Gleneagles, shushing the Scottish fans while making putt after putt.

Out of that charged atmosphere they proceeded, halving the first two holes with Reed saving a par on the first with a big 20-footer over the ridge. The Irishman finally cashed in with a birdie on three, but instead of going all emotional, he celebrated with a barely perceptible wave of his hand. Reed looked on incredulously.

"That's all?" he asked him. "This is not going to be just a fun day. When I win a hole, you're going to know it."

That broke the tension. McIlroy laughed. It was a spirited match, and, while it appeared to the gallery that the two combatants were at each other's throats, they were actually enjoying the great golf. They were spurred on by each other, rather than sparring against one another. No stretch of any Ryder Cup match in history can rival how well they played the four holes from five through eight where McIlroy made four birdies–and lost ground.

On the drivable par-four fourth, McIlroy pulled 3-wood and got to the front of the green. Reed slung a driver to pin high, 12 feet away. McIlroy left his ling eagle putt short, and Reed evened the match by making his. True to his word, he went "insane." And so did the fans. Reed was in tight for a birdie on the par-five sixth, three feet uphill. "I mean, you could make it with your eyes closed," he said. Undeterred, McIlroy poured his birdie putt into the hole and let loose. Reed tapped in, and in a bit of one-upmanship, bowed to the crowd as McIlroy had done.

"We're all laughing about it," Reed recalled a few years later in a video produced by the PGA of America. "We get to the next tee, and he looks at me, and he goes, 'Well, my bow was better.' I go, 'Mine was. It was American bow on American soil.' And he just starts laughing. We both start laughing."

The good golf and great fun continued on seven, where McIlroy rolled in a birdie putt on top of Reed's, then impersonated his opponent's shush gesture from Gleneagles. But nothing topped what happened at eight. McIlroy got a bad break when his ball landed just short of scaling the right ridge and rolled all the way back to the front of the green, about 65 feet away. Reed was already pin-high, about 25 feet from the cup. When he saw what McIlroy had left, he turned to Kessler Karain, his caddie and brother-in-law, and told him his opponent was going to make the bomb. "No, he's not," Karain said. McIlroy sent the putt on its way with a hard stroke. It never wavered from his line. "When the putt was five feet from the hole, Kessler just looks at me, because we know at that point it's in. It's the perfect speed. It's going to be right in the heart."

McIlroy clenched both fists in ecstasy and screamed, "C'mon." He cupped his hand to his ear, as if to say to the crowd, "I can't hear you," while striding back up the hill. But Reed still had his putt, and it was also far from a tap-in. Karain suggested a cup and half break. "No, it's a cup. I got it," Reed told him. "All right," Karain replied. "Then go and do it."

Reed, certain it was in about four feet from the hole, turned to McIlroy and wagged his finger before the ball dropped, as if to say, "Not today." McIlroy waited for him off the green. They bumped fists and put their arms around each other. Samuel Ryder may have objected to some of the gestures, but he would have nonetheless approved of the sentiment.

"I feel like that that is probably the biggest thing that we showed, not only with the great golf, but how much we respect each other, the sportsmanship," Reed said. "We're out there having a good time, and, yeah, we're here trying to win but we're putting on a show and playing some absolutely amazing golf."

The rest of the round was less spectacular, particularly so far as Rory was concerned. Reed executed the better bunker shot on twelve (he was magic from the sand all day) and went ahead when McIlroy missed a curling eight-footer. McIlroy should have had the advantage with his length on the par-five sixteenth, but he pulled his drive into a bad lie in the rough, then hit a wedge fat with his third shot. Once again, Reed got up and down from the bunker for a birdie to go 2-up with two to play. Reed's bogey extended the match to eighteen, where both players hit their approach shots inside six feet. After measuring to see who was away, Reed poured his in to win the match. "All right, perfect, make it, it's over," he said to himself before stroking the putt. "I live for those kind of moments."

The point was a dagger, an early spot of red on the scoreboard when the Europeans needed to see the blue wave that would have rolled in along with Stenson's win over Spieth and Pieters' win over Holmes, both, 3-and-2. With the third match not yet completed, Europe added another point with Cabrera-Bello's 3-and-2 win over Walker. Had McIlroy beaten Reed, the Europeans would have had the first four flags on the board. As it happened, though, they would manage to eke out just one more win the rest of the day.

Fowler stanched the bleeding with a 1-up win over Rose in the fourth match, which pitted the Nos. 9- and 11-ranked players in the world. Neither man held more than a 1-up lead throughout the day, but Rose's putting touch deserted him. He grazed the hole on several makeable attempts, including a 10-footer on sixteen, where Fowler went 1-up with a nice up and down for birdie. Fowler drained a clutch putt from 20 feet on thirteen to remain all square and held his nerve on several shorter ones. The score was 10 ½-9 ½ when they arrived at the final green. Rose had a final 15-footer to halve the match but left it short, before Fowler tapped in from two feet to win the match and restore a two-point lead. At that point, it looked bleak for Europe, up in two, even in one and 2-down in each of the last five matches.

Garcia played Mickelson to a draw in a compelling match worthy of more importance, with nineteen birdies between them in eighteen holes, each finishing 10-under. Then it was left to Moore, Love's somewhat controversial final pick, to provide the Cup-clinching point against Westwood in just the seventh match of the day. The crowd exploded but the US team's celebration was somewhat muted, largely because the result was so decisively lopsided. The Americans would close things out by winning five of the last six matches. The well-earned six-point victory, the Americans' biggest since 1981, vindicated Mickelson, validated the task force and gave everyone associated with the US Ryder Cup some much-needed relief. Mickelson, who went 2-1-1 for the week, with fourteen birdies over his last twenty-seven holes, was in a far different mood than at Gleneagles.

The press conference began with a question hurled at Phil: "What do you think of Captain Love's leadership style?" When Mickelson demurred with a simple, "We had a great week this week," his teammates followed with mock applause. Shortly after, when asked about the pressure he was under all week, Mickelson sent the room into laughter: "The pressure started when some dumb ass opened his mouth two years ago in the media center."

Mickelson went on to describe how the task force had set the team up for success two years hence in France, calling the challenge "a whole different feat that's going to require a whole different level of play, of solidarity, of fortitude." Love interrupted him by popping the cork on a champagne bottle. Mickelson heard it and looked across at his captain. "That's my cue to shut up," he said with a bashful grin.

It was up to Love to explain how the task force had transformed the culture, as it were.

"Just because we got kicked around for so long," he said. "You keep losing, you feel like you've got to do something different. It was a little bit of rebuilding, a little bit in shift of attitude, but from (vice-captain) Raymond Floyd to Rickie Fowler in those first meetings, we said we're going to do whatever it takes to get this one on the right track. You know what, we're not going to win every one of them but we're going to go into it with a better attitude from here on forward."

The proof, at least for one year, was on paper. Fowler, who was 0-3-5 in two previous appearances, was 2-1-0. Snedeker, who was 1-2 at Gleneagles, was 3-0 at Hazeltine. Only three Euros, McIlroy, Pieters and Cabrera-Bello, left Minnesota with winning records for the week. The results also hinted to a brighter US future. The two American, rookies, Moore and Koepka, were a combined 5-2-0. The six European rookies were 7-9-1, with six of those wins coming from Pieters and Cabrera-Bello.

The European camp admitted it was fairly beaten and that, in fact, it was probably a good thing for the Ryder Cup that the US had restored a measure of competitive balance. The British press went easy on Clarke, mildly criticizing his choice of his old chum Westwood over Russell Knox and for keeping Cabrera-Bello and Wood out of the Saturday afternoon session. But Clarke had no regrets.

"Hindsight is a wonderful thing but even with that we wouldn't have made any changes," he said.

"A putt missed here, or a putt holed outside your opponent, that makes all the difference. Unfortunately for us we didn't quite hole them, and the Americans did."

There was, however, a good deal of leftover carping over the behavior of the galleries.

"They have been quite poor. I'm not going to lie," Garcia acknowledged. "Obviously it's unfortunate because I think that eighty-five percent of the people are great, and I love playing in America. My girlfriend is American. But that fifteen percent that is really bad, it makes them look bad. And I feel ashamed for my girlfriend, because I know how bad she feels when she hears all the things, but it is what it is. It's as simple as that."

"When you are teeing off at 7:35 in the morning and you see people on the first tee with a beer in their hands and matches aren't finishing until five o'clock in the afternoon there can be problems," added McIlroy, although he had turned the heckling into an advantage, unlike the unfortunate Willett.

No one was more adversely affected by it all with Willett losing all three of his matches. A photo of him sitting glumly at the final Euro press conference, his chin in his hand, said it all. His brother had done him no favors, although Willett's last tweet concurred with his sentiments:

"Very strange week here at the Ryder Cup. Tried my best but played poorly. Unfortunately some American fans showed that @PJ_Willett was in fact correct. Nothing to blame my bad play on but still shows that sometimes fans don't know when to call it a day. Shame really!!"

Dan Jones of the *Evening Standard* had a different take.

"European moaning about American crowds, which continues even in the aftermath of a 17-11 larruping that would more properly recommend silent contemplation, makes us look like a bunch of saps," he wrote. "To go to the US for a sporting contest and come back complaining that they can't keep their mouths shut is like jumping in the sea and complaining about damp socks. As for all the wailing about the damage done to the spirit of golf and the apparent death of good sportsmanship, please, spare me."

The Europeans and their fans would get the chance to turn things around on the US at the next Ryder Cup at Le Golf National outside Paris. Their 19-11 rout there proved that the greater American task had yet to be completed.

DAY 1
FOURSOMES
Jordan Spieth/Patrick Reed (US) defeated Henrik Stenson/Justin Rose (E) 3-and-2 Phil Mickelson/Rickie Fowler (US) defeated Rory McIlroy/-and-y Sullivan (E) 1-up Jimmy Walker/Zach Johnson (US) defeated Sergio Garcia/Martin Kaymer (E) 4-and-2 Dustin Johnson/Matt Kuchar (US) defeated Lee Westwood/Thomas Pieters (E) 5-and-4 **United States wins session 4–0**
FOURBALLS
Justin Rose/Henrik Stenson (E) defeated Jordan Spieth/Patrick Reed (US) 5-and-4 Sergio Garcia/Rafa Cabrera Bello (E) defeated J.B. Holmes/Ryan Moore (US) 3-and-2 Br-and-t Snedeker/Brooks Koepka (US) defeated Martin Kaymer/Danny Willett (E) 5-and-4 Rory McIlroy/Thomas Pieters (E) defeated Dustin Johnson/Matt Kuchar (US) 3-and-2 **Europe wins session 3–1** **United States 5, Europe 3**
DAY 2
FOURSOMES
Rory McIlroy/Thomas Pieters (E) defeated Rickie Fowler/Phil Mickelson (US) 4-and-2 Br-and-t Snedeker/Brooks Koepka (US) defeated Henrik Stenson/Matt Fitzpatrick (E) 3-and-2 Justin Rose/Chris Wood (E) defeated Jimmy Walker/Zach Johnson (US) 1-up Patrick Reed/Jordan Spieth (US) halved with Sergio Garcia/Rafa Cabrera Bello (E) **Europe wins session, 2 ½–1 ½** **United States 6 ½ Europe 5 ½**

FOURBALLS

Rory McIlroy/Thomas Pieters (E) defeated Brooks Koepka/Dustin Johnson (US) 3-and-1
J.B. Holmes/Ryan Moore (US) defeated Danny Willett/Lee Westwood (E) 1-up
Phil Mickelson/Matt Kuchar (US) defeated Martin Kaymer/Sergio Garcia (E) 2-and-1
Patrick Reed/Jordan Spieth (US) defeated Justin Rose/Henrik Stenson (E) 2-and-1
United States wins session 3–1.
United States 9 ½ Europe 6 ½

DAY 3

SINGLES

Patrick Reed (US) defeated Rory McIlroy (E) 1-up
Henrik Stenson (E) defeated Jordan Spieth (US) 3-and-2
Thomas Pieters (E) defeated J.B. Holmes (US) 3-and-2
Rickie Fowler (US) defeated Justin Rose (E) 1-up
Rafa Cabrera Bello (E) defeated Jimmy Walker (US) 3-and-2
Phil Mickelson (US) halved with Sergio Garcia (E)
Ryan Moore (US) defeated Lee Westwood (E) 1-up
Br-and-t Snedeker (US) defeated -and-y Sullivan (E) 3-and-1
Dustin Johnson (US) defeated Chris Wood (E) 1-up
Brooks Koepka (US) defeated Danny Willett (E) -and-4
Martin Kaymer (E) defeated Matt Kuchar (US) 1-up
Zach Johnson (US) defeated Matt Fitzpatrick (E) 4-and-3
United States wins session 7 ½–4 ½

UNITED STATES WINS RYDER CUP, 17–11

Acknowledgments

First off, if not for the suggestion and encouragement of my publisher at Tatra Press, Chris Sulavik, this book would not have been written. He provided unconditional support for my last book, City of Champions, and did enough arm twisting for me to do it one more time. Thanks, also, to his wife, Emily Church, for her contributions and to designers Mimi Bark and Maria Ilardi for making it look so great. Special thanks to the staffs at Worcester Country Club, Southport & Ainsdale, Portland Golf Club and Lindrick Golf Club for the use of their archives. My family is a constant source of encouragement. My mom Ann, who just turned 102 (just a bit older than the Cup itself), has always been my best salesperson. My wife Lillian is a reliable sounding board. My son and daughter Henry and Julianne, their spouses, Alice Ann and Jason and my grandkids, Ruby, Rose, Elliot and Iris are an inspiration, my sister Sandy always there with support. This book was written largely off research and owes much to the descriptive words and thoughts of golf journalists dating back some one hundred years. I'm particularly indebted to all those with whom I shared Ryder Cup press rooms, many of whom are quoted within. They include but are not limited to Mark Cannizzaro, Damon Hack, Ed Sherman, Joe Logan, Mark Herrmann, George Willis, Bill Pennington, Robert Lusetich, Kevin Manahan, John Paul Newport, Jimmy Roberts, Mike Whitmer, Jim McCabe, Tod Leonard, Ron Kroichick, Jaime Diaz, Ron Green Jr., Scott Michaux, Bob Harig, Tedy Greenstein,

Sam Weinman, Ann Ligouri, Michael Bamberger, Dave Shedloski, Len Shapiro, Jason Sobel, Mike Buteau, Mike Kern, Joe Juliano, Craig Dolch, Dave LeGarde, Bob Verdi, Dave Hackenberg, Brad Townsend, Kevin Roberts, Melanie Hauser, Gary D'Amato, Marino Parascenzo, Jeff Rude, Alex Micelli, Doug Ferguson, Thomas Bonk, John Hopkins, Derek Lawrenson, Jay Flemma, Martin Davis, the late, great Dave Anderson, Furman Bisher, Vartan Kupelian and Dai Davies as well as the late John Feinstein, Steve DiMeglio and Jeff Babineau, whose too-soon deaths came just as this book was completed. Thanks, as well, to Julius Mason and Bob Denney at the PGA of America and to Mitchell Platts of the then-European Tour for running those press rooms and to Kerry Haigh of the PGA for his eagle eye. Thanks to Gia Sangani at Sky Sports for an important clarification. Also, I can't ignore my teammates on the US media squads which I captained to a 4-1 record in the Rolex Cup over the years (sorry, my Euro friends, but I just had to mention that one in the spirit of the trans-Atlantic rivalry). A shout goes out to good buddy Dan Sellers for one particular line in the book and thanks to everyone at North Jersey Country Club (home course to myself and 1927-29 Ryder Cupper Johnny Golden), where I find inspiration much more easily than birdies. Finally, thanks to everyone—players, officials, spectators and media—who have made the Ryder Cup such a fascinating study for almost a century.

Bibiography

1927

Books

Bubka, Bob and Clavin, Tom. (2014). *The Ryder Cup: Golf's Greatest Event.* New York: Diversion Books

Callow, Nick (2020). *The Ryder Cup; The Complete History of Golf's Greatest Competition.* London: Welbeck.

Clavin, Tom. (2005). *Sir Walter: Walter Hagen and the Invention of Professional Golf.* New York: Simon and Schuster.

Feherty, David with Frank, James A. (2004) *David Feherty's Totally Subjective History of the Ryder Cup.* New York: Rugged Land.

Hagen, Walter. (2018). *The Walter Hagen Story by The Haig, Himself.* Papamoa Press.

Newspapers

Athletic News, Atlanta Journal, Boston Globe, Boston Herald, Daily Mirror, Detroit Free Press, Edinburgh Evening News, Evening Dispatch, Evening Gazette, Evening Standard, Hull Daily Mail, Leicester Evening Mail, Linconshire Echo, Manchester Evening News, Minneapolis Sunday Tribune, New Orleans Item, New York Herald Tribune, New York Times, Paterson Morning Call, Paterson News, Pittsburgh Daily Post, Port Chester Daily Item, Rochester Democrat and Chronicle, Seattle Daily Times, Springfield Republican, Tacoma Daily Leader, The Guardian, Weekly Dispatch, Worcester Evening Gazette

Periodicals

Golf Illustrated, Golf Weekly

Websites

Archive.org, Bunkered.Co.UK, Golf.Com, GolfCompendium.Com, Golftoday.co.uk, MaxFaulkner.Net, NYTimes.Com, RyderCup.Com, WorcesterCC.Org.

Wire Services

Associated Press, North American Newspaper Alliance, United Press

1937

Books

Callow, Nick (2020). *The Ryder Cup; The Complete History of Golf's Greatest Competition.* London: Welbeck.

Clavin, Tom. (2005). *Sir Walter: Walter Hagen and the Invention of Professional Golf.* New York: Simon and Schuster.

Cotton, Henry. (1948). *This Game of Golf.* London: Country Life.

Dobereiner, Peter (1992) *Maestro: The Life of Henry Cotton.* London: Hodder and Stoughton.

Dodson, James. (2012). *American Triumvirate: Sam Snead, Byron Nelson, Ben Hogan, and the Modern Age of Golf.* New York: Alfred A. Knopf.

Feherty, David with Frank, James A. (2004) *David Feherty's Totally Subjective History of the Ryder Cup.* New York: Rugged Land.

Hagen, Walter. (2018). *The Walter Hagen Story by The Haig, Himself.* Papamoa Press.

Kenny, Kevin. (2016). *Ralph Guldahl: The Rise and Fall of the World's Greatest Golfer.* Jefferson, North Carolina: McFarland and Company.

Nelson, Byron. (2006). *How I Played the Game: An Autobiography.* Lanham, Maryland: Taylor Trade Publishers.

Rees, Dai, with Ballantine, John. (1968) *Thirty Years of Championship Golf.* London: Stanley Paul and Company.

Snead, Sam, and Tarde, Jerry. (1962) *The Education of a Golfer.* New York: Simon and Schuster.

Newspapers

Atlanta Journal, Biddeford Daily Journal, Birmingham Gazette, Brooklyn Daily Eagle, Buffalo Courier Express, Chicago Tribune, Daily Independent, Daily Mail, Daily Mirror, Daily Telegraph, Daily Times, Dallas Morning News, Detroit Free Press, Evening Chronicle, Evening Dispatch, Evening Express, Evening News, Evening Sentinel, Evening Standard, Evening Star, Fort Worth Star Telegram, Harrisburg Telegraph, Fort Worth Star-Telegram, Leicester Evening Mail, Liverpool Daily Post, Liverpool Echo, London Star, Manchester Evening News, Midland Daily Telegraph, New York Daily News, New York Sun, South Wales Evening Post, Sunday Dispatch, Sunday Pictorial, The Alberdare Leader, The Guardian, The Observe Sun, The Washington Post, Western Daily Press and Bristol Mirror, Wester Mail.

Periodicals

Golf Digest

Websites

BBCSport.com, GolfCompendium.Com, Golfingherald.com, Golfonline.com, Ourventuraboulevard.com, PunkGolf.com, Sandagolfclub.co.uk, TheWanderingGolfers.Com, YouTube.Com

Wire Services

Associated Press, Canadian Press, International News Service, Ledger Syndicate, Newspaper Enterprise Association, United Press

1947

Books

Barkow, Al. (2010). *Sam: The One and Only Sam Snead.* Lanham, Maryland: Taylor Trade Publishers.

Burke, Jackie Jr., with Yocum, Guy. (2006). *It's Only a Game: Words of Wisdom from a Lifetime in Golf.* New York: Gotham Books.

Burns, Peter, and Hodge, Ed. (2016) *Behind the Ryder Cup: The Players' Stories.* Edinburgh: Polaris Publishing.

Callow, Nick (2020). *The Ryder Cup; The Complete History of Golf's Greatest Competition.* London: Welbeck.

Cotton, Henry. (1948). *This Game of Golf.* London: Country Life.

Dobereiner, Peter (1992) *Maestro: The Life of Henry Cotton.* London: Hodder and Stoughton.

Dodson, James. (2012) *American Triumvirate: Sam Snead, Byron Nelson, Ben Hogan, and the Modern Age of Golf.* New York: Alfred A. Knopf.

Feherty, David with Frank, James A. (2004) *David Feherty's Totally Subjective History of the Ryder Cup.* New York: Rugged Land.

McMillan, Robin (2011) *Us Against Them: Oral History of the Ryder Cup.* New York: Harper Collins.

Nelson, Byron. (2006). *How I Played the Game: An Autobiography.* Lanham, Maryland: Taylor Trade Publishers.

Rees, Dai, with Ballantine, John. (1968) *Thirty Years of Championship Golf.* London: Stanley Paul and Company.

Snead, Sam, and Tarde, Jerry. (1962) *The Education of a Golfer.* New York: Simon and Schuster.

Newspapers

Asbury Park Press, Belfast Telegraph, Columbus Dispatch, Daily Mail, Daily Mirror, Daily Telegraph, Dallas Morning News, Dayton Daily News, Evening Express, Evening Gazette, Evening Standard, Evening Telegraph and Post, Fort Worth Star Telegram, Herald Express, Joplin Globe, Journal American, London Daily Express, London Star, Manchester Evening News, New York Daily News, Oakland Tribune, Oregon Journal, Palo Alto Times, Paterson Morning Call, Philadelphia

Inquirer, St. Louis Globe Democrat, Statesman Journal, The Dayton Herald, The Desert Sun, The Guardian, The Observer Sun, The Oregonian, The Press and Journal, The Spokesman Review, The Tacoma News-Tribune, The Vancouver Province, The Vancouver Sun, Western Daily Press and Bristol Mirror, Western Mail, Western Morning News. Yorkshire Post and Leeds Mercury

Periodicals

Professional Golfer, The 1947 Ryder Cup Program

Websites

GlobalGolfPost.Com, Golf Digest, Golfweek, HistoryScotland.Com, LiverpoolEcho.Com, PortlandGolfClub.Com, RyderCup.Com, TurnberryGolfClub.Net, USGA.Org, Willotheglenongolf.blogspot.com, YouTube.Com

Wire Services

Associated Press, International News Service, Reuters, Newspaper Enterprise Association, United Press International

1957

Books

Belton, Brian. (2007) *The Ryder Lions: The Story of Britain's 1957 Ryder Cup Victory.* London: Pennant Books, Limited.

Bolt, Tommy, with Mann, Jimmy. (1971) *The Hole Truth; Inside Big Time, Big Money Golf.* Philadelphia: JP Lippincott and Company

Bubka, Bob and Clavin, Tom. (2014) *The Ryder Cup: Golf's Greatest Event.* New York: Diversion Books

Burke, Jackie Jr., with Yocum, Guy. (2006) *It's Only a Game: Words of Wisdom from a Lifetime in Golf.* New York: Gotham Books.

Callow, Nick (2020). *The Ryder Cup; The Complete History of Golf's Greatest Competition.* London: Welbeck.

Feherty, David with Frank, James A. (2004) *David Feherty's Totally Subjective History of the Ryder Cup.* New York: Rugged Land.

McMillan, Robin (2011) *Us Against Them: Oral History of the Ryder Cup.* New York: Harper Collins.

Pelham, Bill. (2014) *Burke and Demaret: The Wit and Wisdom of Golf's Most Colorful Duo.* Xlibris.

Rees, Dai, with Ballantine, John. (1968) *Thirty Years of Championship Golf.* London: Stanley Paul and Company

Newspapers

Birmingham Post, Daily Graphic, Daily Mirror, Daily Telegraph, Dayton Daily Herald, Durham Sun, Evening Express, Evening Standard, Halifax Daily Courier, Leicester Evening Mail, Liverpool Daily Post, London News Chronicle, Los Angeles Times, Miami News, Nottingham Evening News, Post Green, Rock Hill Herald, San Diego Evening Tribune, San Diego Union, St. Petersburg Times, South Yorkshire Times, Sunday Dispatch, Sunday Express, The Guardian, The People, The Standard-Star, Western Mail

Periodicals

Golf Digest, Golf Illustrated, Sports Illustrated

Websites

BBCSport.com, BroBible.Com, ESPN.Com, GolfCompendium.Com, GolfMonthly.Com, GolfPunk.Com, Golfshake.Com, Independent.Co.UK, LindrickGolfClub.Co.UK, MaxFaulkner.Net, RyderCup.Com, TheHerald.Com, TheWanderingGolfers.Com, WorksopGuardian.Com.

Wire Services

Associated Press, Reuters, United Press International

1969

Books

Alliss, Peter. (2022) *Peter Allis—Reflections of a Life Well Lived.* London: G2 Rights.

Bubka, Bob and Clavin, Tom. (2014) *The Ryder Cup: Golf's Greatest Event.* New York: Diversion Books

Callow, Nick (2020). *The Ryder Cup; The Complete History of Golf's Greatest Competition.* London: Welbeck.

Feherty, David with Frank, James A. (2004) *David Feherty's Totally Subjective History of the Ryder Cup.* New York: Rugged Land.

Hill, David with Seitz, Nick. (1977) *Teed Off.* Englewood Cliffs, NJ: Prentice-Hall.

Jacklin, Tony. (2021) *My Ryder Cup Journey.* New York: Pegasus.

McMillan, Robin (2011) *Us Against Them: Oral History of the Ryder Cup.* New York: Harper Collins.

Nicklaus, Jack with Wind, Herbert Warren. (1969) *The Greatest Game of All.* New York: Simon and Schuster.

Sagebiel, Neil. (2014) *Draw in the Dunes.* New York: St. Martin's Press.

Snead, Sam, and Tarde, Jerry. (1962) *The Education of a Golfer.* New York: Simon and Schuster.

Trevino, Lee. (1982) *They Call Me Super Mex.* New York: Random House

Newspapers

Belfast Telegraph, Birmingham Evening Mail, Cambridge Evening News, Cleveland Plain Dealer, Daily Mail, Daily Mirror, Daily Telegraph, Evening Standard, Florida Times-Union, Liverpool Daily Post, Liverpool Echo, London Daily Express, London News Chronicle, The Times of London, Los Angeles Times, Manchester Evening News and Chronicle, Memphis Press Scimitar, Miami Herald, New York Times, Pittsburgh Press, Tacoma News Tribune, The Guardian, The Observer, The People, Vancouver Province, Washington Evening Star, Western Daily Press.

Periodicals

Golf Digest, Golf Illustrated, Sports Illustrated.

Television Networks

BBC

Websites

BBCSport.com, ESPN.Com, Forbes.Com, GolfCompendium.Com, RyderCup.Com., YouTube.Com.

Wire Services

Associated Press, Reuters, United Press International.

1985

Books

Bubka, Bob and Clavin, Tom. (2014) *The Ryder Cup: Golf's Greatest Event.* New York: Diversion Books

Callow, Nick (2020). *The Ryder Cup; The Complete History of Golf's Greatest Competition.* London: Welbeck.

Feherty, David with Frank, James A. (2004) *David Feherty's Totally Subjective History of the Ryder Cup.* New York: Rugged Land.

Langer, Bernhard (2002) *Bernhard Langer My Autobiography.* London: Hodder & Stoughton.

Jacklin, Tony (2021) *My Ryder Cup Journey.* New York: Pegasus.

McMillan, Robin (2011) *Us Against Them: Oral History of the Ryder Cup.* New York: Harper Collins.

Tait, Alistair (2012) *Seve: A Biography of Severiano Ballesteros.* New York: Random House.

Torrance, Sam (2003) *Sam. The Autobiography of Sam Torrance, Golf's Ryder Cup Winning Hero.* London: BBC Books.

Trevino, Lee. (1982) *They Call Me Super Mex.* New York: Random House

Newspapers

Abilene Reporter, Atherstone Herald, Belfast Telegraph, Chicago Tribune, Daily Mail, Daily Mirror, Evening Express, Evening Mail, Evening Post, Liverpool Echo, The Times of London, New York Daily News, New York Times, Tacoma News Tribune, Sports Argus, The Age, The Independent, The Guardian, The Observer, The Press and Journal, The Scotsman, The Telegraph.

Periodicals

Golf Digest, Golf Illustrated, Sports Illustrated.

Television Networks

BBC, NBC

Websites

CNN.Com, ClubTee.Com, ESPN.Com, Forbes.Com, GolfCompendium.Com, GolfShake.Com, RetroSports.Com, RyderCup.Com, YouTube.Com

Wire Services

Associated Press, Reuters, Scripps Howard News Service

1987

Books

Bubka, Bob and Clavin, Tom. (2014) *The Ryder Cup: Golf's Greatest Event.* New York: Diversion Books

Callow, Nick (2020) *The Ryder Cup; The Complete History of Golf's Greatest Competition.* London: Welbeck.

Faldo, Nick (2004) *Life Swings.* London: Headline Book Publishing.

Feherty, David with Frank, James A. (2004) *David Feherty's Totally Subjective History of the Ryder Cup.* New York: Rugged Land.

Langer, Bernhard (2002) *Bernhard Langer My Autobiography.* London: Hodder & Stoughton.

Jacklin, Tony (2021) *My Ryder Cup Journey.* New York: Pegasus.

McMillan, Robin (2011) *Us Against Them: Oral History of the Ryder Cup.* New York: Harper Collins.

Tait, Alistair (2012) *Seve: A Biography of Severiano Ballesteros.* New York: Random House.

Torrance, Sam (2003) *Sam. The Autobiography of Sam Torrance, Golf's Ryder Cup Winning Hero.* London: BBC Books.

Woosnam, Ian (2002) *Woosie: My Autobiography.* London: Willow.

Newspapers

Atlanta Journal, Birmingham Evening Mail, Boston Globe, Boston Herald, Chicago Tribune, Columbus Dispatch, Cleveland Plain Dealer, Daily Mail, Detroit Free Press, Evening Post, Hartford Courant, Indianapolis Star, Las Vegas Review, Leicester Mercury, Liverpool Echo, Liverpool Daily Post, Liverpool Mercury, Manchester Evening News, Miami Herald, New York Times, News Letter, Palm Beach Post, Pittsburgh Post Gazette, Pittsburgh Press, Press Journal, Sandwell Evening Mail, Sunday Telegraph, Surry Herald, Springfield News Herald, Sports Argus, Stuart News, Tallahassee Democrat, Tampa Tribune, The Guardian, Washington Post.

Periodicals

Golf Digest, Sports Illustrated.

Websites

CNN.Com, ESPN.Com, GolfCompendium.Com, GolfMonthly.Com, GolfShake.Com, RetroSports.Com, RyderCup.Com, The42.Com, YouTube.Com

Wire Services

Associated Press

1991

Books

Azinger, Paul (1995) *Zinger.* New York: Harper Collins.

Bubka, Bob and Clavin, Tom. (2014) *The Ryder Cup: Golf's Greatest Event.* New York: Diversion Books.

Callow, Nick (2020) *The Ryder Cup; The Complete History of Golf's Greatest Competition.* London: Welbeck.

Faldo, Nick (2004) *Life Swings.* London: Headline Book Publishing.

Feherty, David with Frank, James A. (2004) *David Feherty's Totally Subjective History of the Ryder Cup.* New York: Rugged Land.

Langer, Bernhard (2002) *Bernhard Langer My Autobiography.* London: Hodder & Stoughton.

McMillan, Robin (2011) *Us Against Them: Oral History of the Ryder Cup.* New York: Harper Collins.

Sampson, Curt (2012) *The War by the Shore: The Incomparable Drama of the 1991 Ryder Cup.* New York: Gotham Books.

Tait, Alistair (2012) *Seve: A Biography of Severiano Ballesteros.* New York: Random House.

Torrance, Sam (2003) *Sam. The Autobiography of Sam Torrance, Golf's Ryder Cup Winning Hero.* London: BBC Books.

Woosnam, Ian (2002) *Woosie: My Autobiography.* London: Willow.

Newspapers

Atlanta Journal Constitution, Beaufort Gazette, Boston Globe, Charleston News, Charleston Post Courier, Charlotte Observer, Chronicle and Echo, Chicago Tribune, Cincinnati Enquirer, Daily Post, Daily Telegraph, Detroit Free Press, Evening Post, Evening Sentinel, Evening Standard, Greenville News, Los Angeles Times, Manchester Evening News, Miami Herald, Myrtle Beach Sun News, Naples Daily News, New York Times, Newsday, News Letter, Observer Sun, Palm Beach Post, Palm Desert Post, Philadelphia Daily News, Philadelphia Inquirer, Port Chester Daly Item, Press Journal, Raleigh News and Observer, San Diego Union, Stains and Ashford News, Sunday Independent, Sport On Sunday, Tallahassee Democrat, Tampa Bay Times, Tampa Tribune, The Courier and Advertiser, The Guardian, The Observer, The People, The Scotsman, The State, The Telegraph, Tucson Citizen, Washington Post.

Periodicals

Golf, Golf Digest, Golfweek, Links Magazine, Sports Illustrated

Websites

BleacherReport.Com, ESPN.Com, GlobalGolfPost.com, GolfMonthly.Com, IrishExaminer.Com, PGATOUR.COM, RyderCup.Com, TheGolfPaper.Com, YouTube.Com

Wire Services

Associated Press

1997

Books

Bubka, Bob and Clavin, Tom. (2014) *The Ryder Cup: Golf's Greatest Event.* New York: Diversion Books

Callow, Nick (2020) *The Ryder Cup; The Complete History of Golf's Greatest Competition.* London: Welbeck.

Feherty, David with Frank, James A. (2004) *David Feherty's Totally Subjective History of the Ryder Cup.* New York: Rugged Land.

McMillan, Robin (2011) *Us Against Them: Oral History of the Ryder Cup.* New York: Harper Collins.

Ryan, Shane (2022) *The Cup They Couldn't Lose. New York: Hachette Book Group*

Tait, Alistair (2012) *Seve: A Biography of Severiano Ballesteros.* New York: Random House.

Newspapers

Birmingham Post, Boston Globe, Chicago Tribune, Daily Express, Daily Press, Daily Record, Desert Sun, Evening Mail, Evening Post, Evening Standard, Gloucester Echo, Houston Chronicle, Kansas City Star, Los Angeles Times, Miami Herald, Myrtle Beach Sun News, New York Daily News, New York Post, New York Times, Newsday, Palm Beach Post, Philadelphia Inquirer, Pittsburgh Post Gazette, Scottish Daily Express, Sunday Mirror, Sunday Telegraph, Tampa Bay Times, The Guardian, The Independent, The People, The Record, The Signal, The Scotsman, The State, Washington Post, Western Daily Press, Williamsburg Times Dispatch.

Periodicals

Golf, Golf Digest, Golfweek, Links Magazine, Sports Illustrated

Television Networks

NBC

Websites

BleacherReport.Com, Bunkered.Co.UK, Defector.Com, ESPN.Com, GlobalGolfPos.Com, GolfMonthly.Com, IrishExaminer.Com, PGATOUR.COM, RyderCup.Com, TheGolfPaper.Com, YouTube.Com

Wire Services

Associated Press, Scripps Howard News Service

1999

Books

Bubka, Bob and Clavin, Tom. (2014) *The Ryder Cup: Golf's Greatest Event.* New York: Diversion Books

Callow, Nick (2020) *The Ryder Cup; The Complete History of Golf's Greatest Competition.* London: Welbeck.

Feherty, David with Frank, James A. (2004) *David Feherty's Totally Subjective History of the Ryder Cup.* New York: Rugged Land.

James, Mark with Hardy, Mark (2000) *Into the Bear Pit.* London: Virgin Books Ltd.

McMillan, Robin (2011) *Us Against Them: Oral History of the Ryder Cup.* New York: Harper Collins.

Robbins, Kevin (2019) *The Last Stand of Payne Stewart.* New York: Hachette Book Group.

Newspapers

Birmingham Post, Boston Globe, Boston Herald, Chicago Tribune, Detroit Free Press, Dallas Morning News, Daily Mail, Daily Mirror, Daily Post, Daily Telegraph, Evening Standard, Fort Worth Star Telegram, London Evening Standard, The Times of London, Los Angeles Times, New York Daily News, New York Post, New York Times, Newsday, Sunday Telegraph, Tampa Bay Times

Periodicals

Golf, Golf Digest, Golfweek, Links Magazine, Sports Illustrated

Television Networks

NBC, Sky Sports

Websites

BBC.Com, CNN.Com, ESPN.Com, GlobalGolfPost.Com, GolfCompendium.Com, GolfMonthly.Com, GolfShake.Com, NBCSportsBoston.Com, NewEnglandGolf.Com, PGATOUR.Com, RyderCup.Com, TCC1882.Org, YouTube.Com

Wire Services

Associated Press, Scripps Howard News Service

2008

Books

Azinger, Paul and Braund, Ron (2010) Cracking the Code. Decatur, Ga.: Looking Glass Books.

Bubka, Bob and Clavin, Tom. (2014) *The Ryder Cup: Golf's Greatest Event.* New York: Diversion Books

Callow, Nick (2020) *The Ryder Cup; The Complete History of Golf's Greatest Competition.* London: Welbeck.

McMillan, Robin (2011) *Us Against Them: Oral History of the Ryder Cup.* New York: Harper Collins.

Newspapers

Boston Globe, Charlotte Observer, Chicago Tribune, Daily Mail, Lexington Herald Leader, Louisville Courier News, Los Angeles Times, The Times of London, New York Daily News, New York Post, New York Times, Newsday, Ottawa Citizen, Palm Beach Post, Tampa Tribune, The Guardian, The Independent, The Telegraph, Washington Post

Periodicals

Golf, Golf Digest, Golfweek, Irish Golfer, Links Magazine, Sports Illustrated

Television Networks

NBC, Sky Sports, The Golf Channel

Websites

BBC.Com, Bunkered.Co.UK, ESPN.Com, EuropeanTour.Com, GlobalGolfPost.Com, Golf.Com, Golf365.Com, PGATOUR.COM, RyderCup.Com, RyderDiary.Com, YouTube.Com

Wire Services

Associated Press

2012

Books

Azinger, Paul and Braund, Ron (2010) Cracking the Code. Decatur, Ga.: Looking Glass Books.

Bubka, Bob and Clavin, Tom. (2014) *The Ryder Cup: Golf's Greatest Event.* New York: Diversion Books

Callow, Nick (2020) *The Ryder Cup; The Complete History of Golf's Greatest Competition.* London: Welbeck.

Holt, Oliver (2012) *Miracle at Medinah. Europe's Amazing Ryder Cup Comeback.* London: Headline Publishing Group.

Newspapers

Boston Globe, Charlotte Observer, Chicago Sun Times, Chicago Tribune, Daily Telegraph, Evening Standard, Gloucester Echo, The Times of London, Miami Herald, Myrtle Beach Sun News, Milwaukee Journal, Myrtle Beach Sun News, New York Daily News, New York Post, New York Times, Palm Beach Post, The Guardian, The Independent, USA Today.

Periodicals

Golf Digest, Golfweek, Sports Illustrated

Television Networks

NBC, Sky Sports, The Golf Channel

Websites

BBC.Com, ESPN.Com, GlobalGolfPost.Com, GolfCompendium.Com, PGATOUR.COM, RyderCup.Com, SkySports.Com, YouTube.Com

Wire Services

Associated Press, Reuters

2016

Books

Callow, Nick (2020) *The Ryder Cup; The Complete History of Golf's Greatest Competition.* London: Welbeck.

Feinstein, John (2017) *The First Major; The Inside Story of the 2016 Ryder Cup.* New York: Doubleday

Newspapers

Atlanta Journal Constitution, Chicago Tribune, Evening Standard, Fort Myers News Press, Los Angeles Times, Miami Herald, Minneapolis Star Tribune, New York Post, New York Times, Palm Beach Post, St. Paul Pioneer Press, South Wales Argus, The Guardian, The Independent, USA Today.

Periodicals

Golf Digest, Golfweek, Sports Illustrated

Television Networks

NBC, Sky Sports, The Golf Channel

Websites

BBC.Com, CNN.Com, ESPN.Com, GlobalGolfPost.Com, GolfCompendium.Com, GolfMonthly.Com, PGATOUR.COM, RyderCup.Com, SkySports.Com, TheGuardian.Com, YouTube.Com

Wire Services

Associated Press